Death
and
Dollars

Death
and
Dollars

*The Role of Gifts and
Bequests in America*

Alicia H. Munnell
Annika Sundén
Editors

BROOKINGS INSTITUTION PRESS
Washington, D.C.

ABOUT BROOKINGS
The Brookings Institution is a private nonprofit organization devoted to research, education, and publication on important issues of domestic and foreign policy. Its principal purpose is to bring knowledge to bear on current and emerging policy problems. The Institution maintains a position of neutrality on issues of public policy. Interpretations or conclusions in Brookings publications should be understood to be solely those of the authors.

Copyright © 2003
THE BROOKINGS INSTITUTION
1775 Massachusetts Avenue, N.W., Washington, D.C. 20036
www.brookings.edu

Library of Congress Cataloging-in-Publication data

Death and dollars : the role of gifts and bequests in America / Alicia H. Munnell and Annika Sundén, editors.
p.   cm.
Includes bibliographical references and index.
ISBN 0-8157-5890-1 (cloth : alk. paper)
ISBN 0-8157-5891-X (pbk. : alk. paper)
1. Inheritance and succession—United States. 2. Wealth—United States. 3. Charitable uses, trusts and foundations—United States. 4. Charitable bequests—United States. I. Munnell, Alicia Haydock. II. Sundén, Annika E.
HB715.D4   2003
339.2′2--dc21   2002156373

9 8 7 6 5 4 3 2 1

The paper used in this publication meets minimum requirements of the American National Standard for Information Sciences—Permanence of Paper for Printed Library Materials: ANSI Z39.48-1992.

Typeset in Adobe Garamond

Composition by
Betsy Kulamer
Washington, D.C.

Printed by
R. R. Donnelley
Harrisonburg, Virginia

Contents

1

Introduction

ALICIA H. MUNNELL

S trong economic growth, a stock market boom in the 1990s, and the shift toward defined contribution pension plans means that more and more individuals will have significant wealth upon retirement. How they use that wealth will determine not only their own well-being, but also the living standards of their children, the resources available to philanthropies, and the level of investment capital in the economy. To predict the impact of policy changes on future wealth accumulation, it is important to understand not only the disposition of wealth, but also why people save in the first place. Do they accumulate wealth to support themselves in retirement or do they save to leave a bequest to their children?

This volume explores the reasons why people save, how they decide to allocate their wealth once they retire, and how givers select their beneficiaries. It also assesses the extent to which the estate tax and annuitization of retirement wealth affects the amount and nature of wealth transfers. Finally, it looks at the impact of wealth transfers—first on the amount of aggregate saving and capital accumulation, and then on the distribution of wealth among households. To place the U.S. experience in context, the analysis begins with a historical and an international perspective.

Several important issues appear repeatedly throughout the volume: The first is the motive for saving. The big question is whether bequests result from a deliberate bequest motive or from unpredictable deaths that occur before consumers without bequest motives consume all of their resources. If people do save to leave bequests, the question is why. They could be motivated by pure altruism, where their transfers reflect a selfless concern for their beneficiaries. Alternatively, bequests could result from a strategic or exchange motive where the giver is trying to influence behavior or get recognition in return. Another alternative is a "warm glow" motive, where people get pleasure from the mere act of giving. Finally, people may hold wealth, and die with wealth, simply because they like it, or perhaps because it brings them prestige and power.

The motive matters. For example, if bequests are accidental, an increase in the estate tax should have no effect on wealth accumulation. If bequests are the result of altruistic or warm glow motives, an increase in the estate tax is likely to reduce total accumulation and transfers. Similarly, the Ricardian Equivalence proposition, which asserts that a tax change has no effect on consumption, saving, or interest rates, requires that consumers have bequest motives that arise from pure altruism toward their children. If bequests are simply the accidental by-product of unpredictable deaths, then the Ricardian equivalence proposition will not hold.

The effort to sort out motives brings up the second issue: money versus people. The question is whether one is trying to explain the motives of most of the population or the motives of those—namely, the very rich—who bequeath most of the money. The bulk of the empirical work comes from household surveys, which generally do not include the very wealthy, so the results may explain what drives the behavior of most households but not the motive for the bulk of bequests.

The third issue is the trade-off between bequests and *inter-vivos* gifts. The literature suggests considerable substitutability between the two options, particularly for the wealthy. Some evidence indicates a movement among wealthy donors towards *inter-vivos* gifts to philanthropic organizations. Thus any analysis of the quantitative impact of transfers on wealth accumulation must consider gifts as well as transfers at death.

The final issue is the decisionmaking unit. In the case of a single person, the analysis is easy. One person is making a decision, and the bequest usually goes to the next generation. But often the decisionmaker is not a single unit, but a married couple consisting of two individuals with different life expectancies and different preferences. In most cases, the husband is likely to die before the wife, which means that the bulk of the estate goes to the wife and then to the children. In other words, while couples do engage in joint decisionmaking, they have different preferences and die at different times and therefore cannot be treated as a single unit with respect to transfer behavior.

As the authors address their specific topics and touch on the issues described above, several conclusions emerge: First, gifts and bequests are important; they may account for about half of total wealth. Second, rich people make most of the wealth transfers. They are thoughtful about how much they pay in taxes and how they dispose of their wealth. They care about philanthropic causes and view their charitable contributions as more than a way to avoid paying estate taxes. But tax minimization and thoughtfulness about disposition do not necessarily imply that they accumulate their wealth *solely to leave a bequest*; they could also simply value wealth per se. Third, most nonrich people probably have some lexicographic preferences about the disposition of their wealth; they want to ensure they have adequate resources to take care of their own needs, and if money is left over, they would like it to go to their children. Fourth, little support has emerged for the pure altruistic model of bequests; people do not offset public sector transfers, and they tend to leave equal bequests to their children rather than compensating those well endowed. Fifth, institutions matter. In the case of the rich, the estate tax probably reduces saving and increases bequests to charity. In the case of the nonrich, the shift to defined contribution plans will at a minimum mean that they have more wealth in their hands when they die, and therefore they will leave larger accidental bequests. It might also increase their interest in leaving an estate for their heirs.

Saving and bequest behavior remains a fertile ground for future research. Major differences of opinion remain on such important issues as the effect of bequests on the distribution of wealth. The shift toward defined contribution plans may have an equalizing effect by increasing bequests from middle-income households, but what about the impact of the bulk of estates? An equally important issue is why people do not buy annuities. These issues need to be resolved as the baby boom generation arrives at retirement with bigger bundles of cash than ever before.

Although questions remain, the following papers provide an exciting summary of existing knowledge, push the debate forward, and link topics in a unique and comprehensive way.

The U.S. Experience in Perspective

Before exploring the reasons for and economic effects of bequests in the United States, two papers put the current U.S. experience in perspective by offering first a historical and then an international view. It turns out that motivations for making wealth transfers change over time, and the workings of bequests are very dependent on the institutions within different countries.

J. Bradford DeLong characterizes today's consensus view of bequests in the United States as follows: Bequests influence, but do not decisively determine, both wealth accumulation and wealth inequality. Bequests are motivated primarily by the desire to improve the lot of one's children—all one's children, although strategic and compensatory bequests are also possible. Bequests as a part of American life are viewed with some suspicion. This consensus view is new, says DeLong; 250 years ago practically every aspect of bequests was different.

Before the Industrial Revolution, the fundamental purpose of bequests was not to make all one's descendants better off or to make children behave appropriately, or to compensate for unequal endowments, but rather to maximize the wealth and power of the eldest male of the lineage for all future generations. The mechanisms to accomplish this goal were known as *primogeniture*, the principle that the eldest son inherited almost everything, and *entail*, the legal requirement that the current wealth holder transmit the principal value of the estate unimpaired to his heirs. Bequests were central to the workings of society and in no way distasteful.

In practically every pre–Industrial Revolution society, bequests played an overwhelming role in wealth accumulation and wealth distribution. Very low rates of economic growth meant that net investment was a minuscule 1.5 to 2.2 percent of annual output. At the same time, DeLong estimates that shorter generations meant that between 16 and 24 percent of annual output—more than ten times the contribution of net investment to wealth—was turned over in bequests each year. These rough calculations suggest that bequests accounted for about 90 percent of wealth acquisition before the Industrial Revolution compared to 45 percent today. With little ability for individuals to accumulate wealth, the system of primogeniture and entail meant that wealth holdings remained extremely concentrated in the hands of a few.

Migration to the New World changed perceptions about the purpose of bequests. The old patterns were not consistent with a land-rich, rapidly growing, frontier economy. The family needed everyone to clear and improve the land, but younger children would have little incentive if they were precluded from enjoying the fruits of their labor. They could always move further west and acquire their own land. Within two or three generations, the principle of primogeniture was replaced with the idea that estates should be divided equally among all the children, or at least among all male children. Moreover, the ability to accumulate wealth through the acquisition of land and one's labor meant that bequests were less important in wealth accumulation and wealth distribution.

The coming of the Industrial Revolution to America produced large increases in the concentration of wealth, which led to questions about the legitimacy of passing huge estates to one's heirs. By the twentieth century, inherited wealth was viewed with some suspicion; even a number of the very rich supported high statutory rates on large estates. Although the estate tax, which began in 1916 in the shadow of World War I, has never raised much money, it serves as a message and an obstacle to large bequests. Today, after a sharp rise in inequality in the 1980s and 1990s, the estate tax is scheduled for repeal. The question is whether the scheduled repeal means that views about inherited wealth, which have been remarkably mutable over the centuries, are changing once again.

DeLong's discussants agree with his overall story about the changing nature and role of bequests. Peter A. Diamond proposes two topics for some further analysis: The first is protection of widows, which has a long history that originally centered on the concept known as *dower*. Dower is the right of the wife to a life estate in one-third of the lands of her husband. Dower persisted in England until 1925, and in the United States, dower was added to and expanded and eventually became the spousal *forced share* that is part of American inheritance law today. The second avenue for further research is the behavior of the nonwealthy. How has the age of the recipient changed over time and how important are bequests as a share of total wealth?

With regard to the wealthy, Diamond offers three comments: First, he does not think that accidental bequests or bequests to improve the well-being of one's descendants can explain why the wealthy leave such large estates. He believes that wealth itself enters the utility function of the wealthy. That is, the wealthy accumulate assets and hold onto them because they get pleasure from their holdings. Second, even though the estate tax has raised limited revenue, it may have curtailed large estates. Recent research suggests that the wealth of the top 2 percent of the wealth holders has grown more slowly than average wealth per capita. The estate tax also encourages contributions to charities, which may be a further inhibiting factor. Finally, Diamond thinks the enthusiasm for repeal may be short lived once the fiscal realities take hold.

Jonathan Skinner, agreeing with Diamond, thinks that the estate tax revenues from the wealthy few may be just too tempting as persistent deficits reemerge. He then turns to DeLong's discussion about the declining importance of agricultural land and primogeniture for wealth accumulation over the last three hundred years. While DeLong gets the essence of the story correct, he may overstate the importance of land in total wealth. It is true that most of the labor force was employed in agriculture, but productivity was so low that the value of land was minimal compared to the capital used in commerce. Peter Lindert provides data on total wealth from probate, tax, debt, and ownership records for 1670 and 1875.[1] The data fit with DeLong's story in that the share of the capital stock held in land declines significantly over this period, and by 1875 a much larger share of wealth arises from life-cycle accumulation of merchants, entrepreneurs, and professionals. The surprising fact is that even in 1670, about half the capital stock is held by the nonagricultural sector, such as merchants, professionals, industrial and building trades, shopkeepers and laborers, and much of this capital could be viewed as arising from conventional life-cycle saving.

Skinner then discusses DeLong's contribution to the contentious debate about the relative importance of bequests and life-cycle motives in explaining overall wealth accumulation. DeLong's calculations show that the accounting exercises, beginning with Kotlikoff and Summers and continuing with Modigliani and Kotlikoff, tell us little about motives.[2] All those involved in this debate would find a much larger role for bequests in 1670 than today. But that does not mean that people cared more about their children, or that decedents left more accidental bequests. The debate about motives is a nondebate, according to Skinner. Money is fungible, and a dollar set aside at age fifty can be used as a cushion in case of poor health or some other contingency, and if these adverse events do not occur, the dollar can flow to one's children as a bequest. Saving for bequests and precautionary saving are not substitutes, but could well be complements. This combination of motives probably explains wealth accumulation in 1670, as well as in 2002, and will probably explain it in the future.

Pierre Pestieau provides an international perspective on gifts and bequests. The institutional setting surrounding wealth transfers in the United States and Europe differs in two important dimensions: the way transfers are taxed and the freedom to select beneficiaries. The United States levies an estate tax on the total estate of the donor, regardless of the characteristics and number of recipients. Most European countries, with the exception of the United Kingdom, levy an inheritance tax on the share received by the beneficiary, with rates and thresholds dependent on the relationship between the donor and the beneficiary. Estate taxation is generally paired with total freedom to bequeath to anyone, and the right to disinherit with an explicit will. In contrast, inheritance taxation often comes with the obligation to leave wealth to one's children, if any, and with equal sharing of most of the estate.

1. Lindert (1986).
2. Kotlikoff and Summers (1981); Modigliani (1988); Kotlikoff (1988).

The estate tax is easy to administer, and freedom of bequests allows parents to compensate for differences in income or need. The inheritance tax is more equitable in the case of large families, but forced sharing does not allow parents to offset unequal endowments.

In terms of economic effects of wealth transfers, Pestieau reports the following: Studies using the same methodology for European countries and the United States generally conclude that bequests constitute a larger share of total wealth in Europe than in the United States. This finding must be accepted with caution, however, since most estimates for European countries fall within the very broad range of estimates for the United States. Nevertheless, assuming an altruistic motive for giving, larger private transfers would be expected to offset the greater public intergenerational transfers for social security and health care in the European countries. Despite the apparent greater importance of bequests in Europe, wealth is more concentrated in the United States than in Europe.

In both the United States and Europe, *inter-vivos* gifts are much less important than bequests. Gifts appear to be somewhat compensatory in the U.S., but not in France, which is somewhat surprising since in both countries bequests are generally divided equally among children (voluntary in the United States; mandatory in France). Almost no studies allow researchers to identify the most important bequest motives. In terms of the effect of the number of children on bequest size, studies for both the United States and France find a negative relationship between the amount received by a child and the number of siblings. Finally, regardless of the type of wealth transfer tax, the yield is uniformly low—generally less than 0.5 percent of GDP.

Pestieau cautions that most of the conclusions should be viewed as tentative. Even in the United States, where considerable research exists, many questions are still unresolved about the motives for and effects of wealth transfers.

Peter R. Orszag notes that international comparisons play a role in the debate about eliminating the estate tax. Specifically, opponents of the estate tax, citing the high U.S. marginal rate, argue that wealth transfer taxes are much more burdensome in the United States than in other developed countries. Pestieau, however, shows it is impossible to characterize a tax on the basis of one parameter such as the tax rate. For example, because of a lower exemption level, wealth transfer taxes as a percent of GDP are higher in France than in the United States. Moreover, while opponents claim that high wealth transfer taxes reduce national saving, no such pattern is evident across countries.

Although Pestieau finds little evidence for variations in motives across countries, Orszag suggests one reason why accidental bequests might be lower in Europe. Orszag's sense is that motives are lexicographic in that actual bequests result from some combination of accidental and altruistic motives. That is, people accumulate wealth as a precaution against substantial end-of-life expenses, particularly health care expenses, but also hope that these expenses will not occur and they will be able to leave a significant bequest to their heirs. To the extent that precautionary saving is lower in countries with national health insurance, accidental bequests may also be lower.

In short, bequests in the United States occur in a very different institutional environment than in Europe, and within the United States, the role of bequests and the public's view of bequests have changed significantly over the centuries.

How Do People Make Gifts and Bequests?

This section explores the reasons for wealth transfers and how givers select their beneficiaries. The three papers consider whether bequests are left by accident or on purpose, how people decide between philanthropic organizations and family, and finally, who gets the bequest within the family and the extent to which basic biological criteria—such as gender—play a role.

Michael D. Hurd assesses whether individuals have an important bequest motive or whether bequests arise from precautionary saving and imperfect annuity markets. He presents a simple life-cycle model and assumes that altruism is the motive for bequests, if any bequest motive exists. In his model, consumers get utility from their own consumption, and separately from bequests to children, bequests to relatives, and bequests to institutions.

The life-cycle model makes the strong prediction that the elderly should decumulate their wealth as mortality risk increases; failure to draw down assets would provide evidence of a bequest motive. An altruistic bequest motive implies that elderly people with children should decumulate their wealth at a slower rate than those without children. Hurd reports the results of a number of studies that show the elderly with children decumulating at the same rate as or more rapidly than those without. He interprets these results as evidence against a bequest motive.

Hurd also offers two new pieces of evidence to support his case of no bequest motive. The first is the pattern of homeownership among the elderly. Hurd looks at homeownership rather than housing equity, because equity is subject to reporting error and capital gains. He presents cross-section ownership rates from three waves of the Study of the Asset and Health Dynamics among the Oldest Old (AHEAD). For the population as a whole, homeownership declines by about 2 percent per year between age seventy and eighty-five. Since this rate of decumulation is very close to that for nonhousing wealth, Hurd concludes that it provides no evidence of a bequest motive.

Hurd next looks at projected wealth decumulation, which he estimates from a household's wealth holdings and survey questions on the subjective probability of leaving a bequest of $10,000 or $100,000 reported in AHEAD. He compares the expected bequest with existing wealth holdings to calculate how much people plan to decumulate before they die. Hurd argues that expected decumulation is a better measure than actual decumulation, because it is not subject to various economic shocks, such as the enormous stock market boom of the 1990s. He then tests whether the projected rate of decumulation is slower for those who should have a greater bequest motive, and finds that decumulation is no higher for those without children than for those with children, and the number of children has no effect on the rate of decumulation.

Hurd's overall conclusion is that people without children appear to behave very much like those with children in terms of the rate at which they draw down assets, including housing. Since Hurd assumes that because those without children must not have an operative bequest motive, elderly people with children must not either.

Andrew B. Abel highlights an important limitation to Hurd's analysis, and then presents some evidence in support of a bequest motive. As Hurd acknowledges, his results apply only to people included in the household surveys of the elderly, and these surveys generally do not include the very wealthy. Because the distribution of wealth is highly concentrated, even if Hurd is correct, the absence of a bequest motive may apply to the bulk of bequests, but not to the bulk of the money transferred.

Abel then looks at annuities and life insurance to see if they shed any more light on bequest motives, since in the absence of a bequest motive people should fully annuitize their wealth. He argues that the fact that annuities are expensive is not sufficient to explain why most people do not purchase them. Overpricing may eliminate demand for those with a bequest motive, but annuities have to be monumentally expensive to do the same for those without a bequest motive. More precisely, the load would have to be large enough so that the price of annuities exceeds the price of bonds; recent studies of annuities imply that this is not the case. Therefore, consumers without a bequest motive should buy annuities. The fact that they do not suggests a widespread bequest motive, unless other reasons exist for not purchasing them. One reason, of course, is the risk of very large medical or nursing home expenses. To the extent that these risks are important, improvements in long-term care and catastrophic health insurance may encourage the purchase of annuities. In any case, Abel argues that his model suggests that a bequest motive does exist.

As further support for the notion that consumers have a bequest motive, Abel turns to data on TIAA-CREF annuities purchased in 2000. Many annuities offered by TIAA-CREF include a "years certain" or "guaranteed payment" option. For example, a single-life annuity with a ten-year guarantee will provide periodic payments for life if the annuitant lives at least ten years; if the annuitant dies before ten years, it will provide his heirs with payments for the remainder of the ten-year period. In 2000, 80 percent of men and 75 percent of women elected an annuity with some form of guarantee. The proportions are even higher if the sample is limited to those with some form of joint annuity, where the fixed payment generally benefits the children. Abel interprets the purchase of annuities with guarantees as evidence of a bequest motive.

Jonathan Gruber also challenges Hurd's conclusion of no bequest motive. First, he notes that Hurd's results on homeownership are virtually identical to those of other researchers. Hurd finds that housing wealth declines at about 2 percent per year and concludes that the rate does not suggest an active bequest motive. In contrast, Steven Venti and David Wise find housing wealth decumulation of 1.76 percent per year after age seventy-five, and conclude that housing equity is not drawn down for consumption.[3] The difference between the two studies rests on the interpretation of the results, and it is impossible to tell whose interpretation is right without a true underlying model of consumption needs in old age.

Second, Gruber challenges Hurd's conclusions from his estimates of projected wealth decumulation. Recent research documents considerable substitutability between gifts and bequests, which suggests that part of the decumulation of those with children may be in the form of gift-giving. The more fundamental question is the hypothesis that the bequest motive is stronger for those with children. It is not obvious to Gruber that among those planning to leave a bequest, that the bequest motive is stronger for households with children, and even less obvious that it is stronger with more children. The effect of children depends on the model; Hurd has assumed altruism as the motive for bequest, but the literature includes other options. For example, the warm glow model, where the donor gets utility simply from providing the bequest, does not imply that more children would lead to larger bequests.

Paul G. Schervish and John J. Havens shift the focus from why people accumulate wealth to how they decide what to do with it. The shift in focus also involves a shift in the population under investigation from the vast

3. Venti and Wise (2000).

majority of the households to the households that control the vast majority of the money. In exploring how people decide to allocate their wealth between charitable institutions and their children, the authors bring a social psychological perspective and extensive in-depth interviews. One set of interviews focused on 130 millionaires in the mid-1980s, another involved forty-four randomly selected people from the Boston area who reported weekly on care and giving over the course of a year from 1995 to 1996, and the third set of interviews was conducted with twenty-eight high-tech entrepreneurs and executives in 2001 about their attitudes to wealth and philanthropy.

From these interviews and other literature, they derive a general theoretical framework for giving: the "identification theory." This theory has two components: The first is that giving to families, friends, and charity is a manifestation of the more general concept of care. Second, identification with the needs of others is the major motivation for giving to both charitable organizations, and to friends, relatives, and to others in need. Identification motivates giving and caring behavior by families and individuals across all levels of wealth and income. The identification theory is more general than the motives for giving—altruism, exchange, or warm glow—generally cited in the economics literature. Motives do not lie along an axis from altruism to self-interest but rather an axis from isolation to engagement.

The second part of their argument is that while identification holds across the economic spectrum, the realms of identification and hence the allocation of gifts differ for those who have redundant resources; that is, those who can provide for their desired standard of living and still have financial resources left over. Such financially secure individuals, who are responsible for the bulk of charitable giving, do not have to trade off consumption expenditures for gifts. They also tend to have control of their time and can create their own opportunities for philanthropy; they are not limited, like the nonwealthy, to supporting predefined institutions and organizations.

Schervish and Havens argue that the very wealthy appear to be shifting gifts away from children and toward charities, and from bequests to *inter-vivos* giving. These shifts may in part reflect new techniques used by fundraisers for charitable organizations and by financial planners through the development of innovative giving vehicles. The new techniques involve the wealth holders in a process of discernment to clarify their own financial needs and to identify their philanthropic objectives and priorities for the allocation of their wealth. This self-reflective financial advising could significantly increase the amounts being left to charitable organizations in the future.

James Andreoni argues that the core components of identification theory are similar to the motives described by economists: altruism, exchange, and warm glow. "Care," in the Schervish-Havens identification theory, is very close to the economists' concept of altruism. People express their care for people or organizations through gifts, and Andreoni likens the joy people get from helping those with whom they identify to the economists' notion of warm glow. But the interviews also make clear that care can be intended to shape and influence others, so the process of giving also has a strategic or exchange motive.

Although the core components of identification theory are similar to current economic concepts, Andreoni asserts that the social psychological approach enriches the economic analysis in three ways: First, the interviews provide a nice analysis of how economic objectives are formed. Second, identification theory makes clear that giving is a dynamic social activity. Third, the dynamic interaction between givers, and heirs and beneficiaries, which emerges from the interviews and the data, means that identification can be manipulated and influenced. To Andreoni, the major innovation emerging from the Schervish-Havens work is the potential to create a new literature on fund-raising. That is, the social psychological literature should encourage economists to think about the lifelong relationships between givers and their beneficiaries, and how preferences are shaped by these relationships.

Charles Clotfelter notes that two other literatures address the division of estates between heirs and charitable organizations. One is the theoretical literature that offers alternative models of behavior for charitable giving:

—Donors care about the provision of public goods;

—Donors care about the well-being of their heirs;

—Donors want to affect the behavior of their beneficiaries;

—Donors get a warm glow from giving.

The second is the empirical literature that assumes preferences as given, and within an assumed model of behavior, tests for the importance of factors such as income, tax rates, wealth, age, and marital status. This literature shows that people respond to the relative costs of alternatives, and they tend to donate more if the price is lower. This literature also yields some other stylized facts:

—Charitable bequests are a small percent of total bequests, except for the very rich;

—Religious groups receive the most in the lowest wealth classes, but their share drops to near zero at higher levels of wealth;

—Decedents who are survived by a spouse tend to leave less to charity;

—Charitable bequests are higher the more affluent the children.

The Schervish-Havens in-depth interviews offer an opportunity to understand the complexity of human decisionmaking. Schervish and Havens observe a variety of motivations underlying charitable giving and attempt to blend them together under the identification theory. Although Clotfelter finds the notion of blending love of self with love of family and community appealing, he agrees with Andreoni that the authors overdraw the distinction between their model and those that exist in the economics literature. Moreover, Schervish and Havens, like other researchers, face the challenge of showing how the empirical regularities described above emerge from their model of behavior.

Donald Cox shifts the discussion from charity versus family to the distribution of bequests within the family. He summarizes what the existing literature says about the allocation of bequests among family members and then explores the potential role that basic biology might play. The stylized facts that have emerged from research to date are as follows:

—Most bequests are shared equally among the children;

—Unlike bequests, *inter-vivos* giving tends not to be shared equally; they are targeted to children who are liquidity constrained;

—Demographic characteristics of children, such as gender, are often important determinants, even after controlling for income.

While these findings are broadly accepted, they create some puzzles. For example, if altruism is the primary motive for wealth transfers, the pattern of *inter-vivos* giving would be expected to vary strongly with the income of the children—vis-à-vis the parents and each other. The altruistic model also predicts that among parents who make transfers to their children, a $1.00 increase in parents' resources coupled with a $1.00 decrease in children's resources should raise transfers from parents to children by a dollar. However, researchers have been unable to find anything close to a dollar-for-dollar response to an increase in transfers; in fact, the highest estimate for the United States is 15 cents. Of course, an even bigger challenge for the altruistic model is to explain why bequests are distributed equally.

Although much of the empirical work in the United States includes demographic variables, these variables are generally entered as controls and rarely discussed in relation to any theory of behavior. Cox contends that greater consideration of male-female differences could provide useful insights. He suggests that researchers might want to consider at least a biological motive for transfers; that is, parents and grandparents invest in children in order to maximize the likelihood of passing along their genes. Within this framework, he explores three implications of biology for intergenerational transfers: The first is how uncertainty about paternity could affect the incentives of fathers, mothers, and grandparents to invest in children. The second is how differing reproductive prospects of sons versus daughters could affect parental investment in the two. The third is the extent to which parent-child conflict, which stems from children's strong genetic interest in themselves, might affect transfers. Each of these predictions presents testable hypotheses.

One implication of parental uncertainty is that mothers, who are more certain of the biological link, are more likely to make transfers than fathers. Cox examines this hypothesis by looking at the transfers from grandmothers to their grandchildren. The notion is that maternal grandmothers are more likely to make transfers than paternal grandmothers because they are more certain of the genetic link. The evidence supports this prediction, but the pattern is also consistent with a variety of commonsense explanations as well. For example, the mother of young children might feel more comfortable turning to her own mother for support than to her mother-in-law.

In terms of investing in children, Cox starts with the Trivers-Willard hypothesis. This model from biology predicts that parents differentially invest in boys versus girls depending on which sex has the most favorable reproductive prospects. Cox argues that investment in education is one way, albeit less extreme, to apply the Trivers-Willard model. The hypothesis is that parents will vary how much they invest in children of each sex depending on how successful they expect them to be in the world. Cox finds that poor people are more likely to educate daughters, while rich people are more likely to educate sons. He attributes this finding to the expectation that daughters have a better chance of marrying up to escape poverty than sons who lack the resources to marry at all. Conversely, investments in sons from rich families will only enhance their chances to "go forth and multiply." Once again, the results are also consistent with alternative nonbiological explanations, such as the differential returns to schooling reported in the human capital literature.

Finally, parent-child conflict in families stems from the fact that children have a stronger genetic interest in themselves than in their parents or siblings. This self-interest creates the possibility for conflict and the potential for people to make transfers, not for reasons of altruism or exchange, but simply to avoid nasty interactions. Cox presents some evidence from the 2000 wave of the Health and Retirement Study (HRS) that suggests that conflict, or the avoidance of conflict, may play a role in transfers between generations.

Kathleen McGarry doubts whether a biological motive plays a significant role in transfer decisions, but applauds Cox for offering a theory with testable implications. With regard to parental uncertainty, she suggests that the same prediction about maternal grandmothers could be extended to grandfathers;

that is, maternal grandfathers should provide more support than paternal grandfathers. In fact, it should be possible to establish a ranking of probabilities of transfers: maternal grandmother first, then either maternal grandfather or paternal grandmother, and finally paternal grandfather (who does not know for certain that his wife's son is his child, nor that the grandchild belongs to his son). This ranking is testable for transfers of time.

In terms of money transfers, the ranking suggests that the maternal side should unambiguously make greater transfers. Cox's data, however, show that while couples lower in the income distribution receive more from the wife's parents, those higher up receive more from the husband's parents. Cox suggests this twist reflects less confidence in paternity for poor people than for rich people. But McGarry offers another explanation. To the extent that the recipient couple's income is largely determined by the husband, it is probably more highly correlated with the income of the husband's parents than with that of the wife's. Since high-income husbands are likely to have high-income parents who can afford generous transfers, and low-income husbands are likely to have low-income parents who do not make generous transfers, it is not surprising that the husband's parents dominate at the high end and the wife's parents dominate at the low end.

Another area where the biological model provides testable predictions, which Cox does not address, is transfers to stepchildren and adopted children. If the biological model dominates, these children should not receive any transfers at all. The one study that explores the issue finds that adopted and biological children are treated equally.[4] Some survey evidence on stepchildren suggests a preference for biological children, not necessarily because of genetics, but because stepchildren have another parent from whom they will get transfers and the donor is trying "to be fair."

The biological model also makes it difficult to understand the prevalence of bequests over *inter-vivos* giving. The notion would be to make transfers early so that the assistance influences the quantity and quality of one's children. Similarly, bequests are overwhelmingly divided equally across children, with no preference for those with more children or a particular gender. Despite these puzzles and others, McGarry concludes that the notion of a biological motive merits further investigation.

Theodore Bergstrom also finds intriguing, if not fully convincing, the notion that biological differences between the sexes are likely to result in predictable differences in economic relations among family members. He too

4. Judge and Hrdy (1992).

applauds the fact that Cox's hypothesis provides testable implications. With regard to paternity uncertainty, Bergstrom is interested in the incidence of children conceived outside of marriage. Cox notes one study that says between 5 and 30 percent of American and British children have been adulterously conceived, but notes that even these imprecise estimates are poorly documented. How much is going on, and where it is going on, has implications for some of the data reported by Cox.

Bergstrom finds the Cox data showing bias toward the maternal line interesting regardless of the reason, and suggests some further avenues of exploration. For example, divorce might offer an explanation. Grandmothers are more likely to have dealings with grandchildren that live with their own child than with their child's former spouse. If mothers generally gain custody, this would explain some of the bias toward maternal rather than paternal grandchildren. Age of the grandparents and distance from the grandchildren would also be useful to consider.

With regard to investments in sons versus daughters, Bergstrom does not find Cox's application of the Trivers-Willard model persuasive, but can offer no other explanation. Finally, on the issue of conflict, Bergstrom agrees that conflict is important and rejects the argument put forth by Gary Becker that even totally selfish children can be forced to act in the reproductive interests of their parents. Bergstrom concludes by adding one source of disparate treatment of children not mentioned by Cox—namely, in-laws. Hamilton's kin selection theory says that a wife values her sibling's children half as much as her own, while her husband will have no genetic stake in them whatsoever. This means that the genetically related spouse will have much more interest in supporting nieces and nephews than the spouse without the genetic link.

Impact of Taxes and Pension Benefits on Gifts and Bequests

These papers shift the discussion from the inner workings of the household—their decisions about saving and about the disposition of their wealth—to external factors that affect bequests such as taxes and benefits.

Wojciech Kopczuk and Joel Slemrod explore the impact of the estate tax on wealth accumulation and transfers. They note from the outset that their analysis applies only to the rich since no more than 6 percent of decedents in any year have ever paid the estate tax and currently that number is limited to the top 2 percent. The most important features of the 2001 estate tax are:

—Current law imposes an integrated set of taxes on estates, gifts, and generation-skipping trusts;

—Bequests to spouses and to charitable institutions are tax free;

   —A credit provides the equivalent of an exemption for the first $675,000 of transfers;

   —The tax rate on transfers over $675,000 is 37 percent and rises to 55 percent on taxable transfers above $3 million;

   —A surtax of 5 percent applies to taxable estates between $10 million and $17 million.

The Economic Growth and Tax Relief Reconciliation Act of 2001 includes major changes to the estate tax, and suffice it to say that the future of the estate tax is uncertain.

   Given recent legislative interest in the estate tax, a series of studies has tried to assess its effects on wealth accumulation and giving. These studies suggest that the estate tax reduces the accumulation of estates by as much as 10.5 percent and increases charitable contributions by as much as 12 percent. Moreover, even though the tax provides substantial reasons to favor *inter-vivos* gifts over bequests, most wealth transfers occur through bequests. Kopczuk and Slemrod add to the existing literature in three ways: First, they explore the relationship over time between reported estates of the top one half of one percent of decedents as a share of total wealth and the estate tax rate. Reported estates are clearly negatively related to the estate tax rate, which is consistent with earlier studies that suggest the estate tax reduces accumulations. The key question, of course, is whether wealthy individuals are actually saving less in response to the estate tax or simply making their reported estate smaller through some form of avoidance. Nevertheless, the results are suggestive.

   Second, Kopczuk and Slemrod estimate time-series equations to explain the effect of the estate tax on charitable contributions. Because charitable contributions are deductible from the taxable estate, the estate tax lowers their price relative to noncharitable bequests; the price effect would be expected to increase charitable bequests. At the same time, the estate tax reduces the total wealth available for bequests; this would be expected to reduce all bequests, including bequests to charity The ratio of charitable con-tributions to gross estate has drifted up over time. If this drift can be attrib-uted to increasing wealth, then the regressions indicate that the estate tax rates have a significant positive effect on charitable giving. Moreover, given the progressivity of the rate structure, for most reforms the price effect will change proportionately more than the so-called net-of-tax wealth effect, implying that a tax decrease will reduce charitable contributions. The overall results of the Kopczuk-Slemrod analysis is that the tax has increased charita-ble contributions, and the effect could be larger than the 12 percent found in recent studies.

Third, Kopczuk and Slemrod analyze a model of the optimal distribution of bequests between spouses and the role of QTIP trusts. This is an important contribution, because it recognizes that the decisionmaker is not a single unit, but typically a married couple consisting of two individuals with the husband likely to die before the wife. In their model, a husband facing death gets utility from his widow's consumption after he dies, and the value he places on nonspousal bequests made by him or his widow. Solving this model subject to a budget constraint, and assuming that the husband and wife have similar tastes, indicates that the two estates should be set so that the husband's and wife's marginal tax rates are equal. This result changes to the extent that the husband and wife disagree about the wife's consumption as a widow; the husband and wife place different values on giving to children; the couple places a significant option value on retaining resources for the surviving spouse; or they expect very large capital gains between the death of the first spouse and the second. The availability of QTIP trusts is also important in that these trusts allow the husband to leave resources to his wife and still control the ultimate destination of the bequest.

The authors check their predictions against the data and find that husbands leave significantly more to their wives than tax minimization would suggest. This is puzzling, especially since the large transfers often do not benefit the wife in that they are placed in a QTIP trust that restricts the wife's control. The inefficiency of the large spousal transfers seems at odds with the apparent responsiveness of charitable contributions to the price considerations embedded in the estate tax. In short, the estate tax appears to be an important determinant of bequests, but more work is needed to understand intrafamily dynamics.

Ray D. Madoff addresses some of these questions: She agrees with Kopczuk and Slemrod that the technical division of assets is responsive to tax considerations, but cautions that the technical division may provide little information about the transfers of resources between husband and wife. Credit shelter trusts allow decedents to take advantage of the unified credit yet offer enormous discretion about how much benefit is given to the surviving spouse. Similar flexibility is available with respect to transfers qualifying for the marital deduction. In other words, the husband can take full advantage of the unified credit and the spousal deduction without being subject to significant limitations on his dispositive plan. Very little trade-off is required between resource allocation and tax minimization.

In contrast, Madoff notes that tax equalization involves real costs to taxpayers. Tax equalization, which is accomplished by paying some taxes on the death of the first spouse, requires diminishing the resources available to the surviving spouse by the amount of the tax. Without equalization, the couple's combined tax liability will be higher, but the burden of the reduced resources will fall on the children. One great advantage of the QTIP trust, not mentioned by Kopczuk and Slemrod, is that it allows couples to defer the difficult decision about when to pay taxes until nine months after the death of the first spouse. At that time, the surviving spouse may herself be in poor health and indifferent to reduced resources; in which case assets can be subjected to taxes in the first spouse's estate. Alternatively, she may feel that she needs the resources, and the resources can be transferred undiminished by payment of estate taxes. This reluctance on the part of couples to reduce the resources available to the surviving spouse is consonant with people's reluctance to make taxable gifts even though the effective tax rate on gifts is significantly lower than on transfers at death.

James Poterba offers some thoughts on identifying motives for establishing QTIP trusts. He suggests that distinguishing between couples who have been married only once, and those where at least one partner has been married before, should provide some insights. In the latter case, a QTIP provides an obvious mechanism for the first to die to ensure that part of the estate goes to his or her natural children. Another possible motive for a QTIP is the desire to transfer management of assets to experienced trustees rather than leaving it in the hands of a less financially sophisticated spouse. Finally, it would be useful to know the extent to which QTIPs actually constrain the consumption of spouses below their desired level or alter the pattern of desired bequests.

With regard to other parts of the Kopczuk-Slemrod paper, Poterba emphasizes that the ability of the wealthy to reduce their reported estates seriously complicates efforts to estimate the impact of the estate tax on wealth accumulation. For example, recent research shows that when the unitary credit increases, people affected by the change appear to reduce their *inter-vivos* giving.[5] Various estate planning strategies can also reduce the size of the estate. Since these strategies always involve some loss in control, they are more likely to be adopted when rates are higher and the tax savings greater.

With regard to charitable giving, Poterba emphasizes the fragility of the Kopczuk-Slemrod results in that the significance of the estate tax rate disappears when the equations include a time trend. The difficulty with any type of time-series analysis is that tax rates do not vary much over time, and removing trend variation makes it difficult to identify behavioral effects. Nevertheless, Poterba shares the belief that lower marginal estate tax rates will lead to lower charitable contributions.

5. Bernheim, Lemke, and Scholz (2001).

That the estate tax affects wealth transfers is not surprising in that it changes the resources available for gifts and bequests and the price of allocating resources one way or another. However, Alicia H. Munnell, Annika Sundén, Mauricio Soto, and Catherine Taylor argue that the estate tax is not the only part of the U.S. financial infrastructure that influences bequests; the changing nature of the private pension system is also likely to have an important effect. They contend that the dramatic shift from defined benefit to defined contribution plans will increase bequests as retirees receive more of their pension benefits as lump sums rather than annuity payments.

Munnell and others contend that the shift to lump-sum distributions will affect bequests in two ways: First, unintended bequests will rise because people are reluctant to spend accumulated wealth. This reluctance is evident in the small size of the U.S. annuity market, the aversion of older homeowners to reverse annuity mortgages, the holdings of life insurance by retirees, and the limited dissaving in retirement. In the past, any reluctance to turn assets into income streams was mitigated by the fact that most retirement wealth, such as Social Security and private pensions, came in the form of annuity payments. But this countervailing force has diminished as more and more private sector pension plans provide lump-sum benefits. As a result, people will die with more assets than they would if they received their pensions as annuities, and greater assets in the hands of decedents will produce greater bequests. The second way in which a rise in lump-sum payments will increase bequests is by increasing intended bequests. The authors argue that people's interest in bequests increases when they gain access to accumulated assets. Accumulating wealth out of current income to leave a bequest is too difficult, but if people receive a pile of wealth, leaving a bequest becomes a plausible option. Thus Munnell and others contend that both intended and unintended bequests are likely to increase.

The increase in bequests due to the increase in lump-sum payments is potentially large. Using data from the Survey of Consumer Finances (SCF), the authors estimate that by 2004, assets in the hands of decedents each year will be roughly 6 percent higher ($28 billion in 2004) than otherwise because of the projected shift to defined contribution plans between 1992 and 2004. Roughly half this amount is transferred across generations, and since the increase in wealth is far more important for lower and middle quintiles of the wealth distribution, the increase in bequests should reduce wealth inequality.

The authors present a series of regressions to show that the composition of pension wealth affects people's subjective probability of leaving a bequest as reported in the Survey of Consumer Finances and the HRS. The first relates plans to leave a bequest to the ratio of defined contribution and IRA wealth as a share of total pension and Social Security wealth. As hypothesized, bequeathable pension wealth as a share of total pension wealth has a positive and large effect on the probability of leaving a bequest. The second set of equations relates the same variables to the probability of leaving a bequest of $10,000 or more and the probability of leaving a bequest of $100,000 or more as reported in the HRS. Again, bequeathable pension wealth as a share of total pension wealth has a significant positive effect on the probability of leaving a bequest.

The remaining question is whether the increase in bequests will be financed by lower consumption in retirement or greater saving during the work life. To address this question, Munnell and others estimate saving and wealth equations including various forms of defined benefit, defined contribution, and Social Security wealth. The results suggest that workers react very differently to their defined contribution accumulations than they do to the present value of annuity pensions. They do not reduce their other saving in anticipation of payments from defined contribution plans as they do in response to promised Social Security and defined benefit pension payments. Thus it appears that households will finance their increased bequests by more saving during their work life.

The authors recognize that it may seem strange to worry simultaneously about people cashing out their defined contribution accumulations when they change jobs during their work lives, and to worry about people's reluctance to spend defined contribution accumulations in retirement. They argue that different worries may be appropriate for different types of people. Those who make it to retirement with large accumulations are likely to be the savers, while those with a propensity to cash out during their working years are likely to be the spenders. In any event, they conclude that an increasing number of people will receive lump-sum payments from their pension plans, and this change will increase bequests and have important implications for both this generation and the next.

Amy Finkelstein agrees that the increase in lump-sum payments will increase bequests but raises four concerns about the analysis: First, she notes that it matters whether the increase in bequests is intended or unintended. If bequests increase simply because households are reluctant to annuitize their accumulations due to the high load factors in the annuity market, this increase represents a welfare loss. On the other hand, if intended bequests rise because the utility of bequests increases with more bequeathable wealth, the increase in bequests would be welfare neutral. If unintended bequests increase because the increase in defined contribution plans reduces excess annuitization, the outcome would represent a welfare gain.

Given that the welfare outcomes hinge on the motive for the bequest, it would be useful to know how much of the projected increase is intended versus unintended. Finkelstein argues that neither of the authors' empirical exercises produces such a breakdown. First, not all the increase of wealth in the hands of decedents should be characterized as a potential increase in unintended bequests. Second, the equations explaining expectations of leaving a bequest should not be characterized as explaining intended bequests. Households may recognize that they will hold more assets as precautionary saving in response to the decreased annuitization and understand that their bequests will increase even if they do not intend them to. Thus while the exercises shed light on the effect of bequeathable wealth on bequests, they cannot be interpreted as evidence of an effect on intended bequests.

Finkelstein's third concern is whether the relationships observed in the 1990s will be stable over time. Specifically, the shift to defined contribution plans may have effects other than those that work through the decline in annuitization. The shift occurred during a period of rapid run-up in the stock market, and the large gains might have increased interest in bequests if households engage in any form of intergenerational risk sharing. If so, the desire to leave a bequest might be lower if markets did not perform as well.

Finally, Finkelstein raises the inevitable question of how much of the relationship between pension wealth, on the one hand, and saving and nonpension wealth, on the other, is spurious. That is, defined contribution plans are voluntary and allow workers to decide how much to contribute; individuals with a taste for saving may be more likely to participate and contribute higher amounts to their defined contribution plans. Similarly, individuals with a taste for a saving are more likely to save more and accumulate greater nonpension assets. Therefore, unless the equation controls adequately for a taste for saving, the regression will show a positive relationship between defined contribution wealth and saving and nonpension wealth even if one does not determine the other. The authors recognize the potential bias and attempt to address it through instrumental variables, but Finkelstein is not convinced that they have solved the problem.

Olivia S. Mitchell cites another version of the same type of problem. She notes that workers covered by any type of pension tend to be more risk-averse, more productive, and have longer planning horizons than average. This means that the variable representing bequeathable pension wealth as a share of total pension wealth may be reflecting these characteristics, and these characteristics rather than more lump-sum payments leads to the increase in expected bequests. While Munnell and others try to address this issue by including a pension coverage variable, it may not reflect all the differences between covered and noncovered workers. For example, pension-covered workers are more likely to have health insurance, and if bequeathable pension wealth as a share of total pension wealth is related to health insurance, and the presence of health insurance allows people to think they will leave a larger bequest, the coefficient of the share variable will overstate its effect on expected bequests.

Mitchell also believes that households are too optimistic in survey responses about how much they will ultimately leave as a bequest. The average household has only $60,000 in nonfinancial assets and an equal amount in housing. The household nearing retirement may have to use a significant portion of these resources to support itself. Therefore, Mitchell is skeptical of the HRS responses indicating 41 percent of households expect to leave a bequest in excess of $100,000. It would be fruitful to compare households' expectations of bequests with bequest realizations.

Taking the findings of Munnell and others at face value, Mitchell notes they have potentially important policy implications. The analysis indicates that wealth in a defined contribution plan is more likely to be saved than spent. As employers move to automatic enrollment in defined contribution plans, inertia may get workers to save more during their work lives. Munnell and others suggest that households will continue to hold these funds in retirement, increasing long-term saving and wealth. The implication is that building a defined contribution component into Social Security might do the same.

Impact of Gifts and Bequests on the Economy

The final section shifts from examining the impact of economic institutions on bequests to exploring the impact of bequests on the economy. It starts with a discussion about how much bequests contribute to aggregate wealth and then turns to their effect on the distribution of that wealth among households.

William Gale and Samara Potter discuss empirical estimates of life-cycle wealth and transfer wealth and then question the usefulness of the accounting exercise even if it provides precise answers. They begin with the classic paper by Kotlikoff and Summers in which the authors establish a simple accounting framework that attributes any excess of lifetime earnings over consumption to life-cycle wealth and any excess of inheritances over bequests to transfer wealth.[6] Using data on average earnings and consumption by age across different cohorts, they conclude that life-cycle saving is at most 20 percent. This means that 80 percent of wealth comes from gifts and bequests.

6. Kotlikoff and Summers (1981).

Modigliani sharply criticizes their methodology and conclusions.[7] He argues that parents' payments for college should not be counted as transfer wealth, that interest accrued on previous transfers should be attributed to life-cycle, not transfer wealth, and that they did not accurately measure the consumption of durable goods. Making these corrections, Modigliani concludes that 80 percent of aggregate wealth can be explained by life-cycle wealth. Subsequent estimates by other researchers of life-cycle wealth also show enormous variation in magnitude.

Gale and Potter then explore other methods of estimating transfer wealth. One alternative is to ask people how much of their wealth was inherited. Studies looking at these survey data generally conclude that transfer wealth accounts for no more than 20 percent of the total. Gale and Potter note that this approach is plagued with difficulties. First, these surveys focus only on wealth received through inheritance and ignore *inter-vivos* gifts. Second, transfers received are generally significantly underreported, for example, as compared to transfers given. Third, it is not clear how respondents define the size of transfers received; that is, do they adjust these transfers to reflect subsequent earnings on the inherited amounts? William G. Gale and John Karl Scholz, using the 1983 and 1986 SCF, estimate that *inter-vivos* gifts account for 20 percent of net wealth and intergenerational bequests for 30 percent.[8] More recent estimates from the 1998 SCF produce a lower number. Gale and Potter conclude that trying to divide aggregate wealth between life-cycle saving and transfers yields a wide range of estimates.

They next ask what we would learn if we could calculate precisely the true values of these wealth components. Their answer is not much. First, the Kotlikoff-Summers accounting definitions do not provide economically meaningful information. For example, their definitions assume that all transfers received are either saved or paid out as transfers but not consumed, and that all earnings are either saved or consumed but not transferred. This assumption is at odds with the life-cycle model, according to which some transfers received might be consumed or result in changes in labor supply, and some wages might be used to provide transfers. Thus life-cycle wealth as defined by Kotlikoff and Summers does not necessarily correspond to what the life-cycle model would predict.

Second, knowing the precise magnitude of transfer wealth provides no information about the motives for the gift or bequest, because even if the transfer component is large, it could arise entirely from accidental bequests

---

7. Modigliani (1988).
8. Gale and Scholz (1994).

within the life-cycle framework. Gale and Potter believe that the patterns of *inter-vivos* giving, estate planning, annuity choices, and other evidence suggest that not all bequests are accidental, but they acknowledge that researchers have had substantial difficulty validating the specific implications that arise from alternative bequest motives. The important point is that all values of transfer wealth are consistent with either accidental or intended bequests and with any motive for intended bequest.

Understanding motives for transfers is critical because the response to government policy depends crucially on the reason for the bequest. For example, if bequests are accidental or because people get utility from holding wealth, changes in the estate tax will have no effect on saving. On the other hand, if transfers arise from altruism, an increase in the estate tax would likely reduce saving for bequests. The difficulty is that precise estimates of the amount of transfers say nothing about the motive, and without understanding the motive, it is impossible to predict responses to policy changes. Thus while transfers are probably a significant portion of wealth and merit attention and research, simply trying to get better estimates of the share of transfer and life-cycle wealth will not resolve the key issues about the motivation for saving and transfers and the effect of government policy on transfers and wealth.

Peter A. Diamond agrees with Gale and Potter that the accounting issue does not shed any light on interesting economic questions, but acknowledges that the Kotlikoff-Summers paper stimulated a lot of useful work. He reiterates the Gale-Potter point that motives are key to determining the impact of policy on saving. For example, if some people simply like to hold wealth— Diamond's preferred motive for the very wealthy—and therefore die with it, an increase in estate taxes will have no effect on their saving, although it will affect recipients.

Diamond also argues that the distinction between intended and accidental bequests used by the authors and others is not helpful. If an individual derives utility from both consumption and bequests, then the ultimate size of the bequest depends upon when he dies. It is not correct to characterize the excess of actual over intended bequests as accidental, because the entire bequest was intended in a probabilistic sense. So the question is how the distribution of possible bequests responds to changes in the economic environment.

This leads to the point that some annuitization is not inconsistent with a bequest motive. For example, annuitizing an amount equal to planned consumption sets the amount of the bequest with certainty, assuming no unforeseen contingencies. Conversely, annuitization is not a sign of an absence of bequest motive. This can be seen in the selection of an annuity that guarantees payment for a fixed number of years, a very popular option, that increases the price of the annuity and again makes the bequest probabilistic, depending on the time of death. While the popularity of the "years-certain" option is difficult to explain in the context of a standard utility-maximizing framework, it highlights the need for exploring a number of ways to model the decision concerning consumption, savings, and bequests. This kind of modeling, rather than accounting exercises, is the way to shed light on the role of transfers in aggregate wealth accumulation.

Laurence J. Kotlikoff, one of the authors of the original paper, agrees that the accounting exercise does not answer questions about motive or effect of government policy, but that was never the point of the original Kotlikoff-Summers article. The authors were just trying to figure out whether intergenerational transfers were important enough to merit further consideration. The paper concludes that transfers are the major source of wealth, and the results appear to have stimulated a great deal of important research.

Kotlikoff argues that we have learned a lot about the determinants for intergenerational transfers in the last twenty years. Researchers have found little empirical support for the Ricardo-Phelps-Barro model of intergenerational altruism. The old do not increase their bequests in response to government transfers financed by their children. Similarly, family members do not engage in much risk-sharing, which is an automatic implication of intergenerational altruism. Finally, parents generally ignore differences in the economic resources of their children and leave them equal amounts. *Inter-vivos* gifts are made primarily by middle-class families in the form of college support, and by the superrich in the form of business interests. This may be altruism, but to Kotlikoff, it seems more like the parental interest in transferring a particular item.

Kotlikoff believes that bequests are driven primarily by imperfect annuitization, and reports recent simulation results that support this hypothesis. In the simulation, parents have no interest in bequests, but any money left over at the end of life because of incomplete annuitization goes first to the surviving spouse, and when the last spouse dies, to the children in equal shares. The model generates realistic results for the flow of bequests relative to GDP, the distribution of wealth, and the share of wealth held by the top 1 percent of households.

Although the issue of motive remains unresolved, Gale and Potter and their discussants agree that intergenerational transfers constitute a significant share of total wealth. The next question is how those transfers affect the distribution of aggregate wealth. On his way to answering that question, Edward N. Wolff notes the following: First, wealth in the United States is extremely concentrated, with the top 1 percent of richest households holding about 40 percent of net worth. Second, the concentration increased notice-ably during the 1980s and continued to rise, albeit at a much slower rate, in the 1990s. Third, financial net worth, which excludes housing, is even more concentrated. Fourth, median net worth increased little between 1989 and 1998. Finally, snapshot comparisons where comparable data exist show that wealth holdings in the United States are also more concentrated than in France, Germany, Canada, and Japan.

Wolff then turns to the SCF to assess the role of bequests and *inter-vivos* gifts on the distribution of wealth. The first step is to calculate the value of wealth transfers received in the past. Wolff assumes that past inheritances grow by an average real rate of 3 percent, a number he views as a compromise between allocating all the returns to lifetime earnings and attributing all the returns to the transfer. The next step is to estimate lifetime earnings, and then calculate transfers as a percent of earnings by quintile. The results show that transfers are significantly larger for those with low lifetime earnings than for those with higher earnings. This suggests that transfers reduce inequality. Since simulating the effect of eliminating wealth transfers on lifetime resources would require a full behavioral model of household savings, Wolff uses a decomposition analysis to get at the question. This analysis shows that the correlation between wealth transfers and current wealth holdings exclud-ing transfers is negative, which means that households with lower wealth holdings exclusive of transfers receive higher transfers. At the same time, the distribution of wealth transfers is much more skewed toward the wealthy than net worth excluding transfers. The magnitude of the transfer effect, however, dominates that of the skewness, so the net impact of transfers has been to reduce wealth inequality.

John Karl Scholz challenges the conclusion that transfers equalize the dis-tribution of wealth. The key question is what would the world look like in the absence of the transfers. Wolff's calculations imply that a low-income person who has $10,000 of net worth and a transfer received ten years ago with a current value of $9,000 would be expected to have $1,000 in the absence of the transfer. Similarly, a high-income person with $100,000 of net worth and a transfer received ten years ago of $50,000 in today's terms would be expected to have $50,000 in the absence of the transfer. Thus the ratio of high-income to low-income net worth falls from fifty to one in the absence of transfers to ten to one with transfers. The problem is that this exercise assumes both the low- and high-income recipients save all of their inheri-tances. In fact, low-income recipients are likely to consume a large part of any inheritance and would experience little increase in net worth. Thus elim-inating inheritances would have no adverse impact on the wealth of the low income, but would reduce the wealth of the high income by $50,000 and therefore, Scholz argues, would have an equalizing impact on the distribution of wealth.

Scholz raises two other issues: First, he questions Wolff's adjustments to align the SCF with the Federal Reserve's Flow of Funds. The Flow of Funds household sector is calculated as a residual and therefore is not an obvious benchmark; even if it were, it is not clear that a proportional increase, which assumes uniform underreporting, is the right adjustment. Second, Scholz thinks Wolff provides a misleading characterization of the economic changes during the 1990s. Median net worth may have increased by only 1.6 percent per year from 1989 to 1998, but using this figure ignores the fact that households move through the wealth and income distribution as they age. Median net worth for thirty-five- to forty-four-year olds in 1989 increased at an annual average rate of 3.3 percent between 1989 and 1998, when these households were between fifty and fifty-nine years old.

John Laitner also challenges Wolff's finding that bequests and *inter-vivos* gifts are equalizing based on a theoretical model of household behavior from his own work, which shows that altruistic transfer behavior greatly increases the concentration of wealth. The Laitner model has four principal elements: Each household has a finite life span and engages in life-cycle saving and dis-saving. Each household's utility depends on its own consumption and that of its descendants. A household's net worth and transfer cannot be negative, and earning ability varies across households. Simulations with this model calibrated to U.S. data imply that life-cycle saving explains about two-thirds of wealth creation and that transfers increase concentration of wealth.

The intuition for this result is the following: In a model without transfers, if household A earns twice as much as household B, we would expect life-cycle wealth to be twice as great. With transfers, however, the high-earning household also saves to leave a bequest, so household A is likely to accumulate more than twice as much as B at each stage. Thus from the donors' side, transfers increase inequality. In terms of the recipients, transfers will reduce inequality in that household A will leave larger bequests to its low-earning children. To get an understanding of the overall impact requires looking at the behavior of both donors and recipients. Laitner claims that Wolff gets his result of transfers being equalizing because he looks only at recipients.

Conclusion

The conclusion that emerges from these papers is that wealth transfers are big and important. They probably account for about half of total wealth in the economy. Transfers can occur for a variety of reasons: a positive bequest motive, such as altruistic, warm glow, or strategic; accidental bequests due to precautionary saving and incomplete annuitization; or simply because people like wealth and die holding it. Studies provide some support for all three alternative explanations, but none verify all the predictions of the various models. Moreover, these reasons need not be mutually exclusive; in fact, for the nonrich, the most likely explanation is that people hold wealth for precautionary reasons, but if they do not need it, are delighted for it to go to their children.

Understanding how people make their consumption, saving, and bequest decisions is crucial for predicting how people will respond to major changes. For example, the plan to phase out the estate tax will increase saving and wealth accumulation if people are motivated to save in order to leave an altruistic bequest to their children. If rich people get rich simply because they value wealth per se, phasing out the estate tax will have no impact on the donors (although it will increase funds in the hands of recipients). How people respond to macro policy changes, such as an increase in deficit spending, also depends on whether people have altruistic savings motives or not.

For the elderly population, an immediate issue is why they do not purchase annuities. Price is part of the answer, but probably is not the whole story. Why do they care so much about dying before they have gotten their money back if they do not place a value on bequests?

The papers in this volume bring the reader up to date with what is known about the role and impact of gifts and bequests and they also move the story forward. At the same time, they make clear that many questions remain unresolved about the motives for and effects of wealth transfers.

PART 1

The U.S. Experience in Perspective

2

A History of Bequests in the United States

J. BRADFORD DELONG

When we look at the system of bequests as it operates in the United States today, most of us would be willing to accept five broad conclusions:

1. Bequests play an important but not an overwhelmingly decisive role in the wealth accumulation of any particular cohort.

2. Bequests play an important but not an overwhelmingly decisive role in the creation of wealth inequality within any particular cohort.

3. People leave bequests, especially large bequests, for three reasons, in declining order of importance: First, to make their children—all their children—better off and happier; next, to use the carrot of a promised bequest to make their children or other descendants behave appropriately; and last, to insure against inequalities of skill or fortune that give some of their heirs better life chances than others.

4. Bequests are sometimes seen as "dirty," which contradicts American values, and the high notional marginal tax rates on large-scale bequests that have ruled in America since the Great Depression are, from a sociological perspective, a way of expressing this distaste for bequests and inherited wealth.

The author would like to thank Peter Diamond, Sean Flynn, Alicia Munnell, Christina Romer, and Jonathan Skinner for helpful comments.

5. Yet as one would expect of any arena for political decision in which a few are massively affected by public policy, the details of America's estate tax have kept their bite relatively weak, and its leveling effect on the distribution of wealth relatively small.

This paper argues that all five of these major aspects of our system of bequests today are relatively new and that none of them were present four, three, or even one century ago. In the past, the system of bequests worked very differently, had a very different place and role in economic and social life, and was built on top of very different assumptions about what bequests were *for*—what their basic purposes were.

To demonstrate these points, this paper takes a brief tour of bequests in the Anglo-Saxon world in the post-Medieval past. The first stop is early modern England, between 1600 and 1800, where bequests played an absolutely decisive role in the wealth accumulation of each cohort. They played an absolutely decisive role in the creation of wealth inequality within each birth cohort: their fundamental purpose was not to make all one's descendants better off, or to induce all one's descendants to behave appropriately, or to compensate for inequalities of nature or fortune among one's heirs, but instead to maximize the wealth and power of the eldest male head of the lineage in future generations. *Primogeniture*, the principle that the eldest son got nearly everything, and *entail*, the legal institutions that bound the current possessor to transmit the principal value of the estate unimpaired to his heirs, made the current "owner" not the master of the property, but the servant of the male lineage's long-term wealth accumulation program. Bequests at that time were not considered distasteful or contrary to established values.

Indeed, in practically every pre–Industrial Revolution society, bequests were of decisive importance to every rich lineage. Low rates of net saving meant that the overwhelming bulk of the wealth holdings of any cohort came through bequests. With few opportunities to accumulate wealth except through bequests, those particular lineages that adopted primogeniture-based bequest systems were likely to see their positions in the relative wealth distribution rise. To the pre–Industrial Revolution rich, and to the pre–Industrial Revolution middle class and poor as well, the stakes at risk in the bequest game were relatively large, and the prizes uneven. How well one manipulated the bequest system was nearly the only factor in whether one's children rose or fell in the ranking of wealth and status.

The second stop on our tour is nineteenth-century America, in which the pieces of the early modern English pattern of bequests were broken, and the shards reassembled into the pattern that still dominates American inheritance today. A rapidly expanding economy meant that bequests were no longer the only factor affecting each birth cohort's total wealth accumulation, or affecting the distribution of wealth within each particular birth cohort. The conditions of America assisted in the collapse of primogeniture and the elimination of doctrines like entail. But nineteenth-century America also saw the rise of an ideology of wealth that put inherited wealth under particular suspicion, and rendered it and its possession somewhat dubious.

The migration to the New World appears to have been accompanied by a rapid shift in the perception of the purpose of bequests. In a matter of two or three generations, a bias toward primogeniture (almost all assets to the eldest male) was replaced by a presumption of *multigeniture* (equal division among the children—or at least among the male children). The migration from a land-scarce, slowly growing economy to a land-rich, rapidly growing frontier-settler economy significantly reduced the relative role of bequests as a determinant of peak wealth accumulation. Clearing and improving local land or moving to the frontier were strategies for upward mobility at least as effective as plotting how to inherit from a rich father or, for example, how to marry the Lord of Pemberly with an income of £10,000 a year.

In short, even while America remained a primarily agricultural society, the place of bequests in its economy and society had already profoundly shifted. An economy in which the rich were the lucky—those who had chosen the right wealthy parents—had been replaced by one in which, in theory at least, the rich were supposed to be those who had demonstrated thrift and industry, and also those who had more than their share of entrepreneurial luck as well.

The coming of the Industrial Revolution to America brought still further changes in the system of bequests. Large increases in the economy's capital intensity and an extraordinary rise in the concentration of wealth during the Gilded Age did raise the salience of bequests as a determinant of the distribution of wealth within any particular cohort, even if it did not re-attain its early dominance as a determinant of the total wealth of any cohort. The industrial statesmen, or robber barons, of the late nineteenth century had staked their claim to the legitimacy of their accumulated wealth as the result of acts of bold foresight, Schumpeterian innovation, and a little luck. This made things somewhat difficult for their heirs: the passing on of the Rockefeller, the Mellon, and lesser fortunes did not seem to fit with the ideology of America as a land of equality of opportunity.

Thus the coming of social democracy to America brought with it high notional statutory rates of tax on bequests. The standard Lockeian arguments did not seem to establish a right to this particular form of property.[1] However, the standard legislative dynamics gave concentrated interest groups a good chance of rewriting the legislative fine print in their favor, so that the base on which the estate tax was levied was narrow. Opportunities to avoid the estate tax remained ample: at the end of the twentieth century, a couple with five married grandchildren could transfer $4 million to them over a period of twenty years free of estate tax, plus make additional transfers to other descendants, make payments for education and other expenses, and utilize other tax avoidance strategies.[2] From at least one perspective, the estate tax at the end of the twentieth century is best seen not as a revenue-raising measure, but as a symbol of social disapproval of inheritance, and an attempt to alter the incentives of the rich in such a way as to encourage charitable giving.

It is in this context that we look forward to the promised and now enacted repeal of the federal "death tax" to take effect in less than a decade, to be immediately followed by the reimposition in the following year of today's current estate tax laws and rates. The sharp rise in income and wealth inequality in the 1980s and 1990s raised the salience of the estate taxes among those who might wind up paying them, and strongly increased the demand for estate tax repeal. The narrow base of the estate tax means that revenue losses from estate tax repeal are not large, and limits the potential for forming coalitions to maintain current estate tax law in the interest of avoiding the further impairment of federal revenues. Nevertheless, it remains odd that the bold assertion that one of the rights of Americans is to inherit a large fortune does not call forth the same ideological counterreaction as the transmission of the large fortunes of the Gilded Age. Perhaps we are today seeing the beginnings of another shift in how inherited wealth is viewed in America, a shift of the same order of magnitude as that which in the seventeenth and eighteenth centuries shattered the English system of inheritance in the first generations after the migration to the New World.

---

1. That rights to property are derived from everyone's right to whatever he or she has created. See John Locke (1689, ch. 5, §27) "The labour of his body, and the work of his hands . . . are properly his. Whatsoever . . . he hath mixed his labour with . . . thereby makes it his property. . . . [F]or this labour being the unquestionable property of the labourer, no man but he can have a right to what is once joined to, at least where there is enough, and as good, left in common for others."

2. Using the gift tax exemption allowance for each grandparent to give $10,000 a year to each grandchild and his or her spouse tax-free.

Back before the Industrial Revolution

In chapter three of *Pride and Prejudice*, Jane Austen introduces her hero, Mr. Darcy.[3] The last, by far the most lengthy, and by far the most important part of her initial description of him is ". . . the report, which was in general circulation within five minutes after his entrance (into the ballroom), of his having ten thousand a year." Mr. Darcy has inherited an estate, Pemberly, from his late father. From this estate, he derives an income of £10,000 a year.[4] It is this inheritance that leads "the ladies . . . (to declare) that he was much handsomer than (his friend) Mr. Bingley." Mr. Bingley, by contrast, has inherited only half as large a fortune from his late father. Note the striking disjunction between how virtually everyone would be introduced today, in which the principal question is "what does he or she do?" and the introductions in the still overwhelmingly pre-industrial world of Jane Austen, in which the principal question was "what has he inherited?" or "what will he inherit?"

Bequests versus Accumulation

The explanation of this is straightforward. Jane Austen's novel is mirroring the world in which she and her ancestors lived. Before the Industrial Revolution, the relative distribution of wealth was much more dependent upon bequests than it is today. Indeed, it is not going too far to say that bequests were *the* crucial factors influencing the distribution of wealth, and thus the distribution of economic and often political power. A much greater proportion of society's wealth was acquired by the members of any particular birth cohort through bequests than through accumulation or entrepreneurship or any alternative channel.

Sound quantitative estimates of the share of inherited wealth in any birth cohort's total wealth accumulation or in the proportion of wealth inequality generated through bequests are not available for pre-industrial early modern England. But a few illustrative calculations will convincingly demonstrate that the role played by bequests must have been overwhelming. Societies before the Industrial Revolution saw shorter life expectancies and generation

---

3. Austen (1813).

4. That is, if landed wealth is capitalized at the conventional twenty years' income, Mr. Darcy's fortune is worth some £200,000. According to Lindert's (1986) estimates, the average holding of the top 1 percent of households, at the time Jane Austen was writing, was £100,000. This makes Mr. Darcy quite a catch, and puts him at about the 99.75 percentile of the British wealth distribution; perhaps 5,000 households in all Britain were richer.

lengths. They saw a ratio of nonhuman capital wealth to production that was surely not less than it is today. They also saw extraordinarily low rates of net capital accumulation. These three features of pre-industrial societies together guaranteed that bequests were the single most important factor determining the wealth and wealth distribution of any particular birth cohort.

First, begin with the length of a "generation," that is, how long the average piece of wealth remains in the possession of a member of one particular birth cohort. The shorter the "generation," the more important bequests will be in the relative wealth accumulation of any cohort. The amount of wealth gained through bequests is equal to the total capital stock divided by the length of a generation, and the amount of wealth gained through accumulation is simply equal to net investment, and is invariant to the length of a generation. At first glance, it is not clear what effect the longer life expectancies found today—life expectancies at birth in the 1970s compared to pre-industrial life expectancies at birth in the 1930s, according to Livi-Bacci—have on the length of a generation.[5] One retains one's wealth until one is older, yes, but one also receives one's inheritance when one is older. However, it is clear that pre-industrial generation length was shorter, as bequests descended over-whelmingly from the deceased male wealth holder to his eldest male child (or other eldest male heir).[6] Today, by contrast, inheritances descend from the deceased wealth holder to all his or her children or other heirs in approximately equal shares. With roughly equal numbers of children surviving to adulthood today and in the pre-industrial past, the spread in years between the eldest surviving male and the middle child makes it overwhelmingly likely that pre-industrial generation length was shorter by a matter of years.

Second, consider rates of population growth back before the Industrial Revolution. The consensus estimate of population growth in Eurasia in the period between 1500 and 1800 averages 0.25 percent per year.[7] Angus Maddison's estimate of the rate of growth in output per worker from 1500 through 1800 is 0.125 percent per year.[8] This is an upper limit to pre–Industrial Revolution early modern growth rates; any faster rate of growth

5. Livi-Bacci (1992).

6. With the only significant exception being the provisions for widows discussed by Peter Diamond in his comment (this volume)—of especial interest because these widows' provisions were a nonmarketable right that survived the extinction of other customary, feudal, and nonmarketable restrictions on property for centuries.

7. See Livi-Bacci (1992). Moreover, even that low rate vastly outstrips what demographers believe were average rates of population growth found back in the pre-1500 Middle Ages.

8. Maddison (2000).

over that period would imply that standards of living in the period between 1000 to 1500 would have been too low to support human life.[9]

Assuming a constant capital-output ratio, the slow rate of growth of total output of approximately 0.375 percent per year places stringent limits on the amount of net investment possible in any pre-industrial society. Because the capital stock grows at the same rate as total output, the share of output devoted to net investment equals the proportional rate of growth of output times the capital-output ratio. At a society-wide reproducible capital-to-annual-output ratio of 2:1, such rates of growth imply net investment shares of 1.5 percent of output. At a society-wide reproducible capital-to-annual-output ratio of 3:1, such rates of growth imply net investment shares of 2.2 percent of output. The conclusion is inescapable: except in those few pre–Industrial Revolution economies experiencing extraordinary mercantile booms in trade and population, such as fifteenth-century Venice, seventeenth-century Amsterdam, or eighteenth-century London, the accumulation of capital through net saving was simply not large enough to be an important component of any birth cohort's wealth.[10]

By contrast, bequests were a major component of acquired wealth before the Industrial Revolution. With a societywide total capital-output ratio of 3:1 and a generation length of twenty-five years, about 12 percent of a year's output changes hands and passes down through the generations through inheritance every year.[11] With a societywide total capital-output ratio of 4:1, some 16 percent of a year's output changes hands through inheritance every year. Estimates of the ratio of wealth to output before the Industrial Revolution are guesses. How many years' worth of output was the stock of reproducible capital? How many years' worth of output was the capitalized value of land? How many years' worth of output was the capitalized value of labor

9. See Pritchett (1997).

10. Why were rates of investment so low? That they were low cannot be doubted. The population history of humanity is well known. See Livi-Bacci (1992), and the near-stagnation of material standards of living and productivity for the bulk of the population is recognized by an analytical tradition dating back to Malthus (1798), recently reinforced by Pritchett (2000). Economic historian Gregory Clark has speculated that substantial rates of capital depreciation, perhaps half again or higher than today's benchmark rate of four percent per year, is half of the answer. An absence of opportunities for investments that paid high rates of return must be the other half, but why remains obscure.

11. If one twenty-fifth of society's wealth is held by those who die, this is equal to 12 percent of a year's output. This is, of course, only a rough order-of-magnitude calculation. But it does its job.

Figure 2-1. *Approximate Net Shares in the Wealth Acquisition of a Rising Cohort*

Percent

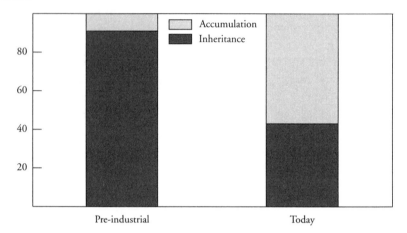

Source: Author's calculations.

control rights?[12] My guess is that every year, bequests turned over to the receiving cohort were equal to between 16 and 24 percent of annual output. This is more than ten times the contribution of net investment to wealth.

Contrast the dominance of inheritance over net investment before the Industrial Revolution with the lack of such dominance today. Today investment is a more important component of a cohort's wealth accumulation than inheritance. Rates of growth of GDP per capita average 3 percent per year or more, and the population growth rate is approximately 1 percent per year. At a ratio of reproducible capital to output of between three and four, net investment must amount to between 12 percent and 16 percent of total output, while approximately 12 percent of a year's total output passes to the receiving cohort by means of bequests and *inter-vivos* transfers. This balance between accumulation and bequests is in sharp contrast to the more than 1:10 ratio of the pre–Industrial Revolution past.

These estimates are illustrative calculations only. Their value lies not in the exact numbers, but in the astonishingly large contrast in the relative role of

12. It is important not to forget that bequests transmitted not just wealth but poverty—serfdom and slavery were inherited as well. Slaves were subject to the same rules of inheritance as other personal property. The obligations of serfdom followed different—feudal—rules.

bequests and accumulation between the slowly growing, low-net-investment economies of the pre-industrial age and the economies of today.

Primogeniture and the Concentration of Wealth

The much larger relative role of bequests in wealth accumulation is not the only or the major difference between pre-industrial England and modern-day America. The use, or the purpose, of bequests, was different, as well. Today economists model the principal purpose of bequests as raising the well-being of one's descendants, and of all one's descendants.[13] It thus seems natural today that the ruling principle governing bequests will be that of equal division: equal division of estates follows from what seems to us to be the very basic assumptions of declining marginal utility of wealth on the part of one's descendants, and symmetry of one's regard and concern for one's children.

Yet equal division was anathema among the estateholders of pre-industrial England. Instead, the default rule was primogeniture: the unitary transmission of the overwhelming bulk of the property to a single heir, the eldest male in the line of descent.[14] The feudal origins of primogeniture seem reasonably clear. A fief was granted to an individual in return for service—either the service of a knight in a lord's army, or the service of a lord and his knights in the army of some lord further up the feudal pyramid. When one fiefholder died, it was natural to look to his heir to step into his place, but the personal and reciprocal nature of the quasi contract that made up the feudal landholding meant that only one person could fill the role. Hence primogeniture: if you were seeking one child to fill the father's place in the feudal hierarchy,

---

13. However, researchers have offered other motives. See Bernheim, Shleifer, and Summers (1986) for a theory of bequests as another tool to be used in the within-family game of influence and control to try to ensure that one's descendants behave appropriately. Becker and Tomes (1986) argue that parents use bequests as a way to insure their children against inequalities produced by nature and fortune, bequeathing more to poorer children. Menchik (1980), however, finds that at the estate stage (but perhaps not at the *inter-vivos* transmission stage), the norm of equal division to potential heirs is very strong.

14. A variety of considerations of sentiment and utility modified and softened the application of the principle of primogeniture. See, for example, Chu (1991); Huston (1993); and Bonfield (1986). Dowries for daughters were an expected charge. Estates inherited from an extinct collateral branch of the lineage might descend not to the already well-provided-for eldest son but to a younger brother. Among the rich, marriage bargains would frequently contain provisions assigning life estate interests to the widow—the mother of the heir—allowing her substantial material independence.

choose a male and choose the oldest male. Certainly Adam Smith saw this feudal-military rationale as the reason for the development of primogeniture after the fall of the Roman Empire, for "when land . . . is considered as the means . . . of power and protection, it was thought better that it should descend undivided to one . . . The security of a landed estate . . . depended upon its greatness," and justified the departure from the principle of equal division, which Smith saw as the "natural law of succession."[15]

Yet this cannot be a complete solution. The feudal rationale for primogeniture may have been its original cause, but primogeniture itself outlived feudalism. The last remnants of feudal military tenures were abolished in the seventeenth century. Nevertheless, primogeniture survived. Thompson reports that in nineteenth-century England the overwhelming majority of even new millionaires, newly self-made men whose ancestors had never kissed the hands of and received a military fief from any of the barons of King John, followed the principles of primogeniture as they handed their estates down to their heirs.[16] Families like the Rothschilds that did not practice primogeniture were the exception, not the rule. The landed rich of England, at least, held strongly to primogeniture for more than half a millennium after the disappearance of its supposed feudal-military rationale.

The only paternal utility function that would make sense of such a bequest rule would be one that focused not on making all of one's children happy, but on maximizing the social position and resources of the eldest male descendant. One derives utility not from thinking about how happy and well-off all your children will be, but from thinking about the wealth and power of your successor as head of the lineage. If one assumes that such preferences can be and are culturally transmitted down the lineage, it is reasonably clear how a taste for primogeniture could continue to dominate the economy even given a propensity for what Adam Smith calls the "natural law of succession: equal division of property among all children based on equal natural love for each." Those who divide their property among their children see all branches of the lineage revert to the mean in wealth over time. Those who concentrate wealth in the hands of the eldest surviving son see the rest of their descendants undergo a rapid descent in wealth and social status, but also see a rise in the relative status and wealth of the beneficiary of primogeniture. Following the principle of primogeniture cannot raise the average wealth of one's descendants, but it does greatly concentrate wealth.

15. Smith (1776).
16. Thompson (1990).

Concern for the long-term wealth of the lineage was strong enough to frequently override the material interests of even the eldest male heir himself. From the sixteenth through the nineteenth century in England, a large and increasing proportion of landed property came to be held under the form of the *entail*. Under this legal institution the male lineage head and current wealth holder was not the owner of the property in any real sense. He could not sell it. He could not mortgage it beyond strict limits. He held a life interest in the property, but was under the obligation to pass it on unimpaired to his eldest son. The eldest son would then in turn be asked to continue the entail: to assign—before his father died—his ownership interest in the property to his eldest male descendant, and to accept in his turn, a life interest only in the property when it came to him after his father's decease. Historians judge that by the middle of the eighteenth century, it was more likely than not that a piece of English property that passed in direct line from father to son was entailed, and thus passed from one life tenant to another.[17]

The purpose of the entail was to eliminate, as far as possible, the right of any eldest male in the chain of lineage descent to do anything to dissipate the wealth and property of the lineage. Thus the aim of the bequest game, as played through the legal institution of the entail, was not to boost the average utility and material well-being of one's descendants, and not even to boost the utility and material well-being of the heir blessed by primogeniture, but instead to gather and maintain as large and lucrative a property and fortune as possible in the hands of the eldest male line of descent of the lineage.

Indeed, if Mr. Darcy's large inheritance—and the "truth, universally acknowledged, that a single man in possession of a good fortune must be in want of a wife"—is one of the mainsprings of the action of *Pride and Prejudice*, the institution of the entail is the other. The heroine Elizabeth Bennet's father has an estate one-fifth as large as Mr. Darcy's, but only a trivially small proportion of that estate will ever descend to any one of his four daughters, for it is "entailed, in default of heirs male, on a distant relation." Should Mr. Bennet die, his wife and daughters face an 80 percent cut in their income. This is a source of great tension and dismay within the Bennet household; they do not like their distant cousin who is to inherit in the name of preserving the estate and lineage intact, and they are, or at least Mrs. Bennet is, desperate to marry her daughters to men who promise to inherit substantial property before the death of her husband and the consequent financial collapse of the family.

The institutions of primogeniture and entail, combined with the tendency

17. See Clay (1968).

Figure 2-2. *Wealth Held by the Top 10 Percent of Households in England and Wales, 1650–1975*

Percent

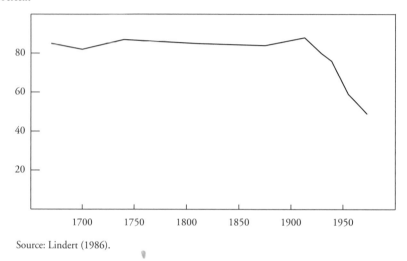

Source: Lindert (1986).

of the heiresses that did exist to marry heirs, appears to have given pre-industrial England an absolutely extraordinary degree of concentration of wealth. According to Peter Lindert, the top 10 percent of households in England and Wales held between 80 and 90 percent of total wealth between the mid-seventeenth and the early twentieth centuries (see figure 2-2).[18] The declines in the concentration of mercantile, commercial, and industrial wealth were offset by a secular rise in the concentration of landed property, on which entail could bind and for which primogeniture was most often applied.[19] Such levels of wealth concentration were rarely attained in America, only at the peak of U.S. wealth inequality during the Gilded Age, if then. The concentration of wealth in England is only half as great today, as measured by the share held by the top 10 percent of households.

How much of a difference the bequest system of pre-industrial England, with its three components of the dominance of inherited wealth, primogeniture, and entail, made for the distribution of wealth, or indeed of utility in pre-industrial England, is unclear. What is clear is that the particular equilibrium found in pre-industrial England was a sensitive one. It could not survive transplantation to colonial America.

18. See Lindert (1986).
19. Lindert (1986).

Coming to America

Before the end of the eighteenth century, colonial America had already broken with the pre-industrial English pattern of bequests along several important dimensions. The first element to fall was primogeniture. The move to
America saw the rapid end of the belief that the purpose of bequests was to
maximize the social position of the lineage head down through the generations. Equal division, the "natural law of succession" as Adam Smith saw it,
quickly took hold. The second element to fall was the centrality of bequests
in each cohort's wealth accumulation. The inescapable fact was that a rapidly
expanding frontier-settler economy would inevitably see bequests rank far
lower as a component of one's peak accumulation of wealth.

The Fall of Primogeniture

In England, primogeniture had contributed to the concentration of wealth
and the power of the lineage head among the rich, and thus had flourished
even after the end of its supposed feudal-military rationale. Primogeniture
had contributed to the maintenance of farm sizes sufficient to support a family among the yeomanry: division of the farm would, it was feared, soon leave
each descendant with too little to maintain a family. Neither of these reasons
seemed to have much purchase in British-settled colonial America. In the
northern colonies, primogeniture was never established, and what traces of it
did exist vanished almost immediately after the initial settlements. In the
southern colonies, primogeniture remained a default legal principle down to
the time of the Revolutionary War. Georgia abolished primogeniture in
1777; North Carolina, Virginia, Maryland, and New York in the years 1784
through 1786; South Carolina in 1791; and Rhode Island in 1798.[20] However, it is unclear to what extent the Revolutionary War–era end of primogeniture as a default legal doctrine represented a change in practice, or simply
brought lagging legal formalities into accord with actual practice.

Alston and Schapiro speculate that the rapid disappearance of primogeniture in the northern colonies was the result of the need for large amounts of
family labor to clear land and establish farms.[21] Younger sons would be more
willing to remain and help with the family project if they believed that they
were likely to receive a share of the property on their father's death. By contrast, a presumption that primogeniture would apply would send younger
sons out in search of other economic opportunities at an earlier age. And a

20. See Alston and Schapiro (1984).
21. Alston and Schapiro (1984).

rapidly expanding economy with a westward-moving agricultural frontier offered many other economic opportunities.

However, evidence in favor of this speculation is relatively weak. Some contemporary observers did see this land-clearing and family-labor motive as a reason to shift from primogeniture to the natural law of succession. At the end of the seventeenth century, Governor Talcott of Connecticut said that "much of our lands remain yet unsubdued and must continue to do so without the assistance of the younger sons, which in reason cannot be expected if they have no part of the inheritance. . . ." But primogeniture remained the default legal rule in the southern colonies until the American Revolution.[22]

It seems as likely that the shift from an economy in which bequests were the overwhelming source of wealth acquisition by a birth cohort to one in which it was roughly balanced by saving and accumulation played an important role in changing support for primogeniture. As long as bequests are the principal and overwhelming source of wealth, division of the property among more than one male heir virtually guarantees that all of one's descendants will lose relative wealth and social position. Hence to the extent that maintaining the dignity of the lineage is an important value, wealth holders will have strong incentives to sacrifice the interests of younger sons to that of the prospective lineage head, which will have a large payoff if one values having at least one rich and high-status descendant.

Expansion, Upward Mobility, and Ideology

Once it is possible for descendants to maintain their relative wealth and status without relying almost completely on bequests—as must be the case in a rapidly growing settler economy—then the factors that have always limited and softened primogeniture are likely to come into play. Population in the American colonies had a doubling time of twenty-five years or less and an annual population growth rate of about 3 percent per year. This means that

22. Alston and Schapiro (1984) hypothesize that the southern colonial attachment to primogeniture arose from two reasons: First, the large-scale availability of slaves diminished the need to tie younger sons to the property being developed in order to mobilize labor for land clearing and improvements. Second, the staple export crops grown by southern slave plantations were produced under substantial economies of scale. Hence, wealth concentration provided extra benefits—and thus bequest rules, like primogeniture, that favor concentration of wealth. It is not clear to me, however, that economies of scale in plantation agriculture are large enough to sustain this hypothesis.

net investment played at least as large a role in the wealth accumulation of any particular cohort as did bequests.

How did Americans think about upward mobility under the changed conditions of a rapidly expanding settler economy? In pre-industrial England, upward mobility had been seen as something exceptional and unusual. Class position and relative economic standing was given by who one's parents were, and what one's birth order was, and thus by what one's prospective inheritance was. With the coming first of the commercial revolution and then of the great nineteenth-century Industrial Revolution, upward mobility became possible. Long and inconclusive debates have taken place among historians about the extent and possibilities for upward mobility in pre-twentieth-century England. I have always been impressed by Thompson's findings that even in the second half of the nineteenth century, British millionaires tried, with few exceptions, to adopt the patterns of life and ideologies of the landed aristocracy: primogeniture, intermarriage with the gentry, and "complete withdrawal from (the) business (in which they had made their fortunes) by the second or third generation."[23]

America was very different. Perhaps by the start of the nineteenth century, and certainly by the era of Andrew Jackson, few in the dominant north of the United States wanted to be identified with static class distinctions. By the middle of the century, politicians like Abraham Lincoln would make the fluidity of class distinctions a standard part of their speeches and visions. As Lincoln put it in one of his stump speeches, nearly everybody started out as a laborer and nearly everyone could, with sufficient industry and a small amount of luck, make something of himself: acquire property, learn a profession, or build a business. In Lincoln's words, "The man who labored for another last year, this year labors for himself, and next year will hire others to labor for him."[24]

The divisions between rich and poor in the northern United States, in Lincoln's view, were much more a gap between the established and the young than a permanent gap between those destined to be rich and those destined to be poor for their entire lives. "Southern men declare that their slaves are better off than hired laborers amongst us," Lincoln wrote. "How little they know whereof they speak! There is no permanent class of hired laborers amongst us. Twenty-five years ago, I was a hired laborer . . . (A)dvancement—improvement in condition—is the order of things in a society of equals." Lincoln's view was surely idealized, and also out of date. In all likeli-

23. Thompson (1990).
24. See Foner (1985).

hood, the top one percent of households already held twice as large a share of total national wealth in 1860 as they had in 1774.[25] But Lincoln was not wrong in seeing that America's rapidly expanding settler economy had fundamentally different dynamics of inheritance, mobility, and wealth distribution than pre-industrial England had possessed.[26] The fact that Civil War–era America defined itself as the land of, in Eric Foner's phrase, "free soil, free labor, free men" was to have powerful consequences for how the twentieth-century American government was to regard inheritance.[27]

The Gilded Age and After

The coming of the Industrial Revolution to America in the second half of the nineteenth century brought with it a slow, but sustained and large, increase in the concentration of wealth. Estimates of the share of wealth held by the richest one percent of Americans on the eve of the Revolutionary War center around 15 percent as seen in figure 2-3.[28] Between 1776 and the end of the Civil War, the concentration of wealth increased. America in the aftermath of the Civil War was, perhaps, a society whose wealth was as concentrated as it was in the post–World War II era.[29] Then came a second industrial revolution: an enormous upward leap in the economy's capital intensity and in wealth inequality, carrying the concentration of wealth in the decade before World War I to levels that have probably never been seen since.[30] In the years around and after World War I, as the founding entrepreneurs, plutocrats, and malefactors of great wealth of the Gilded Age died off, inheritance became an important issue not in terms of its increased quantitative significance in the wealth acquisition of the rising cohort, but in terms of the concentration of wealth.

The great fortunes of the Gilded Age were justified by the fortunemakers both to themselves and to others as their just rewards, in a Lockeian sense,

---

25. See Jones (1980).

26. Pre–Civil War northern American politicians also liked to draw a contrast between the fluid north and the slave-ridden south, where the existence of slave property reduced the wages of white non-slaveholders and created a nearly impassable class gulf between plantation owners and the rest. It is hard to find large differences in mobility between the northern and the southern white populations before the Civil War.

27. Foner (1985).

28. Jones (1980).

29. Soltow (1989).

30. Abramovitz and David (1973).

Figure 2-3. *Wealth Held by the Richest One Percent in the United States, 1774–2000*

Percent

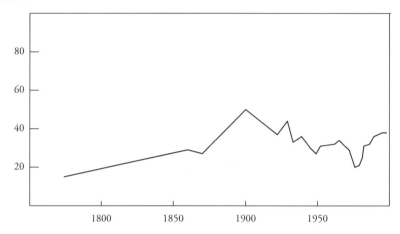

Source: 1774—Alice Hanson Jones (1980); 1860–70—Lee Soltow (1989); 1922 to the present—Edward Wolff (1992), as updated by Wolff; 1990—author's estimate based on size of largest fortunes.

for the tasks that they had accomplished. John D. Rockefeller had, it was said, earned his fortune. He had made his money by the sweat of his brow and by his acts of Schumpeterian entrepreneurial vision in grasping the extraordinary economies of scale potentially present in the production and distribution of petroleum and petroleum products, not to mention the distribution of well-placed sums to members of the Pennsylvania legislature. Leland Stanford had earned his fortune by masterminding the construction of the transcontinental railroad (never mind that the publicly traded Central Pacific Railroad had vastly overpaid for the construction services it bought from a company narrowly held by Leland Stanford, Mark Hopkins, Colis Huntington, and Charles Crocker).[31]

But the same Lockeian argument did not seem to apply to the fortune of John D. Rockefeller Jr., or to the other inheritors of the Mellon, Guggenheim, and other fortunes. The way the Prince of the Robber Barons, Andrew Carnegie, put it was that an extraordinary entrepreneur was rewarded with an extraordinary fortune because his vision and enterprise had made him worthy of deciding on how such a fortune should be spent to better society. His wealth was a public trust to be used for public betterment; hence the

31. Josephson (1934).

Carnegie libraries, endowments, buildings, and universities that we still see scattered over America. To not spend one's fortune on public improvements, but to leave it to one's heirs, was to betray this public trust. As Carnegie put it, "He who dies rich" and leaves a fortune to his heirs "dies in disgrace." Carnegie applauded the ". . . growing disposition to tax more and more heavily large estates left at death." He saw this as a ". . . cheering indication of the growth of a salutary change in public opinion." In Carnegie's view, "Of all forms of taxation, this seems the wisest."[32]

Thus it should be no surprise that the coming of social democracy to America was accompanied by the creation of an estate tax. Such a tax made sense in terms of America's underlying value of equality of opportunity: America's upper class should be made up of those who have been skillful and lucky in their deeds. Those who had chosen the right parents were not automatically entitled. Gradually, as wars and national emergencies came and went, the estate tax acquired higher and higher notional statutory rates. The permanent (so far) estate tax was passed in 1916 in an attempt to compensate for the nonprogressive impact of the then-existing federal tax system, based as it was primarily on tariffs and secondarily on excises.[33] The 1916 version of the estate tax had a marginal tax rate of 10 percent on the largest estates, which applied to estates over $5 million; in relative income terms, equivalent to about $500 million today. During World War I the marginal tax rate on the largest estates was raised to 25 percent, and the marginal tax rate on the largest estates was then raised to 70 percent during the New Deal and 77 percent during World War II.

In spite of high statutory marginal rates on large estates, the U.S. federal estate tax has never raised more than 5 percent of federal tax revenues. A combination of a narrow base confined to only the highest-valued estates coupled with many channels through which income can be transferred down the generations tax-free have kept it from being a major source of federal revenue, in spite of high marginal estate tax rates since the Great Depression. It seems, instead, as though its primary function has been a political statement that "equality of opportunity" is a good thing to aim for—that wealth and economic power should spring from one's own accomplishments, and not from the fact that one has in some sense chosen the right parents. Its secondary function has been to put a moderate-sized obstacle in one channel for the intergenerational transfer of wealth and power.

32. Carnegie (1889).
33. There had been earlier, explicitly temporary, estate taxes passed to raise revenue during the Civil War and the Spanish-American War.

Figure 2-4. *Maximum U.S. Estate Tax Rate, 1990–present*[a]

Percent

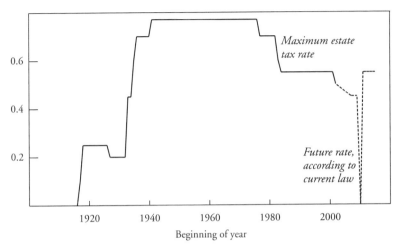

Source: Commerce Clearing House.

a. In 1987 Congress in effect raised the maximum rate from 55 percent to 60 percent for some estates by phasing out the initial exemption on taxable estates between $10 million and $21.4 million.

In this context, the tax legislation passed in 2001 has been especially interesting. It promises the end of the "death tax" in less than a decade, and then its immediate reimposition the following year. The estate tax proposals of 2001 drew remarkably little opposition and remarkably little ideological dissent, but this time there was little opposition to the estate tax's *repeal*, and little dissent based on the belief that the estate tax is a useful marker emphasizing the core American value of equality of opportunity. Does this represent a temporary change or a permanent shift in Americans' attitude toward the legitimacy of large bequests?

It is possible that the nineteenth-century American belief of Andrew Carnegie and others—that inherited wealth, especially large-scale inherited wealth, is somehow illegitimate—is the unusual and temporary view. After all, Adam Smith observed a tendency in human nature to identify with and applaud the happiness of the rich and celebrated.[34] In his view, "A stranger to human nature who saw the indifference of men about the misery of their inferiors, and the regret and indignation which they feel for the misfortunes and sufferings of those above them would be apt to imagine, that pain must

34. See Smith (1759).

be more agonizing, and the convulsions of death more terrible to persons of higher rank, than to those of meaner stations."

Conclusion

A historical look back at the pattern of bequests in the Anglo-Saxon world over the past several hundred years has to reinforce one's sense of how mutable human motivations are, and how different and institution-dependent are the workings of the major forces that govern our economy. Most economists today, when they think about bequests, think that they are an influence, but not the decisive determinant of wealth accumulation; an influence, but not the decisive determinant of wealth inequality; motivated primarily by individuals' desires to see their children—all their children—lead better lives; and finally, a part of American economic life that is looked upon with some suspicion. Yet none of these was true in pre-industrial England. At that time, bequests were the decisive determinant of wealth accumulation, as well as the decisive determinant of wealth inequality, primarily motivated by a desire to see the power and wealth of future male lineage heads grow, and a very natural and normal part of economic and social life.

Before the Industrial Revolution, inheritance loomed much larger as a component of each cohort's wealth in the past than it does today. Low rates of accumulation and relatively high ratios of nonhuman capital wealth to annual income guaranteed that the overwhelming bulk of wealth came through inheritance. Yet the use that the pre–Industrial Revolution rich made of the inheritance system strikes as us odd: they used it not to enhance the well-being of their descendants as a group, but instead to try to maximize the social position of the prospective head of the lineage: the line of descent of the eldest male.

Eighteenth-century America saw a sharp break with this pre-industrial pattern. Primogeniture remained the default rule longest in the American South, but even in the American South, nearly all traces of it had vanished completely by 1800. Equal division (among sons at least) meant that inheritance played a smaller role in the concentration of wealth. And the dynamics of a rapidly expanding settler economy meant that bequests played a smaller part in the wealth of any cohort.

The Gilded Age of the late nineteenth century in America saw a sharp upward leap in the concentration of wealth accompanied by a substantial increase in the capital intensity of the economy. Thus bequests became more salient, yet they remained embarrassing. The Lockeian argument that John D. Rockefeller had earned his fortune by the sweat of his brow and his acts of

Schumpeterian entrepreneurial vision (plus the distribution of well-placed sums to the members of the Pennsylvania legislature) did not apply to the fortunes of his children. Hence the coming of social democracy to America was accompanied by high statutory tax rates on large bequests.

Now we face another turn of the wheel. Current tax law promises the end of the federal estate tax in less than a decade and then its sudden rebirth the following year. Whether we are seeing a momentary blip or a permanent change is not clear. What is clear, however, is that history gives us little confidence that bequests will play the same role—economic, social, fiscal, or ideological—in twenty-first century America that they played in the twentieth century.

COMMENT BY
Peter A. Diamond

This paper considers wealth and transfers across generations in three eras: pre-industrial Europe, colonial America, and America since the Gilded Age. It also considers President Bush's estate tax cuts in historical perspective. My comments identify two potentially important aspects of bequests that are not discussed: the treatment of widows and the behavior of the nonwealthy, and then elaborate a little on the behavior of the wealthy and the effectiveness of the estate tax.

The Treatment of Widows

By focusing on intergenerational transfers, the paper does not address bequests to spouses. The protection of widows is a long-standing and widespread phenomenon, and the marital deduction in the current estate tax is a reflection of that tradition. In the past, with its lower life expectancy, women were widowed (and remarried) at much younger ages. With significant age differences between husband and wife in many cases, some bequests to widows went to much younger cohorts.

Early history of the treatment of widows centers on *dower*. Dower was the right to a life estate in one-third of the lands of which the husband was "seised in fee" at any time during the marriage, so long as the fee was one which the heirs of the marriage, if any, could have inherited.[35] Dower was

---

35. "In early times dower was optional with the husband. He could endow his wife at the time of marriage or not, as he chose. Hence the antique importance of including in the marriage ceremony the words, 'and with all my worldly goods I thee endow.'" Casner and Leach (1969, p. 262).

abolished in England in 1925, though it had ceased to be of much practical importance over the course of the preceding couple of centuries.

Dower was operative in most, if not all, of the American colonies. "As late as 1850, . . . New York's highest court declared that a wife who divorced her husband because of his adultery was still entitled to dower."[36] It was not abolished (speaking as a general matter, and leaving out the states that adopted community property), but rather was added to in the nineteenth century by statutory provisions. These provisions allowed the widow to elect in lieu of dower either to take what was given to her under her husband's will or to take against the will one-third of his probate estate outright. This provision developed into the spousal *forced share* that is characteristic of the American law of inheritance today.[37]

It would be interesting to consider the evolution of protection of widows and its counterpart in pensions for widows, both public provision and regulation of private provision. And it would be interesting to speculate on how society will adapt to the increases in divorce, remarriage, and dual career families.

Behavior of the Nonwealthy

By focusing on wealth, DeLong's attention is on the very small fraction of people holding the bulk of tangible wealth. A focus on the behavior of the vast majority of people would be enlightening for different issues. It would be informative to examine the age distribution of recipients and how important bequests are as a share of their total wealth, both relative to wealth at the time they receive bequests and relative to lifetime resources. Among the nonwealthy, longer life expectancies imply that bequests are received at much later ages on average. This changes their role. The nature of *inter-vivos* gifts has presumably changed dramatically as well. The dramatic increase in provision of higher education makes *inter-vivos* gifts somewhat different from what they were in the past, or at least more widespread. The affluent have always provided for younger sons through the purchase of military commissions and clerical positions. As DeLong notes, a variety of considerations have softened the pure application of primogeniture.

Land availability and the frontier affected the bequest behavior of the non-rich in America. In early colonial times, land was widely available and labor was in very short supply. This had two implications: an economic role for many children to work the land and a desire to attract additional settlers.

36. Hartog (2000, p. 71).

37. For a review of the contemporary situation, see Donahue, Kauper, and Martin (1993, pp. 505–09, 547–53).

A pattern (which I assume to be common) was to move out from established settlements to found new ones. Land was distributed to new settlers—as much land as they could fruitfully use. That left considerable land collectively held. Additional settlers were given land; indeed, land was used to attract more settlers. When a point was reached that land became sufficiently well used to be valuable, the remaining collective land was divided between land to be publicly held and land given to existing landholders; it became too valuable to give away. This had three implications: One was that the generation in such a place first was likely to be much richer than the next generation. Second, many farms were large enough to divide and still provide a good living, at least in the early years of settlement. Third, the ability to move further west meant that not receiving land did not have the importance it did in Europe.

But items other than land, such as tools of the trade, necessities for daily living, and luxuries, also figured in bequests. For many of the poor, these must have been important as well. The use of the legal institution of probate for household items suggests the importance of these objects.

Wealth of the Wealthy

Why do the wealthy leave bequests? What role has the estate tax played? Why did the United States adopt an estate rather than an inheritance tax? In contrasting the motivation of early and late cohorts, DeLong writes: "People leave bequests . . . first, to make their children . . . better off and happier, second, to use the carrot of a promised bequest to make their children or the other descendants behave appropriately, and last, to insure against inequalities of skill or fortune that give some of their heirs better life chances than others." But this does not square with Chris Carroll's view, which I share, that we cannot make sense of the savings of the very wealthy with either of these perspectives.[38] To make sense of that behavior using the standard models, Carroll suggests that wealth itself enters the utility function, leaving wealthy people happy to die with wealth so they can hold it right to the end. This is a critical perspective to keep in mind when thinking about the positive and normative aspects of estate taxation of the very wealthy.

In their recent paper, Piketty and Saez argue that the higher in the wealth distribution one looks, the less the growth of real wealth in the twentieth century.[39] They argue that the estates in the 98th percentile almost keep pace with what they guess is average wealth per capita, but the higher they look

38. Carroll (2000).
39. Piketty and Saez (2001).

above this point, the lower the increase. They suggest that income and estate taxes play a significant role in preventing the restoration of the previous distribution before the shocks of the first half of the century. In addition, the estate tax seems likely to contribute to charitable donations instead of bequests to children, which also might have contributed to preventing a restoration of the previous concentration at the very top. Both these phenomena imply that the estate tax has affected the concentration of wealth—a view at odds with that presented in DeLong.

It would be intriguing to know how the United States settled on an estate tax rather than an inheritance tax. This does not fit with the "underlying value of equality of opportunity" referred to by DeLong.

DeLong raises the question of the lack of general public response to the one-year repeal of the estate tax. I suspect (hope) this is not a permanent end of the estate tax, but rather a political vote that will not become a durable outcome as the fiscal realities unfold in the next nine years. The attempt to change the vocabulary from estate tax to death tax seems to have played a role in blunting the public response, but the lack of hearings in the Republican rush to legislate may have been significant as well. The very good times and surplus also made the repeal easier, since it would be hard to eliminate the estate tax if that required some other tax increase for marginal budget balance. The sudden fortunes through dot coms of Democratic supporters may have been behind a bipartisan view that estates were taxed too heavily, although the parties disagreed on two counts: how much tax to retain and whether the major problem was the exemption level or the rates at the top. A generally positive attitude toward bequests is also reflected in the argument made for Social Security individual accounts that they can be bequeathed. As the debate on estate taxation continues, it is instructive to have such a long historical view as DeLong has given us.

COMMENT BY
Jonathan Skinner

When it comes to answering the really important questions, economic historians have a big advantage over everyone else. For traditional macro- and micro-economists, a forty-year frame is a long time, but for economic historians, a forty-year period is just a data point. In Bradford DeLong's paper, he demonstrates once again the intellectual returns to standing back and taking the longer picture in attempting to understand both patterns of bequests in the long term, as well as the evolution of tax policy towards inheritances and wealth transfers.

In these comments, I focus on three distinct issues: The first is the long-term shift in the importance of agricultural land and primogeniture for wealth accumulation during the past three centuries. DeLong makes a compelling case for this transformation, documenting both the likely shifts in the level and composition of intergenerational transfers based on mortality rates, productivity growth, and the composition of wealth. In this view, the pre-industrial economies relied largely on agricultural output, so that much of the capital stock consisted of land. In theory, life-cycle accumulation could take place through productive investments in agricultural technology, but as DeLong argues persuasively, productivity growth was low during this pre-industrial era, making it unlikely that much life-cycle accumulation occurred in the agriculture sector per se. Combined with high mortality rates, and with an emphasis on primogeniture—passing along assets to the eldest son— the stylized pre-industrial story woven by DeLong points strongly to an economy in which capital accumulation takes place largely through bequests to the eldest son, not through life-cycle accumulation. Gradually, with the rise of the industrial age, this pattern shifted into the one we are more familiar with now, where life-cycle accumulation and longer life spans reduce the reliance on intergenerational flows in aggregate capital accumulation.

This is a convincing story. However, as is usually the case for any single hypothesis that attempts to explain economic behavior over three centuries or more, it is probably a more textured story than at first blush. One reason is that, while much of the labor force was employed in agriculture in the pre-industrial era, the productivity of agriculture was so low that the capitalized value of agricultural land was minimal in comparison to the capital used in commerce in towns. In a remarkable study, Peter Lindert measures wealth from probate, tax, debt, and ownership records between 1670 and 1875 to match existing wealth to specific occupations.[40] We first look at the wealth in 1875, after the Industrial Revolution. Titled gentry and farmers together held just 12 percent of wealth, while the merchant and profession class held one quarter, and industrialists and building trades held nearly one-quarter. Nearly one-quarter of wealth cannot be assigned to any specific occupation; widows or single women held some of it.[41] The distribution of wealth in 1875 clearly fits with the DeLong story; by this time, the capital stock held

40. Lindert (1986, figure 2-5).

41. The calculations were performed by multiplying the estimated average personal estates of living men and women by earnings category times the corresponding number of people in each category (Lindert, 1986, table 1, p. 1137). Farmers comprised yeomen and husbandmen as well.

Figure 2-5. *Distribution of Wealth in England, 1875 and 1670*

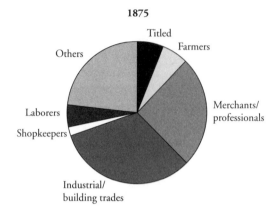

1875

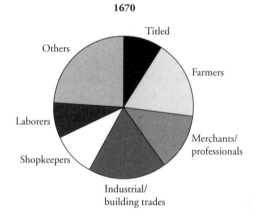

1670

Source: Lindert (1986, p. 1137).

in land is a marginal fraction of the aggregate capital stock, and a much larger proportion of wealth arises from life-cycle accumulation of merchants, entrepreneurs, and professionals.

Figure 2-5 shows patterns of wealth accumulation from Lindert for 1670, and thus before the Industrial Revolution.[42] The trend identified by DeLong

42. Lindert (1986). For professional and building trades, sample sizes were too small to determine average personal estates in 1670, so I assume that the wealth holdings of these groups were the same proportion relative to mean wealth in 1810 (where full information is available) as they were in 1670. For example, from Lindert (1986, p. 1137) the wealth of professionals in 1810 was 607 pounds, and the average

is clear from this graph; titled gentry and farmers together held 27 percent of wealth in 1670, more than double the percentage in 1875, and it seems likely that a larger fraction of the "other" category also held wealth in the agricultural sector. But while the trend is right on target, a surprisingly large fraction of wealth is still held by the nonagricultural sector: merchants, professionals, industrial and building trades, combined with shopkeepers and laborers, hold about half of the national capital stock. This capital, particularly merchant and industrial capital, was subject to the vagaries of booms and busts, shipwrecks, wars (which could provide either a bonus or a body slam for specific firms), failure of financial institutions, and other contingencies facing capitalists of the era.

Of course, these are measures of wealth, and not an allocation of working capital. Titled gentry may have held shares of industrial firms, while industrialists are likely to have owned agricultural land. Nonetheless, these distributional figures point to a more important role for the merchant and trade class in pre-industrial society. In a new book, Meir Kohn argues that much of the growth in agricultural productivity (and hence agricultural land prices) came about because traders and merchants reduced the transaction costs of trading agricultural outputs, thus allowing the agricultural sector to specialize and reap large gains in efficiency.[43] In sum, the merchant and industrial classes still held a large share of aggregate capital even in the pre-industrial era, and it is not unreasonable to think about this type of capital in a more modern life-cycle context.

DeLong takes advantage of the long sweep of European history, but lessons can be learned from other countries as well. Charles Yuji Horioka documents the sharp differences in how assets were bequeathed in pre-industrial Japan. For example, during the early part of the Tokugawa period, 1603 through 1868, equal division of bequests was common; only later was that replaced by male primogeniture. In other regions of the country, families followed postremogeniture, in which the youngest son received a larger share of the bequest.[44] Since pre-industrial Japan was still largely agricultural, understanding these patterns in the context of Japanese eco-

---

wealth of all men was 303 pounds. (This ratio remained relatively constant over the nineteenth century; in 1875 the values were 1,201 and 636, respectively.) Since average wealth of all men in 1670 was 100 pounds (expressed in 1875 prices), I impute wealth of professionals in 1670 to be 100x607/303 = 203 pounds. A similar adjustment is made for building trades.

43. Kohn (2002).

44. Horioka (2001).

nomic history could provide a richer and more general model of bequests and inheritances.

The second issue is what explains the long-term changes in government policies toward inheritances and estates. This is again an important question where the historical perspective is particularly valuable, and once again, I think DeLong gets it exactly right. In 1819, Ricardo was concerned that taxes on estates could "prevent the national capital from being distributed in the way most beneficial to the community."[45] As DeLong notes, the tide had turned by the time of the late nineteenth and early twentieth century, when observers argued in favor of such taxes to control the proliferation of "social drones" feeding off the accumulated nectar of very successful industrialists.[46]

While how the public perceives bequests in the long term has clearly changed and provided a necessary popular basis for effecting wealth taxes, in practice, the actual enactment of inheritance or bequest taxes (the former levied on the estate of the decedent; the latter on the recipient of the bequest) is often stimulated as a result of budgetary necessities. A bequest tax was introduced during the Civil War to raise needed revenue for the North, and later repealed after the war. The current tax on estates was begun in 1916, in the shadow of World War I, and spurred on by the presence of a $177 million federal budget deficit; presumably the changing political views on bequests allowed it to remain in place.[47]

We can also use similar historical perspective to ask the reverse question: what might have caused public support of the estate tax to diminish? If it were unfair to tax estates in 2001, surely it would have been unfair in 1980.[48] One possibility is that top marginal federal income tax rates have fallen during the past several decades, but that maximum estate tax rates have not kept pace, so that estate tax rates are now entirely out of line with conventional federal income tax rates.[49] This argument certainly has merit; marginal rates of 55 percent provide large incentives for (inefficient) tax planning. From a revenue standpoint, however, the estate tax has not been assuming a much larger role in federal tax collections. Figure 2-6 shows estate tax, expressed as a percentage of total federal revenue, based on data from the Statistics of

45. Ricardo (1819, p. 192); quoted in Johnson and Eller (2001, p. 4).

46. Professor Gustavus Meyer, quoted in Johnson and Eller (2001, p. 7).

47. Johnson and Eller (1998).

48. See Gale and Slemrod (2001) for an excellent discussion of the estate tax debate.

49. I am grateful to Jane Gravelle of the Congressional Research Service for making this point.

Figure 2-6. *Estate Tax Revenue as a Percent of Income Tax Revenue*
Percent of income tax revenue

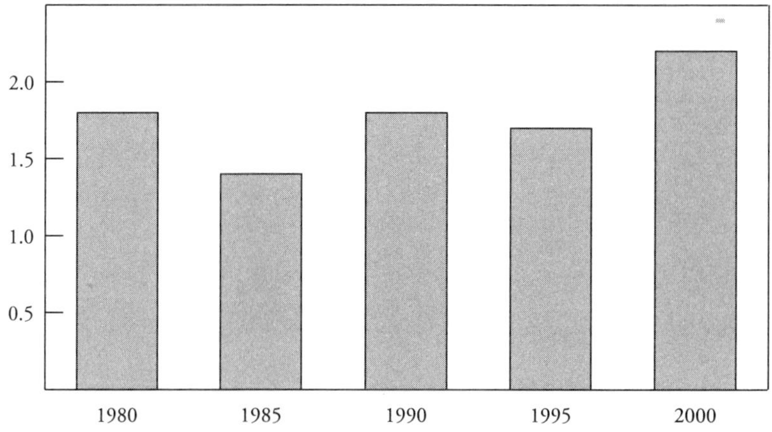

Source: Internal Revenue Service, Statistics of Income (various years).

Income published by the Internal Revenue Service. While this proportion has been inching upward in recent decades, its current rate, slightly over 2 percent, is still not much higher than its level back in 1980.

Another possibility is simply that more people are becoming subject to the estate tax, thus expanding the ranks of descendants who have direct financial interest in protesting the tax. Again, no apparent upward trend can be found in the percentage of decedents subject to the estate tax. In 1972, as shown in figure 2-7, more than 6 percent of deaths were subject to the tax, while in 1993 (the most recent data) fewer than 2 percent of deaths were subject to this tax.[50]

Perhaps the best explanation for the renewed interest in repealing the estate tax is the remarkable gains in asset holdings among those still living who would be subject to the tax bite in the future. Edward Wolff demonstrates that the number of households holding $5 million or more in assets nearly tripled between 1992 and 1998, leading to a dramatic rise in precisely those estates subject to the high marginal tax rates.[51] Whether the Bush administration's target of diminishing and presumably eradicating the estate tax by 2010 is later reversed by revenue needs of future administrations remains to be seen. However, if history is a guide, the allure of a tax that

50. Johnson and Eller (1998).
51. Wolff (this volume).

Figure 2-7. *Deaths Subject to Estate Tax*
Percent

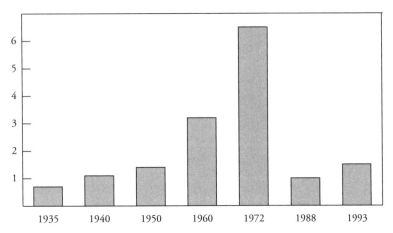

Source: Johnson and Eller (1998).

raises substantial revenue on a still very small number of wealthy taxpayers may be too tempting to pass up.

The third and final question is: How has DeLong's paper shed light on what is a contentious debate regarding the relative importance of life-cycle and bequest motives in explaining overall capital accumulation? Beginning with Laurence Kotlikoff and Lawrence Summers, and Franco Modigliani, and others discussed elsewhere in this volume, the controversy has often revolved around accounting exercises that compare the composition of aggregate wealth that occurs because of bequests, and the amount occurring because of life-cycle accumulation.[52] This accounting exercise has often been interpreted as telling us something about the importance of the bequest motive or the life-cycle motive in capital accumulation. The nice thing about DeLong's panoramic view of capital accumulation is that it lays bare how little these accounting exercises *do* tell us about motives for saving. Were Kotlikoff, Summers, and Modigliani to conduct their exercise for the year 1670 in England, undoubtedly they would find—consistent with DeLong's study—a much larger role of bequests and inheritances in aggregate capital accumulation, and a much smaller role for life-cycle motives. Would this suggest that in 1670, people cared much more about their children? I doubt it

52. For earlier cites, see, for example, Kotlikoff and Summers (1981); Modigliani (1988); and Kotlikoff (1988).

very much; indeed, one could argue that, given the many risks facing the average farmer or landed gentry in 1670, that surviving the next war or famine was foremost in their minds. Yet one would be hard-pressed to view bequests in 1670, as in 2001, as pure life-cycle saving that was left as an "accidental" bequest either; people both then and now care about their children. Indeed, one recent study suggests wealthy people will even hold off dying for a few days to allow more after-tax bequests to flow to children or other causes.[53]

I suspect that this debate between life-cycle motives for saving (resulting in "accidental" estates) and bequest motives for saving is in fact a nondebate. A dollar set aside at age fifty, for example, can serve many purposes. The accumulated wealth may be used to cushion poor health, to guard against the inflation-induced erosion of pension benefits, or other reasons. The odds are, however, that these adverse outcomes will not occur, since on average, individuals die with positive assets, allowing them to leave something for their children, relatives, or charitable causes.[54] Bequests and precautionary saving against future contingencies are not substitutes, but could well be complements. This was as likely true in 1670 as it was in 1800 and 2001: that over the long sweep of history, households have struggled with setting aside enough to tide them through the rainy day, and if the fates smile upon them, to leave a tidy estate to their descendants. I do not see any reason why this combination of motives will not encourage wealth accumulation for the next several centuries as well.

53. Slemrod and Kopczuk (2001).
54. Dynan, Skinner, and Zeldes (2002).

3

The Role of Gift and Estate Transfers in the United States and in Europe

PIERRE PESTIEAU

In Europe, as in the United States, wealth transfers generally are not a big issue in the political debate, except when plans surface to reform estate or inheritance taxation. A major theme of the most recent U.S. presidential campaign and the Italian parliamentary campaign was whether or not to phase out the so-called death tax. Both George W. Bush and Silvio Berlusconi, the proponents of such a drastic reform, won their elections.[1]

During the U.S. and Italian campaigns, it was interesting to hear the same arguments on the legitimacy of death taxation for both countries. The proponents for repealing it claim this would remove an unfair, immoral, and inefficient tax. This tax, according to them, adds to the suffering of mourning families; it hurts people of equivalent wealth differently depending on their acumen at tax avoidance; it penalizes the frugal who pass wealth on to their children; and it reduces everybody's incentive to save and to invest. By contrast, supporters of the tax argue that it is fairly based on the equal opportunity principle; that it is a small but effective counterweight to the concentration of wealth; and that it has few disincentive effects since it is payable only at death.

---

1. The Economic Growth and Tax Relief Reconciliation Act voted in 2001 actually repeals the estate tax effective in 2010. The Italian inheritance tax was also repealed in 2001.

One question is whether the issue of inheritance—its economic effects, its legitimacy, its tax treatment—is perceived in the same way in different countries. As I discuss below, the legal institutions regulating gifts and bequests are somewhat different in the United States and Italy. At first, the similarity of the debate appears to imply that institutions do not affect behavior. That would be surprising in the light of recent developments in political economy. Continental Europe (the United Kingdom is closer to the United States than to most European countries) has legal institutions regarding inheritance that are different from those in the United States, which may explain some limited divergence in behavior.

In addition to institutional differences, the United States and most European countries differ with regard to the size of intergenerational transfers by the public sector. Transfers such as public debt, pay-as-you-go Social Security, and health care (for the elderly) in countries like Italy or Belgium, for example, are much higher than they are in the United States. This difference can lead to contrasting levels and patterns of bequest.

The first section of the paper presents a taxonomy of legal institutions regulating gifts and bequests. It also summarizes the main types of bequests, considering that the economic effects of private intergenerational transfers depend on the motives governing them. Since quantitative information on wealth transfers is not very good, and comparisons are difficult, this discussion deals mainly with the United States, the United Kingdom, France, and whenever possible, with other Continental European countries. The following section deals with particular questions to which the United States and Europe may give different answers: the quantitative importance of bequests, the effect of bequests on inequality, the compensatory nature of gifts and bequests, and the way they are divided among heirs. A final section concludes.

Institutions and Motives

The nature of wealth transfers is undoubtedly affected by the legal institutions that govern their transmission, and the potential economic effects depend directly on the motive for the transfer. As a prelude to international comparisons, therefore, this section looks at alternative institutions and motives.

Legal Institution

Political economy is a growing field that deals with the effect of institutions on policy outcomes. A considerable amount of work has been done linking

Table 3-1. *Legal Institutions Regulating Wealth Transfers*

Freedom of bequest	Taxation		
	None	*Estate*	*Inheritance*
Absolute	Canada	United States, United Kingdom	. . .
Restricted to children and equal sharing	. . .	. . .	France, Germany

Source: Masson and Pestieau (1995).

budgetary institutions and budget deficits, fiscal federation, and the size of the government, electoral rules and fiscal policy, to take three well-known examples.[2] In the same vein, it would be interesting to link the legal institution regulating bequests and the actual practice of gift and estate transfers.

Legal institutions vary greatly from country to country. With regard to the institutional setting for private wealth transfers, two important dimensions are the freedom of bequest and the taxation of transfers. Table 3-1 joins these two dimensions, showing how countries such as the United States and the United Kingdom can be contrasted with France and Germany.[3]

At death, two main types of taxes are levied on wealth transfers. The first is the estate tax, which is levied on the total estate of the donor, regardless of the characteristics and the number of recipients. This tax is used both in the United States and in the United Kingdom. The second type is the inheritance tax levied on the share received by the recipient. Inheritance taxation typically includes a variety of rate scales and thresholds that depend on the relationship between donor and recipient. Most European countries, with the exception of the United Kingdom and to a lesser extent Italy, have inheritance taxation.

Table 3-2 provides some information on the structure of inheritance taxation in a number of European Union countries. Tax rates that are applied when wealth is transmitted to children or to strangers "in blood" vary from country to country, as does the level of exemption. The taxes provide special treatment for spouses and charitable contributions.[4] The final columns of

2. Persson and Tabellini (2000).
3. Masson and Pestieau (1997).
4. Tax rates applied when wealth is transferred to a charitable organization, rather than to an individual, vary considerably from country to country. As in the United States, transfers to charities in the United Kingdom are exempt from the estate tax, while in Ireland and Italy, transfers to charities are exempt from inheritance and gift

table 3-2 record the extent to which *inter-vivos* transfers are subject to the same treatment as bequests.[5]

In general, estate taxation gives one total freedom to bequeath one's wealth to anyone or anything. Disinheritance is possible, as long as the decedent prepares an explicit will. Inheritance taxation, on the other hand, often comes with the legal obligation to bequeath one's wealth to one's children, if any, and with an equal sharing of most of the estate. Donors have some freedom to do as they wish with a small fraction of the estate, but this fraction declines with the number of children. As the relation between recipient and donor gets more distant, the inheritance tax treatment becomes less and less generous.

The relative merits of the estate-type and the inheritance-type taxation are clear. The first is simple and relatively easy to administer, leaving all discretion to donors to dispose of their wealth as they wish. This means that it is possible to compensate some children over others for differences in income or need and that it is possible to disinherit one's children. By contrast, the inheritance tax is more equitable than the estate tax in that it lightens the tax load of large families. Yet, it does not allow for compensatory treatment of children with uneven endowments.[6]

Basically, estate taxation reflects a concept of the family and of the state that is quite different from the one that governs inheritance taxation. If one trusts parents to be fair in disposing of their estate, and if one believes that intrafamily inequality is as important as interfamily inequality, then what is desirable is a combination of freedom of bequest and a very low estate tax. On the other hand, if one does not trust parents to make compensatory transfers within the family, and wealth varies enormously across families,

---

taxes. However, Austria and the Netherlands apply flat rates of 5 and 11 percent, respectively, to such transfers, and preferential measures apply to these transfers in France and Luxembourg. Rates on transfers to charities in Sweden may be preferential but still range from 10 to 30 percent. Other countries offer no preferential measures, which may explain why charitable contributions are much lower in continental Europe than in the United States.

5. For the sample of countries considered, gifts are included in the inheritance tax base when they are made between two and ten years before death. Gifts that are made before this period are subject to the same tax rate as inheritances, but with a substantial exemption for each child and each year. In France, a parent can give an average of EUR 4,600 to each child every year (if the donation is made more than ten years before death). In the United States, a parent can give $10,000 to each of an unlimited number of individuals without incurring a gift tax.

6. Cremer and Pestieau (1988) argue that tax rates that decrease with the degree of consanguinity can be redistributive.

Table 3-2. Wealth Transfer Taxation: Tax Rate and Exemptions

Country	Inheritance (spouse and children)[a]					Gifts	
	Exemption (euro)[c]	First rate of tax (percent)	Minimax[b] (euro)[c]	Top tax rate (percent)	Rates for strangers in blood (percent)	Rates higher or lower[d]	Preceding years included
Belgium	12,400	3	495,600	30	30–80	Same	3
France	76,200 (45,800)	5	1,707,500	40	60	Same	10
Germany	306,800 (204,100)[e]	7	25,565,000	30	17–50	Same	10
Netherlands	266,700 (7,700)[f]	5	761,900	27	41–68	Same	2
Spain[g]	15,900 (47,800)[h]	7.65	696,500	34	Same[i]	Same	3

Source: Smith (2001).

a. Amounts in brackets are the allowances for children where they differ from the spousal allowance.
b. Minimum taxable amount at which the maximum rate applies.
c. Converted by using exchange rates as of July 1, 2001.
d. When they are not included in the overall tax basis, gifts are tax exempted below a ceiling.
e. Special maintenance allowances are available to spouses and children under 18.
f. Gifts from parents to children are exempt to euro 7,700 over two years and may give euro 19,000 once in a child's lifetime if the child is between 18 and 35.
g. Dependents under 18 are exempt. Those over 18 are treated the same way as the spouse.
h. If a child is under 13, the allowance is euro 47,800, and for those over 13 it is euro 15,900 plus euro 4,000 for each year. Disabled heirs or donees may receive an additional amount from euro 47,800 to euro 149,900 depending on the disability.
i. Effective rates are higher because there is no basic deduction.

then high inheritance taxation with mandatory equal sharing seems to be the best solution.[7]

The regulation of estate division can have surprising implications. It has been shown that in agricultural France, equal sharing, unlike total freedom of bequeathing, has induced families to have fewer children. The traditional objective of parents in an agricultural environment has been to keep the estate from being divided. This was possible with primogeniture, but not with equal sharing. Therefore, the only choice left was to have one child or at most two children.[8] During the English Middle Ages, the frequency of remarriage, along with existing societal values, traditionally led to the mistreatment of stepchildren by stepparents. To prevent disinheritance, equal division was imposed. When both the demographic and the societal evolution made such situations less likely, England moved back to unrestricted bequeathing. By contrast, most of continental Europe maintained restrictive equal sharing.[9]

Transfer Motives and Implications

To understand the importance and the role of gifts and estate transfers, one needs to have a clear grasp of the donor's motives and intentions. Depending on motive, the effects of bequests on income inequality, capital accumulation, and education could be different. The following briefly examines a number of bequest motives offered in the literature, and sketches their implications, focusing on those that are testable, and the contrast in motives between the United States and Europe.[10]

ALTRUISTIC BEQUESTS. Parents care about the likely lifetime utility of their children; hence about the welfare of future generations. Accordingly, wealthier parents make larger bequests, and for any given level of parent's wealth, children with higher labor earnings receive smaller bequests. Parents also have a tendency to leave different amounts to different children in order to equalize their incomes. Finally, pure altruism leads to the Ricardian equivalence, whereby parents compensate any intergenerational redistribution by the government through matching bequests.

JOY OF GIVING OR PATERNALISTIC BEQUESTS. In this case, parents are motivated not by altruism but by the direct utility they receive from the act of giving. This phenomenon, also referred to as "warm glow" giving, can be

7. See more on this in Cremer and Pestieau (2001).
8. Rosenthal (1991).
9. Brenner (1985).
10. This is developed in Masson and Pestieau (1997). See also Laferrère (1999).

explained by a virtuous feeling connected with sacrifice, a need to help one's children, or to control their lives. Formally, these bequests appear in the utility function as a consumption expenditure incurred in the last period of life. *Ceteris paribus*, they are subject to income and price effects, but they have no compensatory effect.

EXCHANGE-RELATED MOTIVES OR STRATEGIC BEQUESTS. In their canonical form, exchange-related models show children choosing a level of "attention" with respect to their parents in exchange for the prospect of a potential bequest. Such exchanges can involve all sorts of nonpecuniary services, and can be part of a strategic game between parents and children. Strategic bequests, as originally presented, imply that parents get as much attention as possible from their children by playing them against each other. Strategic or exchange bequests depend on the wealth and the needs of the donor; they are not compensatory and they do not need to result in an equal distribution among children.

NO MOTIVE OR ACCIDENTAL BEQUESTS. Up to this point, bequests, whatever their motive, are planned and voluntary. Unplanned or accidental bequests, however, can result from a traditional life-cycle model. Accordingly, people save during their working lives in order to finance consumption when retired. Bequests occur only because wealth is held in bequeathable form due to imperfections in annuity markets, or because of the need for precautionary savings. The main implication of this form of bequest is that even a 100 percent estate tax rate should have no disincentive effect on the amount.

Table 3-3 gives an overview of some of the key implications of wealth transfers for each of these four types of motives. The disparity between generations and among siblings is only equalized with pure altruism. Although, by default, accidental and paternalistic bequests create equal estate division, altruistic and exchange-related bequests do not. Accidental and exchange bequests have no effect on wealth distribution, whereas altruistic—pure or paternalistic—motives reduce inequality. Taxation of accidental bequests is nondistortionary and does not affect saving; only pure altruistic bequests lead to the Ricardian equivalence.

These four canonical motives are not the only ones that can be found in the literature. In particular, to characterize the behavior of very wealthy individuals who are more driven by the desire to leave a legacy than by parental altruism, one talks of *capitalistic* motives.[11] In fact, children are not needed to observe that kind of behavior.

11. Masson and Pestieau (1997).

Table 3-3. *Implications of Bequest Motives*

	Types of bequests			
	Altruistic	*Paternalistic*	*Exchange*	*Accidental*
Panel A: Effect of Bequests on Intrafamily Disparity				
Disparity between parents and children	Equalizing	Neutral	Neutral	Neutral
Disparity among siblings	Equalizing	Neutral	Neutral	Neutral
Equal estate division	No	Yes	No	Yes
Effect on wealth distribution	Positive	Moderate but positive	Weak and uncertain	Uncertain
Panel B: Effect of Fiscal Policy on Consumption and Saving				
Public debt on consumption	Neutral	Positive	Positive	Positive
Inheritance taxation on saving	Negative	Negative or zero	Negative	Zero

Source: Masson and Pestieau (1997).

Economic Effects of Wealth Transfers

Research on wealth transfers in the United States addresses a number of issues regarding the importance of, motivation for, and economic effects of wealth transfers. This section summarizes those results and compares them with what is known for European countries.

Quantitative Importance of Bequests in Wealth Accumulation

Laurence J. Kotlikoff and Franco Modigliani have hotly debated the quantitative importance of bequests in wealth accumulation; the former claiming that the share of inherited wealth in the United States is close to 80 percent; the latter estimating it as below 20 percent.[12] The reason for such a huge discrepancy is that the two authors agree neither on the relevant unit of decision and the definition of a transfer, nor on the way to evaluate transfers received in the past.[13]

On the first point, Modigliani considers only inheritance and *major* gifts (those that add to children's wealth, not to consumption between *independent* households). Kotlikoff wants to add all transfers received above the age of eighteen, including college education fees, which roughly doubles the

12. Kotlikoff (1988); Modigliani (1988).
13. Kessler and Masson (1989); Kessler, Masson, and Pestieau (1991).

amount of transfers. Given the conventional definition of bequest, Modigliani's definition seems more compelling, while allowing for the fact that his evaluation may be somewhat underestimated.

On the second point, Modigliani wants to count bequests' contributions to total wealth as only the sum of received transfers in real terms. Kotlikoff wants to add to this the accumulated interest on transfers, once again doubling the figures; the discrepancy in the results is approximately one to four. Who is right? Apparently no one is, since each convention relies on an arbitrary accounting decomposition of wealth in inherited and self-accumulated shares.[14]

With such a range of estimates, comparisons are not easy. Recently, Edward Wolff estimated that two-thirds of the growth in household wealth in the United States is accounted for by intergenerational transfers.[15] Studies for other countries indicate a greater share of inherited wealth. James B. Davies and France St. Hilaire apply an accounting approach to the Canadian data and find a 35 percent share for inherited wealth without capitalizing, and a 53 percent share when inheritances are capitalized.[16] John Laitner and Henry Ohlsson find that the inherited wealth of households as a fraction of their total wealth in Sweden was 51 percent in 1981.[17] Using similar data and computations for the United States, they estimate that share at 19 percent in 1984.

Denis Kessler and André Masson measure the decrease in total saving that would follow a uniform reduction in bequests.[18] Estimates derived with this approach are between 40 percent and 35 percent for France, and lower for the United States. On the other hand, Anetta Reil-Held obtains a low 10 percent for the share of inherited wealth in aggregate wealth in Germany, which is surprising since Germany is known for having an elderly population that saves.[19]

Since the existing estimates for European countries typically lie within the range of estimation for the United States, a comparison is difficult. However, several studies have applied the same methodology to European countries and to the United States. They have concluded that inheritances constitute a greater share of wealth in the European countries than in the United

14. Blinder (1988); Gale and Potter (this volume).
15. Wolff (1999).
16. Davies and St. Hilaire (1987).
17. Laitner and Ohlsson (1997).
18. Kessler and Masson (1989).
19. Information can be found in Reil-Held (1999); and Borsch-Supan (1992).

States.[20] Faster-growing and predominantly private economies, such as the United States, seem to have a higher share of aggregate wealth associated with lifetime accumulation. Finally, Barthold and Ito compare the importance of bequests in wealth accumulation in Japan and in the United States.[21] They conclude that in both countries it belongs to the same range of 25 to 40 percent. The main difference is that in Japan, the bulk of wealth transmission consists of real estate.

The Importance of Gifts Relative to Bequests

The importance of *inter-vivos* gifts is a highly controversial issue in the research done for the United States.[22] As discussed above, the differences in definition are insufficient to account for the conflicting conclusions.

In various papers, Nigel Tomes states that gifts are probably only of minor importance, the only possible exception being those of the wealthiest individuals.[23] Douglas Bernheim, Andrei Shleifer, and Lawrence Summers see "the apparent insignificance of gifts" as an element supporting their model of strategic bequest.[24] On the other hand, Mordecai Kurz, Donald Cox, and Donald Cox and Frederik Raines claim that an enlarged conception of *inter-vivos* transfers, including in kind or in cash transfers received by an adult child over eighteen in the same household, makes them more important than inheritance, in a ratio of three to two.[25] More surprisingly, William Gale and Karl Scholz, while considering only interhousehold transfers worth more than $3,000, find that *inter-vivos* transfers "account for at least 20 percent of U.S. wealth and possibly more" and inheritances roughly 30 percent.[26]

In France, estate duty statistics indicate that the total amount of *declared* *inter-vivos* transfers each year represents approximately one-third of the total amount of *declared* inheritances, or one-quarter of total transfers. However, this evaluation is incomplete, since small inheritances as well as many gifts, especially those handed over directly, and various parental aids—sometimes important—are not declared.

20. See, for example, Kessler and Masson (1989) for France; and Laitner and Ohlsson (1997) for Sweden.
21. Barthold and Ito (1991).
22. See Gale and Potter (this volume).
23. Tomes (1981, 1988) makes this assertion in the context of his study of intergenerational transfers by noting that gifts, about which he has no information, will not invalidate his results.
24. Bernheim, Shleifer, and Summers (1985).
25. Kurz (1984); Cox (1987, 1990); Cox and Raines (1985).
26. Gale and Scholz (1994, p. 156).

In any case, it is clear that in France, the rate of diffusion of gifts, and their relative importance with respect to inheritance, has increased over the last forty years. Reasons for the long-term development of gifts, other than the increase in average wealth of households, may include the rise in life expectancy and the lengthened period where generations—parents and adult children—overlap, and perhaps the development of Social Security. However, over the short run, the frequency of gifts appears sensitive to changes in taxation. Their number was greatest in 1981, before the introduction of the wealth tax; it declined afterward until 1986; and rose again with the reestablishment of tax advantages on gifts relative to inheritance.[27]

Gifts in France seem to be an upper-class phenomenon. Among the people who died in 1987, less than 10 percent made gifts. However, the proportion rises to more than half among the top 1 percent of the bequest distribution. This privileged group, which accounts for 19 percent of total bequests, is responsible for more than 54 percent of the total amount of gifts.[28] Gifts appear more frequently among farmers and wealthy self-employed people who bequeath their professional assets. They are less frequent among wage earners, especially blue-collar workers, where they correspond mainly to an anticipation of inheritance. Luc Arrondel and Francois-Charles Wolff distinguish reported and unreported *inter-vivos* gifts.[29] They find that reported gifts, unreported gifts, and bequests each contribute about one-third of overall intergenerational resource transmission.

The Compensatory Nature of Inter-Vivos Transfers

To determine whether *inter-vivos* transfers, considered in isolation, are dependent upon the economic situation of the recipient requires considering both the probability of a transfer and the amount of that transfer.

For the United States, Cox, and Cox and Tullio Jappelli, claim that transfers between parents and adult children—loans and gifts—are generally targeted to children who are *liquidity-constrained*, insofar as their *permanent* income—and therefore their consumption needs—exceeds their *current* resources (income or assets).[30] They find that, *for a given permanent income* of the child, the probability of receiving a transfer decreases both with current

---

27. Laferrère 1991. The consequence of the favorable tax treatment of *inter-vivos* gifts relative to bequests has been studied by McGarry (2001); and Poterba (2001), who show that donors do not take full advantage of available tax breaks.

28. Arrondel and Laferrère (1994).

29. Arrondel and Wolff (1998).

30. Cox (1990); Cox and Jappelli (1990).

income and with the ratio of financial assets to income. On the other hand, these variables have no significant statistical effect on the amount of the transfer received.

The picture is different when one does not control for the child's permanent income. Cox, and especially Cox and Mark R. Rank, concludes that the transfer decision is *compensatory*, the probability of receiving a transfer declining—other things being equal—as the recipient's income rises.[31] But the transfer *amount* is *anticompensatory*, increasing as the child's current income increases. Kathleen McGarry and Robert Schoeni find that *inter-vivos* transfers are greater when given to less well-off children.[32] Joseph G. Altonji, Fumio Hayashi, and Laurence Kotlikoff also observe that compensation in *inter-vivos* giving tends to be compensatory, while bequests are divided generally equally among children.[33]

Finally, Steven Hochguertel and Henry Ohlsson estimate probit and Tobit models using U. S. family panel data on gifts.[34] They find that gifts are compensatory in the sense that children are more likely to receive a gift if they work fewer hours and have a lower income than their brothers and sisters. These results carry over to the amounts given.

A French study by Arrondel and Masson that deals with the issue of compensatory giving reaches similar results: the frequency of gifts is compensatory, but the amount bestowed is anticompensatory.[35] Such behavior might be more consistent with exchange-motivated than altruistic models of transfers, since it does not help the less successful child.

Apparently, the study by Arrondel and Masson is the only one that considers the relation between different forms of transfers, whether bestowed or received. The results are striking. Parents who have helped their children are more likely to make a gift later on, and to leave a significant bequest at death. Also, the probability of helping children financially is higher for those who have already made a transfer, and repeated assistance or gifts over a lifetime are quite common. Similarly, children who have already been helped are more likely to receive a gift, or to benefit from another form of assistance. At the same time, the probability of receiving an inheritance is higher for recipients and heirs. Yet this complementarity does not extend to

31. Cox (1987); Cox and Rank (1992).

32. McGarry and Schoeni (1994).

33. Altonji, Hayashi, and Kotlikoff (1997).

34. Hochguertel and Ohlsson (2000).

35. Arrondel and Masson (1991). See also Arrondel and Masson (2001), who reach the same conclusions.

amounts: for instance, the amount of gifts bestowed or received is not significantly higher for helpers or helped children. In other words, the same subpopulation of French families appears to monopolize private intergenerational transfers received or bestowed. Not only do they combine the different forms of transfers, they also multiply them. This noncompensatory nature of gifts in France is a bit surprising. Given that bequests have to be equally divided among children, one would expect that parents would achieve some compensation through gifts. This is the way it is in the United States, where equal division of bequests is observed without being mandatory.

The Relation between the Number of Children and the Size of Bequests

Few studies deal specifically with the effect of the very existence of children. Using U.S. panel data, Michael D. Hurd has found that on average couples with independent children dissave during retirement proportionally more than childless couples, other things being equal (including the amount of wealth annuities at retirement).[36] Yet this striking conclusion favoring accidental bequests for childless couples is not really valid for two reasons: first, couples without children may continue to save for precautionary reasons against major catastrophes such as illness or invalidity, while in other families, children may provide a "safety net." Second, altruistic parents may decumulate more rapidly during their retirement period because of partly unobserved *inter-vivos* transfers made to their liquidity-constrained children, rather than passing their wealth to them at death.[37]

On the basis of French estate data, Arrondel and Anne Laferrère have focused on the specific behavior of the rich (the top 1 percent or so) who are mainly—formerly or actually—self-employed, own most of the stock, and make many more gifts and bequests than others.[38] The idea is that "the very wealthy . . . may not have an operable bequest motive . . . because they already consume as much as they want to or can . . . ; thus changing the concern they have for the welfare of their heirs will not change their consumption behavior or wealth holdings."[39] In other words, very wealthy people make capitalist bequests. The empirical analysis corroborates this: below the top 1 percent, the size of bequests is lower for childless couples and increases with children's income (anticompensation). But among the richest percentile,

36. Hurd (1987).
37. See Bernheim (1991).
38. Arrondel and Laferrère (1994).
39. Hurd (1990, p. 621).

the size of bequests no longer depends on the presence of children, or on their income.

On the other hand, the relation between the bequest and the number of children is not clear, neither in the United States nor in France. The only exception is the Bernheim, Shleifer, and Summers study, which finds that bequests are much more important and sensitive to the level of the children's attention when there are at least two children.[40] In any case, most American studies, as well as French ones, find a significant negative correlation between the amount of inheritance or transfers received by a child and the number of siblings.[41] This is often interpreted as the consequence of the quantity-quality trade-off in the "demand" for children.

Sören Blomquist estimates Tobit models for inherited amounts using Swedish micro data.[42] He finds that the number of siblings has a significantly negative impact on the inherited amount. Laitner and Ohlsson also estimate Tobit models for inherited amounts using Swedish microdata.[43] The findings are the same: significantly negative impacts of the number of siblings on inherited amounts. They also get the same result using U.S. microdata. Finally, Robert Alessie, Anna Lusardi, and Arie Kapteyn obtain more or less the same result for the Netherlands.[44]

Do Bequests Compensate for Unequal Income among Children?

In France, people are forced by law to share their estate equally among their children, and they can freely allocate only a limited part of it—called *quotité disponible*—by writing a will. In the United States, equal sharing is the rule in intestate cases, namely, those cases where the decedent has not prepared a will, but people are free to divide their estate as they wish by making a will, taxation being invariant to the way an estate is divided.

The first difference between the two countries is the proportion of testate cases. In the United States, about two-thirds of decedents have a will. In France, it is less than 10 percent, with the proportion increasing dramatically for the richest people and for the childless decreased

Let us consider the U.S. testate cases. Tomes, whose work is based on heirs'

---

40. Bernheim, Shleifer, and Summers (1985).

41. For information on the American studies, see Adams (1980); Tomes (1981); and Wilhem (1996). For information on the French studies, see Arrondel and Laferrère (1992); Arrondel and Masson (1991).

42. Blomquist (1979).

43. Laitner and Ohlsson (2001).

44. Alessie, Lusardi, and Kapteyn (1998).

declarations, concludes that exact equality exists in less than half of the cases.[45] Other authors, who confine themselves to information contained in probate records, find a much greater incidence of equal sharing. In families with two children, for example, exact equality is observed in approximately 70 percent of the cases as opposed to only 22 percent in Tomes.[46] Primogeniture represents less than 10 percent of the cases, and the frequency of equal sharing is higher among wealthy households. Finally, the transmission of an indivisible professional asset often leads to unequal sharing only if no other wealth is available to compensate children deprived of the professional bequest.

Thus the evidence suggests that equal sharing is the most frequent official practice in the United States. What remains to be seen is whether the subjective responses of the heirs are accurate, or whether parents use unofficial means—assistance and undeclared gifts—to favor a particular child.

In France, less than 8 percent of the estates are unequally divided.[47] These cases concern mainly the rich (by contrast to the U.S. situation), and the self-employed with several children and a nonliquid or indivisible bequest (professional assets, real estate). Moreover, inheritance shares remain generally equal, the redistribution among siblings achieved mainly through previous gifts in 80 percent of the cases.

The question remains whether unequal shares compensate the less-privileged child. Some evidence for the United States suggests that girls, assumed to receive less education or to care more for parents, are slightly advantaged. Yet Paul Menchik, and Mark Wilhem do not find any significant correlation between children's observable characteristics and the relative amount of inheritance received.[48] Indeed, both the French and the American studies, apart from Tomes's, can explain when unequal estate division occurs, but not the rationale underlying the observed distribution.

The Importance of Altruistic Bequests in Total Bequests

Empirical studies of bequests use additional information concerning the composition of wealth, opinion, or intention variables, or the influence of the level of parental education to determine the importance of altruism in bequest behavior.

---

45. Tomes (1981, 1988).

46. To be exact, in families with two children, the exact equality figures are 63 percent in Menchik (1980a) and 87 percent in Joulfaian (1994).

47. Arrondel and Laferrère (1992).

48. Menchik (1980a); Wilhem (1996). This ambiguous conclusion is also found for France by Arrondel and Laferrère (1992).

The composition of bequests or bequeathable wealth should provide some information as to the cause or motive of the transmission. But clear-cut cases—such as an estate consisting mainly of life annuities (accidental bequest), a widower declaring important life insurance (altruistic model), a large fortune composed primarily of stocks and shares and other high-yield assets (capitalistic bequest)—are quite rare. Moreover, the nature of the asset must be precisely determined to be of any value; for instance, the beneficiary of life insurance should be known.

Thus it is not surprising that very few studies use information on the nature of assets held in order to test inheritance models. On the basis of U.S. panel data, Bernheim does find that higher Social Security benefits tend to be associated with a higher level of life insurance purchases.[49] Moreover, the purchase of life insurance is more frequent among older couples with independent children, especially so when children are worse off than the parents. These results are consistent with the presence of altruistic compensatory motives for bequest. However, in a recent paper, Jeffrey Brown shows that Bernheim's results do not hold for term life insurance only, as opposed to whole life insurance.[50]

The simplest and most direct way of determining whether future bequests correspond to a genuine transmission motive is to question households about their intentions or opinions. Although economists are often reluctant to use subjective information in their analyses, such variables appear in several American studies, as well as in some French ones.[51] These studies suggest several lessons: First, in the absence of an in-depth psychological interview, it is essential that such subjective information be obtained in a context where people are asked about their actual intentions. Getting a person to just give his general opinion on transmission is not likely to lead to much, as amply shown by the econometric insignificance of the regression in the Menchik, Irvine, and Jianakoplos American study.[52] On the other hand, a retired person asked to speak about her assets and how she intends to dispose of her estate will provide more satisfactory results, as seen in the French wealth surveys 1986 and 1992.[53]

Second, opinions and intentions give more significant results when used

49. Bernheim (1991).
50. Brown (1999).
51. For information on these variables in the American studies, see Menchik, Irvine, and Jianakoplos (1986); McGarry (1999); Laitner and Juster (1996).
52. Menchik, Irvine, and Jianakoplos (1986).
53. Perelman and Pestieau (1991); Arrondel and Perelman (1994).

as explanatory variables rather than as dependent ones, even though the "bequest intent" in French surveys can be successfully explained by household characteristics: wealth, income, self-employed status, and especially inheritance received.

Third, in France the bequest intent is found to increase with the amount of bequeathable wealth, the level of portfolio diversification, and the probability of owning homes and holding other nonliquid or indivisible assets. But opinions in French surveys used as explanatory variables can also have significant effects on the amount of wealth, especially those referring to "retrospective" behavior captured by a statement such as: "Would it upset you to leave your kids a lesser amount of wealth than you received from your parents?"

If human capital and financial transfers are substitutable, the level of parental education should, other things being equal (notably the level of parental resources), reduce the amount of bequests, since more educated parents are more efficient at producing learning or earning skills in their children. For the United States, Tomes obtains a specific negative effect regarding the education of parents on the inheritance received by the child.[54] Tomes specifically shows that, at given parental resources, the overall amount of the estate and intergenerational savings is negatively correlated with the education of the father or mother.[55] But these results, which lend support to the altruistic model, have only been obtained by members of the Chicago Beckerian school.

For France, Arrondel and Masson get mixed or opposite results: a higher level of parental education increases the amount of gifts bestowed; on the other hand, it has an ambiguous effect on the size of bequeathable wealth, depending on econometric specification and population selection.[56]

Finally, a recent comparison between Japan and the United States by Charles Horioka and others reports that altruistic motives are weak in Japan, both absolutely and relative to the United States.[57] On the basis of microdata, they show that Japanese bequests can be explained mainly by lifetime uncertainty and by exchange considerations during old age.

Differences in Wealth Distribution

Wealth distribution figures for the United States and continental Europe inevitably prompt questions about the causes of the observed differences, and

54. Tomes (1981).
55. Tomes (1982).
56. Arrondel and Masson (1991).
57. Horioka and others (2001).

Table 3-4. *Percentage of Wealth Share of Top 1 Percent of Households*

Country	Year of the study	Surveys	Year of the study	Estate multipliers
United States	1983	33	1981	30
France	1986	26	1977	19
Denmark	1975	25	. . .	. . .
Germany	1983	23	. . .	. . .
Italy	1987	13	. . .	. . .
Ireland	1987	10	1966	30
Sweden	1985	11	. . .	. . .
United Kingdom	. . .	. . .	1993	17

Source: Davies and Shorrocks (2000).

particularly of the role of inheritance and estate taxation.[58] Table 3-4 summarizes the most recent data on wealth concentration obtained from surveys and estate multiplier estimates.[59] The broad conclusion is that wealth is less concentrated in continental Europe than in Britain and in the United States. In all these countries, wealth inequality has headed downward since 1920, with an upturn in the United States since the 1970s. Focusing on the United States and France, Kessler and Wolff attribute the lower concentration of wealth in France to the lesser importance of corporate share ownership in France due to the greater share of productive capital in the hands of the public sector.[60]

As for the downward trend in wealth concentration observed over the past century, the fact that most of the reduction in inequality comes from the falling share of the top 1 percent suggests that estate and inheritance taxes are influential. This is significant since the effect of inheritance on wealth and income inequality is still controversial in political debates.

An alternative explanation offered by Thomas Piketty for France, and Piketty and Emmanuel Saez for the United States, attributes the downward trend to a number of large shocks from which large fortunes never fully

58. For international comparisons, see Wolff (2001).

59. The estate multiplier method is quite simple. Assuming that individuals of a particular age and sex dying in a given year are representative of the living population and that the reported estate is correct, the overall wealth distribution is obtained by blowing up the estate data by a mortality multiplier equal to the reciprocal of the mortality rate. The dead are thus used as a random sample of the living. The main problem is that this approach misses the estates of those not liable to death taxation.

60. Kessler and Wolff (1991).

Table 3-5. *Wealth Transfer Taxes as a Percentage of Total Tax Revenues and GDP, 1998*

Percent

Country	Share of GDP	Share of total tax revenue
United States	0.36	1.16
Belgium	0.39	0.86
France	0.51	1.13
Germany	0.13	0.34
Italy	0.08	0.17
Netherlands	0.32	0.78
Spain	0.20	0.57
United Kingdom	0.21	0.57

Source: Organization for Economic Cooperation and Development (OECD). 2000. *Revenue Statistics 1965-1999*, Paris.

recovered due to steep progressive taxation (income more than wealth transfer taxation).[61]

Impact of Wealth Transfer Taxes on Government Revenues

Wealth transfer taxation is different in the United States from Continental Europe. Besides the difference analyzed above between estate and inheritance taxation, estate taxation in the United States is known to concern only the very wealthy households. Generally speaking, the deductible—the amount below which there is no taxation—is 10 times higher in the United States than in France and 50 times higher than in Belgium. Regardless of the type of wealth transfer taxation, the yield is uniformly low. Table 3-5 provides for a sample of Organization for Economic Cooperation and Development (OECD) countries and the relative yield of wealth transfer taxation, which barely exceeds 1 percent of total revenue.[62] It is noteworthy that Italy collects only 0.17 percent, which could mean that abandoning the death taxation would have little consequence in Italy, unlike the United States, where the yield is 1.16 percent.

Over time, the evolution of estate, inheritance, and gift taxes has not been uniform. Figure 3-1 and figure 3-2 show stability in Germany, the United States, and the United Kingdom, after a drastic decline for the latter in the early 1970s. By contrast, France has seen a slight increase with the arrival of the Left in the government in 1981. Clearly, wealth taxes do not reduce reliance on other taxes. In some cases, such as half the European Union

61. Piketty (2000); Piketty and Saez (2001).
62. See Kopczuk and Slemrod (2001) for a table with all OECD countries.

Figure 3-1. *Estate, Inheritance, and Gift Taxes as a Percent of Total Tax Revenue, 1965–97*

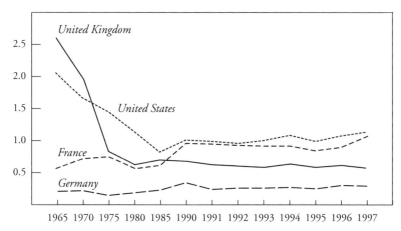

Source: Organization for Economic Cooperation and Development (OECD). 1999. *Revenue Statistics 1965-1998*, Paris.

Figure 3-2. *Estate, Inheritance, and Gift Taxes as a Percent of GDP, 1965–97*
Percent

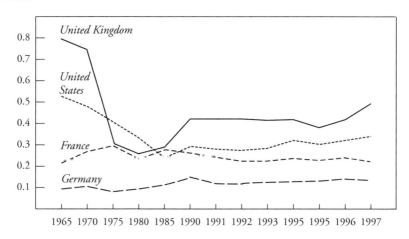

Source: Organization for Economic Cooperation and Development (OECD). 1999. *Revenue Statistics 1965-1998*, Paris.

Table 3-6. *Net Wealth Taxes on Individuals as a Percentage of Total Tax Revenues and GDP, 1998*

Percent

Country	Share of GDP	Share of total tax revenue
United States	. . .	. . .
Belgium	. . .	. . .
France	0.13	0.29
Germany	0.01	0.03
Italy	. . .	. . .
Netherlands	0.19	0.46
Spain	0.17	0.50
United Kingdom	. . .	. . .

Source: Organization for Economic Cooperation and Development (OECD). 2000. *Revenue Statistics 1965-1999*, Paris.

countries, inheritance taxes are imposed in conjunction with an annual wealth tax, but as shown in table 3-6, wealth tax yields are even lower than those of wealth transfer taxes.[63]

Table 3-5, even if it were made more complete, would not allow for a fair comparison of the wealth transfer tax system across countries. The top marginal rate in the French inheritance tax is lower than the top marginal tax rate in the U.S. estate and gift tax. However, the exempt amounts are much higher in the United States than in France. Besides, in the United States the tax base is the whole estate, whereas in France it is the amount received by each heir. Note also that in France, rates are substantially higher on "strangers in blood," and the exemptions much lower. Finally, in France, assets such as agricultural and forestland, term life insurance benefits, and artwork donated to the government are exempted from inheritance taxation. One could look at the end result, namely the revenue collected by the tax, which amounts to 0.51 percent of GDP in France relative to 0.36 percent in the United States. Given that according to most estimates, the wealth-GDP ratio is higher in the United States than in France, one can conclude that the French system is more stringent than the American one. By way of illustration, Kessler and Pestieau estimate that the effective inheritance and gift tax rates are equal to 6.25 percent in France, whereas standard statutory tax rates are around 40 percent.[64]

It would seem that in the balance between avoidance and evasion, Americans favor avoidance, and Europeans, evasion. This contrast raises an inter-

63. See Smith (2001) for more information.
64. Kessler and Pestieau (1991).

esting question. Given that the death tax yield is the same in the United States and Europe, is it better to elude its burden by giving away money to foundations or by investing it in tax havens such as Luxembourg or Switzerland? In addition to tax evasion, the European Union is engaged in an important race to the bottom regarding financial capital income taxation. This can have some effect on wealth transfer taxation, as has been the case in the United States with state taxation. The difference is that the European Union does not have a supranational government to regulate such tax competition. For example, tax competition is invoked in Italy in favor of repealing the inheritance tax. In Belgium, the Flemish region has lower rates and higher exemptions than the rest of the country.

Conclusion

The conclusion that emerges from this survey is that the findings are few and imprecise, which is not surprising. Even in the United States, where the academic debate over the motives and the implications of inheritance is more intense than anywhere else, most questions are still wide open. By comparison, European countries lack data, making it impossible to test theoretical hypotheses. In many instances, European economists who study the issues of inheritance use U.S. data. When they focus domestically, they are very much influenced by the dominant paradigm, and their main concern is to show that the behavior of their own country is like that of the United States. Finally, as the French case shows, research is often restricted to a limited number of closely connected people, and this does not lead to controversy. One can hope that, with the development of research networks supported by the European Commission, the future will show a substantial effort to develop databases that are complete and comparative.

Despite these problems, one can agree on two differences: First, voluntary bequests seem to play a slightly more important role in Europe than in the United States. Life-cycle accumulation relative to wealth transmission is more visible in the United States than in Europe. Second, regardless of the legal setting, one observes equal estate sharing and poor yield of wealth transfer taxation everywhere.

COMMENT BY
Peter R. Orszag

Wealth transfer taxes have recently received substantial attention in the United States. The Economic Growth and Tax Relief Reconciliation Act of 2001 dramatically liberalizes the wealth transfer tax system, and repeals the estate and generation-skipping taxes effective in 2010, although the taxes technically then go back into effect in 2011.

In the debate surrounding this legislation, advocates of repealing the estate tax argue that the United States imposes a heavier tax on estates than other countries, and therefore—in the logic of the advocates—the tax should be repealed. For example, the American Council for Capital Formation (ACCF) issued a report which concludes "that the U.S. death tax rate is higher than almost all of the twenty-four countries surveyed," which "lends support to the conclusions of many academic scholars and policy experts that the estate tax should be repealed or reduced. . . . Reform or repeal of the death tax could also help increase the low U.S. saving rate."[65]

The topic of Pierre Pestieau's paper—the role of wealth transfer taxes in different countries—is thus directly relevant to the policy debate over estate and gift taxes in the United States. Those who rely on international comparisons to advocate repeal of the estate tax in the United States would do well to read Pestieau's paper, which argues that it is difficult to reach any firm conclusions. Before commenting on Pestieau's paper, I want to make two points about the type of evidence presented by the ACCF in the U.S. debate:

First, international comparisons of wealth transfer taxes are extremely complicated, and a single parameter is not sufficient to compare the stringency of the tax system across countries. As just one example, the ACCF focuses only on the top marginal tax rate. By that measure, the U.S. system is more stringent than the French one: The top marginal tax rate in the French inheritance tax system is lower than the top marginal tax rate in the U.S. estate and gift tax system. By other measures, however, the relative rankings change. For example, the exempt amounts are much higher in the United States than in France, and the revenue collected is 0.51 percent of GDP in France relative to 0.36 percent in the United States.[66] It is thus difficult to

The author would like to thank Robert Cumby and William Gale for helpful conversations.

65. American Council for Capital Formation: "An International Comparison of Death Tax Rates" (www.accf.org/deathtax699.htm [June 1999]).

66. See Joint Committee on Taxation, "Description and Analysis of Present Law and Proposals Relating to Federal Estate and Gift Taxation," JCX-14–01, March 14, 2001, table 5.

Figure 3-3. *Estate Taxes and National Saving*

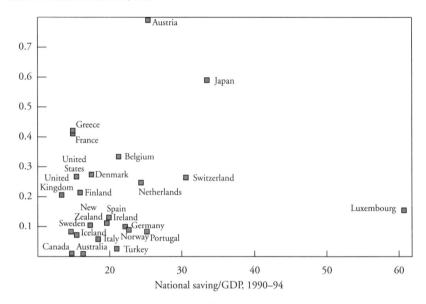

Estate or inheritance tax/GDP, 1992

National saving/GDP, 1990–94

Sources: Estate, inheritance, and gift taxes from OECD, *Revenue Statistics, 1965–1993,* and national saving data from OECD, *OECD Economies at a Glance: Structural Indicators,* Paris, 1996.

determine which system imposes a "heavier" tax, and arguably the French system is more stringent.

Second, the relationship between wealth transfer taxes and national saving is more intricate than advocates of repealing the estate tax suggest. William Gale and Maria Perozek show, and Pestieau emphasizes, that the effects of estate taxes on saving depend on the donor's motives, and that no general conclusion can be reached about the theoretical sign, let alone the empirical size, of the impact.[67] This ambiguity is underscored by a plot of wealth transfer taxes relative to GDP and national saving relative to GDP across countries. Although one should not read too much into such a simple correlation, figure 3-3 does not suggest any striking negative relationship between these two variables.

I agree with most of the conclusions in the paper, especially with its emphasis on the difficulties inherent in its fundamental objective. comparing the importance, motive for, and impact of wealth transfers across countries. In the context of that general agreement with the paper's points, let me note a few areas of concern:

67. Gale and Perozek (2001).

First, I am concerned about the conclusions regarding the relative importance of bequests in the United States and other countries. The paper notes that estimates for the share of inherited wealth in the United States vary between 20 percent and 80 percent, and that the estimate is sensitive to the definition of "inherited wealth." It notes that "with such a range of estimates, comparison is not easy." I agree completely. In the very same paragraph, however, the paper argues that "studies for other countries indicate a greater share of inherited wealth." Since the estimates for other countries typically lie within the range of estimates for the United States, it is not clear that the conclusion is warranted.

It is perhaps worth emphasizing that, especially in an international context, trying to draw conclusions about the impact of taxation from the share of inherited wealth based on *ex post* data may be particularly challenging because of other confounding variables. Based only on anecdotal experience, I suspect that a combination of the "accidental bequest" and "altruistic bequest" motives provides the most powerful explanation for bequests in the United States. Individuals accumulate wealth as a precaution against substantial end-of-life expenses (especially medical expenses), but also with the hope that such expenses will not occur and therefore that they will be able to leave a significant bequest to their heirs.[68] This explanation is consistent with the fact that individuals with potentially taxable estates do not take full advantage of the annual gift exclusion (which is consistent with the "accidental bequest" motive), that the average propensity to give gifts is lower for those in poor health, and that the deceased do not leave their full estate to foundations (which suggests at least some "altruistic bequest" motive).[69] *Ex ante*, the motivation is thus mixed. *Ex post*, the data will suggest either a large bequest or not, depending on whether the individual suffered high medical or other expenses at the end of life.

In an international setting, individuals living in countries without nationalized health systems may have more of an incentive for precautionary saving against high end-of-life medical expenses than individuals living in countries

68. Note that a well-functioning annuities market would not address this concern in the absence of a well-functioning long-term health insurance market (or an annuity that provided payments based on health expenses). The "dual motivation" for saving is also explored in Jonathan Skinner (2001, p. 501–02). Note that Michael Hurd and James Smith (1999) raise questions about the extent to which illnesses are associated with substantial changes in assets.

69. See Richard Schmalbeck (2001) for citations on the relatively low use rates of the annual exclusion. Charitable contributions averaged only 6 percent of gross estate values in 1998. See Gale and Joel Slemrod (2001, table 1.4).

with such nationalized health systems. In the United States, Medicare provides no long-term health care insurance, and Medicaid is only available to those with relatively low levels of assets.[70] The dual motivation for saving mentioned above may therefore be more prominent in the United States than in other countries, making it difficult to reach any conclusions from cross-country comparisons of inherited wealth shares.

In other words, countries in which a larger share of end-of-life medical expenses is financed by a public system may have smaller unintended bequests and smaller overall bequests, all else equal, than countries in which a smaller share of end-of-life expenses is covered by the public system. Furthermore, even for countries with similar public health systems, the *ex post* inherited wealth figures may be affected by differences in the distribution of mortality and morbidity shocks. The consequence is that any effort to link *ex post* inherited wealth data to national tax systems must also control for characteristics of the health care system, and the distribution of health shocks, which vary across countries.

Second, on a somewhat related point, the structure of the wealth transfer tax may be endogenous. Figure 3-4 shows that countries with more progressive tax systems (measured as the difference between the top marginal tax rate and the average marginal tax rate, in percentage points), on average, raise more revenue from their estate and inheritance taxes than other countries. The size of the estate and inheritance taxes across countries may thus be systematically related to other underlying characteristics of the countries, which could further complicate efforts to analyze the impact of the tax structure per se.

In other words, figure 3-4 should remind us that we must explore *why* different countries have different wealth transfer tax systems before we can fully understand the implications of those different systems. The paper contains an interesting reference to historical explanations for "equal sharing" provisions in Europe, but a more extensive examination of why different wealth transfer tax systems evolve would help identify the full set of factors that might otherwise confound cross-country analyses.

Third, I would caution against concluding that a small revenue share means that abandoning "death taxation would have little consequence," as the paper suggests. In most cases, inheritance or estate taxes are imposed in conjunction with gift taxes, as is necessary to avoid gaming of the system

---

70. It should be noted that even nationalized health systems often do not cover or at least fully cover long-term care. Nevertheless, as long as the share of end-of-life medical expenses financed by the public system varies across countries, the *ex post* inherited wealth data will likely be affected.

Figure 3-4. *Estate Taxes and "Progressivity" of Tax System*

Estate or inheritance tax/GDP, 1992

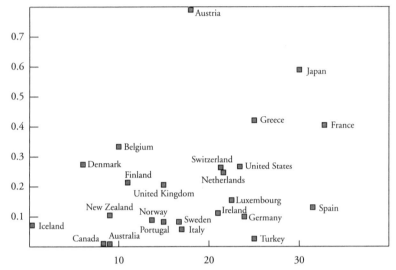

Top marginal tax rate minus average worker marginal tax rate

Source: OECD, *OECD Economies at a Glance: Structural Indicators,* Paris, 1996.

through *inter-vivos* transfers. If gift taxes are eliminated at the same time as inheritance or estate taxes are, the outcome within a progressive tax structure could be a massive loss of revenue—even if the gift and inheritance taxes collect little revenue.[71] For example, those with high marginal tax rates and substantial capital gains could gift the assets to trusted friends with lower marginal tax rates. The capital gains could then be realized at a lower tax rate, and the assets transferred back to the original owner. Gift and inheritance taxes may thus protect much more revenue than they directly collect.

In conclusion, this paper sets itself an ambitious goal and provides much useful information about bequests in different countries. The objective of the paper is so ambitious, however, that despite Pierre Pestieau's commendable efforts, I remain concerned about some of the conclusions.

71. Blattmachr and Gans (2001); Buckley (2001); and Lav and Friedman (2001). See also David Cay Johnston, "Questions Raised on New Bush Plan to End Estate Tax," *New York Times,* January 29, 2001, p. A1.

PART 2

How Do People Make Gifts and Bequests?

4

Bequests: By Accident or by Design?

MICHAEL D. HURD

The life-cycle model of consumption is the standard model for the analysis of consumption and saving over the life cycle.[1] The model specifies that people save during their working lives, and then consume their savings in retirement. The claim that a large fraction of household wealth is the result of inheritances has stimulated substantial interest in a bequest motive for saving. While large bequests are not necessarily at odds with simple life-cycle saving, they could also indicate that people are actively saving in order to make such transfers.

If people alter their consumption behavior with the objective of leaving a bequest, the nature of the life-cycle model is changed; an important determinant of consumption among the elderly, mortality risk, will no longer operate in the same way, and the time horizon for making consumption decisions will lengthen. In some extreme versions, mortality risk does not matter at all because the elderly person acts like the head of a dynasty that is infinitely long lived.

The existence of a bequest motive has implications for scientific investigations: It changes the nature of modeling, of estimation, and of data requirements. The presence of a bequest motive also has important implications for

The author would like to thank the National Institute on Aging for providing additional support for data and model development.

1. Modigliani (1988).

the consequence of public policy. Intergenerational inequalities can be partially offset by transfers through an increase or a reduction in bequests. For example, current retirees benefit from generous Social Security benefits relative to their contributions, and those benefits are paid for by their children. However, the retirees could save part of their Social Security benefits and bequeath it back to their children in partial compensation.

The empirical magnitude of the effect of a bequest motive for saving is controversial, as it is almost bound to be. A bequest motive is not observed directly and can only be inferred from behavior. However, in the absence of a well-functioning annuity market, large bequests could be the result of uncertainty about the date of death: highly risk-averse people will hold substantial amounts of wealth to guard against a shortfall in consumption should they live substantially beyond life expectancy. For such people, bequests are "desired" in the following sense: they plan and desire to leave a bequest because were they to die with no wealth, their consumption would be low late in life.

Because some utility function parameters such as risk aversion can lead to large bequests even in the absence of a bequest motive for saving, it is not reasonable to measure a bequest motive by studying the magnitude of bequests or the rate of saving in the population. The only reasonable empirical goal is to find how observable characteristics that should be associated with the strength of a bequest motive alter saving and bequest behavior. If over a number of data sets and in a number of situations, saving and bequest behavior is not altered by these characteristics, then a bequest motive is not likely to be an important determinant of behavior, and therefore, of bequests.

This paper begins with a discussion of the importance of the magnitude of any bequest motive for public policy. Then it reviews the life-cycle model augmented to include a bequest motive for saving. The goal is to specify how a bequest motive should affect outcomes. The following section presents some evidence from past findings about the strength for a bequest motive. It also reports on some new findings about the extent to which the elderly hold onto their homes: an apparent lack of housing decumulation has been taken as evidence for a bequest motive because of the importance of housing in the portfolios of the elderly, and because of the special role that a particular house may play in the extended family. The next empirical section presents results about expected bequests, followed by the conclusion.

Bequests and Public Policy

In the standard life-cycle model, intergenerational linkages are weak, and the time horizon of households extends only to its maximum survival age. Therefore, when households make decisions they do not take into account consequences that will take place in the distant future when they make their decisions. A strong bequest motive extends the time horizon of the household, and in some versions of the model, the time horizon becomes infinite. This extension in time horizon will change the decisions of the households, particularly in intertemporal allocations.

A bequest motive will most directly aggregate saving rates, because a bequest motive causes households to hold more wealth. That is, a cohort with a bequest motive will consume less and bequeath more than a cohort that lacks a bequest motive. The immediate effect is to increase the saving rate of the cohort, and because those entering retirement have substantial wealth, the increase in the saving rate could be substantial. If the younger generation that will receive the bequest reduces its own saving in anticipation of the bequest, the effect on the aggregate saving rate would be mitigated, but increased saving by the older generation is unlikely to be completely offset by the reduction in saving by the younger generation.

Because of the change in time horizon, intergenerational transfers such as Social Security and Medicare will produce different outcomes with a bequest motive than without. For example, an increase in Social Security benefits that is financed in a pay-as-you-go system by means of taxes will be seen by the older generation as a windfall gain in lifetime resources. If that generation has no bequest motive, it will increase its consumption and could consume the entire increase in Social Security benefits.[2] If the older generation has a strong bequest motive, it may not change consumption at all and bequeath the entire increase in Social Security benefits back to the younger generation. In a similar way, an increase in Medicare benefits financed by a tax on the working-age population would have the effect of a windfall gain for the retired generation. To restore the balance of resources between the generations, the older cohort would have to reduce nonmedical consumption, increasing bequests with the net result that the increase in Medicare costs would be shared by the generations. Thus a strong bequest motive can operate to reduce the intergenerational inequalities that are associated with the public programs targeted to the elderly. The choice between financing government expenditures through taxes or through debt will depend on the time horizon of the public. In the absence of a bequest motive, the older generation will tend to favor debt financing, while the younger generation may be relatively indifferent. A strong bequest motive should make the older generation also indifferent.

2. Hurd (1993).

A bequest motive can have more subtle interactions with other types of behavior. For example, suppose the marginal utility of bequests is relatively constant compared with the marginal utility of consumption. The presence of a bequest motive will cause more wealth to be held. In the event of unexpected expenditures for health care that are financed out of wealth intended for a bequest, the household will lose some utility. But because the marginal utility of bequests is approximately constant, while the marginal utility of consumption exhibits diminishing returns, the loss in utility would be much smaller than were the costs financed by reducing consumption where a large reduction would cause a large increase in marginal utility. Thus a quantitatively important bequest motive will reduce the demand for precautionary saving.

The effect of an estate tax will depend on a bequest motive, but the effect is likely to be complex and depend on the level of wealth. Of course, in the United States, the estate tax is only relevant for a small fraction of households, but it is relevant for a substantially greater number of dollars. Among households of moderately high wealth, an increase in the estate tax should decrease bequests, increase *inter-vivos* giving, and increase consumption. Bequests and *inter-vivos* giving are not perfect substitutes among moderately high-wealth households because an *inter-vivos* gift cannot be recalled should the household live unexpectedly long and require more resources for consumption. Among higher-wealth households where *inter-vivos* giving is already at a maximum, a tax on bequests will cause an increase in consumption. Among very high-wealth households where the marginal utility of consumption is close to zero or even at zero, an increase in the estate tax will have no effect.[3]

Although a bequest motive can neutralize the intergenerational transfers that would otherwise be induced by government policy such as Social Security, the transfers are only neutralized on average: in each generation some households will have no strong ties to the preceding or following generation. In these circumstances, an increase in Social Security benefits will give a windfall to the older generation, and the younger generation will gain no increase in bequests to compensate for the higher taxes.

3. This simple outline ignores more complex responses such as the establishment of trusts or foundations, which are likely to be responsive to an estate tax. The fact that households give their estates to foundations or to their families rather than to the government is not really evidence for an important bequest motive; were bequests completely accidental, a very weak preference to give to foundations or families over government would lead to the same behavior.

Bequest Behavior in a Life-Cycle Model

The following discussion of bequest behavior is based on a life-cycle model of consumption that has the following features and assumptions: life-time utility is based on time-separable utility from consumption and from bequests; the only uncertainty is date of death; resources are initial bequeathable wealth and a stream of annuities; bequeathable wealth cannot become negative, and, therefore, borrowing against future annuities is not allowed.[4] The model has no provision for the choice of labor, so it is only appropriate for retired persons. Although models for couples and for singles differ in important ways, they make the same qualitative predictions for understanding a bequest motive, so the following discussion does not distinguish between the two types of households.

The solution to the model yields a path of desired consumption and an associated path of wealth.[5] When households have no bequest motive, their utility comes only from consumption, and the most important implication of the model is that at a sufficiently advanced age, the paths of consumption and wealth will decline. This happens because the probability of death increases with age so that it becomes increasingly risky to hold wealth. The age at which consumption and wealth begin to decline, and the rate of decline, depends on the interest rate and the parameters of the utility function.

Having a bequest motive means that someone gains utility from the knowledge that wealth will be left to someone at death. Whether a bequest motive has a quantitatively important effect on savings and consumption behavior depends on the relative magnitudes of the marginal utility of consumption and the marginal utility of bequests. If the marginal utility of bequests is relatively small, a bequest motive will have little effect on consumption and saving behavior. However, the relative marginal utilities are not constant, but will depend on the levels of bequeathable wealth, annuities, and the other determinants of consumption.

The literature has identified a number of explanations for a bequest motive. The donor may be altruistic and care about the utility of the inheritors.[6] That is, parents may care about the consumption levels of their children and grandchildren. In the case of altruism, the characteristics of the

4. Yaari (1965).
5. I have analyzed this model extensively in other work, so here I will just give a summary of the main findings as they relate to a bequest motive for saving; Hurd (1989, 1995, 1997).
6. See Robert Barro (1974); Gary Becker (1974).

recipients of the bequests should help determine the strength of a bequest motive. Thus if a single child is the target and the child is well-to-do, the parent may decide that an increase in bequests to the child will cause very little increase in the child's utility because of the already high level of consumption by the child. Therefore, the marginal utility of bequests would be small. Should the parents' marginal utility of consumption be large, the effect on consumption or wealth holdings from the bequest motive would be small or even zero. Although the parent would have a bequest motive, it would be difficult to estimate it empirically because it would have little effect on behavior. The consumption and wealth paths of such parents would be indistinguishable from the consumption and wealth paths of someone who had no bequest motive; the bequest motive would not be operable.[7]

A second explanation for a bequest motive is that people care about bequests per se: people simply desire to leave a bequest. Even if this explanation were plausible, the idea lacks theoretical structure so it becomes difficult, if not impossible, to test. In contrast to the altruistic explanation, which suggests that behavior should vary with the observable characteristics of potential bequest recipients, the case of bequests per se provides no such suggestion.[8] Because of the drawbacks of basing a bequest motive on bequests per se, the following discussion assumes that bequests are altruistic.

A bequest motive reduces the risk associated with holding wealth, and this causes more wealth to be held. The mechanism for holding more wealth is to reduce consumption: thus a bequest motive causes the consumption and wealth paths to decline less steeply, and depending on the parameters of the model, wealth could even increase. An important observation is that although someone may have a bequest motive, he or she could still consume all bequeathable wealth. This would happen when the marginal utility of consumption is considerably greater than the marginal utility of a bequest, and it probably should be expected when bequeathable wealth is small relative to annuity income. If bequeathable wealth is great, the marginal utility of consumption will be small, so that even weak bequest motives will influence the consumption and wealth paths.

This model of bequests can explain a number of stylized facts. Broadly speaking, the three types of targets for bequests are: children, other relatives, and institutions such as churches or foundations. To fix ideas, suppose a

7. Abel (1987).

8. From this point of view, strategic bequests are similar to altruistic bequests in that both should depend on the characteristics of the bequest target; Bernheim, Shleifer, and Summers (1985).

potential testator has one child, one relative, and one target institution. Suppose further that he or she has different marginal utility functions for each recipient, specifically that the marginal utility of a bequest to a child will be greater than the marginal utility of bequests to a relative, which will be greater than the marginal utility of bequests to institutions.

Bequests will be a highly superior good in this model. When bequeathable wealth is small, consumption by the parent will be small, and therefore the marginal utility of consumption will be large relative to the marginal utility of a bequest. The observed wealth path for this type of household would be approximately the same as the wealth path of someone who had no bequest motive. Wealth will decline, eventually reaching zero, after which consumption will be financed out of annuities and bequests will be small. Furthermore, any variation in bequeathable wealth will modify the consumption path in a way that is not very different from the path were there no bequest motive whatsoever.

With increasing initial wealth, consumption would increase, causing the marginal utility of consumption to decline. At some wealth level the marginal utility of consumption would become comparable to the marginal utility of bequests, and further increases in wealth will partly be held for desired bequests and partly consumed. At this point, the bequest motive becomes operable. Furthermore, the higher level of wealth will, of itself, cause accidental bequests to increase. Thus observed bequests will increase sharply in wealth, and they will be targeted to the child rather than to the relative or to the institution because of the higher marginal utility of bequests to the child.

At some wealth level, bequests will continue to increase in wealth, but now they will be divided between the child and the relative because the child will have "enough" wealth. Should wealth become very large, not only will the child have enough wealth, but also the entire dynastic line will have enough. Then the institution will become the target for further increases in wealth, and because institutions are large, the marginal utility of bequests to institutions is approximately fixed. Any further increases in wealth will be bequeathed: the elasticity of bequests will be one.[9]

In summary, this model predicts a progression of bequests as wealth increases: bequests increase from none to moderate and targeted to a child, to large and targeted to a child and to a relative, to very large and mostly targeted to institutions. It should be noted that the progression is not caused by any variation in tastes for bequests; the marginal utility functions for

9. Hurd (1989).

bequests are the same for all potential bequeathers. Instead, the progression is caused by variations in economic resources.

In an altruistic framework, the marginal utility of bequests will be altered by the characteristics of the recipients of the bequests, especially the characteristics of the children. In particular, the marginal utility of bequests to children will remain high when the household has many children: it is bequests per child that determine the rate of decline of the marginal utility of bequests to children.

The behavioral model does not distinguish between consumption of owner-occupied housing services and consumption of other goods. Yet, owner-occupied housing has several differences from other goods. It simultaneously provides a flow of services and acts as an asset. It is a large asset, and adjusting holdings involves substantial transaction costs. Despite the differences between housing and nonhousing wealth, home ownership should be taken into account in empirical studies. Housing is the largest asset of many people, and therefore represents a store of value that can be converted to consumption of other goods should someone live to extreme old age. It can be bequeathed, and should act as a good substitute for other assets in satisfying a bequest motive. Because of the likely attachment of both parents and children to a particular house, in many cases that house provides greater utility as a bequest than does a monetary asset of equal value.

Previous Findings about Consumption and Wealth Decumulation

The life-cycle model without a bequest motive predicts declining consumption and wealth paths as households age, so the most direct evidence for a sizable bequest motive would be that consumption and wealth increase even at advanced old age. Panel data are needed to examine this prediction because in cross section, cohort and differential mortality will obscure life-cycle trajectories. But even in panel data, empirical investigations are difficult because macroshocks such as the stock market boom in the late 1990s could cause consumption and wealth to increase even though individuals anticipated dissaving. Therefore, panel data from many years are needed so that macro shocks would average out.

Change in a partial measure of consumption can be calculated from the 1969–79 Retirement History Survey (RHS). The RHS has direct measures of the following categories of consumption: food purchased in grocery stores, food from vendors and home delivery, food purchased away from home, nonfood items purchased in grocery stores, gifts and donations, recreation

Table 4-1. *Change in Average Bequeathable Wealth*

Data set	Annual rate of wealth change (percent)	Source
RHS 1969–79 (singles)	−4.5	Hurd, 1987b
RHS 1969–79 (couples)	−1.6	Hurd, 1987b
Federal Reserve 1963, 1964[a]	−1.2[b]	Mirer, 1980
NLS Mature men 1966–76	−5.0	Diamond and Hausman, 1984
SIPP 1984, 1985 (singles)	−3.9	Hurd, 1991
SIPP 1984, 1985 (couples)	−1.8	Hurd, 1991

a. Data from the Federal Reserve are from the Survey of Financial Characteristics of Consumers and Survey of Changes in Family Financing.
b. The −1.2 is median wealth change.

and membership fees, and gasoline and other transportation expenses (but excluding automobile purchases). The covered categories compose about 34 percent of total consumption by retired singles and couples approximately 60 to 74 years of age.[10]

The unit of observation is a two-year change in consumption by a household where the respondents are retired. The majority of people are in their late sixties and early seventies. Averaged over ten years, the annual rates of change are −3.5 percent for singles and −3.9 percent for couples. Consumption declines at a rather high rate, and consumption by couples declines more rapidly than by singles, although the life-cycle model makes no prediction about the relative rates.

Table 4-1 shows wealth change from four panel data sets. The median age of single persons in the ten years of the RHS was about sixty-five. At an annual dissaving rate of 4.5 percent, it takes about fifteen years to decumulate half of initial wealth. Most of the singles are females who had a life expectancy of about eighteen years at age sixty-five; were the rate of decumulation to remain constant at 4.5 percent per year, they would still have about 44 percent of initial wealth at age eighty-three.

The rate of decumulation by couples is less than by singles. An explanation for this is that the expected lifetime of the household (time until both die) is greater than the expected lifetime of a single person. To see how this could affect wealth change, consider an extreme case in which the returns-to-scale in household consumption are complete: that is, two can live as cheaply as one. Then the appropriate mortality rate for the couple to use in its consumption calculations is the probability that both members of the household

10. Hurd (1992, table 5.9).

will die, which is very much lower than the probability that either will die. Therefore the desired consumption path of the couple could still be rising at age sixty-five, whereas the desired consumption of either a single male or female could be falling. The result could be a flat or slowly falling wealth path of the couple until one spouse dies. Then the survivor would switch to the more steeply falling path of a single individual.

This prediction, however, depends on the returns-to-scale assumption. Consider the opposite assumption of no returns-to-scale whatsoever: The couple's utility is just the sum of the utility of the husband and of the wife. If both have the same utility function, the optimal allocation in each time period is that both consume the same amount. Except for mortality discounting, this will be the same amount as what will be consumed by the surviving spouse. Thus consumption by the couple could be as much as twice the consumption by a single person. Then, holding wealth constant, the rate of wealth decline will be greater among couples than among singles. The conclusion is that although couples seem to dissave more slowly than singles, it is not necessary under the life-cycle hypothesis that they do.

Dissaving by the retired elderly is found in other panel data: Peter Diamond and Jerry Hausman used the National Longitudinal Survey and found rates of dissaving after retirement that are higher than in the RHS, about 5 percent per year.[11] Thad Mirer used a one-year panel from the 1962 and 1963 Federal Reserve wealth surveys to study wealth change of retired elderly.[12] The median rate of dissaving was 1.2 percent per year. In the Survey of Income and Program Participation (SIPP), the rates of dissaving are remarkably similar to the rates in the RHS. Table 4-2 has annual rates of dissaving by age and marital status from the SIPP. The rate of dissaving increases with age, except for couples seventy-five or over. Couples dissave less rapidly than singles.

In contrast to the results described above, several studies have shown no decline in wealth among the elderly. Erik Hurst, Ming Ching Luoh, and Frank Stafford found positive wealth change among those sixty-five or over in the Panel Study of Income Dynamics (PSID) from1984 to 1994.[13] Their results, however, are not comparable with those from tables 4-1 and 4-2. First, they have computed the average of the individual-level changes in wealth as a fraction of "permanent" income. The normalization by permanent income has consequences of an unknown nature because permanent income is a constructed variable rather than an observed variable. Second, the average of individual-level ratios is not robust to observation error in the

11. Diamond and Hausman (1984).
12. Mirer (1980).
13. Hurst, Luoh, and Stafford (1998).

Table 4-2. *Annual Percentage Change in Average Real Wealth, SIPP 1984*
Percent

Age range	Singles	Couples	All
65–69	–0.1	2.3	1.3
70–74	–4.8	–5.9	–5.3
75+	–6.0	–3.7	–5.1
All	–3.9	–1.8	–2.9

Source: Hurd, 1991. Calculated from 1984 SIPP, waves 4 and 7. Includes housing and nonhousing wealth.

divisor of the ratios. In contrast, the results from the RHS and SIPP are based on ratios of average wealth, which are robust to observation error on wealth. Third, the results of Hurst, Luoh, and Stafford do not control for retirement; yet, the life-cycle model does not predict dissaving among workers even at advanced ages.

Steven Haider and others found large wealth increases in panel data from 1993 through 1998 for the population age seventy or over.[14] However, because of the large unanticipated capital gains during that time, those results should not be interpreted as evidence against the life-cycle model. Although the weight of evidence on wealth change is consistent with the life-cycle model, the results do not rule out the possibility that people save to leave a bequest. The empirical implication of a bequest motive for saving is that the declining consumption and wealth trajectories will be flattened, not that they will necessarily slope upward.

One way to test for a bequest motive is to compare the consumption level of someone who has children or close relatives with the consumption of someone who does not. A measure of the difference in their bequest motives would be the difference in the consumption or wealth trajectories of the two individuals. This kind of test has the appealing characteristic of being based on observed behavior. It does not depend on whether people actually give bequests, which because of uncertainty about the date of death would happen anyway, or on whether they say they would like to give bequests. The test depends on whether the desire to give bequests leads to differences in consumption and wealth trajectories.

Similar trajectories could mean that the individuals care equally about the welfare of their heirs. However, similar trajectories could also mean they care differently, but the bequest motive is not operable: as in ordinary demand analysis, the optimum can be a corner solution. Someone may care about the

14. Haider and others (2000).

welfare of his heirs, but when he weighs the utility of his own consumption against the utility from a bequest, he may choose the same consumption path as someone who has no heirs. That is, desired bequests could be zero even though someone has heirs he cares about; his bequest motive is not operable.[15] In an economy in which incomes rise with each generation, it would not be surprising to find that each older generation has no desire to leave a bequest simply because it anticipates the succeeding generation will have adequate consumption without a bequest. In this setting, bequests will be accidental, the result of uncertainty about the date of death, even though the older generation cares about the welfare of the younger generation.

A test based on the difference between paths cannot distinguish between an inoperable bequest motive and no bequest motive whatsoever. Whether this distinction is important depends on how the results will be used. In some circumstances, it is not important to distinguish between them; for example, the effects of a small change in a policy may be well approximated by assuming that no one switches from having an inoperable bequest motive to having an operable bequest motive, which is the same as assuming that those with an inoperable bequest motive have no bequest motive at all. The effects of a large change in policy, however, may not be well approximated by this assumption.

Because children receive the great majority of bequests, a natural way to classify elderly individuals by the strength of a bequest motive is by whether or not they have children. A test based on wealth comparisons requires panel data; it would not make sense to compare the wealth of two individuals of the same age in cross section because one person expended an unknown amount on child raising, and, furthermore, we know from the labor supply literature that family earnings vary by the number of children. Therefore, variation in wealth by parental status is to be expected even in the absence of a bequest motive. Table 4-3 shows the change in bequeathable wealth among retired singles and couples over the ten years of the RHS. As the last row shows, the bequest motive is not supported according to this test; parents should dissave at a slower rate than nonparents, but they do not.[16]

15. Abel (1987); Hurd (1987a).

16. Parents may be able to dissave more rapidly than nonparents because their children will act as insurance against an excessively long life. Then two effects (bequest motive and insurance) may generally cancel, making the rates of dissaving by parents and nonparents approximately the same. My reservation about this explanation for the lack of difference is that we observe very few transfers from children to parents in data. Also, parents may have already provided substantial *inter-vivos* gifts.

Table 4-3. *Average Annual Real Wealth Change, RHS*[a]
Percent

Parental status	Singles	Couples
Children	–4.8	–1.7
No children	–3.9	–0.2
Bequest motive	No	No

Source: Hurd, 1987.
a. Retired singles and couples. Bequeathable wealth excluding housing.

An alternate way to find the influence of a bequest motive is to look at consumption data because a strong bequest motive will flatten the consumption path. Table 4-4 shows the average change in consumption in RHS panel data. On average, consumption declined. Among singles, consumption by parents declined less than consumption by nonparents, which supports a bequest motive, yet the changes among couples do not support it.[17] In neither case is the difference statistically significant.

The tests reported in table 4-3 and table 4-4 have been criticized because they assume that people who do not have children have no bequest motive. In my view, it is not feasible to estimate a bequest motive that is common to everyone. Such a bequest motive would alter the consumption and wealth paths, but the paths could be indistinguishable from the paths of someone lacking a bequest motive but with greater risk aversion. Furthermore, if everyone has the same desire to bequeath to relatives and institutions but parents have an additional bequest target, the marginal utility of bequests to children cannot be larger than the marginal utility of bequests to other relatives or institutions; otherwise we would observe a difference in the consumption and saving behavior. An implication of this is that parents should bequeath to other relatives or institutions with approximately the same frequency that they bequeath to their children. Yet parents give about 90 percent of their bequests to their children.[18] It is particularly implausible that the marginal utility of bequests to children would be about the same as the marginal utility of bequests to other recipients, because the economic circumstances of children vary widely. Such variation should cause differences in consumption and saving behavior or differences in the targets of bequests. My conclusion from these empirical results is they offer no support for an operable bequest motive.

17. A comparison of levels of consumption is not valid because of differences in wealth and annuities.
18. Hurd and Smith (2001).

Table 4-4. *Consumption and Consumption Change, RHS 1969–79*[a]

	Singles		Couples	
	No children	Children	No children	Children
Initial consumption (C_0)	22.7	21.4	37.9	38.6
Second-period consumption (C_2)	21.4	20.8	36.0	36.2
$C_2 - C_0$	–1.3	–0.6	–1.9	–2.4
(Standard error)	(0.34)	(0.23)	(0.54)	(0.30)
t statistic for equality of consumption change	1.68		0.72	
Bequest motive	Yes		No	
No. of observations	1,160	2,484	563	2,451

Source: Hurd, 1992.

a. Consumption in dollars per week (1969 prices). Consumption in seven categories, about 34 percent of total consumption.

Additional Evidence on Bequest Motives

Under the strict life-cycle model as formulated by Menahem Yaari, a single person with no bequest motive should annuitize all of his wealth, yet we see few purchases of annuities in the private market and substantial holdings of bequeathable wealth.[19] The lack of annuitization has been taken as evidence in favor of a bequest motive. It is beyond the scope of this paper to review the arguments and evidence about annuitization as it relates to a bequest motive. I will, however, give some reasons why the lack of annuitization could be caused by factors other than a bequest motive.

Annuities are priced so that they are actuarially unfair to the average person in the population.[20] They are also very illiquid, which means that individuals need precautionary saving as well. Annuities are not indexed, so they are highly vulnerable to loss from inflation, which makes them a risky investment for a retired person. Yaari's argument is based on a single fixed interest rate, yet a wide range of interest rates exists, and alternative investments have offered high rates of return. In fact, at times, long-term bonds would have produced a higher flow of income while preserving liquidity and principal. Many individuals are already heavily annuitized because of Social Security and pensions, and for them the value of further annuitization is reduced.[21]

19. Yaari (1965).
20. Mitchell and others (1999).
21. Hurd (1987b).

Table 4-5. *Average Bequeathable Wealth, Face Value of Life Insurance and Percent of Wealth Insured, AHEAD*

Marital status and age	No. of observations	Wealth (percent)	Face value of life insurance (thousands of dollars)	Wealth insured (percent)
Singles				
70–74	1,080	136.9	5.2	1.4
75–79	1,019	109.0	3.0	1.0
80–84	864	98.7	2.2	0.8
85+	741	88.3	2.2	0.9
All	3,704	110.6	3.3	1.1
Couples				
70–74	1,713	271.1	12.3	1.6
75–79	1,065	245.6	9.5	1.4
80–84	663	217.9	7.0	1.2
85+	298	159.0	4.5	1.0
All	3,739	245.5	9.9	1.5

Source: Author's calculations based on AHEAD wave 1.

Finally, in a very wide range of circumstances, people prefer money today to an illiquid future stream even when the present values are the same. The lack of annuitization is widespread despite variations in economic circumstance or the stated importance of a bequest motive. In my view, it would be premature to ascribe the lack of annuitization to a bequest motive.

B. Douglas Bernheim interprets holdings of life insurance in the elderly population to show that people desire to reduce the forced annuitization caused by Social Security and that these holdings were evidence for a bequest motive.[22] Whether or not some individuals have purchased life insurance in order to leave a bequest, it is useful to examine the quantitative magnitude of any such intended bequests. In the population aged seventy or over, the fraction of people that hold life insurance is rather large, about 57 percent in 1993, but holdings decline with age: among those eighty-five or over about 42 percent own life insurance.[23] Part of these holdings is whole life insurance, which represents both wealth and insurance. Table 4-5 shows bequeathable wealth, the face value of life insurance holdings, and my estimate of the

22. Bernheim (1991). Brown (1999) has presented new results that do not confirm Bernheim's findings.

23. My calculations based on the Study of the Asset and Health Dynamics among the Oldest Old (AHEAD) wave 1.

amount of wealth that is insured in the population aged seventy or over.[24] Most relevant for a bequest motive are life insurance holdings of singles because bequests among couples are to the surviving spouse. Overall, the fraction of wealth that is insured is about 1.1 percent, or somewhat over one thousand dollars. These results are almost identical to results based on the RHS, where singles had life insurance of about 0.8 percent of total resources.[25]

My conclusion is that even if life insurance is held to offset the annuitization from Social Security, the total amounts involved are so small that life insurance does not provide evidence of a quantitatively important bequest motive.

The Role of Home Ownership for Bequests

The role of housing in bequests may be different from the role of nonhousing wealth because of the flow of services that a house provides before death and because of sentimental attachment to a particular house. Whether housing is downsized as people age is not well established in the literature. Louise Sheiner and David Weil estimate that among households entering old age and owning a home, just 41 percent still own a home when the surviving spouse dies.[26] However, a good deal of the decumulation of housing wealth occurs in the last year of life, suggesting that it was not due to life-cycle behavior induced by rising mortality risk; but it was rather due to deteriorating health and inability to live independently. A study by Steven F. Venti and David A. Wise concludes that the elderly do not reduce ownership or equity as they age.[27] Their conclusion is based on the RHS, in which the maximum age is seventy-three, so it may be that the respondents had not reached an age at which downsizing had begun. Based on the Study of the Asset and Health Dynamics among the Oldest Old (AHEAD), Venti and Wise conclude that the elderly do not reduce housing equity as they age.[28]

Instead of housing wealth, this paper will examine the rate of home ownership. This avoids the problem with reporting errors and capital gains affecting housing equity. If substantial transitions from owning to renting take place, there may be a reduction in the consumption of housing services, but

24. See Hurd (1991) for an explanation of the calculation of the insurance component of life insurance.
25. Hurd (1997, table 16).
26. Sheiner and Weil (1992).
27. Venti and Wise (1989).
28. Venti and Wise (2001).

Table 4-6. *Home Ownership Rates, Cross-Section, AHEAD, by Marital Status*
Percent, unless otherwise noted

Marital status	Age	Wave 1	Wave 2	Wave 3
Single	70–74	67.0	71.1	75.4
Single	75–79	63.4	65.0	68.1
Single	80–84	59.8	61.1	62.5
Single	85+	49.5	51.1	53.3
All single	70+	60.5	61.3	62.7
Married	70–74	91.2	91.7	85.6
Married	75–79	87.5	86.7	87.1
Married	80–84	84.5	85.2	85.0
Married	85+	77.2	79.0	76.8
All married	70+	88.0	87.1	85.4
All	70+	74.7	74.3	72.7

Source: Author's calculations based on AHEAD waves 1, 2, and 3.

this analysis will not attempt such a measurement because of the difficulties of comparing the flow of services from renting with the flow of services from owning. Rather, the purpose of the analysis is to establish whether any evidence for downsizing as reflected in ownership rates exists.

Table 4-6 has cross-section ownership rates from three waves of AHEAD.[29] Single individuals are approximately age seventy or over in wave 1 and age seventy-five or over in wave 3. Because of compositional and cohort effects, the cross-section rates by age are not accurate indicators of transitions over time. Both singles and couples who own homes tend to have lower mortality than renters, so that the surviving households in successive cross sections would have increasing rates of home ownership. New widows or widowers tend to have higher rates of ownership than singles, which increases rates of home ownership among singles. The oldest cohorts probably had lower rates of home ownership when they were seventy than seventy-year-olds in AHEAD.

Despite these barriers to a straightforward interpretation, the declines in ownership with age shown in table 4-6 are so pronounced that they suggest a

29. AHEAD is a panel survey of people born in 1923 or earlier and their spouses; Soldo and others (1997). At baseline in 1993, the age-eligible respondents are approximately seventy or over. Wave 2 was conducted in 1995 and wave 3 in 1998. The survey collected extensive information on income, assets, health, family connections, and other resources. It includes some innovative questions about subjective probabilities such as survival probabilities.

Table 4-7. *Home Ownership Rates, Panel, AHEAD, by Marital Status Transition*
Percent

Panel A. Marital status	Distribution of marital status	Wave 1 rate	Wave 2 rate
Married to married	43	89.1	87.4
Married to single	4	81.8	74.9
Single to single	42	61.6	59.3
Married to deceased	5	83.0	...
Single to deceased	7	53.4	...
No. of observations	6,486		

Panel B. Marital status	Distribution of marital status	Wave 2 rate	Wave 3 rate
Married to married	40	89.4	84.8
Married to single	3	79.3	72.1
Single to single	42	62.5	59.4
Married to deceased	6	78.7	...
Single to deceased	7	53.4	...
No. of observations	5,702		

Source: Author's calculations based on AHEAD waves 1, 2, and 3.

life-cycle reduction in home ownership. This conclusion is reinforced by a comparison of home ownership rates for the cohort born between 1906 and 1911 as measured in 1979 in the RHS and as measured in 1993 in the AHEAD. In 1979, when the cohort was aged sixty-eight to seventy-three, 70.6 percent of households owned a home according to the RHS; in 1993 when the cohort had reached age eighty-three through eighty-eight, 64.1 percent of the cohorts owned a home (not shown) according to AHEAD wave 1.[30] This synthetic cohort comparison makes no correction for differential mortality. Because homeowners have higher survival rates than those who do not own, the true life-cycle reduction is greater than the synthetic cohort comparison suggests.

Table 4-7 shows ownership as a function of marital status transition for AHEAD waves 1 to 2 (panel A) and for waves 2 to 3 (panel B). The second line of the table shows the difference in mortality: the home ownership rate in wave 1 among those couples in which one spouse dies before wave 2 is 82 percent compared to 89 percent for couples where both spouses are alive. Among single individuals who die between waves 1 and 2, the ownership rate is 53 percent, but it is 62 percent among singles who survive. Even with dif-

30. Hurd and Shoven (1985).

Table 4-8. *Average Two-Year Net Hazard Rates out of Home Ownership*

Marital status transition	Age	Hazard
Married to married	70–74	0.027
	75–79	0.038
	80–84	0.043
	85+	0.057
	All	0.036
Married to single	70–74	0.067
	75–79	0.061
	80–84	0.131
	85+	0.103
	All	0.088
Single to single	70–74	0.005
	75–79	0.033
	80–84	0.079
	85+	0.062
	All	0.043

Source: Author's calculations based on AHEAD waves 1, 2, and 3.

ferential mortality, widowing increases the rate of home ownership among all singles: widows or widowers have an ownership rate of 75 percent in wave 2, whereas singles who survive from wave 1 to wave 2 have a rate of 59 percent.

The table also shows that home ownership rates decline when marital status does not change: among couples who survive from wave 1 to wave 2, the ownership rate declines from about 89 percent to 87 percent, and the rate of decline is greater from waves 2 to 3. This acceleration in the rate of decline is suggested by the life-cycle model: couples are about two years older on average in wave 2 than in wave 1. The rate especially declines when an individual has been widowed. Singles also show declines. The life-cycle model suggests that the rate of wealth decumulation will increase with age. Table 4-8 shows that the rate of transition from housing ownership (the hazard rate) does increase with age, holding marital status constant. The table has two-year hazards, which are the average of the wave 1 to 2, and 2 to 3 hazards. For couples, the hazard increases from 2.7 percent for the age group seventy to seventy-four to 5.7 percent for the age group eighty-five or over. Among singles, with the exception of a small downturn in the age group eighty-five or over, the hazards increase in age.[31]

31. In the population, the average hazard would increase somewhat more with age than the rates that hold marital status constant because of the greater weight put on singles at more advanced ages.

Figure 4-1. *Projected Home Ownership Rates*

Percent

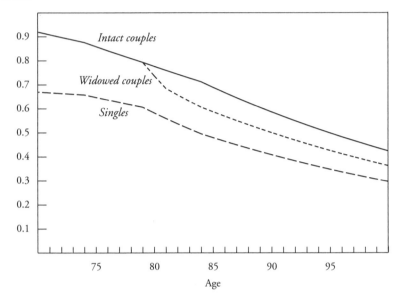

Source: Author's calculations based on AHEAD waves 1, 2, and 3.

The hazard rates in table 4-8 can be used to illustrate how ownership rates would evolve as households age and a spouse dies. The typical path of the home ownership rate among couples after age seventy would be fairly flat because of the low probability of transiting out of ownership, but the probability would increase with age. At some point, one of the spouses would die, and then the transition probability would temporarily increase, as indicated by the much higher hazard rates for the marital transition of married to single. Following that temporary increase, the surviving spouse would follow the transition rates of singles.

Figure 4-1 shows some simulations of ownership rates for three populations. The top curve is for couples in which both spouses survive until age 100.[32] The slope increases with age because the transition rates increase with age as shown in table 4-8. Should the couple survive until age eighty-five, the rate of home ownership would be about 69 percent, and the average annual rate of decumulation would be 1.5 percentage points. This rate is only

---

32. Home ownership rates are calculated by applying the net transition rates out of home ownership to the baseline rate of ownership of 91 percent among couples who are seventy to seventy-four.

slightly lower than the observed rate of wealth decumulation seen in panel data sets. The second path pertains to a population of couples in which both spouses survive until eighty but then one spouse dies. The ownership rate then declines sharply over a two-year period due to the elevated hazards as shown in table 4-8. Then the surviving spouses follow the transition rates of singles. At age eighty-five, the ownership rate of the surviving spouses would be about 59 percent. The path of ownership among singles begins at 67 percent, which is the average ownership among singles aged seventy to seventy-four, and then it declines at an accelerated rate, particularly after age eighty. At age eighty-five, the rate is projected to be about 48 percent.

Weighting the projected rates by the fraction of the population that is married (using the age eighty to eighty-four fractions) indicates that the rate of home ownership would be about 53 percent at age eighty-five based on a population with an ownership rate of 83 percent at age seventy. Thus over fifteen years, the rate of home ownership in the population would decline by about 30 percentage points, or 2 percentage points per year. Table 4-1 shows that these rates are similar to rates of total wealth decumulation. My conclusion is that, as measured by the rate of ownership, housing is decumulated as households age, and that the rates of decumulation are similar to the rates of decumulation of total wealth. As assessed by that standard, housing does not appear to be treated any differently from total wealth.

Subjective Probability of Bequests

This section uses information on households' subjective probabilities of leaving a bequest to shed further light on how households decumulate wealth as they age.[33] The AHEAD asks respondents about their subjective probability of leaving a bequest of at least $10,000.[34] If the probability is at least 31 percent, respondents are asked about the probability of leaving a bequest of at

33. This section is based on work with James P. Smith. See Hurd and Smith (2001).

34. The question is: "Using a number between 0 and 100, what are the chances that you (or your husband, wife, or partner) will leave an inheritance of at least $10,000?" where 0 means absolutely no chance, and 100 means absolutely certain. Validity tests of these questions have shown that in cross section, the responses vary sharply with actual wealth, so that the well-to-do give high probabilities and the poor give low probabilities and in panel data sets, they evolve in a manner that is consistent with their being valid predictors of bequests. See Smith (1999); Hurd and Smith (2001).

least $100,000, and if the probability is less than 31 percent, the probability of leaving a zero bequest. In the case of a couple, each spouse was asked the questions independently.

In some ways, the subjective probabilities of bequests are superior to actual wealth change for the study of life-cycle saving behavior. Respondents are likely to have normal rates of return in mind when they think of an anticipated wealth path, whereas actual wealth change is subject to economywide unanticipated rates of return. For example, it is difficult to believe that households anticipated the very large wealth gains in the stock market during the mid- to late 1990s. The *ex post* rates of wealth change would not have been anticipated or chosen, and therefore may bear little resemblance to normal life-cycle wealth changes.

A comparison of the probabilities of bequests at the target amounts of $10,000 and $100,000 with the share of households that have wealth as great as the target amounts will provide additional evidence about intended wealth decumulation, and how intended wealth decumulation varies with the number of children.[35] The results for AHEAD wave 1 are presented in table 4-9.

Among singles without children, about 74 percent had wealth of $10,000 or more while the average subjective probability of a bequest of $10,000 was only 51.4. The fact that the percentage of the group that had wealth of at least $10,000 is 23 points larger than the subjective probability of leaving a bequest of that amount means that the group anticipates dissaving before death. Among singles with any children, 72 percent had wealth at least as great as $10,000 and 45 percent of bequests will be greater than $10,000; the difference is about 28 percentage points. Judged by these differences, singles without children anticipate less dissaving than singles with children. This result offers no support for a bequest motive for saving.

According to the theoretical discussion above, the marginal utility of bequests should increase with the number of children, causing a reduction in dissaving as the number of children increases. As measured by the difference in the share of households with wealth of at least $10,000 and the average bequest probability, no obvious pattern of declining dissaving with respect to the number of children emerges. In fact, the greatest rate of dissaving is among those with four or more children. Among married people, those with no children anticipate slightly more dissaving than those with children, but the differences are small. With the exception of four or more children, dissaving is reduced as the number of children increases. When the bequest target

35. Because of some inconsistencies in the questions across waves, the data about the target of zero bequests will not be used.

Table 4-9. *Percent with Wealth as Great as Target and Bequest Probabilities: AHEAD, 1993*

Marital status	No. of children	N	Percent with wealth as great as target	Average bequest probability	Difference
Panel A. Target $10k					
All		6,335	83.0	55.4	27.6
Single		2,791	72.8	46.3	26.5
Married		3,544	92.8	64.3	28.5
Single	0	544	74.2	51.4	22.8
	1	429	75.0	48.9	26.1
	2	654	78.1	53.3	24.8
	3	416	74.0	48.2	25.8
	4+	748	64.8	33.1	31.7
	Any	2,247	72.4	45.0	27.5
Married	0	398	93.4	63.4	30.0
	1	490	92.5	64.8	27.7
	2	936	95.2	68.8	26.3
	3	772	92.7	67.8	25.0
	4+	948	90.2	56.6	33.7
	Any	3,146	92.7	64.4	28.3
Panel B. Target $100k					
All		6,221	49.4	27.0	22.4
Single		2,741	35.0	19.6	15.4
Married		3,480	63.4	34.2	29.2
Single	0	533	39.7	24.4	15.3
	1	421	35.0	19.8	15.2
	2	640	40.7	23.7	17.0
	3	409	37.9	19.2	18.7
	4+	738	24.5	12.4	12.1
	Any	2,208	33.8	18.4	15.4
Married	0	392	65.3	36.6	28.7
	1	481	67.2	34.0	33.2
	2	909	66.2	38.0	28.2
	3	760	65.0	36.6	28.4
	4+	938	55.9	27.3	28.6
	Any	3,088	63.1	33.9	29.2

Source: Author's calculations based on AHEAD wave 1.

Table 4-10. *Share of Wealth Expected to Bequeath*

Marital status	No. of children	AHEAD 1993
Single	0	0.638
	1 or more	0.572
	1	0.596
	2	0.612
	3	0.551
	4+	0.514
Married	0	0.584
	1 or more	0.569
	1	0.542
	2	0.603
	3	0.596
	4+	0.518

Source: Author's calculations based on AHEAD wave 1.

is $100,000, the measure of dissaving is about the same among singles without children and with children. For couples there is no support for a bequest motive as seen in panel B.

Another way of examining a bequest motive is to compare the share of wealth that is expected to be bequeathed for households with and without children. Assume that the distribution of wealth within the intervals less than $10,000, $10,000 to $100,000, and greater than $100,000 remains constant as the population ages. Then, expected bequests can be calculated as the weighted average of the probability of leaving a bequest of less than $10,000, the probability of leaving a bequest between $10,000 and $100,000, and the probability of leaving a bequest of more than $100,000. To calculate the expected share of wealth that will be bequeathed, expected bequests are divided by wealth.

Table 4-10 shows the share of wealth expected to be bequeathed as a function of the number of children in the household. In 1993, singles with no children expected to die with about 64 percent of their wealth. Singles with one or more children expected to die with 57 percent of their wealth, so that those with children expect to dissave at a slightly higher rate than singles without children. The average share of wealth that will be bequeathed is about 60 percent and shows little systematic variation with the number of children, thus offering no support for a bequest motive for saving. Among couples, the average share that will be bequeathed is about the same as among singles, and no obvious pattern as a function of the number of children exists.

Conclusion

The two types of results presented in this paper are both relevant for an assessment of the empirical importance of a bequest motive. The life-cycle model makes the strong prediction that when mortality risk becomes sufficiently high, wealth should be decumulated. Failure to find decumulation would be strong evidence against the simple life-cycle model, and, because a bequest model is the leading alternative, evidence for a bequest motive. A lack of housing decumulation would be evidence against the life-cycle model because housing is the most important asset for many people. The results presented here, based on AHEAD in 1993, 1996, and 1998 clearly show housing decumulation.

The second type of evidence based on the subjective probabilities of a bequest show that households anticipate dissaving before they die, and the magnitude of the anticipated rate of decumulation is approximately consistent with that found in actual wealth change and in housing decumulation. Furthermore, the number of children has no apparent effect on anticipated rates of decumulation. Even allowing for the fact that couples who have no children may have different tastes for dissaving from couples who do have children, the bequest model indicates that bequests should increase with the number of children. No such pattern was evident.

When wealth levels are low, the bequest model is consistent with no differences in dissaving among households with and without children. In that case, the marginal utility from a bequest is much smaller than the marginal utility from consumption, so that varying the marginal utility from bequests has little, if any effect on consumption. For all practical purposes, the bequest motive is not operable.

On the other end of the distribution are very wealthy households. Household surveys such as AHEAD are unlikely to include very wealthy respondents simply because such people are more likely to refuse to participate. This group has increasing wealth regardless of age, but the primary cause may not be a bequest motive; rather it is that the marginal utility of consumption has reached zero, and further consumption would make marginal utility negative. Large bequests for the very wealthy are not really the result of a bequest motive in the sense that altering the marginal utility of bequests would not alter actual bequests.

The results here and previous results show no evidence for an important bequest motive for saving. It is, however, important to note that these results are based on household surveys that are unlikely to include very wealthy households. Because the distribution of wealth is highly skewed, most of the bequests flow from households that are not included in the surveys. Thus the conclusion is about the behavior of most households, not necessarily about the determinants of the flow of most of the wealth.

COMMENT BY
Andrew B. Abel

From the viewpoint of understanding consumption and saving behavior and analyzing the effects of various tax changes, it is important to determine whether bequests result from a deliberate bequest motive or from unpredictable deaths that occur before consumers without bequest motives consume all of their resources. For instance, the Ricardian equivalence proposition, which asserts that a lump-sum tax change has no effect on the allocation of consumption and saving, or on interest rates, requires that consumers have bequest motives that arise from altruism toward their children. If bequests arise simply as the accidental by-product of unpredictable deaths, then the Ricardian equivalence proposition will not hold.

Michael Hurd addresses the question of whether bequests are intentional or accidental by describing a simple theoretical model and using that model to guide his comparison of two aspects of the behavior of elderly people without children to the behavior of those with children: wealth decumulation and the size of intended bequests relative to current wealth. In the model, consumers obtain utility from their own consumption and separately from bequests to children, bequests to relatives, and bequests to institutions. Hurd's model implies that elderly people with a bequest motive should decumulate their wealth more slowly than those without a bequest motive. His table 4-3 reports that elderly people with children, whom he identifies as people who might have a bequest motive, actually decumulate wealth more rapidly than elderly people with no children, whom he identifies as not having a bequest motive. Hurd interprets these results as evidence against a bequest motive. He then examines the rate at which home ownership declines as people age, and finds that home ownership declines at about the same rate that wealth is decumulated. However, he does not separately examine home ownership for elderly people with children and without children,

The author thanks John Ameriks for helpful discussion, for providing the data summarized in table 4-11, and for helpful comments on a previous draft; he thanks Olivia Mitchell for helpful discussion.

so from the viewpoint of examining a bequest motive, this analysis appears to be a red herring.

Hurd also examines surveys of elderly people that report the current wealth of individuals and the size of the bequest they expect to leave, whether it is accidental or intended. These data do not provide any clear indication that elderly people with children expect to bequeath a larger share of their current wealth than is the case for elderly people without children. The overall conclusion of the empirical analysis in the paper is that childless elderly people seem to behave and report expectations in a way that suggests that they will bequeath as much as people with children. If childless people do not have operative bequest motives (Hurd allows for the possibility that very wealthy people may have operative bequest motives toward other relatives or to institutions), then elderly people with children do not have operative bequest motives either. The bequests made by both childless elderly and elderly with children are accidental bequests in Hurd's classification.

Without trying to formally or exhaustively examine alternative explanations of the empirical results described above, I will mention one potential explanation. In addition to any saving for the purpose of making bequests, elderly consumers may hold precautionary savings to guard against the risk of having to incur very large medical or personal care expenditures later in life. Elderly people with children may be able to engage in informal (perhaps even unspoken) intergenerational intrafamily risk sharing, in which the grown children may provide some assistance, financial or otherwise, to their elderly parents in the event of a severe adverse health shock. Elderly people without children may not have access to such risk-sharing arrangements and thus would have larger precautionary saving than those people with children. Thus there is no obvious presumption that elderly people with children and a bequest motive will hold more wealth than childless elderly people without a bequest motive and with large precautionary saving.

Interpreting the empirical work through the lens of the theoretical model, Hurd concludes that low-wealth people do not have operative bequest motives, high-wealth people leave bequests that are primarily accidental rather than intentional, and very-high-wealth people have operative bequest motives. This heterogeneity means that most people do not have operative bequest motives, and that most bequests are accidental. However, since a small share of the population holds most of the wealth, most of the wealth that is bequeathed is the result of operative bequest motives of the very wealthy. Therefore, for instance, a change in the rate of estate taxation would not affect the amount bequeathed by most people, but might have a substantial impact on the total amount of wealth bequeathed because it might affect the bequest behavior of the very wealthy.

Hurd singles out a particular asset—housing—in his examination of bequest motives. For the remainder of this discussion, I focus on a different class of assets that may shed more direct evidence on the question of whether bequests are accidental. Specifically, I focus on survival-contingent assets such as annuities and life insurance, and examine how the holdings of these assets are related to the presence or absence of bequest motives.[36] For example, if consumers do not have bequest motives, then they should hold all of their wealth in annuities. Hurd points out that self-purchased annuities are not widely held, and he argues that a primary reason for the limited use of annuities is that they are expensive, not that people have bequest motives. However, being expensive—more precisely, being actuarially unfair—is, in general, not sufficient to prevent consumers from purchasing annuities. Unless annuities are extremely expensive (to a degree that I formalize), their high price alone is not enough to prevent consumers without bequest motives from purchasing them.[37] I present a stylized model to illustrate this point.

Consider a consumer who has already consumed during the current period and has wealth equal to W_0. The probability that the consumer will die before the next period is π and the probability that the consumer will survive until the next period is $(1 - \pi)$. Let W^S denote the consumer's wealth in the next period if he survives, and let W^D denote his wealth in the next period if he dies. The consumer chooses a portfolio to maximize expected utility in the next period, which is

$$(1 - \pi)\ V(W^S) + \pi\Phi(W^D),\tag{1}$$

where $V(W^S)$ is the discounted utility if the consumer survives until next period and $\Phi(W^D)$ is the discounted utility if the consumer dies and leaves a bequest W^D next period. The utility function $V(W^S)$ can be viewed as the present value of utility of consuming in the next period and any subsequent periods, as well as the expected present value of the utility of any bequest after next period. The utility function $\Phi(W^D)$ can depend on the resources of the consumer's children, as in the altruistic formulation of bequest

36. After the conference, Hurd added a discussion of life insurance, including table 4-5.

37. If significant fixed costs are associated with purchasing annuities, reflecting perhaps the costs of learning about annuities, then these costs may prevent some consumers from buying annuities.

motives, or it can be independent of children's resources, as in joy-of-giving bequest motives. The only uncertainty the consumer faces is whether he survives until the next period.

The consumer must choose how to allocate his portfolio among three assets: riskless bonds, annuities, and life insurance. A riskless bond can be purchased at price p_B in the current period and is worth one unit of the consumption good in the following period. Each unit of life insurance can be purchased at price p_L in the current period and has a payoff of zero in the following period if the consumer survives and a payoff of one unit of the consumption good in the following period if the consumer dies. Each unit of annuity can be purchased at a price p_A in the current period and has a payoff of one unit of the consumption good in the following period if the consumer survives and a payoff of zero in the following period if the consumer dies. I assume that the consumer cannot short sell the survival-contingent assets, such as life insurance and annuities. The prices of life insurance and annuities are

$$p_L = (\pi + \theta_L)p_B \tag{2}$$

and

$$p_A = (1 - \pi + \theta_A)\, p_B, \tag{3}$$

where $\theta_L \geq 0$ and $\theta_A \geq 0$ represent the "load" or transactions costs on life insurance and annuities, respectively. If $\theta_L = 0$, then life insurance is actuarially fair. If $\theta_A = 0$, then annuities are actuarially fair.

The consumer allocates his wealth W_0 to the purchase of riskless bonds, life insurance, and annuities, so the budget constraint is

$$p_B B + p_L L + p_A A = W_0. \tag{4}$$

If the consumer survives until the next period, his wealth consists of his bonds and his annuities, so that $W^S = B + A$. If the consumer dies before the next period, the bequest consists of his bonds and his life insurance so that $W^D = B + L$.

Figure 4-2 illustrates the consumer's decision problem, with W^S measured on the horizontal axis and W^D measured on the vertical axis. The consumer can attain point E, where $W^S = W^D = W_0/p_B$ by purchasing riskless bonds and no annuities or life insurance. The consumer can maximize W^S by holding zero bonds and life insurance and using all of his wealth to buy W_0/p_A annuities, as shown by point F. The slope of line segment EF is

Figure 4-2. *Consumer's Decision Problem*

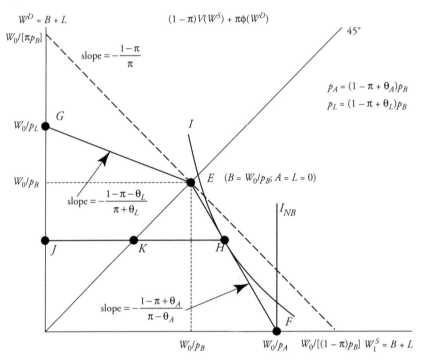

$$-\frac{\left(\dfrac{1}{p_B}\right)}{\left(\dfrac{1}{p_A}-\dfrac{1}{p_B}\right)}=-\frac{1-\pi+\theta_A}{\pi-\theta_A}\,.$$

If $\theta_A \geq 0$, then any point on the segment EF can be attained by a unique portfolio of the three assets: $L = 0$, $B = W^D$, and $A = W^S - W^D \geq 0$. Alternatively, the consumer can maximize the bequest, W^D, by holding zero bonds and annuities and using all of his wealth to buy W_0/p_L units of life insurance, as shown by point G. The slope of line segment GE is

$$-\frac{\left(\dfrac{1}{p_L}-\dfrac{1}{p_B}\right)}{\left(\dfrac{1}{p_B}\right)}=-\frac{1-\pi-\theta_L}{\pi+\theta_L}\,.$$

The unique (if $\theta_L > 0$) portfolio corresponding to any point on the segment GE can be found by setting $A = 0$, $B = W^S$, and $L = W^D - W^S \geq 0$. The consumer's budget line GEF is kinked if life insurance or annuities are priced above their actuarially fair prices, that is, if θ_L or θ_A is positive. For comparison, the perfect markets case with actuarially fair survival–contingent assets ($\theta_L = \theta_A = 0$) is represented by the dashed line through point E with slope $-(1 - \pi)/\pi$.

With the utility function in equation (1), W^S and W^D are effectively normal goods, and the indifference curves representing preferences over these goods have the standard shape as illustrated by indifference curve I in figure 4-2. The optimal combination of W^S and W^D is represented by point H. To attain point H, the consumer holds a portfolio with bonds, B, given by the distance JK and annuities, A, given by the distance KH. In this example, the fact that annuities are overpriced relative to actuarial fairness does not eliminate the demand for annuities. However, if annuities were more expensive, modeled here as an increase in the load θ_A, then the segment EF of the budget line would rotate clockwise around point E and become steeper. If this segment of the budget line becomes steep enough (not shown in the figure), the consumer would be driven to a corner solution at point E, and would purchase neither annuities nor life insurance.

I have shown that overpricing of annuities may eliminate the demand for annuities by a consumer with a bequest motive. Now I consider a consumer without a bequest motive. Formally, a consumer without a bequest motive has $\Phi(W^D)$ identically zero. The indifference curves for such a consumer are vertical lines, as shown by indifference curve I_{NB} through point F in figure 4-2. Indifference curves further to the right represent higher utility. The consumer's optimal point is located at the rightmost point of the budget line, which is point F, where the consumer fully annuitizes his wealth.

Can a high enough price eliminate the demand for annuities by a consumer who does not have a bequest motive? Yes, if the load θ_A is large enough that $p_A > p_B$, then bonds strictly dominate annuities and no one would buy annuities. Recall that an increase in θ_A causes the segment EF to rotate clockwise around point E. When θ_A gets as large as π, $p_A = p_B$, and the segment EF is vertical. If θ_A exceeds π, then $p_A > p_B$, the segment EF slopes upward, and the rightmost point on the budget line is point E. In this case, even a consumer without a bequest motive would not buy annuities. Now the question is whether annuities are actually this expensive; that is, are annuities, in fact, dominated by bonds? The results of Olivia Mitchell, James Poterba, Mark Warshawsky, and Jeffrey Brown imply that annuities are not dominated assets.[38] Specifically, in their table 4-6, Mitchell and others show that a consumer without a bequest motive and without preexisting annuities would be willing to give up between 29 and 40 percent of wealth at age sixty-five to purchase actuarially fair annuities. However, the "overpricing" of annuities in 1990 and 1995 effectively required the sacrifice of less than 25 percent of wealth to purchase actuarially fair annuities, so the consumer would prefer to buy annuities. Of course, these calculations assumed a specific utility function, but the fact that a well-behaved utility function for which the consumer wants to buy annuities exists means that annuities are not dominated assets. This result means that segment *EF* does, in fact, slope downward, as drawn in figure 4-2.

Since annuities are not dominated assets, consumers without bequest motives should buy annuities. Put differently, the limited participation in the annuity market is evidence of widespread bequest motives, unless other reasons that consumers might find annuities unattractive are present. Because annuities are irreversible contracts, one factor that reduces their attractiveness is the risk, mentioned earlier, of very large medical and personal care expenditures. If shortly after using all or most of his wealth to buy annuities, a consumer has a sudden need for large expenditures, he will not be able to use the wealth tied up in annuities. However, this wealth would have been available for these expenditures if he had not purchased annuities. Future developments in the provision and pricing of long-term and catastrophic health insurance may mitigate this risk and encourage the purchase of annuities.

I close the discussion of annuities with some additional evidence supporting the notion that consumers have operative bequest motives. I use data on TIAA-CREF annuitants, most of whom are probably in the intermediate of Hurd's three wealth classes. That is, these consumers do not have extremely high wealth, nor is their wealth so low that the non-negativity constraint on bequests is likely to bind. Hurd concludes that such people do not have operative bequest motives.

Many annuities offer a "years certain" or "guaranteed payment" option. For example, for a single-life annuity with a ten-year guarantee period, if the annuitant lives at least ten years, he will receive periodic payments for the rest of his life; if he dies before ten years, his heirs receive payments for the remainder of the ten-year period. Table 4-11 presents data on the distribution of immediate, life-annuity contracts issued by TIAA-CREF to pension

38. Mitchell and others (1999).

Table 4-11. *Distribution of New Immediate Annuities, TIAA-CREF, 2000*
Percent

Pension participant	Men		Women	
	Guarantee	No guarantee	Guarantee	No guarantee
Single life	19.0	9.9	47.9	21.2
Full to survivor	44.2	6.7	17.9	2.3
Half to second annuitant	3.8	1.0	4.4	0.6
Two-thirds to survivor	12.9	2.5	4.6	1.1
All types of annuity	79.9	20.1	74.8	25.2

Source: Personal communication from John Ameriks of TIAA-CREF.

participants in 2000.[39] For men and women separately, the data in each cell show the fraction of life annuity purchasers who select each combination of annuity and guarantee option. By a four-to-one margin for men, and a three-to-one margin for women, annuity purchasers elect a guarantee period. John Laitner and Thomas Juster point out that annuities purchased on two lives—in this table, full to survivor, half to second annuitant, and two-thirds to survivor—are typically purchased for husband and wife, and the guarantee generally benefits the children, so the guarantee period on these annuities seems to be the most direct evidence of a bequest motive.[40] In table 4-11, among annuities purchased on two lives, annuities with a guarantee period outnumber those without a guarantee by an even larger margin (six-to-one for men, and six and three-quarters-to-one for women) than for all types of annuity taken together.[41] I interpret these data as evidence of a bequest motive, though they might reflect a difficult-to-formalize attitude such as "It would be a shame to have my lifetime saving disappear if I happen to die only two years after buying this annuity."

39. I thank John Ameriks of TIAA-CREF for providing these data in a personal communication.

40. Laitner and Juster (1996).

41. Laitner and Juster (1996, table 1) report data on annuities, separately for annuitants with children and without children, based on a survey conducted in the fall of 1988. They find that 95 percent of joint annuities purchased by annuitants without children and 96 percent of joint annuities purchased by annuitants with children, include a guarantee, so the presence or absence of children does not have much effect on this aspect of bequest behavior, though for single-life annuities, only 24 percent of annuitants without children and 65 percent of annuitants with children elect a guarantee.

I have concentrated on annuities as a source of evidence on bequest motives, but life insurance may also provide evidence. In the simple model in this discussion, anyone who chooses to buy life insurance at a price higher than its actuarially fair price ($\theta_L > 0$) must choose a point on segment GE of the budget line in figure 4-2. A point on segment GE can be optimal only if the consumer has a bequest motive. This observation suggests that retired consumers who have life insurance have a bequest motive. Even taking account of any tax advantages that might be offered by some types of life insurance (and ignored in the simple model presented here), I speculate that it would be difficult to justify the purchase of life insurance by elderly consumers without some sort of concern for their heirs. Hurd reports that 42 percent of people aged eighty-five or over have life insurance, but, as shown in his table 4-5, this life insurance has a value that is only about one percent of the wealth of these people. Hurd concludes that these small holdings of life insurance fail to provide evidence of a quantitatively important bequest motive. However, according to the model in this discussion, even a very small holding of life insurance is evidence of a bequest motive. Before reaching firm conclusions about the strength of bequest motives, we would need to examine the pricing of life insurance policies to determine the size of their transaction costs and also the size distribution of these holdings among the elderly.

COMMENT BY
Jonathan Gruber

One of the most fundamental questions in the literature on savings is the strength of the bequest motive. Dozens of articles, many of them by Michael Hurd, have been devoted to assessing the existence of a sizable bequest motive. Evidence for the United States suggests that a large share of wealth is bequeathed, although the debate continues over the size of the share. However, studies that examine the role of bequests for overall wealth tend not to address the question of whether bequests are *intended* or *accidental*. It is difficult to distinguish between these two types of bequests. The objective of Hurd's paper is to bring to bear two new pieces of evidence on this question. It should be emphasized that this is not only an enormously important problem, but also an enormously difficult one.

While it is always easy to criticize, I do not have many suggestions for alternative ways to test for a bequest motive, and Hurd deserves enormous credit for continuing to innovate in his never-ending search for the right answer. The first piece of evidence in this paper is an examination of housing decumulation. Other researchers have suggested that the elderly do not decumulate their housing assets as they age, which is consistent with a bequest motive.[42] Using data from the Study of Asset and Health Dynamics among the Oldest Old (AHEAD), Hurd presents new evidence that this is not the case. Previous studies that have examined the decumulation of housing have focused on housing equity. Hurd takes a different approach and examines the pattern of downsizing through moving, that is, the change in the rate of home ownership in the elderly population. Yet despite the tone of the paper, the results are almost identical to previous work. Hurd finds modest declines in housing wealth of about 2 percent per year after age seventy. Contrast this with a straw man against which Hurd sets himself, a recent paper by Steven Venti and David Wise, which finds declines of 1.76 percent per year after age seventy-five.[43]

The modest difference in results, yet the enormous difference in rhetoric between Hurd's paper and previous papers, highlights the fundamental difficulty in using rates of decumulation to infer a bequest motive. Venti and Wise conclude from their finding that housing equity is not generally used to finance consumption. In contrast, Hurd concludes that housing equity is decumulated at the same rate as nonhousing wealth, and takes this finding to imply that housing decumulation does not suggest an active bequest motive. However, to assess who is right, we need a true underlying model of consumption needs in old age and how these needs change over time. This is far beyond anything we have available to date.

The second piece of evidence of a bequest motive is novel and more intriguing. Hurd uses a clever comparison between wealth levels and expected bequest levels. The AHEAD asks respondents about the chances of leaving bequests of various sizes. Given existing wealth holdings, these expectations can be used to infer the expected level of asset decumulation by groups. If a bequest motive is present, the expected asset decumulation should be slower for groups with a larger bequest motive. The question is why this is a better approach than using actual wealth decumulation, as the author has already done on numerous occasions? The answer is that actual wealth decumulation is subject to random shocks, which may not reveal anything about intended behavior. For example, the stock run-up in the 1990s may have made it look as though the elderly were accumulating wealth toward a bequest motive, when really, this was a random shock to wealth much as early mortality would be. Hurd's approach avoids this problem and

42. See the review in Venti and Wise (2001).
43. Venti and Wise (2001).

offers a clever new way of thinking about *intended decumulation*. From this analysis, Hurd concludes that intended decumulation is no higher for those with and without kids, and no higher for those with more relatives and fewer kids. Once again the conclusion is that observed behavior is inconsistent with a bequest motive.

But this test runs into two important difficulties. The first is *inter-vivos* gifts. It is possible that families with kids intend to leave less when they die because they plan to give more while they are still alive. Some new and forthcoming papers in the *Journal of Public Economics* present interesting new evidence on the substitutability between bequest and *inter-vivos* giving.[44] One paper is by Ben Page, who finds that individuals in states with higher bequest taxes make larger *inter-vivos* transfers, presumably as a means of avoiding the estate tax. A paper by James Poterba finds that those with higher marginal estate tax rates, those with fewer assets in illiquid forms that can be shielded from the estate tax and those with fewer capital gains that can be shielded from the estate tax are more likely to make *inter-vivos* transfers, all else equal.[45] These findings make exercises such as the one Hurd performs in this paper somewhat problematic, in that the higher decumulation rate among the elderly with children may occur because of *inter-vivos* gift giving. This point could be addressed in a straightforward way in the AHEAD data by using data on transfer payments. I urge the author to examine how this type of analysis would affect his conclusions.

It might be tempting to go further and claim that Poterba's or Page's findings are evidence for a bequest motive; indeed, my first draft of these comments did say that! However, estate tax avoidance does not imply a bequest motive.[46] Consider persons who have no utility of bequests while alive, but who know they cannot possibly run through their assets before death. Those persons might still be interested in maximizing the size of their post-tax "accidental" estate, without having an active bequest motive.

A second issue with the test in Hurd's paper is the following: how plausible is the assumption that bequest motives are stronger for those who have children, or for those who have more rather than fewer kids? The contention that those with children have a stronger bequest motive strikes me as plausible. Among those who expect to leave some bequest, it is not as obvious that the bequest motive is stronger if one has children. It is even less obvious that the bequest motive is stronger with more children. This depends very much

44. Page (2002, forthcoming).
45. Poterba (2001).
46. I am grateful to Peter Diamond for pointing this out to me.

on the model of bequests. In Hurd's model, the marginal utility of bequests rises with the number of children. This could be true, for example, if the utility from bequest is a function of the child's marginal utility of consumption. But in a "warm glow" model, where the utility from bequests is a function of giving the bequest, regardless of how the child feels about it, it is not clear that more children would lead to larger bequests. I would urge Hurd to, at a minimum, try to surmount these data problems and incorporate those who intend to leave zero bequests, which would make his case more compelling.

Although both of these tests are interesting, they are not dispositive. Does a better answer exist? It is not clear. But it seems to me that the right direction for examining this issue is to look at how asset decumulation and intended bequests change as the child's circumstances change. In any model without an active bequest motive, asset decumulation patterns and intended bequests would not change as children have negative or positive shocks to their life circumstances. However, in the altruistic model, they would; if I care about my child's marginal utility of consumption, then a permanent negative shock to them should raise the intended bequest and slow the rate of asset decumulation. Of course, in the warm glow model, they might not change, so a failure of this test would not rule out a bequest motive, but passing this test would clearly indicate one. This is related to work that Laurence Kotlikoff did in the early 1990s, which examines how linked the marginal utilities of consumption were across generations, but with the updated data now available from HRS, we should be able to improve and refine these tests.

Let me conclude with a question. I would also like Hurd to address this question in his paper: If no bequest motive exists, what implication does that have for policy? One important implication is that it heightens the need to ensure proper annuitization of the elderly under any privatized Social Security system. If a bequest motive is absent, imperfect annuitization could mean a large welfare loss. This is important because the administrative costs of annuitization in the United Kingdom have been shown to be quite high.[47] But those costs may be worth bearing if individuals do not have a bequest motive. It also strengthens the case for an estate tax. The optimal redistributive tax is one that taxes luck, not effort. If everyone fully intends to draw down his or her wealth before dying and not leave a bequest, then whatever wealth one dies with is pure luck and therefore should be taxed at 100 percent. This certainly runs contrary to the current direction of estate tax policy! In addition, it highlights that this should remain an active area of research.

47. Murthi, Orszag, and Orszag (2001).

5

Gifts and Bequests: Family or Philanthropic Organizations?

PAUL G. SCHERVISH AND JOHN J. HAVENS

The growth in wealth over the past decades and the projected wealth transfer over the next half century of at least $41 trillion from estates of final decedents means that the decisionmaking process behind the allocation of transfers—both *inter vivos* and by bequest—to heirs and charity has become of great interest in many quarters.[1] The forthcoming wealth transfer is of significance not just to heirs, but to charities, financial planners, financial institutions, state and federal governments, and wealth holders themselves.[2] It is this latter group, and how they decide to allocate their transfers to heirs and charity, that are the special interest of this chapter.

We draw on our theoretical and empirical research on wealth and philanthropy to elaborate two new directions for understanding transfers to family and charity. The first is to suggest that identification with the fate of others is the primary variable that explains transfers to both family and charity for

1. Havens and Schervish (1999).

2. Primarily out of necessity, we join other researchers in identifying wealth holders as those persons having at least $1,000,000 in family net worth. Few large data sets have a sufficient sample of wealthier individuals to focus solely on the extremely wealthy of $5 million or more, among whom, as we have confirmed in our interview studies, the trends we present here are even more strongly evident.

individuals across the economic spectrum. The second and newer direction is to argue that there is a major change in the decisionmaking dynamics of transfers when individuals reach a self-defined level of financial security. When wealth holders have redundant resources, that is, a substantially large enough lifetime resource stream to provide whatever they desire for themselves and their heirs, then the trade-offs between self and family, on the one hand, and charity, on the other, are obviated. If the first aspect of our argument is about continuity in underlying motivation, the second is about discontinuity in decisionmaking dynamics. Both aspects are sociopsychological in that they introduce and rely on behavioral explanations about the meanings and motivations that generate transfer decisions.

In the first section of this paper, we focus on the identification theory and supporting evidence for it, especially from the yearlong Boston Area Diary Study. Incorporating the identification theory into explanations of transfers to heirs and charity has the advantage of serving as a more general theory within which economic theories can be understood, and as a way to integrate aspects of economic theories of motivation. In the second section, we present empirical evidence concerning the relationship of income and wealth to charitable contributions and to interpersonal transfers. The findings suggest that the very wealthy make such substantial and disproportionate contributions to charity that some additional element, over and above identification, is at play in motivating their charitable giving. In the third section, we identify financial security as the additional factor that provides an impetus for greater charitable giving and helps explain why wealth holders at the high end of the wealth spectrum are disproportionately inclined toward charitable giving. Although the motivation of identification explains giving by individuals across the economic spectrum, the allocation of gifts is different for those individuals who have solved what Keynes calls "the economic problem (of scarcity)" and those who have not.[3] If, due to financial security, the dynamics of wealth-transfer decisions are different for the very wealthy, then devising models that better fit their actual decisionmaking processes may contribute to better interpreting, if not clarifying, the contradictory or ambiguous findings about the determinants of transfer decisions, especially in regard to the role of tax considerations in charitable giving.[4] In the fourth section of the paper, we explore a new direction in financial planning that wealth holders are employing. Financial planning procedures are an intervening behavioral variable that contributes to changing the decisionmaking process for wealth

3. Keynes (1930, p. 366).
4. Tempel and Rooney (2000).

holders in relation to allocating transfers, often resulting in a greater priority being given to charitable giving. In the conclusion, we suggest that as a result of material wherewithal, identification with the fate of others, and new directions in financial planning, wealth holders may be shifting their wealth allocations toward philanthropy rather than heirs, in general, and toward *inter-vivos* charitable contributions and transfers rather than bequests, in particular.

The Identification Theory

This section reviews the identification theory and suggests that it provides a general theoretical framework that shares elements with economic explanations of wealth-transfer decisions; that explains transfer decisions to family and philanthropy as similar in motivation; and that is applicable to decisions by individuals from across the economic spectrum. Most recent economic research concerning transfers to adult family members and philanthropic organizations relies on one of three competing motivational paradigms: altruism, exchange, and warm glow. The altruism paradigm assumes that the family, as an institution, functions to equalize the income of its members and that interpersonal (including intrafamilial) transfers are motivated by altruism, or more generally, that charitable contributions are motivated by altruism.[5] The exchange paradigm assumes some *quid pro quo* motivates both interpersonal transfers and charitable contributions.[6] The warm glow paradigm assumes that interpersonal transfers and charitable contributions make the giver feel good and experience a psychological benefit.[7] Each of these paradigms has its proponents and each has some evidence in its favor; however, none has emerged as the single valid motivation to explain either interpersonal transfers or charitable donations. Without denying the validity of any of these paradigms, we offer the identification theory as a broad, empirically derived motivational paradigm that integrates all three economic motivations.

The identification theory is developed from our extensive ethnographic and survey research on charitable giving, although its roots may be found in the religious and philosophical traditions of the practice of human love.[8] The central tenet of the theory posits that self-identification with others in their needs, rather than selflessness, motivates transfers to individuals and to phil-

5. Cox (1987); Clotfelter (1997).
6. Cox (1987); Clotfelter (1997); Andreoni (2001).
7. Andreoni (2001); Clotfelter (1997).
8. Gilleman (1959); Toner (1968); Pope (1991a, 1991b, 1992).

anthropic organizations and provides givers the satisfaction of fulfilling those needs.

Based on intensive interviews with 130 millionaires in 1986 and 1987 in the Study on Wealth and Philanthropy, we developed and subsequently refined the identification theory as a general framework for understanding interpersonal transfers and charitable behavior.[9] The theory has two major components: First, philanthropic behavior, including both charitable donations and transfers to families, is a manifestation of the broader concept of *caritas* or care—what Toner defines as meeting the true needs of another person.[10] Care radiates from the self and care of self is part of *caritas*. Care is first learned in the relationships of family, and expands to encompass friends, neighbors, associates, and others, and is expressed either directly through interpersonal care, or indirectly through nonprofit organizations. Care may

---

9. Schervish and Herman (1988); Schervish, Coutsoukis, and Lewis (1994). We do not hold that this theory is completely novel or that it contradicts the economic paradigms; indeed, its explicit antecedents can be traced at least as far back as Thomas Aquinas. Rather it provides a broader and perhaps richer context within which to understand transfer behavior, which may at times appear to reflect altruistic behavior, at other times reflect exchange behavior, and at yet other times, reflect warm glow. In fact, the theory has a precursor in economics. More than a quarter-century ago, an iconoclastic economist, Kenneth Boulding, foreshadowed the identification theory when he hypothesized that self-identification motivates both charitable and intrafamilial transfers. Examining the motivation for philanthropic giving, Boulding wrote in 1962: "The name philanthropy itself, which means of course, the love of man, is a clue to the essential nature of the genuine article. When we make a true gift, it is because we identify ourselves with the recipient . . . It is the capacity for empathy—or putting oneself in another's place, for feeling the joys and sorrows of another as one's own—which is the source of the genuine gift. It is because 'no man is an island,' because the very realization of our own identity implies in some sense that there is a common identity in humanity, that we are willing to 'socialize' our sub stance and to share with the afflicted . . . Obviously, the more an individual identifies with some cause, community, or organization, the more likely he is to support it and the greater will be his donations to it. This is why the immediate face-to-face group and the reference groups with which he has identified himself always figure largely in the amounts given by an individual. When he gives to his children, for instance, he gives in a sense to an extension of himself. When he gives to a church of which he is a member, he is expressing his identity with a community a little larger than the family but fulfilling some of the same functions. As he contributes toward it, therefore, he is contributing in a sense toward part of his larger self." Boulding (1962, pp. 61–2).

10. Toner (1968).

also extend to people collectively organized in groups, communities, and nations.

The second major component and the essence of the identification theory of *caritas* is the principle that caring behavior does not reflect selflessness or the absence of self; rather, a self-identification with others. Care results from a recognition that the needs of others are similar to what oneself or one's family has or could have personally experienced. As such, caring for others fulfills the needs of the caregiver as well as the needs of the recipient, providing the caregiver with a kind of emotional satisfaction akin to the "warm glow" motivation specified by some economists. In our research, we find that identification with others develops and is applied primarily through networks of association that bring donors into contact with potential recipients. Through the various constellations of formal and informal associations, some of which we seek out and some of which are thrust upon us, we learn about people in need and come to identify with them. It is not surprising, therefore, that we tend to give, at least at first, to those organizations and individuals we frequently associate with in our daily lives. One of the most consistent findings from our research is that the greatest portion of giving and volunteering takes place in a donor's own community and church, and helps support activities with which the donor is directly associated, and as is often the case, from which the donor directly benefits. Over the course of our research, it has become increasingly clear that differences in levels of giving of time and money are due less to differences in income, wealth, religion, gender, or race, and more to the mix and intensity of one's network of formal and informal associations, and hence to one's identifications, ranging from immediate family to extended family, friends, associates, community groups, and eventually beyond these groups.[11]

Identification in Practice: The Boston Area Diary Study

Evidence that the identification theory is a robust model for understanding the caring behavior of a wide spectrum of individuals at all levels of income and wealth—as well as age, ethnicity, gender, and marital status—comes from the Boston Area Diary Study (BADS) which we conducted during 1995 and 1996. To our knowledge, this is the first methodologically rigorous diary study focusing primarily on giving and volunteering.[12] The BADS

11. Schervish and Havens (1997); Schervish and Havens (2002b).
12. The study was funded by the W. K. Kellogg Foundation and the T. B. Murphy Foundation Charitable Trust. For details on the research methodology and interview protocols see Schervish and Havens (2001a). For further interpretation of the findings see Havens and Schervish (1997); and Schervish and Havens (2002b).

involved repeated intensive interviews with forty-four randomly selected people who were contacted weekly by telephone to report on care given and care received over the course of a year. The study collected information from participants concerning money and goods given to and received from charitable organizations and other persons, except for spouses and dependent children. The study also inquired about time both given and received in unpaid assistance, emotional support, and volunteer activity from organizations and other persons, excluding spouses and dependent children. The findings show that care is a unity or seamless continuum which does not distinguish between recipients except in regard to immediacy of need; and that the individuals and causes that received the most care were those with which our interviewees identified in a personal way.

Table 5-1 summarizes respondents' donations of time and resources given on a regular basis. Care is provided in an array of ways: some are relatively passive, such as praying for others or treating others with civility and respect; others involve direct action, such as taking care of an elderly relative, driving friends and acquaintances who are in need of transportation to a variety of appointments and activities, helping others take care of their children, and providing emotional support to those facing both common and extraordinary tribulations. The statistical findings combined with the additional personal information garnered during the interviews produce three findings:

First, above and beyond the care respondents expressed through contributions of money, goods, and time to and through charitable organizations, the participants spent a considerable amount of money, goods, resources, time, and energy on informal care for individuals other than their spouses and dependent children. Second, formal philanthropy represents merely the surface of the total amount of care that the members of society extend to each other on an informal basis. Third, participants contributed the largest amounts of care to those individuals and charitable causes with which they were most closely identified and involved; for example, giving to family and relatives generally took precedence over friends and acquaintances, and giving to organizations that helped the participants, their family, or their friends generally took precedence over organizations and causes that did not.

Findings on Identification and Wealth Holders

The findings of the BADS are consistent with the findings of our previous and subsequent research based on in-depth interviews with wealth holders.[13]

13. Schervish and Herman (1988); Schervish, Coutsoukis, and Lewis (1994); Schervish, O'Herlihy, and Havens (2001).

Table 5-1. *Contributions of Money, Goods, and Time, Boston Area Diary Study*

Organization or person	Mean annual contribution of money and goods (dollars)	Share contributing money and goods (percent)	Contributions of money and goods as percentage of income	Volunteering and unpaid assistance Share (percent)	Hours
All organizations	1,490	100	2.2	84	9.9
Religious	741	75	1.3	36	6.0
Nonreligious	750	95	0.9	79	5.9
All interpersonal	7,779	98	7.4	100	57.7
Relatives	7,092	93	6.1	100	44.2
Adult child or grandchild	4,834	50	3.8	59	6.7
Parent	294	52	0.6	64	15.7
Other relative	1,964	93	1.6	95	10
Nonrelatives	687	98	1.3	100	13.5

Source: Social Welfare Research Institute, Boston College, 1996.

Even at higher levels of wealth and income than we encountered in the diary study, we find that behind any charitable gift is a story of identification and association. For example, among the younger philanthropists who were interviewed in our 2001 high-tech donors study, the primary impediments to greater charitable involvement were the relative youth of the interviewees, their lack of religious connection, their recent arrival in their communities, and their ownership or participation in a business which depended on national and international, rather than local, markets.[14] Such sparse networks of association simply did not provide them with extensive or intensive outlets for their care or many opportunities for identification. But as their connections grew through peer organizations like Social Venture Partners, or through involvement in their children's schools, so too did their involvement and financial support of charitable causes. After taking care of their families, for example, through outright transfers of capital, scholarships, or living trusts for health care, they looked for outside opportunities to use their wealth to express their personal and family values. Throughout the interviews, we found that, as with the BADS respondents, high-tech donors tended to support the causes which addressed the concerns that they, their families, and those with whom they had been associated, had experienced, often in their childhood. Experiencing the benefits of a good elementary school or college education leads to a concern in later life with early childhood education or research at a university. A lifelong participation in hiking and mountain climbing generates a special care for preserving the environment. The death of a loved one from cancer leads to establishing an oncology center at a hospital. Being a musician leads to contributions to the arts. Explicitly or just beneath the surface of their narratives is an account of how the people and events that have materially and emotionally affected high-tech donors and their loved ones are recapitulated in the people and causes they most care about. Respondents made it clear that their moments of identification extended the sentiments of family feeling to the realms of fellow feeling and respondents often recounted the motives and meanings of their philanthropy in the language of surrogate kinship. Regardless of other differences, those they seek to help are like them, they say, like their parents, and like the people they once knew.

Implications for the Allocation of Transfers

There are important implications of the findings from our BADS and wealth-holder studies for understanding the allocation of transfers between family and charitable organizations. First, individuals across the economic

---

14. Schervish, O'Herlihy, and Havens (2001).

spectrum allocate their financial resources to the people and organizations with whose needs they identify. Allocations for self, family, and charity are all motivated by identification. Second, there tends to be a hierarchical ordering of such identifications and allocations such that personal and family needs generally take priority over the needs of friends and acquaintances, and the needs of organizations with which one has been associated take priority over other organizations. Third, as the needs of the people and organizations to which one has given initial priority become fulfilled, the needs of other individuals and organizations are moved up in priority.

In sum, our research on the philanthropic behavior of the very wealthy, the wealthy, and the nonwealthy has repeatedly shown that the dichotomy of formal and informal philanthropy, or giving to and through formal philanthropic organizations as opposed to giving to family and friends, is a false dualism. Most individuals do not make such sharp distinctions, but perceive their transfers of time, money, and emotional support as occurring in concentric circles of care, beginning with those who are closest to them and extending to others beyond immediate family and friends. Furthermore, our research suggests that the allocation decisions between family and charity spring from a dynamic relationship among social, economic, and demographic variables, which can be influenced, altered, and expanded for all individuals regardless of their socioeconomic and demographic status, especially as they are dependent on moments of identification and connection.

Empirical Relationship between Transfers and Family Income and Wealth

People can give to charitable causes during their lifetime (*inter-vivos* giving) or at their death (charitable bequests). Similarly, they can transfer financial resources to relatives and friends through *inter-vivos* transfers or bequests to heirs. In both cases, such a striking upswing in giving among those in the upper tiers of income and wealth has taken place that it is important to identify not only the fact of such an upswing but also what it implies.

Charitable Inter-Vivos *Giving and Bequests*

In aggregate, for the year 2000 *Giving USA* estimates that charitable contributions amounted to $203 billion from all sources. Three-quarters of this total was contributed by individuals in their lifetime, and another 7.8 percent consisted of charitable bequests.[15] During the past twenty years, aggre-

---

15. American Association of Fundraising Counsel (AAFRC) (2001). The remaining 17 percent was contributed by foundations and corporations.

Table 5-2. *Charitable* Inter-Vivos *Contributions, by Income and Wealth*
Percent, unless otherwise noted

Income	Share of families	Share of families contributing	Group's share of total contributions	Mean family contribution (dollars)
	Panel A: Income greater than 0 (dollars)			
1–19,999	29.4	62.1	5.1	211
20,000–39,999	28.1	75.8	12.1	504
40,000–74,999	26.3	83.7	25.8	1,147
75,000–124,999	11.1	87.9	17.3	1,836
150,000+	5.2	97.0	39.7	8,926
	Panel B: Net worth greater than 0 (dollars)			
1–19,999	22.7	10.5	3.6	190
20,000–74,999	24.7	26.7	7.1	409
75,000–199,999	24.6	40.9	16.4	763
200,000–999,999	23.1	61.6	31.3	1,639
1,000,000+	5.0	85.8	41.6	9,644

Source: Authors' own calculations using the 1998 Survey of Consumer Finances and the 1998 General Social Survey (for contributions less than $500).

gate giving by individuals has grown 79 percent in real terms and aggregate charitable bequests by 168 percent. This section presents data on charitable giving and on the transfers to relatives and friends. Table 5-2 presents data from the 1998 Survey of Consumer Finances (SCF) and the 1998 General Social Survey (GSS) on the distribution of *inter-vivos* charitable giving.[16] The data show that the share of families making charitable contributions increases by income and net worth. The results also indicate that a small fraction of high-income families or high-wealth families make a disproportionately large share of the charitable *inter-vivos* contributions. Families in the top 5 percent of the income distribution made 39.7 percent of the total charitable contributions in 1997, with an average donation of $8,926. Similarly, families in the top 5 percent of the wealth distribution made 41.6 percent of the charitable contributions in 1997 with an average donation of $9,644.

One apparent anomaly is that charitable contributions as a share of net worth decrease with net worth. Families in the bottom half of the wealth distribution contribute about 1 percent of their net worth, while families in the top 5 percent of the distribution contribute only 0.3 percent (not shown). However, as shown in table 5-3, there is a strong positive relationship between charitable bequests and wealth that contrasts sharply with the nega-

16. National Opinion Research Center (1998a, 1998b).

Table 5-3. *Charitable Bequests, Taxes, and Bequests to Heirs and Others, by Asset Value of Estate for 1999 Filings*

Gross estate category (millions)	*Gross estate*				*Charitable bequest*		*Taxes*		*Heirs and other*	
	N returns (thousands)	*Net worth (billions)*	*Fees and surviving spouse (billions)*	*Available estate*[a] *(billions)*	*Amount (billions)*	*Share of available estate (percent)*	*Amount (billions)*	*Share of available estate (percent)*	*Amount (billions)*	*Share of available estate (percent)*
0.6–1	49.9	37.9	7.3	30.6	1.1	3.6	1.3	4.2	28.2	92.2
1–2.5	40.8	58.4	18.3	40.1	2.4	6.0	6.7	16.7	31.0	77.3
2.5–5	8.6	28.2	10.6	17.6	1.5	8.5	5.7	32.4	10.5	59.6
5–10	3.1	20.0	7.9	12.1	1.4	11.6	4.9	40.5	5.8	47.9
10–20	1.1	13.9	5.4	8.5	1.4	16.5	3.8	44.7	3.3	30.8
20+	0.6	31.6	11.3	20.4	6.8	33.3	7.9	38.7	5.7	27.9
Total	104.0	189.9	60.7	129.3	14.6	11	30.3	23	84.4	65

Source: Calculated by John Havens, Boston College, Social Welfare Research Institute, based on tabulated data available on the web page of the Statistics of Income Division of the IRS.

a. Available estate is the estate after fees and transfer to surviving spouse.

tive correlation between wealth and percentage of wealth contributed to charities in the form of *inter-vivos* gifts. Among wealthy decedents, charitable bequests as a percentage of the value of the estates—minus estate fees and spousal deduction—increase as asset levels increase, rising from 4 percent for estates of less than $1 million to 33 percent for estates of $20 million or more.

In addition, as shown in table 5-4, the allocation of bequests has changed over the period 1992 to 1999. In the early part of the decade, wealth holders seemed to shift bequests from heirs to charity, but as shown in panel A, this trend reverses between 1997 and 1999. In particular, as shown in panel B of table 5-4, those with net estates valued at $20 million or more increasingly devote a larger share of their estates to charitable bequests between 1992 and 1997. The share of bequests in charitable estates increased from 33.7 percent in 1992 to 49.1 percent in 1997, but then fell to 33.3 percent in 1999. Some potential reasons for this trend and why it does not necessarily indicate a retreat from charitable giving by the wealthy are discussed later in this chapter.

Inter-Vivos *Transfers to Relatives and Friends*

High-income and high-wealth families also make a disproportionate share of transfers to relatives and friends. According to the 1998 SCF, approximately 12 million households made *inter-vivos* transfers to relatives and friends for financial support amounting to $64 billion during 1997. These transfers range from as little as $20 to more than $1,000,000. The typical transfer for households making transfers is $3,000 and is most often given to the respondent's own children. Households in the top 5 percent of the wealth distribution make 35 percent of all the transfers in dollar terms.[17] Previous research has shown a strong relationship, comparable to transfers to charity, between income and wealth on one hand and the frequency and magnitude of intrafamilial transfers on the other.[18] For very wealthy decedents, the wealth of the decedent is strongly related to both the frequency of making *inter-vivos* gifts and the value of those gifts.[19]

The data in this section may be summarized as follows: A small percentage of wealthy and very wealthy families makes a disproportionate amount of the transfers both to charitable causes and to friends and relatives. These transfers are made both during life and at death. As wealth increases, the share of

17. Havens and Schervish (2001).
18. Altonji, Hayashi, and Kotlikoff (1996).
19. Joulfaian (2000a).

Table 5-4. *Amount and Allocation of Estates Less Fees and Bequests to Spouse, 1992–99*
Billions of 1999 dollars, unless otherwise noted

Year	Available estate[a]	Charitable bequest		Taxes		Bequest to heirs	
		Amount	Share of available estate (percent)	Amount	Share of available estate (percent)	Amount	Share of available estate (percent)
Panel A: All estates							
1992	74.4	8.1	10.9	15.7	21.1	50.6	68.0
1995	79.8	9.5	11.9	17.1	21.4	53.2	66.7
1997	106.09	14.8	13.8	22.8	21.3	69.3	64.8
1999	129.3	14.6	11.3	30.3	23.4	84.4	65.3
Panel B: Estates of $20 million or more							
1992	8.6	2.9	33.7	3.3	38.4	2.4	27.9
1995	9.1	3.7	40.7	3.2	35.2	2.2	24.2
1997	17.5	8.6	49.1	5.3	30.2	3.6	20.6
1999	20.4	6.8	33.3	7.9	38.7	5.7	27.9

Source: Boston College, Social Welfare Research Institute, based on data from Johnson and Mikow (1999), Eller (1996–97), and the web page of the Statistics of Income Division of the IRS.

a. Available estate is the estate after fees and transfer to surviving spouse.

income given to charity while the donor is alive also increases, but the share of *wealth* given to charity while the donor is alive falls. However, wealthy people have traditionally given to charitable causes through charitable bequests, and as the asset value of estates rises, the share of that value devoted to charitable bequests rises substantially. Although the findings confirm that the motivation of both wealth holders and nonwealth holders in making financial transfers revolves around identification and care, the foregoing patterns require that we look for an additional factor that inclines wealth holders to give such large portions of their wealth to charity. We hypothesize that this factor is the matrix of material capacity and sociophysiological dispositions associated with financial security. When wealth holders can underwrite into perpetuity a desired standard of living for themselves and their heirs, the trade-offs and motivational dynamics circumscribing their wealth-transfer decisions become different from those of people who are not financially secure.

Financial Security and Philanthropy

We argue that those who are financially secure enter a new realm of decision-making concerning charitable transfers. By financial security, we mean that individuals have reached a level of wealth where both materially and perceptually they can provide the standard of living they desire for themselves and their family, such that they could survive a major personal or economywide financial setback with their standard of living ensured. If financial security is the material and emotional foundation for dedicating large sums to philanthropy, the next question is: How does financial security translate into financial philanthropy rather than into business investment, greater transfers to heirs, or tax payments? In other words, why do wealth holders who are financially secure tend to allocate a greater proportion of their wealth to charity than those who are not financially secure?

Findings from a survey of 112 individuals with assets at or above $5 million demonstrate that feeling financially secure does not occur at some objective level of financial resources, and individuals vary greatly in the amount of wealth they consider necessary to reach financial security.[20] Although 98 percent of the respondents placed themselves above the midpoint on a scale from zero to ten (from not at all secure to extremely secure), only a relatively low share, 36 percent, felt completely financially secure. The amount of wealth respondents considered necessary to feel completely financially secure ranged from $10,000 to $500 million. The median amount needed for

20. Schervish and Havens (2001b).

financial security was $20 million, or 67 percent more than current wealth, while the mean amount needed was $44 million, or 76 percent more than current wealth. These amounts, of course, vary by how financially secure someone currently feels. Respondents who felt completely financially secure indicated that they would require about 44 percent of their current level of wealth to maintain that security. Respondents who rated themselves as eight or nine indicated that they would require an average additional 60 percent of their current net worth in order to feel completely financially secure, and respondents who rated themselves lower than eight on the scale indicated they would require an average increase of 285 percent in their net worth in order to feel completely financially secure. Another indicator of the psychological dimension of financial well-being is that on average, respondents at moderately high levels of income (up to $10 million family income) and wealth (up to $50 million family net worth) indicated they would require additional wealth in order to feel completely financially secure. Only at very high levels of income ($10 million or more in family income) and wealth ($50 million or more in family net worth) did respondents indicate, on average, that they would feel completely financially secure with less than their current level of wealth.

Despite these perhaps surprising findings about the level of financial resources deemed necessary to guarantee financial independence, the same study shows there is a strong positive relationship between perceived financial security and charitable giving, measured in amount, percentage of income, and percentage of wealth. Table 5-5 shows those with higher net worth give substantially more to charity on average than those with less (although substantial) net worth, and this holds in terms of absolute dollars, as well as in terms of percentage of income contributed and percentage of net worth contributed. More importantly, the table also shows that financial security has a very strong positive relation to charitable giving. The more financially secure a respondent feels, the more is given to charity, not just in absolute amounts but also as a percentage of income and net worth.

Given the positive relationship between financial security and charitable giving, just how does financial security translate into charitable giving? Thomas B. Murphy, an actuary, business owner, and wealth holder, has sought to conceptualize the usually implicit combination of financial and psychological reckoning that he and other wealth holders go through, formally or informally, in determining how much of their resources to donate to charity. Murphy describes a process in which wealth holders determine a stream of resources; a stream of expenditures for self, family, and investment; and a stream of truly discretionary resources that is simply the posi-

Table 5-5. *Charitable Giving by Net Worth and Financial Security*
Percent, unless otherwise noted

Level of financial security[a]	Less than 8	8 or 9	10	All levels
Panel A: Net worth of $15 million or less				
Average charitable donation (dollars)	32,114	69,036	369,778	116,778
Average share of income contributed	5.0	6.6	23.4	9.5
Average share of net worth contributed	0.4	0.5	3.0	1.0
Panel B: Net worth of more than $15 million				
Average charitable donation (dollars)	228,333	1,044,265	3,779,159	2,234,681
Average share of income contributed	7.6	19.2	51.0	32.9
Average share of net worth contributed	0.7	2.0	3.9	2.8
Panel C: All levels of net worth				
Average charitable donation (dollars)	58,872	603,839	2,598,988	1,108,707
Average share of income contributed	5.4	13.5	41.5	20.4
Average share of net worth contributed	0.5	1.3	3.6	1.8

Source: Calculated by John Havens, Boston College, Social Welfare Research Institute, based on data from Bankers Trust, *Wealth with Responsibility Study 2000*.

a. Respondents were asked to rate their sense of financial security on a scale of 0–10 from completely insecure to completely secure.

tive difference, if any, between the stream of resources and the stream of expenditures.[21]

This decisionmaking scenario outlined by Murphy regarding the meaning of financial security and how it translates into charitable transfers reflects what we have repeatedly heard wealth holders report in their intensive interviews. For example, an interview with one wealthy respondent in our 2001

21. "Given the generally accepted assumption that one provides first for oneself and one's family and does so at some level of lifestyle, philanthropy enters into the decisionmaking process in a more formidable manner when the difference between the expected level of income, current and future, and expected level of expense, current and future, to maintain and enhance one's standard of living is substantial and

high-tech donors study, a forty-five-year-old, cashed-out equity partner of a venture capital firm, confirms Murphy's analysis of the transition from accumulation to charitable allocation and demonstrates our view that a substantial behavioral change is taking place in the decisionmaking dynamics of the very wealthy concerning charitable involvement. He defines financial security as "basically having a very, very low chance that you will go broke even if you don't have a job, given an acceptable lifestyle. I have a computer model that I built that reaches out to when we're (he and his wife) ninety years old that factors in inflation, and that plays out all this growth stuff and what the random fluctuations of the stock market could possibly be. And it lays out a thousand versions of the way the world might play out and in only one time out of a thousand will we go broke given the life-style that we've chosen. And that's financial independence."[22]

He goes on to explain that as a mathematician and computer programmer, and as one who is exceptionally risk averse when it comes to long-term financial independence, the elaborate model he has constructed "randomly simulates the way the stock market will play out over the years, using history as a guide for what numbers you should put in there. And the question for me was, do you have enough squirreled away so that basically we can maintain the life-style that we've chosen through our old age and have a very low probability of having either inflation or a lack of appreciation in the stock market make us go broke?"

For the respondent, the amount designed for financial security is a present value resource stream of $6 million, net of prospective taxes, net of inflation, and net of potential negative stock-market shocks.

More important for our argument here is how, in the light of meeting his goals for financial independence, the interviewee has turned to philanthropy as the realm in which he has now begun to focus his intellectual, emotional, and financial capital. Before declaring himself materially and psychologically financially secure, the respondent was already a small contributor to charities, but upon cutting back on his business activity and cashing out his

---

relatively permanent as measured by the subjectively determined criteria of the decisionmaker. . . . The extent to which this difference (discretionary income) between income and expense is positive quantifies the financial resources available for philanthropic activities. The extent to which this difference is perceived as permanent strengthens the case for allocating some of the resources for philanthropy. The extent to which the difference is positive, permanent and growing in magnitude enhances the philanthropic allocation." Murphy (2001, pp. 34–35).

22. From a confidential interview. Schervish, O'Herlihy, and Havens (2001).

equity share in his venture capital firm, he began in earnest to investigate ways to use his money, skills, and time in a more qualitatively systematic and quantitatively substantial manner. It was now time, he recounts, to pursue more wholeheartedly something in the realm of philanthropy that fits the "ideal" of being unambiguously social.[23] The respondent makes it clear, however, that a serious pursuit of philanthropy would have been a "romantic" rather than a "pragmatic" ideal had he not first achieved financial independence.[24]

It is instructive that even with financial security certain, the transition to a sharper focus on philanthropy is neither for the respondent, nor for his financial peers, an automatic step. Financial security, even when understood to be assured, leads to philanthropy only in combination with other motivational vectors. This array of motivations includes identification, gratitude, the prospect of entrepreneurial effectiveness, and the desire to limit bequests to heirs.

Identification

We have already discussed the motivation of identification at some length. But its ability to animate the philanthropy of a wealth holder is clear by a brief look at how the respondent described above connects what he considers to have been the comparative advantage of being well educated with the plight of those whose lack of quality education excludes them from the knowledge

23. As our respondent puts it, "I've always kind of rolled my eyes a little bit when I hear about do-gooders because I have this image in my mind—not grounded at all on any experience—they will be lightweight type of stuff, full of petty politics. So I've always steered away from the world of philanthropy or nonprofit and pooh-poohed it somewhat. But there is a side of me that says that maybe I can tune in a little bit more and do something that is unambiguously socially positive and see how that feels. I would like to see how that feels and if I find myself getting up in the morning very excited about how I am spending my time, if indeed I do find something that is unambiguously socially positive. This is something that struck me really very profoundly: those simple pleasures of being a contributor and being able to map how those contributions fit into the larger scheme of things. Kind of the social welfare, if you will." Schervish, O'Herlihy, and Havens (2001).

24. "You need wealth to actually act on that ideal because, I'm sorry, I enjoy so much the lifestyle you can achieve with wealth. The pragmatist in me, like the squirrel, says, 'save your chestnuts and the sooner you get that done, the sooner you can rise up a Maslovian level and do the other things. And beware trying to rise up the Maslovian level before you are ready to do it. Be very, very sure that you are ready to do it because it is tough to turn back.'"

economy. The respondent recounts that both he and his wife have gotten ahead in life as a result of the intellectual capital they garnered from their extensive top-tier university studies and, because of the many educators in the family, a concern for education has been "imprinted in us." As he puts it:

"I'm very concerned about a bifurcation of the educated and the edu-cated-nots in our society because I see increasingly that our economy is driven by knowledge-worker types, problemsolvers. So I have real concerns about how to democratize education." Especially for the poor, "education is very important 'cause what we're talking about is people who would other-wise be burger-flippers." As was true for him, "the comparative advantage to poor children is an affordable education, which in turn allows them to get jobs in the knowledge economy."

Gratitude

The motivation of identification is complemented by a particularly strong sense of gratitude for unmerited advantages or, as some say, "blessings," in reaching financial success. In our 2001 high-tech donors study we find that most participants do not credit their wealth solely to their own efforts and skills.[25] They understand that at various points in their careers there was always risk of failure. Thus some credit their wealth at least in part to luck and good fortune, or if they are religiously inclined, to God's will or God's blessing. Such experience of blessing and gratitude further animates them to seek ways to help individuals and causes with which they identify.

The dynamics of gift and gratitude leading to care for others is precisely what our respondent describes as motivating his concern for the vocation of education as a "noble thing." "The other piece of it," he continues, moving from identification to gratitude, "is I personally got so much out of my edu-cation. It has enriched me beyond measure. Not only the practical aspects of it, for instance in my career, but also to have a sense of irony, and to build an intellectual richness in life that for me has just meant so much as a gift."[26]

---

25. Schervish, O'Herlihy, and Havens (2001).

26. "The gift of knowledge you might say—the gift of how to think, how to write, how to communicate, how to analyze as well as the gift of all the touchstones that an education gives you—the building of commonality in a community. You know, if everybody has read Shakespeare, there's a commonality that comes out of that which makes for better life. I do believe in having touchstones—that communi-ties have points of reference that are rich and deep which can be commonly held and therefore allow people to not feel alone and to have confidence in the like-mindedness of their fellows." Schervish, O'Herlihy, and Havens (2001).

Hyperagency

In addition to identification and gratitude, another motivation derives from the particularly active way high-net-worth individuals have made their money; namely, the desire to be as entrepreneurially productive in the realm of philanthropy as they have been in the realm of commerce. The majority (approximately 93 percent) of wealth holders acquired most of their wealth through their own skills and efforts (including investments) rather than through inheritance (7 percent).[27] Their major road to wealth has been business, in the sense that they have owned and operated their own businesses, most often as entrepreneurs. [28] Those who have not been directly involved in business see themselves as active investors. Our research findings confirm that the fundamental common trait of wealth holders is what we call *hyperagency*. Hyperagency is the ability to be a producer and a creator of the organizational life of a society rather than simply a supporter and participant. As institution-builders in commerce, politics, and philanthropy, hyperagents do not simply seek to find the best environment within which to work, live, or give. Rather, hyperagents are able to do alone or with a few other individuals what would take others a substantial social, political, or fund-raising movement to achieve. When they choose to do so, hyperagents on their own can start new ventures, apply new ideas and methods, and set new institutional directions for existing organizations; and, as we have often seen in recent years, they can jump into electoral politics, leapfrogging established candidates. The wealthy thus bring to their philanthropy not just an overarching expectation and confidence about being effective, but also a wide range of skills revolving around what our respondent called "questions of how to manage change." Such skills include an understanding of finance, management, investment leverage, personal connections, leadership talent, and a can-do attitude bred by success. In particular, the longer wealthy individuals are members of a community, the more likely they are to have assembled an

27. These estimates are based on data from the 1998 Survey of Consumer Finances of the National Opinion Research Center, which asks respondents detailed questions concerning inheritance. The current value of all inheritances was estimated by adjusting the value of inheritances received for inflation and by assuming a real secular growth rate of 3 percent. This value was at least 50 percent of current total net worth for only 7 percent of families whose net worth was $1,000,000 or more.

28. Based on data from the 1998 SCF we estimate that of the 4.6 million families with a net worth of one million dollars or more, 53 percent owned one or more businesses, as contrasted with the 11 percent of families with less than one million dollars in net worth.

array of informal and formal associations within their communities, and to have become, through board memberships and other leadership positions, intimately knowledgeable about, interested in, and responsible for philanthropic initiatives and nonprofit management and innovation. When coupled to the fact of earlier financial security and longer life expectancy, many wealth holders have both the time and energy to devote deeper thinking and vigor to the people and causes about which they care.

In philanthropy, as in commerce, politics, and civic life in general, the desire to be productive hyperagents is an active motivation that is part of the general inclination of wealth holders to be as publicly purposeful in allocating their wealth as they were privately purposeful in accumulating it. The respondent we describe above demonstrates this third motivation in addition to those of identification and gratitude. His disposition to be involved in philanthropy requires working through a "high performance culture." He says: "I want strong intellectual problem-solvers who are also interested in really getting a lot done. It's not just getting a lot done, but I am just a more cerebrally oriented person, I think, and will find it difficult being effective and happy in a more politically oriented culture or in a more ideologically oriented culture than maybe other people will be." His objective to make a far-reaching impact leads him to look first at local education but, speaking as a hyperagent, he says, "At the end of the day I have an ambition to be able to look at the magnitude, how far reaching the things are that I do. I'd like to see if I could affect thousands of people positively and meaningfully."

Limiting Transfers to Heirs

As noted above, a decline in the shift of bequests from heirs to charity took place between 1997 and 1999. It is difficult to know whether this reversal is a random fluctuation in the 1999 data, a decline in overall giving to charities, or the beginning of a shift among the wealthiest individuals from giving through bequests to *inter-vivos* giving through one of several vehicles for charitable giving. Certainly, in recent years, some reports indicate (although do not thoroughly document) that, as a result of planned giving strategies, wealth holders are moving toward increased *inter-vivos* giving as part of a consolidated lifetime financial plan. The increase in the variety and popularity of planned giving vehicles for donors, as well as the growth in the number and size of private foundations, including personal and family foundations, and donor-advised funds are indicators of this shift.[29] Moreover, our inter-

29. Between 1999 and 2000, the Fidelity Gift Fund assets grew 41 percent, the amount distributed to charities grew 53 percent, and the number of donor-advised

views with high-tech wealth holders and some informal interviews with financial planners and fund-raisers reveal that increasingly upper-tier wealth holders are actively pursuing opportunities to implement their philanthropy while they are alive, rather than largely through their estates.

In addition, for the very wealthy, the allocation of wealth to heirs is already being limited by considerations such as the potentially negative effects of large inheritances on children; and allocations to philanthropy are more frequently occurring by means of a family foundation or through the involvement of the wealth holder and heirs in philanthropy, as a good way to resolve the moral dilemmas that surround the best use of excess wealth.

In the *Wealth with Responsibility Study 2000*, 112 respondents worth $5 million or more were asked about the effect of the estate tax on their allocation of wealth between charitable bequests and heirs.[30] The distribution of responses indicates that if estate taxes were eliminated as a consideration, wealth holders would give more to charity rather than giving all the tax savings to heirs. For example, when asked how they expected to and how they would like to allocate their estates to heirs, taxes, and charity, on average the respondents *expected* 47 percent of assets from their estates to go to heirs, 37 percent to go to taxes and 16 percent to go to charities. Their *desired* allocation, however, was to see 64 percent of their assets go to heirs and 26 percent to charity, with taxes unsurprisingly trailing a distant third priority at 9 percent (unspecified other purposes made up the remaining 1 percent). In other words, in their ideal scenario, their 76 percent reduction in taxes would result

---

funds grew 39 percent. In 2001, the Fidelity Gift Fund became the second largest charity on the *Chronicle of Philanthropy*'s Philanthropy 400, its assets growing to over one billion dollars. In recent years, there has been a huge growth in private foundations, showing that gifts are being made in life rather than at death: 40 percent of U.S. foundations are family foundations; two-thirds of family foundations were formed in the 1980s and 1990s (Foundation Center [2000b]). Independent (not corporate or community) foundations accounted for more than four-fifths of the overall increase in foundation giving in 2000; the number of independent foundations grew 7.2 percent between 1998 and 1999; and the number of operating foundations grew 8.3 percent over the same period (Foundation Center [2000a]). Donors have been taking advantage of charitable vehicles that meet their needs. Just 2 percent of the total population has established a charitable remainder trust (National Committee on Planned Giving [2001]). However, the 1998 *US Trust Survey of the Affluent*, which interviewed 150 people in the top 1 percent of income and wealth, found that 15 percent of respondents had set up a charitable remainder trust and 25 percent were likely to do so in the future (U.S. Trust [1998]).

30. Bankers Trust (2000); Schervish and Havens (2001b).

in a 63 percent increase in bequests to charity. The *Wealth with Responsibility Study 2000* also shows that the desire to reallocate money from taxes to charity is even stronger at the upper levels of wealth: respondents with a net worth at or above $50 million envisioned an even greater shift to charity than those with a net worth below that amount.

Additional evidence that the wealthy are purposely limiting transfers to heirs is provided by this respondent in our 2001 high-tech donors study.[31] He speaks for the majority of those we interviewed in citing his fear that the burden of wealth would overwhelm his children and attests to his intention to limit the resources made available to his heirs, seeing overly abundant inheritances as an extravagance, if not downright injury. The respondent grew up fending for himself with several small entrepreneurial ventures and struck it rich when a larger firm bought his company. Although he is just thirty-five years old and has four children under the age of eight, he is already concerned about ensuring their financial virtue. The fact that his children will grow up affluent is "a bitch," something that is "really scary" and "haunts" him, in part because his own childhood was so different from theirs that he feels simultaneously inadequate and yet determined to deal with the issue of their affluence.

He recalls his own upbringing, where "you had to make your own way . . . There wasn't some rich uncle somewhere who would keep bailing you out of university or anything like that. There are decisions you make and consequences to each one of them and that's really frightening," before turning to his kids, and wondering aloud how he should eventually talk to them about "all the challenges that wealth is going to bring to them." Although his kids are "damn well going to" be taught how to handle wealth responsibly, he is simply clearer about the problems than the solutions for such training. Educating the children about wealth is "really a difficult area for us to think about and we are only a year into this and we certainly don't have the answers there yet." One thing the respondent does know is that he "just can't see anything beneficial" from simply transferring all his wealth to his kids. That would turn out to be "just mostly downside for them; more complexities." At the same time, he has begun to think that involving his kids in philanthropy offers some "practical" potential for teaching his kids how to handle their wealth.

"I think the Social Venture Partners Fund (my wife and I founded) is a good example. If we build this thing right, our kids are going to grow up knowing us as people that took our own unique gifts and got back involved in the community. Not someone that just kind of got a wing of the music

31. Schervish, O'Herlihy, and Havens (2001).

college named after them for a couple million dollars or something easy like that. But that we rolled up our sleeves and took our unique gifts and tried to build something where something didn't exist."

Neither the survey nor ethnographic evidence just presented *proves* that financial security changes the decisionmaking dynamics for those who have solved "the economic problem" for themselves and their families. However, the foregoing statistical and interview evidence does indicate that the allocation of wealth between family and philanthropy may take on a different character for the financially secure, one that does not depend primarily upon estate-tax avoidance, but depends more upon a logic that inclines the very wealthy to view philanthropy as both a positive alternative to bequeathing wealth to heirs and a way to combine philanthropy with the transmission of financial morality through the creation of foundations and philanthropic trusts that will involve the next generation.[32]

New Directions in Financial Planning and Their Impact on Wealth Allocation

Like many of us, wealth holders (especially those who are self-made) typically concentrate on accumulating wealth early in their careers. Only later do they focus as attentively on the allocation and distribution of the wealth they have accumulated. During this subsequent phase they usually seek information and advice about allocation strategies, often from financial or estate planners and sometimes from development officers and fund-raisers for charitable organizations to which they may potentially contribute. This section describes a relatively new methodology used by some financial planners, as well as some fund-raisers, to guide wealth holders through the planning process for allocating redundant resources. We have coined the term "discernment process" as a descriptive name for this new methodology.[33]

Discernment means insight, perception, or sagacity. The discernment method is an approach that helps wealthy individuals gain insight into their finances and their needs with a view to identifying their personal level of financial security and their desires for using their financial resources to express their personal and family values. The goal is to enable individuals to make wise choices concerning the allocation of their redundant financial resources.

The discernment process has three subprocesses. The first subprocess

32. Paul G. Schervish, "Philanthropy Can Thrive without Estate Tax," *Chronicle of Philanthropy*, January 11, 2001, pp. 47–48.
33. Schervish (2001); Schervish and Havens (2002a).

guides wealth holders through an examination and discernment of their financial resources. The second subprocess invites wealth holders to examine their values, goals, desired life-style, and ideals in order to discern their psychological inventory of subjective factors that affect the allocation of their financial resources. The third subprocess involves the development and implementation of a plan, including specific financial instruments, to allocate their resources consistently with their subjective values, goals, and desired life-style for themselves and for their families. More specifically, the discernment methodology of financial planning seeks to enable wealth holders to estimate an expense stream, to view wealth and income as together providing the resources to meet and exceed that expense stream, and to estimate what is left over after financial security has been achieved.[34] It helps obviate the anxiety wealth holders feel about providing for self and family, settles the issue of inheritance for children, and opens up remaining resources (that is, redundant financial resources) to create a social capital legacy composed of explicitly directed transfers to taxes and to philanthropy.

These financial planning processes actually formalize the discernment that many wealthy people go through privately. As implied by Murphy's description of the dynamics of financial security, many high-net-worth individuals are already inclined away from leaving an inheritance to children that exceeds their needs, away from excessive taxation, and toward charity as the best disbursement of their financial legacy.[35] The practice of a discernment model of financial planning reinforces this inclination, since participants arrive at greater clarity both about their financial potential and personal predilections for charitable giving. The positive role of the discernment process in helping the wealth holders identify financial security cannot be underestimated, for it is only when wealth holders reach financial security that they can become confident about the existence, and therefore deployment, of redundant resources. As we have already noted, the *Wealth with Responsibility Study 2000* clearly shows that feeling financially secure is a function of psychological comfort as well as of the level of material wealth. The discernment process, because it involves deep personal reflection in relation to values and money, can give donors the confidence to determine, locate, and allocate financial resources to achieve financial and psychological security for self and spouse and to provide what wealth holders want to give their heirs; then it can give them the freedom to embrace ways to be effective in the public sphere by responding to the following four questions:

34. See Fithian (2000) for an elaboration of these ideas.
35. Schervish and Havens (2002a).

—Is there anything you want to do?

—That you consider important to do to meet the needs of others?

—That you can do more efficiently than government or commerce?

—And that enables you to express your identification with others and gratitude for advantages, and to achieve greater effectiveness and deeper personal happiness?

A discernment-led approach to allocation differs from traditional financial planning in two major respects: First, values rather than tax considerations drive allocation decisions for those who go through the process. Second, rather than accepting a predetermined plan, the wealth holders are at the center of the process and are encouraged to develop their own plan based on their own perceptions of their financial resources and future financial needs, based on their own values, and based on their own philanthropic objectives and priorities.

Will a more self-reflective wealth allocation decisionmaking process lead to a noticeable effect on charitable giving on an aggregate level? Our hypothesis is that the effect will be substantial; it may already be visible in the statistics. First, a large number of families that are already wealthy (in 1998 approximately 5 percent of families, more than 5 million families, had a net worth of at least $1 million). The rapid growth in wealth during the last decade has meant that more and more people are achieving high levels of wealth and confronting in daily life what we call "the spiritual secret of wealth": how to best disburse redundant resources when financial security has been achieved and guaranteed.[36] We expect the trend to continue as personally held wealth continues to grow over the next fifty-five years, though perhaps at a lower rate than during the 1990s. In our 1999 report *Millionaires and the Millennium*, we present projections for wealth transfer through the year 2053. The most conservative estimate of economic growth of just 2 percent produces projections of wealth transfer of $41 trillion, of which at least $6 trillion could be allocated to charity. According to recent calculations, and based on a low estimate of secular growth of just 2 percent, we project that individuals will donate $3.3 trillion in lifetime giving to nonprofit organizations in the next twenty years, or $13.2 trillion in lifetime giving over the next fifty years.[37] Clearly, independent of the effects of the discernment process, there is a boon for charity in the offing.

Second, the behavioral indicators from intensive interviews, from statisti-

36. Schervish and O'Herlihy (2002).

37. Calculated by the Social Welfare Research Institute, Boston College, based on an initial estimate from AAFRC, *Giving USA 2001*, of *inter-vivos* giving in 1998.

cal trends, and from the *Wealth with Responsibility Study 2000* imply that both charitable bequests and *inter-vivos* gifts will increase to the extent that the practice of financial planning offers a methodology that reinforces the behavior already evident. We have seen a growing interest in the wider variety of charitable vehicles available to donors, evidence of donors more frequently using their wealth to have an impact in life rather than after death, the involvement of heirs in philanthropy, and a reluctance to burden heirs with a large legacy in excess of their needs. As more and more donors have the opportunity for self-reflection about their wealth and values in an atmosphere of liberty and inspiration, we expect these trends to continue, resulting in more *inter-vivos* giving to charity and a continuing shift in bequests from heirs to charity.

In sum, the new practices of financial planning revolving around developing and implementing a financial plan by means of a structured set of meetings between client and professionals have the following effects: First, they reduce uncertainty concerning current and future financial status and increase clients' psychological sense of financial security, if for no other reason than that doubt about one's own and one's family's current and prospective financial condition is mitigated. Second, the new planning methods encourage clients to contemplate their own lives and their values in a way that brings identification to a conscious level. Finally, the new planning approach provides expert information concerning the alternative uses of any excess financial resources that clients may have, including how to allocate excess resources to charity in a manner that meets the needs of others, fulfills the inclinations of donors to be socially constructive, and opens an opportunity for the philanthropic education of heirs.

Conclusion

Our purpose has been to set out some new thinking about the motivations for giving to heirs and charity and the dynamics of those transfers among upper-tier wealth holders; that is, among those who are self-consciously financially secure. We argue that the meaning and practice of wealth transfer among the very wealthy need to be understood in a new way, one that reveals why so many current research findings involving the very wealthy are at best, ambiguous, and at worst, mistaken.

We pose an argument with two motifs: The first theme revolves around locating elements of continuity in the wealth-transfer dynamics of wealth holders and the nonwealthy. Wealth holders share with others across the economic spectrum a common motivational matrix for allocating financial resources, which we have termed *identification*. Individuals' caring behaviors are motivated by a convergence of interest with the fate of others, not along the axis of altruism as opposed to self-interest, but along the axis of identification as opposed to isolation. It is not the absence of self but the engagement of self that motivates care for others in need. Moreover, in the identification theory, because care of self, family, and others is viewed by the caregiver as arising from the same underlying dynamics, it is not necessary to attribute different motivations for wealth transfers to different recipients. Rather, what is needed is to uncover the relative amount of financial care people are inclined to allocate to self, heirs, and social needs. The decision-making dynamics of this second process are the paper's second motif.

If the dynamics of identification delineate a common motivation for allocations to self, heirs, and others—and do so for individuals across the economic spectrum—the dynamics of financial security reflect consequential discontinuities in the content and categories of wealth-transfer decisionmaking. It is not so much differences in fundamental motivation as differences in capacity that result in the distinct way the wealthy allocate their financial resources. Research on wealth and philanthropy reveals that those who are both materially and psychologically financially secure eliminate those budget constraints that would entail trade-offs between their own material well-being and that of their heirs, on the one hand, and the well-being of others, on the other. Such wealth holders are increasingly disinclined to simply maximize transfers to heirs, minimize taxes, and treat charitable transfers as a by-product of the other two. Rather, because of enhanced material capacity combined with new methods of self-reflective financial advisement, increasing numbers of wealth holders, at an earlier age and at more realistic levels of wealth, understand themselves as enjoying redundant resources. The implications for behavior and hence for theory, research, and policy are several and notable:

First, economic theories and evidence from analysis of estates across the entire spectrum of wealth and income brackets are indeterminate regarding the motivations behind the allocation of transfers between philanthropy and family. Our analysis indicates that the dynamics of identification and financial security may have special application in explaining the behavior of those at the highest levels of income and wealth, thereby clearing up some of the contradictory and ambiguous findings about how and to whom wealth is allocated.

Second, if findings on the effect of estate taxes conflate the differing decisionmaking dynamics at play at different levels of financial security, then policy proposals based on such research may be misguided. For example, the basic motivation animating the philanthropic behavior of the very wealthy is identification, but precisely what other factors affect that behavior, and how, remain largely speculative. More specifically, much research assumes that marginal estate and income tax rates coupled with charitable deductions influence philanthropic behavior. However, it is not clear that taxes have the same effect on very wealthy individuals who command redundant financial resources as they do on well-to-do, but not wealthy, individuals.

Third, in the past decade a new approach to financial planning, the discernment method, has emerged. This methodology guides wealth holders through a process of self-discovery before the development of specific financial plans. This relatively new process not only reflects but also actually creates the outcomes that formerly have been attributed to conventional independent variables. These new models and methods for financial planning and fund-raising increasingly encourage understanding *inter-vivos* and bequest giving as a unified, endogenous process. We hypothesize that these new approaches are having a profound effect on the timing and magnitude of giving among wealth holders such that they are moving their charitable giving toward the present and thereby away from charitable bequests and toward *inter-vivos* gifts.

Although there are many additional implications for theory, research, and policy, the primary implication of our analysis is that a relatively substantial reconsideration of the dynamics of wealth allocation may be in order. This, we believe, is certainly true in reference to the very wealthy who deem themselves, as they are in fact, financially secure. Economic analysis consistently assumes budget constraints in modeling and explaining financial decision-making. But if it is true that increasing numbers of individuals are completely financially secure and even larger numbers are substantially financially secure or sufficiently affluent to relax budget constraints, then a new approach to conceptualizing wealth-transfer dynamics is crucial for discerning the effects of public policy on the distribution of wealth between individuals and philanthropic organizations. For now, our research suggests that the dynamics of identification, financial security, and financial planning dispose the very wealthy to define their financial independence, to intentionally limit the amounts they want transferred to heirs, and to purposefully dedicate their redundant resources for charitable purposes.

COMMENT BY
James Andreoni

Schervish and Havens bring a social psychology perspective to the economic question of what influences individuals' decisions to allocate their wealth between children and charities. They discuss, often in colorful detail, some of the considerations of real philanthropists. This look into the thoughts and deliberations of givers is a useful exercise that economists perhaps do too little of. The insights for economic research are many. In this comment I highlight a few.

As the authors point out, the building of economic models typically begins with motivations for actions. Then financial constraints are added. Combining the two, the economic model finds the "best" way for individuals to achieve their goals within their means. This generates the usual framework for predicting and interpreting behavior, with the key variables being the incomes of the families and the relative prices of the options in the budget set.

In the arena of estates, economists take the goods to be the gifts and bequests to children and charities. Economists have thought hard about the potential motives of givers. One possible assumption is that individuals are motivated by a selfless concern for the well-being of those who receive their generosity. Economists call this altruism. Alternatively, they may give in order to get something in return. For instance, they may use gifts to influence the life choices of their children, or simply to get them to pay more attention to their parents. Likewise, their attachment to a charity may hinge on influencing its direction, especially for big donors, or being memorialized with their names on buildings. Economists have called this the exchange motive. Finally, they may just give for the pure joy of giving. This motive has been called, only slightly pejoratively, the "warm glow" motive.

The "goods" in the economic analysis are lifetime gifts, both to children and charities, with the choices being how much to give and when to give. Prices are determined by taxes that depend on the type of gift, how it is given, or when it is given. For instance, higher estate taxes make bequests to charity, which are exempt from the estate tax, relatively cheaper. Higher capital gains taxes make holding wealth until death, which erases capital gains, more appealing than giving assets away to children while alive. And, of course, the more the children or charity need the money (or earned it in some exchange), the more resources may be devoted to those needs.

This framework, as Schervish and Havens note, has been successful at capturing the broad aspects of individual behaviors on a general level. Moreover, economists studying motives for giving have found evidence for altruism, exchange, and warm glow. A fair interpretation of the literature is that all three motives likely play some role in most allocations of gifts during a person's lifetime and perhaps also at death. Given a model of behavior, economists then find that prices and income affect decisions in the predicted fashion. When the relative cost of giving to an heir or a charity goes up, people tend to give less; when the level of wealth increases, people give more in all forms.

In contrast to the economic approach, Schervish and Havens present a social psychological model they call *identification theory*. The basic tenet of this theory is that the more an individual "identifies" with a person or a cause, the more care he will express for that target, and as a result the more generous he will be. Care and love are the ultimate goals, with love being a combination of all the care shown to all those with whom one identifies. Moreover, in the model, care is dynamic—it grows and develops over time. It can be encouraged by the donors or by the recipients, and it is strengthened as the involvement with children and charity deepens.

The main way Schervish and Havens use identification theory is to organize information that they have collected from social surveys and interviews with hundreds of very wealthy people. In the interviews with potential philanthropists, Schervish and Havens ask questions about their attitudes and expectations for giving. What emerges from the interviews is that it is the relationships these wealth holders have with their children and their other beneficiaries that determines when and how much they give. Schervish and Havens conclude that these considerations stand beside altruism, exchange, and warm glow and provide a new dimension for analysis.

In this comment I argue first that, except for the level of abstraction, the core components of identification theory are actually quite similar—and perhaps even identical—to altruism, exchange, and warm glow, just as in economic models. However, where identification theory differs is that it makes clear a point that economists have been slow to recognize and include in analysis; that is, all sides of the charity market—givers, heirs, and charities—are all active players in the giving game. They all make individual, moral, and strategic choices, all the while accounting for the potential behaviors of the others. Moreover, the relationships among all three players are long, dynamic, and ever changing. In the remainder of this comment, I discuss in more detail how identification theory complements economic analysis, and what research directions it can encourage and inspire.

How Does Identification Theory Fit into Economic Analysis?

The social psychological approach can enrich economic analysis in three ways: First, it illustrates how economic objectives may actually be formed.

Identification theory is based on a notion of "care." This is the same notion that economists have in mind in assuming altruism. The interviews these authors conduct show how care can enter into an individual's universe and grow. How is care expressed in gifts? Care is expressed where individuals feel the most identification. This, as the authors discuss, is much like the economic notion of warm glow—people get a particular joy by helping those they feel close to. However, care can also be intended to shape and influence others. The wealthy givers, for instance, expressed that they did not want their wealth to rob their children of ambition. They also want to teach children a sense of "giving back" to the communities that helped them gain their largess. Giving to charity is thus seen as a way to influence values, attitudes, and ultimately the behavior of children. Likewise, these people did not just want to give money to a large and anonymous charity. Rather they wanted to get involved and be able to see a real difference made by their dollars. These acts, which use gifts to influence the activities of others, are what economic models of exchange have in mind. Hence the core aspects of identification theory are really building on the same ideas that economists have considered in their extensive literature on the motives for giving. What Schervish and Havens do, however, is to bring some life and color to the stark and minimalist assumptions of economists.

A second way identification theory aids and inspires economic analysis is that it makes especially clear that giving is a dynamic social activity. Relationships are built over a lifetime, both with families and charities. Gifts are sometimes made in order to build these relationships, often despite adverse tax consequences. By identifying with a charity, givers are joining a social sphere. They are building social capital that will bring other joys to their lives and, possibly, other pressures that may shape giving in the years ahead.

The third important contribution of identification theory, and of the interviews and data brought by Schervish and Havens, results from combining the first two points—the dynamic interactions between givers and their heirs and beneficiaries work to shape the altruism, warm glow, and exchange. Certainly, children love their parents and foster that love for its own sake, and the managers of charities surely believe deeply in their causes and work for their own benefit. However, the dynamic nature of the identification means, of course, that it can be manipulated and influenced, even by well-meaning individuals, and perhaps even unconsciously. Charities can foster and build relationships, all the while "selling" their cause. Heirs can visit more often or voice more love. But what do we call it when certain strategic elements enter, even if they enter unconsciously, to cause individuals or charities to alter their behavior in order to get further gain from the giver? I think we can, without cynicism, call this fund-raising.

This is, in my view, the most important aspect of the giving decision that is highlighted by the framework and data in this paper. While the social psychologists will phrase this in appealing terms, such as building care, economists will use words that are much less flattering, such as strategic manipulation. Though our words are cold, our hearts and intentions in this matter are not. A fund-raiser who feels strongly about her cause will push hard to make a donor feel good about it as well. She may choose to focus more time and effort with someone who has more to give. These choices, made out of devotion to the cause, are nonetheless strategic. Likewise, if the wealthy grandparents invite a married couple and their children to a Christmas vacation in Hawaii, the couple may eschew a competing invitation to stay at home and visit the less wealthy grandparents. Although this is not a conscious attempt to build more love from the wealthy grandparents, Havens and Schervish show that it will have a similar (strategic) effect of building that love and identification, with the end result of building their bequests.

Shaping a Model of Fund-Raising

The wonderful interviews conducted by Schervish and Havens clearly point to many aspects of the fund-raising market that can help shape a developing fund-raising literature. Here I highlight a few:

THE POWER OF THE ASK. Schervish and Havens note that an invitation to participate in charitable giving is an important feature of the giving process. This is also supported by surveys about annual giving—when given the option, respondents indicate that the main reason for giving to charity is "because I was asked." With respect to major donors, fund-raisers have a name for this phenomenon. They call it "the power of the ask." A lot of the reason for building a relationship with donors is to understand not only their financial constraints, but to get a sense of the giver's commitment to the organization. The fund-raiser is attempting to determine what level of gift can be extracted from this donor and to then ask for that amount. As they will tell you, fund-raisers are seldom surprised by a donor who offers to give more than is asked from them. In addition, "the ask" often presents an opening round of negotiation over what will be given, how the donation will be used, and what kind of recognition will follow.

COMMUNITIES OF PARTICIPATION. By building a relationship with a charity, donors are entering a complex social environment. They build positive relationships with the recipients of their gifts, but they sometimes build competitive relationships with other givers. We see this often in the giving ladders that charities institute to differentiate the superdonors from the mere major donors. Top givers may be on the boards of directors, the next level may be in the "Executives' Club," the next level may be called "Patrons," and so on. Hence the social comparisons also exist among donors and their peers, and fund-raisers obviously manipulate these strategically for their own benefit.

MEN VERSUS WOMEN. Schervish and Havens did not explicitly address the gender of givers or the fact that the ultimate disposition of the estate often resides with the surviving spouse. Recent research shows, however, that men and women tend to have significant differences in their charitable interests. Can we expect that surviving spouses will carry out the intentions of their deceased partners? The answer to this question will be important to understanding how charities and children build relationships with wealthy couples. It may help us understand how some estates are structured with trusts that tie the hands of a surviving spouse. And, as women become more empowered to feel an equal share of wealth gained by their husbands, we may be seeing a concentration of wealth in the hands of independent-minded widows, which will be important to keep in mind as we study the changes and dynamics in charitable giving.

The New Economic Question

This analysis suggests that fund-raising—how the relationships among giver, heirs, and charities are built and prosper—is an important ingredient to determining how giving choices are made. But what is the economic impact of this fund-raising activity? This is an extremely important question that economists have barely begun to answer, and which they will need to take seriously in future research. Suppose, for example, that fund-raising by charities simply influences which charity the dollars go to without influencing the overall amounts. If, as many suggest, bequests are "accidental," and people do not set savings goals with the intent of leaving bequests, then it may actually be the case that fund-raising only shifts the allocation of the charity dollars without increasing the total number of these dollars. If so, then fund-raising would have a negligible economic impact.

Another possibility is that fund-raising does not increase the total dollars given, but simply affects the timing of donations. This may in turn have an effect on lifetime taxes owed on estates. This raises the economic question of where this extra tax windfall will go, to charity or children or consumption while alive?

On the other hand, evidence might indicate that giving will respond quite strongly to fund-raising efforts. If so, this elevates the role of fund-raising in economic analysis and thinking. Careful studies that try to uncover the impact of fund-raising would, therefore, add significant value to our analysis.

Conclusion

In summary, Schervish and Havens do a service to the study of the disposition of estates, and shed light on the motives and dynamics of the giving decisions. The interviews they conducted point to many important aspects of the giving decision that economists have perhaps given too little attention to. Paramount among these is that the relationships between the givers and their children and the givers and their preferred charities are lifelong. The interviews reveal that many people take these decisions very seriously and personally invest a great deal in the result. These social psychological data should encourage economists to think again about these relationships, and especially about the endogeneity of preferences for charity and children due to strategic manipulation of these relationships. In other words, economists should look more closely at fund-raising by both charities and children.

COMMENT BY
Charles Clotfelter

It has been said, I believe in the spirit of ironic understatement, that there is more to life than economics, and more to economics than taxes. The paper by Paul Schervish and John Havens is very much in the spirit of this aphorism. Although taxes, in particular the estate tax, are lurking in the background, the question addressed by Schervish and Havens is simply the allocation of giving between charitable and noncharitable uses. Three literatures could be potentially helpful in answering this question. The first addresses theoretical models of economic behavior. In the best tradition of microeconomic theory, these models explore the implications of various alternative motivations for charitable giving, including the following: Donors care about the provision of certain public goods; donors care about the well-being of recipients; donors selfishly care only about their own consumption; donors are directed by previous commitment to certain principles of behavior; and donors derive utility from the act of giving itself. This last is the so-called warm-glow theory, and is associated with my fellow commentator, James Andreoni. Although models of this sort provide some rigorous links between motivations and behavior, they lack the empirical substance to allow for estimation or practical implementation.

The second literature that promises to be helpful in explaining how giving is allocated consists of econometric studies of giving and bequests. Numerous studies focusing on both charitable giving by living individuals and charitable bequests have employed data to estimate statistical models. These models typically feature as explanatory variables income, tax rates, sometimes measures of wealth, plus a few other variables such as age and marital status. Usually missing from this list of variables are measures of attitudes, personal associations, and life histories that one might readily suppose would be important in influencing charitable behavior. Nor is it common for such studies to have information on the identity of the organizations receiving such charitable donations.

The relative sparseness of economic models should not be too surprising. In considering motivations, economists, by and large, have paid no more attention to the ticklish question of what motivates people to make charitable gifts than they have to the reasons why households buy apples or oranges, pay to heat their homes, or take vacations. Instead, economists are usually content to take preferences for these items as a given, leaving deeper explanations to the theologians, psychologists, and sociologists. Rather than attempting to model tastes, economic models tend to focus on the effects of price and income, plus a few measurable characteristics. In the case of econometric models of charitable giving, the body of research has shown what was not obvious before: that individuals respond to the relative cost of alternatives; whatever the fundamental reasons underlying charitable donations, individuals will tend to donate more if the price is lower.

This brings us to a third literature, the qualitative research such as that described by Schervish and Havens. Here, sociologists and anthropologists are at work, typically not economists. Research such as this has the potential of delving into motivations for giving and for offering richer explanations of behavior than either the highly stylized theoretical or econometric models.

Although not schooled in the qualitative methods they employ, I find much in the Havens-Schervish model and methodology to admire. In particular, the following implications strike me as very appealing and sensible: that "care" is a continuum, and philanthropy is but one manifestation; that "people do not segregate their care for family and friends from wider concerns"; that personal involvement with an organization is an important (though not the only) avenue to charitable contributions; and that self-love is not inconsistent with generosity.

Their methodology as well is praiseworthy. The kind of personal, in-depth interviews upon which much of their findings are based provide unparalleled opportunities to delve into motivations for giving, to see connections with other behavior, such as supporting family members, and generally to reflect on the complexity of human decisionmaking. In their Boston Area Diary Study, Schervish and Havens interviewed some forty-four individuals every week for a year, questioning them by phone-in interviews that sometimes took over an hour. They were careful to establish and follow strict protocols, and they paid attention to possible biases. The results of this investigation add significantly to our understanding of charitable behavior. For example, table 5-1 provides data on contributions of money and time to charitable organizations and to family members and friends—all expressed in terms that can be compared. I know of no other similar comparison. Certainly, these findings are relevant to the central question posed in the paper. In another study, involving interviews with dot.com entrepreneurs, the authors interviewed individuals with family fortunes ranging from $1 million to over $1 billion, and among them, observed a variety of motivations underlying charitable contributions, ranging from the selfishness of narrow business advantage (the "charity begins at home" self-benefit impulse) to those instincts we might define as altruism. What Schervish and Havens emphasize is the blending of motivations: the convergence of love of self with love of neighbor, or, as de Tocqueville put it, "self-interest properly understood."

To be sure, this line of investigation does not answer all our questions. For example, I think the authors would agree that they are unable to draw a tight connection between their theory and the observed empirical regularities they cite. Their identification theory is more appealing, a priori, than the alternatives of selfless altruism, self-interested strategic giving, or even the warm glow idea. However, it shows little more capacity to explain the observed regularities in the data than the models of economic theory.

I find interesting the authors' cataloguing of empirical tendencies. To their list, let me add several additional stylized facts that are evident in data and statistical research on charitable bequests and charitable giving: Charitable bequests are a very small percentage of all bequests, except for the very rich; whereas religious groups are the recipient of most charitable bequests in the lowest wealth class, their share shrinks to near zero in the highest; decedents who are survived by a spouse tend to leave less in charitable bequests; charitable bequests respond to the level of tax rates; for older individuals, giving in life and giving at death are to some extent substitutes—each will be affected by the price of the other; the income of children also affects giving in life; charitable bequests increase if children are more affluent.

Of the empirical trends that Schervish and Havens discuss, perhaps the most interesting is the increasing tendency, at least until 1999, of decedents to leave bequests to charities instead of individuals, particularly among those with the largest estates. They take this as a harbinger of a trend away from heirs and toward charitable purposes. But note that the average wealth of decedents also increases over the period studied. In real terms, the average estate in 1997 is almost exactly twice as large as in 1992, so what appears to be a secular trend may simply be a manifestation of the higher ratio of charitable bequests to wealth that characterizes the biggest estates.

If I had to quibble with anything in this paper, I would lodge a mild objection to the distinctions they draw between their model and the alternatives. In places, I think they are guilty of overstating these differences. However, this does little to dampen my enthusiasm for their paper or this very promising line of research.

6

Private Transfers within the Family: Mothers, Fathers, Sons, and Daughters

DONALD COX

How does a parent decide how much to support a child? Does it matter whether the parent in question is a father or mother? Or whether the child is a son or daughter? And is it the parent who is really doing the deciding? Might it be that the child has already figured out how much he or she wants, and is now conducting a lengthy campaign to get the parent to hand it over?

Surprisingly, the existing empirical literature on intergenerational transfer behavior contains few answers to these basic questions. Most analyses, for example, are gender-blind, with generic parents and generic children, rather than mothers, fathers, sisters, or brothers. Models that contain husbands and wives usually do not feature anything special about being male or female—they may as well be person 1 and person 2. Not that these limitations have necessarily impeded this fast-growing literature so far. Advances in data collection and ever-expanding empirical interest in the economics of the family have generated significant new knowledge about intergenerational transfer behavior. Recent progress notwithstanding, I argue that the domain of analy-

For comments on an earlier draft, the author wishes to thank Ingela Alger, Jim Anderson, Richard Arnott, Ted Bergstrom, Paul Cicchello, Bill Evans, Jack Hirshleifer, Rakesh Kochhar, Kathleen McGarry, Alicia Munnell, and Annika Sundén.

sis should be expanded to recognize the separate behavior of mothers and fathers, and sons and daughters.

The rationale for the more detailed focus comes from biological considerations. Elementary evolutionary biology predicts that men and women have fundamental differences in concerns and objectives in family life. Elementary sex differences in reproductive biology constitute the basic building blocks of studies of family behavior in many disciplines, but despite recent progress, they get little attention in economic studies of the family. Expanding economic models of family behavior to accommodate biological basics could generate substantial new insight into how families function.

Such knowledge is of considerable policy interest. The *existence, responsiveness,* and *nature* of familial transfers each matter for public policies that redistribute income. For example: if my grandmother qualifies for Medicaid benefits that pay for her stay in a nursing home, is she the true Medicaid beneficiary? Or is it my mother, who in the absence of Medicaid would have had to care for her? Is it better for elderly women to be cared for by their daughters or by nonrelatives? Would it matter whether my mother and her mother got along well or not? What if my grandmother had only sons to rely upon rather than daughters?

The existence of intergenerational transfers complicates labeling public income redistribution programs "programs for the elderly" or "programs for kids." (What if my grandmother spends part of her Social Security check to help put my cousin through automotive repair school?) The (as yet) unknown nature of intergenerational transfers implies that judgments about crowding out are equally tricky. If the public sector diminishes the role of the family, it matters how well the family was functioning in the first place.

One way to improve our understanding of how families operate is to focus more attention on the separate interests and capabilities of male versus female family members by exploring three themes that are prominent in biology: The first is paternity uncertainty. How does it affect fathers' versus mothers' incentives to invest in children? The second is the reproductive and economic prospects of male versus female offspring. Do they create incentives for sex-biased parental investments? The third is parent-child conflict. How could it happen and how prevalent might it be? Along the way, I provide preliminary empirical evidence related to each issue, but keep the investigation deliberately simple, to see if these problems are worthy of further empirical scrutiny.

Nothing in this paper should be construed as a claim that "biology is destiny." The descriptive evidence, for example, is consistent with both biological and nonbiological explanations. Nonetheless, attention to reproductive biology has two considerable virtues: It generates falsifiable predictions, and it guides the discovery of new directions for empirical work. Testing a strictly biologically based approach to assess its predictive power is both a feasible and worthwhile direction for future empirical research on the economics of the family. Before proceeding to some considerations of reproductive biology and the family, it is useful to look at some leading stylized facts, puzzles, and gaps in the intergenerational transfers literature.

What Do We Know about How Parents Allocate Transfers to Children? A Brief Overview

In the past twenty years or so, interest in intergenerational transfers has surged, and economists have uncovered a great deal of information about how those transfers are allocated among children. Some of the leading stylized facts that have emerged from this research are:
  —The majority of bequests are shared equally among children.
  —Unlike bequests, *inter-vivos* transfers appear not to be shared equally.
  —The effect of children's incomes on *inter-vivos* transfers is very small. Studies that find a "compensatory" effect of transfers (that is, more help for poorer children) usually indicates compensation of no more than a few cents on the dollar.
  —*Inter-vivos* transfers appear to be targeted toward those who are liquidity constrained.
  Demographic characteristics of children, such as age or gender, are often found to be important determinants of transfer receipts, even controlling for income. Despite these general conclusions, empirical work on private transfers has also raised numerous puzzles; many empirical findings pose significant problems for existing theories of transfer behavior. For example, consider the finding of meager income effects. Gary Becker's theory of altruistic transfers predicts not just *compensatory* income effects, but *large* ones.[1] To see why, consider an altruistic parent who gives money to each of her two children. In doing so, she in effect decides how much everyone in the family consumes. Essentially, everyone's paycheck goes into a common cookie jar, and she determines how the total is divvied up. Now, suppose the parent's income falls by a dollar, say, because of an increase in her taxes. Suppose the government uses these proceeds to subsidize the children, so that total family income remains unchanged. Since everyone's preferences stay the same, everyone's optimal consumption stays the same. The only thing that *does* change is the parent's transfer to the children. She gives a whole dollar less to them because of the

---

1. Becker (1974).

new tax and subsidy scheme. (By taking a dollar out of the parent's pocket and giving it to the children, the government "crowds out" some private transfers by usurping some of the parent's role as provider to the children.)[2]

The parent's response to these schemes has acquired a name in the empirical literature: the "transfer derivative." Altruistic transfers imply a dollar-for-dollar transfer derivative, that is, a value of one. Transfer derivatives become murkier in a multiperiod model. (Imagine, for example, that the parent who was taxed reduces her transfers to children, but spreads out the reduction over time.) However, if, in addition, children are liquidity-constrained, the original predictions hold once again. Further, the evidence suggests that parental *inter-vivos* transfers are indeed disproportionately (though not exclusively) targeted to liquidity-constrained children.[3] Empirical work on U.S. private transfer behavior has reached the consensus that transfer derivatives are not even remotely close to those predicted by the altruism model. The highest estimate for U.S. data is 15 cents on the dollar; most are less than half that much.[4]

An even more formidable challenge to the altruism model is the tendency for bequests to be shared equally among inheritors, a finding first emphasized in Paul Menchik's pioneering work.[5] The altruism model predicts that parents would give more to their poorer children. Equal sharing is difficult for other models of transfer behavior to explain as well. For example, if bequests compensate for services provided by children, it is hard to see how children could all be compensated equally.

To explain equal sharing, economists tend to fall back on the idea that parents care about treating their children fairly. This is quite plausible, but, as most admit, it is not much of a theory. But concentrating on fairness could lead to fruitful theorizing—the trick is to figure out *why* the desire for fairness might come about.[6]

---

2. This example ignores human capital investment and corner solutions, which can complicate matters. For a far more comprehensive analysis, see Behrman, Pollak, and Taubman (1995). The same goes for a scheme that taxes one child by a dollar and gives the proceeds to the other. The parent would undo this scheme by giving exactly a dollar more to the child who is taxed and giving one dollar less to the child who is subsidized.

3. Cox (1990); McGarry (1999).

4. See Altonji, Hayashi, and Kotlikoff (1997, p. 1153); and Cox and Rank (1992).

5. Menchik (1980).

6. The most recent attempt on this front is the work of Bernheim and Severinov (2000), who postulate that bequests provide to children a signal of their parents' altruism toward them.

It would be premature to use findings such as equal sharing to close the door on such a commonsensical hypothesis as altruism. Part of the reason why transfer derivatives appear so low in the United States might be due to its existing public transfers. Perhaps crowding out is a *fait accompli*, rendering the remaining, infrequent instances of private transfers uninformative about altruism. Further, altruistic motives might only come to the fore when potential recipients are in dire straits, suggesting that nonlinearities in income could have an important role to play.[7]

Income is not the only thing that can affect transfer behavior, but it is easy to see why income effects have received so much priority in the empirical literature. One major line of research in intergenerational transfer behavior is the specter of crowding out. Academics and policymakers want to know if public income redistribution supplants private income redistribution. Further, most theoretical models of private transfer behavior emphasize pre-private-transfer incomes more than any other potential transfer determinant.

Despite their importance, income effects may have captured more than their fair share of attention in the U.S. empirical literature. Other determinants of transfers, particularly demographic characteristics, have been given less emphasis, and existing theory provides little guidance on how to interpret their effects on transfers. Usually, demographic variables are either inserted, with little elaboration, as additional "controls," or they are treated as supplemental proxies for income.[8] Sometimes they are included in empirical work but neither reported nor discussed. One exception is the work of Jere Behrman, Robert Pollak, and Paul Taubman, summarized in a recent collection of their articles and papers.[9] One of these papers investigates the possibility of parental favoritism toward boys; another looks at birth-order effects. But papers like these, which use data from the United States, are rare.

In contrast, the development literature has a long tradition of focusing on demographic variables in studies of family behavior: in particular, differences in the ways boys and girls are treated within the family, and differences in

7. For example, two co-authors and I found extremely large transfer derivatives among poor households in the Philippines, a country with very little public income redistribution. See Cox, Hansen, and Jimenez. 1999. "How Responsive Are Private Transfers to Income? Evidence from a Laissez-Faire Economy." Boston College. Mimeo.

8. An example of the latter is age, which tells us something about a potential recipient's access to credit markets.

9. Behrman, Pollak, and Taubman (1995).

how fathers and mothers treat their children are dominant themes.[10] What does this literature tell us about gender and family transfers? Daughters tend to fare worse than sons in the developing world, though pockets of pro-daughter bias do exist and several studies find little or no bias.[11] Gender-based favoritism appears to be absent in the United States.[12] As far as mother-father differences go, emerging evidence from the developing world suggests that putting more money in the hands of mothers would benefit children, especially daughters.[13] Most of the evidence pertains to developing countries, but a recent study of a change in child benefit disbursement policy in the United Kingdom by Shelly Lundberg, Robert Pollak, and Terence Wales indicates that children fare better when the mother has more control over family resources.[14]

Economic theory is only somewhat useful for interpreting these results. Theory tells us that the results could *not* have emerged from a household consensus—the so-called common preferences model—between mothers and fathers. But it does not tell us much beyond that. To the extent that parental transfers have to do with human capital investment, economic theory provides considerable insight, since human capital models have existed for many years and are highly refined. But outside of human capital, economic theory has little to say except to refer to parental preferences. Since preferences are exogenous in most economic models, this is not much of an explanation.[15] A recent survey by Lundberg and Pollak sums up the state of the art quite suc-

10. See, for example, the painstaking and comprehensive literature reviews of Behrman (1997) and Strauss and Thomas (1995).

11. Again, refer to the Behrman (1997) and Strauss-Thomas (1995) reviews.

12. Behrman, Pollak, and Taubman (1986).

13. Strauss and Thomas (1995) are cautious about these trends; uncovering parental differences in transfers to children poses formidable estimation problems because a spouse's contribution to, and control over, family resources is endogenous.

14. The Lundberg, Pollak, and Wales study also has the considerable advantage of being far less prone to the endogeneity problem referred to above.

15. Inattention to the complexities of preferences is more a virtue of economics than a drawback, because it highlights the role of prices, which is easier to interpret, and keeps a lid on the arbitrariness that might plague models with more complicated consumer psychology. Further, existing economic concepts about preferences, simple as they are, contain a bit of nuance nonetheless. For example, Ben-Porath and Welch (1976) get considerable mileage out of an idea from economics called "convex preferences," which implies that people prefer moderation to extremes. They use it to explore sex preferences in fertility, and more parents who have two boys or two girls are likely to have a third child than parents who already have one of each. Their finding suggests that parents prefer variety.

cinctly: ". . . no new theoretical framework has gained general acceptance as a
replacement for common preference models, and empirical studies have concentrated on debunking old models rather than on discriminating among
new ones."[16]

Insights from Reproductive Biology

Over a century ago William James, considered by many to be the father of
modern psychology, penned the following tacky rhyme:

> Higamous, hogamous, woman's monogamous;
> Hogamous, higamous, men are polygamous.[17]

James's whimsical assertion is hardly true for everyone, everywhere, but he
was nonetheless onto something. Even if a man and woman have the same
objective—say, to produce progeny in sufficient numbers and quality to continue the family line—they differ vastly in their capacity to achieve it. In her
whole life, a typical woman produces only about 400 viable eggs. In just one
day, a typical man produces enough sperm to populate a country the size of
Japan. The fecundity of eighteenth century Britain's Duchess of Leinster,
who had her twenty-first child at age forty-six, pales in comparison to seventeenth century Morocco's Moulay Ismail the Bloodthirsty, who sired 888
children by his many wives and concubines.[18] These oddities point up the
obvious: a motivated, resourceful man can literally "go forth and multiply,"
but a woman can only go forth and add.

Of course, this is just one of many basic sex differences in reproductive
biology. Here are three more: First, except in the strangest of cases, a woman
is always 100 percent certain—and a man never 100 percent certain—that a
newborn child is a biological relative. Next, a woman's expected reproductive
life span is only half that of a man's; and last, a fertile man who has secured a
mate is a mere spasm's worth of effort away from the prospect of getting his
genes into the next generation, while a woman who has just conceived still
faces a marathon of exhaustion, sickness, discomfort, pain, and risks to physical and emotional health.

These elementary facts figure prominently in biological studies of family

16. Lundberg and Pollak (1996, p. 140).
17. Cited in Hrdy (1999, p. 233).
18. Hrdy (1999, p. 84).

behavior. They also play an important role in analyses of family and kin behavior undertaken by many anthropologists, ethologists, psychologists, ecologists, demographers, and primatologists. But they are, for the most part, glaringly absent from most economic studies of family behavior. Economic models of intergenerational transfers are, for the most part, unisex models.

Not that insights have been lacking. Gary Becker's analysis of altruistic parental transfers spawned a whole new subdiscipline in economics, and the family bargaining models pioneered by Marjorie McElroy and others broadened the scope of that subdiscipline.[19] For many of the questions posed in this early work, the recognition of biological differences would have been little more than a distracting nuisance. Despite these early advances, however, and despite the efforts of a small cadre of economists who have adopted and promoted a biological focus, the empirical state of the art of family economics suffers from its chronic inattention to reproductive fundamentals.

In recent years, the landscape has begun to change, and increasing numbers of economic analyses have centered on these fundamentals. Theodore Bergstrom has written several papers that use and extend ideas from evolutionary biology and combine them with economic reasoning to study family behavior.[20] An analysis of a long-standing biological theory of preferences for sons versus daughters—the so-called Trivers-Willard conjecture, which is discussed below—recently appeared in the *Journal of Political Economy*.[21] Aloysius Siow has explored the implications of male-female differences in reproductive life span for gender roles in the labor market.[22] Robert Willis's theory of out-of-wedlock childbearing recognizes the distinct problems and incentives faced by men versus women.[23] But much remains to be done, particularly with respect to taking biologically based models to the data. The following sections concentrate on prominent biological themes, starting with one that is pertinent to fathers and mothers.

Fathers and Mothers

Except for having to worry about rare mishaps like babies getting switched in the maternity ward, a woman is always certain that her newborn is a biological relative. But a man seeking the same certainty would have to do more

---

19. See, for example, Becker (1974); and McElroy and Horney (1981).
20. See, for example, Bergstrom (1996).
21. Edlund (1999).
22. Siow (1998).
23. Willis (1999).

than watch the maternity ward; he would have to guard his mate round the clock daily.[24] In some cultures, past and present, husbands have attempted just that. But barring extreme "mate guarding"—usually draconian practices ranging from intrusive to downright barbaric—a man would have to trust completely his mate's fidelity or else harbor some flicker of concern, however small, that his putative child is not really a biological relative. What are the implications of such uncertainty for familial transfers?

Certainty of paternity is a major theme in the biological literature on family behavior and in some branches of anthropology and psychology, but only a minor one in the economics of the family. Even Gary Becker's monumental *Treatise on the Family*, which helped spur the importation of biological concepts into studies of family economics, makes little mention of it.[25] Similarly, Jack Hirshleifer's comprehensive and prescient discussion of the synergies between economics and biology makes no reference to paternity certainty.[26]

But references are beginning to crop up in more recent economic research. Theodore Bergstrom analyzes uncertain fathers' investment in children in his wide-ranging, interdisciplinary review of the economics of the family.[27] Laura Argys and Elizabeth Peters explore empirically the relationship between the establishment of paternity and fathers' involvement with, and transfers to, children.[28] But no other economic studies deal with the implications of paternity certainty on family behavior. Yet evidence from other disciplines has frequently identified paternity certainty as a prominent force; its connection with family transfer behavior is potentially of great importance for the economics of the family.

24. An alternative would be to get a DNA-based paternity test, something I discuss later.

25. Becker (1991, p. 48) discusses briefly the guarding and seclusion of women in the context of the division of labor within the family, and notes that "Female adultery is a serious offense in traditional societies, mainly because men are reluctant to rear children fathered by others." But there is not much further reference to the problem of certainty of paternity in his *Treatise*, and no analysis of its implications. Becker's earlier (1976) article on economics and sociobiology, which has an explicit focus on basic biological concepts such as kin selection, nonetheless makes no mention of paternity certainty.

26. Hirshleifer (1977).

27. See Bergstrom (1996, pp. 1923–24) for an analysis of a male's decision to support his wife's versus his sister's children as a function of paternity certainty for the Nayars of India, a polyandrous matriarchal society.

28. Argys and Peters (2001).

The following discussion explores the basics of female fidelity and its opposite, cuckoldry, that is, misattribution of fatherhood.[29] What is the evidence on paternity and cuckoldry? What is the evidence on concerns about cuckoldry? How large would the uncertainty have to be to generate significant behavioral effects? What are the implications for parenting? For grandparenting?

A Case Study with Possible Clues: Grandparenting and Public Pensions in South Africa

A recent paper by Esther Duflo shows that not all grandparents are equally generous to their grandchildren.[30] In fact, only one, the maternal grandmother, appears responsive to incentives to support them. Duflo's study was not concerned with paternity certainty per se, but her results nonetheless shed potentially useful light on this issue.

Duflo studied familial transfers that occurred in an unusual natural experiment. Pressure for racial parity in South Africa's public pensions resulted in huge cash transfers to the country's poor elderly, who by early 1993 were receiving from the government more money than they had ever dreamed of—twice the median rural per capita income.[31] Duflo investigated the impact of the expanded pension on young children, motivated by the fact that Black South African elderly often live with their grandchildren in multi-generation or "skip-generation" households where absent parents work elsewhere.[32] She reasoned that these pensioners, many of whom were bringing in more money than anyone else in the household, might be spending some of it on better nourishment for their young grandchildren. Though Duflo's interest was in differences between grandmothers and grandfathers, she also considered whether the grandparent was maternal or paternal.

Only one grandparent's pension eligibility had a statistically significant impact on child well-being—that of the maternal grandmother. Her eligibility for a pension was associated with significantly better outcomes for girls' weight-for-height. The maternal grandmother is unique not only economi-

---

29. This definition differs from what can be found in most dictionaries. Webster's College Dictionary, published by Random House, defines a cuckold as being "the husband of an unfaithful wife," a necessary but not sufficient, condition for cuckoldry as defined here. Instead, I adhere to the definition used, for example, by Wilson and Daly (1992), where cuckoldry refers to the misattribution of fatherhood.

30. Duflo (2000).

31. Case and Deaton (1998).

32. Case and Deaton (1998).

cally but also biologically—she is the only grandparent who can be absolutely certain that the grandchild is hers.[33] The question is whether cuckoldry is a reasonable explanation—after all, how prevalent is it likely to be?

Misassigned Paternity: X, the Unknown

How many children are sired by someone other than their putative father? The short answer is that no one knows. Some estimates are rather high but difficult to believe. It could well be that the average probability of cuckoldry in the United States is quite low, though certainly not zero. While concrete evidence is scarce, myth, misinformation, and speculation about paternity uncertainty abound. Further, since beliefs and expectations are presumably what guide behavior, even "urban legends" about paternity could prove relevant. Both fact and fiction merit scrutiny.

Physiologist Jared Diamond created a minor stir by claiming, in his book *The Third Chimpanzee*, that ". . . between about 5 and 30 percent of American and British babies [have been] adulterously conceived."[34] Diamond cites an unpublished study by "Dr. X," a "distinguished medical scientist" demanding anonymity, who in the 1940s accidentally uncovered evidence of widespread cuckoldry in the course of investigating heritability of human blood groups. Diamond reasoned that this early study probably accessed only a few of the many blood-typing procedures now available, so that blood group discrepancies (such as a type-O wife giving birth to a type-A child, but having a type-O husband) represented the tip of the cuckoldry iceberg.[35]

---

33. Another pattern found by Duflo, which is not directly relevant to paternity but nonetheless important from another biological perspective, is the maternal grandmothers' apparent favoritism toward granddaughters. Only girls benefit from grandmotherly largesse. This is consistent with so-called Trivers-Willard effects, which I discuss further below.

34. Diamond (1992, p. 86).

35. Before the advent of DNA testing, serology was the primary forensic tool for investigating paternity. This method could only reject paternity, and only in cases where offspring characteristics were impossible given characteristics of the potential father. If, as Diamond argues, only a limited number of blood characteristics were investigated by "Dr. X," such rejections reveal only a subset of the progeny of adulterous unions. Just to illustrate, suppose there is a single trait with two phenotypes, P and p, determined by two equally prevalent genotypes, dominant G and recessive g. With random mating, only about a quarter of all illegitimate children could be identified by phenotypic discrepancies. About half would escape detection because the "cuckolder" and the putative father would share the same genotype. In half of the remaining cases, the mother would carry the dominant gene, making it impossible to

Diamond states that Dr. X's results ". . . were later confirmed by several similar genetic studies whose results did get published" but unfortunately does not provide any references to them. A few years later, biologists Robin Baker and Mark Bellis, in their controversial study of the implications of female infidelity, made similar claims about the incidence of misattributed paternity, this time summarizing published serology studies.[36]

Another biologist, Tim Birkhead, cautions against reading too much into the limited evidence on paternity uncertainty. Any unpublished study must be taken with a grain of salt since it would not have been subject to routine scientific scrutiny, and published studies are all based upon serology rather than DNA testing, making results difficult to interpret.[37]

One such blood study, conducted on a sample of parents and children from a small Michigan town and published thirty years ago, illustrates some of the problems Birkhead refers to.[38] A team of three geneticists and an epidemiologist used blood samples collected from 9,000 families to identify possible departures from Mendelian inheritance patterns for eleven different blood groupings. After dropping observations with no parental observations, they sought to identify problematic observations, including errors in data entry, unrecorded adoptions, and the like. The researchers went back to the individuals in families with discrepancies and recollected and retyped one or more blood groupings. These screens left 109 out of 2,507 (4.3 percent) with remaining discrepancies, observations that were dropped from subsequent analyses because blood samples were not consistent with parent-child relatedness. Further, though using eleven blood groups generates a higher incidence of exclusion than the more limited studies referred to by Diamond, the probability of exclusion is still less than 100 percent.[39]

Does this imply a minimum 4.3 percent cuckoldry rate? Not necessarily. The researchers found that first-born children were overrepresented among discrepant children, suggesting that many of them might have been stepchil-

reject anyone's paternity. Only in cases in which the mother carried the recessive gene, and the genotypes of the putative father and the cuckolder differed, could paternity be excluded. With equal prevalence of G and g, and random mating, this probability is the product of two independent fifty-fifty events. Of course, the logic of paternity rejection and the evidence are distinct issues, and the numerical assumptions in this example are just used as illustrations.

36. Baker and Bellis (1995).

37. Birkhead (2000, p. 82).

38. Sing and others (1971).

39. "University of Dundee Department of Forensic Medicine" (www.dundee.ac.uk/forensicmedicine/llbtesting.htm [September 2001]).

dren mistakenly reported as biological children. Despite the care with which the authors treated discrepancies, ascertaining the cuckoldry rate proved elusive. Also, it was not a primary aim of the study, and the authors did not pursue it further.

Despite the inferential advantages now available from DNA testing, any direct attempt to study paternity certainty would be fraught with formidable human-subjects concerns and sample-selection bias. It would be obviously unethical, for example, to publish findings about discrepancies in relatedness obtained from DNA studies conducted in relation to, say, organ transplants between supposed kin. And disease inheritance studies based on molecular methods to establish relatedness are based on self-selected samples. In Birkhead's words, "On being told that the information they provide might reveal true paternity, many would-be volunteers melt away. Those remaining are hardly a random sample and hence provide no basis for an estimate."[40]

An alternative source of evidence is animal studies, which are free from human subjects and sample-selection problems. Recent studies point to widespread female infidelity even among species once thought to be almost exclusively monogamous. Even before the advent of DNA testing, biologists were beginning to overturn conventional wisdom concerning parentage in avian species thought to be paragons of monogamy. For example, the indigo bunting, a species of bird once thought to be almost exclusively monogamous, was found to have an estimated cuckoldry rate of at least 35 percent. Findings like these were uncovered repeatedly for one species after another, once DNA fingerprinting techniques were discovered.[41]

One might think it strange to refer to animal studies in the context of economic analysis of families. After all, what does the parentage of indigo bunting or baboons have to do with our behavior? Economists should be careful not to dismiss such findings easily or to treat them as fanciful curiosities. In addition to being largely exempt from ethical concerns and selection bias, their culture-free settings create better laboratories for learning about biologically based behavior. Further, evolutionary models imply that all living things face the same basic problems of surviving and reproducing. In other disciplines, such as anthropology and psychology, researchers routinely sift through cross-species evidence when studying family behavior.[42]

40. Birkhead (2000, p. 82).
41. Birkhead (2000, pp. 37–38).
42. Becker (1991) argues that some of the uncanny similarities in much of the behavior of nonhuman and human families are not necessarily manifestations of "biological determinism," but could instead result from the ubiquity of economic problems faced by nonhumans and humans alike.

Why might cuckoldry occur? If biology is at the root of infidelity, isn't just the male the one who stands to gain, in terms of extra progeny, from stepping out on his mate? This argument fails once it is recognized that people care about child quality in addition to quantity. Quality and quantity trade-offs, first emphasized in economics by Gary Becker, create a conflict of interest between men and women, even if both sexes value these attributes identically. The price of child quantity relative to quality differs dramatically between men and women. A man can pursue extramarital liaisons to raise the quantity of his progeny, whereas a woman obviously cannot (except in cases of male fertility problems). But she can pursue such liaisons to raise the *quality* of her progeny. And, if some of these high-quality progeny happen to be sons, they may afford her an opportunity to "go forth and multiply" vicariously.

A woman's concerns about child quality is a central theme in anthropological, biological, and psychological theories about female infidelity. The theories most interesting from an economic perspective are those concerned with material resources—anthropological models of how women provision their children. Donald Symons argues that a woman might engage in short-term sexual liaisons in order to secure resources for her existing or future progeny.[43] Sarah Hrdy reasons that a woman might seek to create confusion about paternity in order to secure resources from more than one man. [44] Such arguments suggest that female infidelity is, in economic terms, an "inferior good." In Hrdy's framework, for example, two putative fathers may be preferable to one certain father because one man's expected investment is insufficient. Evidence supporting her argument comes from findings about culturally sanctioned multiple husbands, or "polyandry." This rare practice nearly always occurs in environments so rough that a household with only one man might have difficulty making a go of it.[45]

---

43. Symons (1979).

44. Hrdy (1981). Other explanations for female infidelity are similarly founded upon motives to enhance child quality. For example, there is the "sexy sons" hypothesis, attributed to statistician Ronald A. Fisher (1958). Like Flaubert's Madame Bovary, a woman consorts with handsome, but irresponsible "Fast Freddie" while married to wealthy but unexciting "Steady Eddie." With Freddie's chiseled features and Eddie's money, her son inherits the means to perpetuate the family line by producing several high quality grandchildren.

45. For instance, among poor Tibetan yak herders a man might permit his brother to share his wife if having an extra worker helps ensure the viability of the household. For a recent analysis of the relationship between poverty, sex, and reproduction, see Edlund and Korn (2002).

How Much Could Paternity Uncertainty Possibly Matter?

Applying strictly biological considerations to the problem of paternity uncertainty and familial transfers is bound to be misleading. Economic considerations are essential too. For example, consider the kin selection model of William Hamilton.[46] Imagine (since no such thing has ever been found), a "helping gene," that is, a portion of the genome governing altruistic behavior. Hamilton argues that altruistic behavior between kin was determined by the following implicit calculation "I'll help someone else if expected benefits in terms of 'inclusive fitness' exceed expected costs in terms of inclusive fitness." "Fitness," in turn, is usually defined as the expected number of progeny, and "inclusive fitness" is my own fitness plus a weighted sum of my relatives' fitness. The weights, in turn, are the "coefficients of relatedness," defined as the probability (over and above pure chance) that my beneficiary and I share the same helping gene. For example, because of the genetic shuffling from sexual reproduction, the chance that my daughter inherited my helping gene is fifty-fifty, so my coefficient of relatedness to her would be 0.5.

In brief, Hamilton's rule says to provide help if $c < rb$, where c denotes fitness costs, b denotes fitness benefits, and r is the coefficient of relatedness. Certainty of paternity figures into this rule in a straightforward way. Suppose a man is only 95 percent sure that he is really the father of his daughter. Then his coefficient of relatedness would be only 0.475, compared to his wife's 0.5. When his daughter wants to go to the zoo, or to college, his wife will ask, "Is $c < 0.5b$?" while he will ask, "Is $c < 0.475b$?"

But biological considerations alone are woefully insufficient for explaining relative parental investment. It is well known that economic considerations figure prominently. Heading the list is the division of labor between husbands and wives. Decades ago Becker pointed out that specialization can magnify small differences in underlying preferences and technology, resulting in large differences in behavior. Sex differences in the certainty of paternity could figure in, just like other biological differences that Becker lists in his *Treatise*.[47]

In addition to the division of labor, other economic considerations can be appended to Hamilton's rule. For example, paternity uncertainty creates a public goods problem. The flip side of paternal doubt is the possibility that another father is out there somewhere, and perhaps a devoted one at that. Such prospects create externalities that, at least in principle, further dilute incentives for male investment.

46. Hamilton (1964).
47. Becker (1991).

Lastly, limited time budgets play a role. Departures from strict monogamy create obvious opportunities and trade-offs that divert a philanderer's attention from his children. A husband who arrives home too late to take his kids to the ballgame because a dinner with his attractive new systems analyst went on too long is implicitly sacrificing quality of existing offspring for quantity of future offspring.[48]

Grandparenting and Paternity Certainty

Separating the effects of paternity uncertainty from these distinct though related crosscurrents is a potentially daunting task. One way to help control for (though not completely eliminate) the effects of sex-related division of labor in provisioning to children is to back up a generation and focus on grandparenting. Contrasting maternal versus paternal grandmothers, for example, holds constant the sex of the provider while allowing things like relatedness to vary.

Evidence from three household surveys—the Health and Retirement Study (HRS), the National Survey of Families and Households (NSFH), and the Panel Study of Income Dynamics (PSID)—points to large differences in behavior by maternal or paternal status.

The first finding, from the HRS, is that grandmothers who are exclusively maternal (that is, have grandchildren only by their daughters) provide more hours of childcare than grandmothers who are exclusively paternal (have grandchildren only by their sons). To avoid picking up the effects of grandmothers helping out daughters who are single mothers, the sample was limited to grandmothers with married children. In the first wave of the HRS, respondents were asked if during the preceding twelve months they spent 100 hours or more caring for their grandchildren. Those responding "yes" were then asked to give the amount of time, which was coded as the annual number of hours. Exclusively maternal grandmothers provided 374 hours compared to 290 hours provided by exclusively paternal grandmothers, a difference of 29 percent.

This finding proves little about paternity certainty per se, since far more commonsensical explanations exist. Suppose my wife and I need a babysitter for our daughter, but we divide our labor in such a way that finding one is "her department." Though both our mothers might be available, she feels more comfortable imposing on hers. Indirectly, then, the maternal or paternal differences in grandmother care come from how my wife and I divide our labor.

---

48. See Robert Willis (1999) for extensive analyses of these problems and related issues.

Figure 6-1. *Grandmothers' Involvement with Grandchildren*
Number, unless otherwise indicated

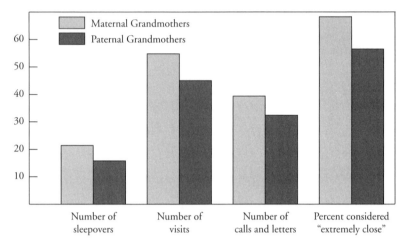

Source: Author's calculations using the National Survey of Families and Households (NSFH).

Maternal or paternal differences extend to other forms of grandmother and grandchild relationships besides hours of care. The second wave of the NSFH includes a special module on contact and affection between grandparents and grandchildren. As with the HRS, I analyze the sample of grandmothers who were either exclusively maternal or exclusively paternal and whose own children are not single parents. The NSFH grandparenting module measures grandparent-grandchild contact (visits separate from letters-plus-phone calls) and the number of times in the past year a grandchild spent the night at the grandmother's house ("sleepovers"). Each measure indicates more contact with maternal grandmothers than paternal ones, as shown in the first three pairs of bars in figure 6-1. Maternal grandmothers had 35 percent more sleepovers and 22 percent more visits and calls-plus-letters.

The NSFH also asked grandparents to report their feelings of affection for grandchildren. On a scale from zero to ten, where zero is "not at all close," and ten is "extremely close," how would you describe your relationship with your grandchild(ren)? The results are displayed in the last pair of bars in figure 6-1. As with the other indicators, this self-reported closeness measure shows the same maternal and paternal differential: 68 percent of the exclusively maternal grandparents chose the extreme portion of the closeness scale compared to 56 percent of their paternal counterparts.

But these additional results still do not rule out more straightforward explanations. Closeness, for example, is likely to be nurtured by repeated contact and care; feelings and actions are not separate.[49] So the results from figure 6-1, while consistent with the idea that paternity uncertainty matters, are hardly conclusive. Instead, they only indicate that further scrutiny is warranted.

I provide a bit more scrutiny with a final piece of evidence, which explores the relationship between incomes of adult children and grandparenting behavior. Recall that there might be reason to believe that paternity uncertainty could be the outcome of a rational strategy of a woman who seeks to provision her children in the face of poverty.[50] Elijah Anderson's ethnography of sexual mores among inner city youth, for example, describes a situation of mutual suspicion between the sexes regarding infidelity.[51]

Accordingly, I explore differences in the familial support provided by paternal versus maternal grandparents, while considering the incomes of the parent (middle) generation. PSID respondents were asked to report in-kind transfers in the form of child care and money transfers received from parents. For the sample of married households with children (age eighteen or younger) and all four grandparents, average hours of care received from maternal versus paternal grandparents are similar to using the HRS data above as seen in the first two bars of figure 6-2. But for transfers of money, the results are reversed—paternal grandparents are more generous with transfers of money.

One likely explanation for this result is related to earlier, commonsensical arguments: A wife calls upon her own mother more often than her mother-in-law to baby-sit. Her mother-in-law makes up for the inequity by giving more money. But focusing just on the households in the lowest decile reverses this paternal advantage in money transfers as seen in the rightmost last two pairs of bars in figure 6-2. Further, the maternal advantage in hours of childcare increases. Unlike the earlier differences, however, it is significant only at the 10 percent level. Further, the difference for childcare is not significant except at the 25 percent level. The sample sizes are small and select— recall that only married households are included.[52] Moreover, part of the

49. Though altruism is mostly treated as an unwavering, exogenous parameter of the utility function, economists have begun to recognize that such preferences are themselves forged by parental choices. For example, see the recent work of Casey Mulligan (1997) on the formation of altruistic preferences.

50. Hrdy (1999).

51. Anderson (1993).

52. Relaxing the requirement that all four grandparents be living, and replacing it with requiring both living grandmothers, doubles the sample size. Using this sample, the difference in differences for the maternal advantage in child care is significant at the .02 level, but that of money transfers, while still positive, is not statistically significant.

Figure 6-2. *Parental Transfers*

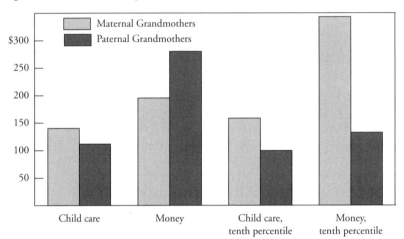

Source: Author's calculations using the Panel Study of Income Dynamics (PSID).

maternal and paternal differences in behavior could come from the effects of different ages, income, location and so on. The simple tabulations only suggest that there might be something to be explained.

Sons and Daughters

While the first implication of biology focused on paternal uncertainty, the second explores the advantages or disadvantages of investing in sons and daughters.

The Trivers-Willard Hypothesis

Consider again Esther Duflo's South African evidence, but this time concentrate on the *recipients* of grandparental largesse—who happen to be the granddaughters.[53] Is it a coincidence that the benefits of pension expansion accrue to them rather than to their brothers? Perhaps, but consider: A daughter from a poor family might stand a better chance of escaping poverty—by marrying "up" the status scale—than a son who lacks the resources to marry at all. Conversely, a son from a rich family might well be in a position to "go forth and multiply."

Such is the logic of the so-called Trivers-Willard effect, an idea formulated in 1973 by renowned evolutionary biologist Robert Trivers and his fellow

---

53. Duflo (2000).

student at the time, mathematician Dan Willard. Trivers and Willard were not concerned with human behavior per se, but instead were interested mainly in whether animals of various species might somehow control the production of female versus male offspring to take advantage of propitious circumstances for one or the other sex. Trivers-Willard effects have been uncovered in both field and laboratory tests for several species. But so far researchers have found little evidence of biased sex ratios for humans.[54]

Parents have considerable latitude for making differential investments in sons versus daughters, even if they choose not to control the sex ratios of their progeny.[55] Edlund cites evidence that points to Trivers-Willard effects in infant and toddler care among North American and German mothers, for example.[56] What about parental investments in older and grown children? In addition to schooling investments, parents can make *inter-vivos* transfers to children and bequests at death.

I investigated the Trivers-Willard hypothesis in a somewhat narrow setting by comparing education levels of male versus female children at varying levels of wealth for the sample of HRS households with just two biological children (one male, one female) from an intact marriage. The results, which are shown in figure 6-3, are surprisingly consistent with the Trivers-Willard hypothesis. Having a daughter who is better educated than a son prevails in the lower ranks, while favoritism toward sons does not emerge until well into the top quartile for parental net worth.[57]

54. One fact that occasionally arises in discussions of sex ratios is the effect of being a U.S. president, a natural proxy for high status and wealth, and the propensity to sire sons versus daughters. Starting with Barbara and Jenna Bush, the daughters of President George W. Bush, and going back in time, presidential families have produced just sixty-three daughters compared to ninety sons, a 59 percent proportion of sons, which teeters on the brink of conventional levels of statistical significance. Does this evidence demonstrate the value of the Trivers-Willard theory for predicting sex ratios in human births? (Or does it reinforce the value of statistical reasoning for preventing type 1 errors?) See Edlund (1999) for more discussion of sex-ratio evidence.

55. But people have other ways of controlling the sex ratios of their progeny, and many of them exact an enormous toll in human suffering: sex-specific pregnancy termination, infanticide, and neglect all play a role. Amartya Sen's (2001) recent estimates point to a catastrophe of unimaginable proportions—as many as 100 million females in the developing world lost from efforts to control the sex of offspring.

56. Edlund (1999).

57. Figure 6-3 plots locally weighted smoothing of the binary variable indicating that the female is better educated (1 if yes, 0 if no) on rank of parental net worth. It also plots, for comparison purposes, the binary variable indicating that the male is

Figure 6-3. *Child Education and Parental Wealth*

Percent

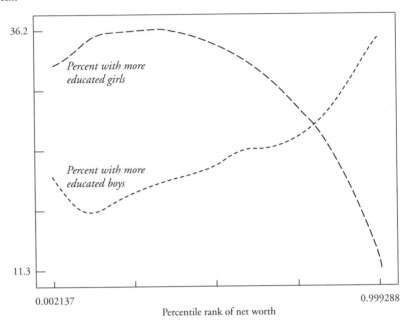

Source: Author's calculations using the Health and Retirement Survey (HRS).

As before, many other explanations are possible. The predominant, and compelling, view in the human capital literature is that schooling is an investment, chosen to maximize expected lifetime earnings. An obvious corollary is that, with well-functioning capital markets, schooling choices are optimal, which implies that no person contributing his or her information to figure 6-3 needed any more or less schooling than he or she got. Perhaps daughters appear "favored" because labor market prospects for male high school dropouts are relatively better than for female dropouts, and both tend to be concentrated among poorer families.

Another measure of transfers to children available in the HRS—intentions to bequeath—indicate no Trivers-Willard effects at all. HRS respondents with only biological children are grouped according to whether they have only male children, only female children, or both, and the desire to leave a

---

better educated. An ordered probit on the ordinal variable (2=male better educated, 1=male-female education equal, 0=female better educated) on rank of parental net worth produced an estimated coefficient of 0.48 with an asymptotic *t* value of 3.30.

Figure 6-4. *Parents Who Intend to Bequeath and Parental Wealth*

Percent

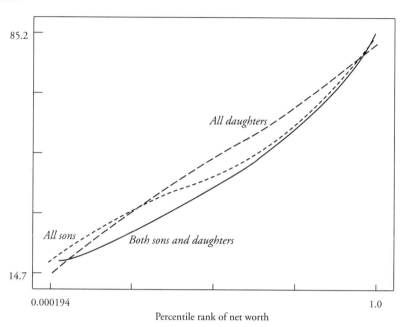

Source: Author's calculations using the Health and Retirement Survey (HRS).

substantial bequest is regressed on the rank of parental net worth as before.[58] The results, which are shown in figure 6-4, reveal no discernible differences in wealth effects by sex composition of the family.[59]

However, bequests might be given too late to have much influence on the reproductive potential of offspring. Further, Kathleen McGarry's recent work comparing *inter-vivos* transfers and bequests indicates that the former are much more responsive to economic and demographic circumstances.[60] It may therefore be worthwhile in future research to use information on *inter-vivos* transfers to test for Trivers-Willard effects.

58. Many HRS respondents have stepchildren, and the problem of giving to stepchildren versus biological children merits separate, detailed attention. Recall, for example, the earlier discussion of Hamilton's rule. I defer the important issue of transfers to stepchildren to another time.

59. These findings are consistent with Menchik's (1980) finding that the majority of bequests to male-female sibling pairs are shared equally.

60. McGarry (1999).

Old-Age Support

Most of the world's elderly in need of financial support receive it in the form of assistance from kin rather than public pensions. Jeffrey Nugent's survey cites individual studies of twenty-four developing countries on four continents (and even a study for Greenland) that provide evidence of the value of children for old-age security.[61] Nugent provides a systematic listing of background conditions that make old-age security an important motive for having children, and prominent institutional factors include the lack of developed capital markets and the lack of old-age pension and disability programs.

But would parents desiring support favor sons or daughters? A case can be made for favoring sons in many instances. For example, Mead Cain estimates that Bangladeshi sons can start pulling their weight as net producers as early as age ten, but that daughters, despite also starting work very young, leave home before having a chance to repay parental investments.[62] But even female exogamy with dowry payments can confer benefits to parents in the form of risk sharing by forging ties with in-laws living far away.[63]

A more straightforward approach to the question might be to rely on the method of "revealed preference." China's 1990 census counts ninety girls for every 100 boys.[64] In Egypt and Iran, the ratio is ninety-seven females for every 100 males; in Bangladesh and Turkey, ninety-five; in India and Pakistan, ninety-three.[65]

Country averages can mask substantial within-country variance. Sen finds, for example, significant variation in sex ratios and sex-specific child mortality across Indian regions and states. He expresses puzzlement at the heterogeneity: "The pattern of contrast does not have any obvious economic explanation. The states with antifemale bias include the rich states . . . as well as poor states. . . ."[66] However, such a pattern could be caused by the conflicting forces of Trivers-Willard effects in rich states and the need for old-age support in poor ones. Sen argues that the worldwide problem of "missing

61. Nugent (1985).
62. Cain (1977).
63. Rosenzweig and Stark (1989).
64. Hrdy (1999, p. 319).
65. Sen (2001); Do proverbs constitute admissible evidence? Consider these: "More sons, more happiness and prosperity" (China); "Eighteen goddess-like daughters are not equal to one son with a hump" (India); "Daughters are no better than crows. Their parents feed them and when they get their wings, they fly away." All quoted in Hrdy (1999, pp. 320–24).
66. Sen (2001, p. 40).

women" is too complicated to be addressed by economic reasoning alone, but economic factors are clearly important. For example, consider the common theme of crowding out referred to earlier: Full crowding out implies that public pensions just cause an equal reduction in private support. Sometimes economists assert that crowding out renders public income redistribution useless, or even counterproductive, if, for example, it raises transactions costs. But a completely different perspective is that the crowding out from public pensions might hold the key to dramatic improvements in the well-being of women. If male-biased sex preferences are in large part determined by the desire for private old-age support, then shifting that support to the public sector could mitigate these biased preferences.

Consider the retired elderly in the United States, for example. Their income sources include Social Security, private pensions, dividends, and the like, but usually little financial support from children. Instead, adult children provide support-in-kind: a drive to the optometrist, for example, or advice with investments. Companionship, emotional support, assistance with problems in daily living—these, not money, constitute familial old-age security in the United States. And the overwhelming evidence indicates that daughters provide much more help than sons.[67] The logic of crowding out suggests that instituting public pensions could tilt parental preferences toward daughters. This conjecture is testable. For example, it might be interesting to compare measures of the desire for, and treatment of, daughters versus sons in the United States before and after Social Security.

Conflict

Exploring some biological roots of family economics has involved some of the nastier aspects of family life: the oppression of wives and neglect of daughters. This section explores further dimensions of family distress. Some of these emanate from a different fundamental theme from biology— Trivers's theory of parent-child conflict. Still others come from extensions of this theory of conflict.

To see why understanding familial conflict can have potential use within the economics of the family, consider the "case of the yelling parent." In a recent study, Frank Sloan, Gabriel Picone, and Thomas Hoerger used data

---

67. Eleanor Stoller's (1983) study of hours of elder care provided by adult children, for example, shows that daughters provide twice as many hours of help as do sons. See related evidence from Kotlikoff and Morris (1989). More recent findings from the HRS and Asset and Health Dynamics among the Oldest Old (AHEAD) data accord with this evidence. See, for example, Soldo and Hill (1995).

from the United States National Long-Term Care Survey (NLTCS) to study the provision of care by adult children to their disabled elderly parents.[68] Part of their aim was to explain variation in hours of help provided by adult children. They regressed hours of informal care provided by children to their parents on a variety of mostly economic and demographic variables, including parent and child wealth, the child's wage rate, sex, marital status, and the like. In addition, they entered the dummy variable: "parent yells when upset." About a third of the parents in their sample were so classified, and yelling turned out to be an important explanatory variable in the regression for informal care. It was associated with an extra thirteen weekly hours of care, a lot by any standard, and large in relation to the average of twenty-nine hours received from the primary caregiving child. Yelling falls outside the typical "altruism-exchange" dichotomy so common in empirical studies of intergenerational transfer behavior.[69] The altruism versus exchange framework has caught on in empirical literature because it seems to cover the bases: I give you something either because I care about you or because I want something in return, or both. This ignores a third possibility: Maybe I just want you to stop bugging me.

At first, this alternative looks like exchange, but it is not. My disabled father yells; I change his blankets. We both would have been better off if he had asked nicely. Yelling is not Pareto optimal; neither is wheedling, nagging, cajoling, or any of the other seven deadly sins of family conflict. Such episodes are wasteful, like strikes or wars. It is preferable to skip them and proceed straight to an agreement.

Such waste makes conflict difficult to analyze in economic terms. John Kennan's thoughtful analysis of strike behavior illuminates the problem, which he calls the "Hicks paradox."[70] To paraphrase Kennan's explanation, consider the following situation: You and I argue constantly, though when the dust settles, we always come to an agreement of some sort. We go to therapy, in search of a theory that predicts when an argument will occur, how long it will last, and what the outcome will be. The therapist supplies us with one. We then use it to circumvent the *Sturm und Drang* and go straight to the outcome. But this makes our therapist's theory cease to hold!

So strong is the economist's affinity for Pareto optimal solutions that

---

68. Sloan, Picone, and Hoerger (1997).

69. In fact, however, Sloan and others were primarily interested in testing the implications of the "strategic bequests" model of Bernheim, Shleifer, and Summers (1985).

70. Kennan (1986).

when he first encountered Robert Trivers's conjecture about parent-child conflict, Gary Becker was inclined to discount it. The theory, which first occurred to Trivers while he was watching pigeons, and which applies more to yelling toddlers than to yelling parents, is summarized in his own words below:

> The parent has been selected to invest in its offspring in such a way as to maximize the number eventually surviving. From the parent's standpoint we can dissolve parental investment into associated benefit and cost. The benefit is the degree to which the investment increases the survival of the offspring at hand, while the cost is the degree to which the investment decreases the parent's ability to invest in other offspring (including those still unborn). Put this way, the parent is naturally selected to avoid any investment in the offspring for which the cost is greater than the benefit, since such investment would decrease the total number of its offspring surviving.
>
> By contrast, the offspring is selected to devalue the cost it inflicts compared to the benefit it receives. This is because the offspring is identically related to itself but only partly related to its siblings. . . .
>
> Because the offspring is selected to devalue the cost of parental investment, it will always tend to favor a longer period of parental investment than the parent is selected to give.[71]

Trivers reasons that such differences in perspective, where mother likes "ego" and "sis" equally, but ego likes himself more, would lead him to temper tantrums and other behaviors aimed at steering extra maternal resources his way. Becker discounts the importance of tantrums, appealing to the logic of his "rotten-kid" theorem.[72] For example: my sister, altruist mother, and I live under the same roof. Conflict, from wherever it may arise, saps shared family resources, and all are made to suffer, even the perpetrator, who therefore should think twice about causing trouble. This is the same logic that might prevent a pet from biting the hand that feeds it or a virus from killing its host. Bergstrom shows that Becker's reasoning has more limited applicability than he supposed.[73] While Becker's theorem arguably qualifies as a behav-

---

71. Trivers (1985, p. 148).

72. Becker (1976, p. 825) writes: "My analysis denies that such a conflict exists when parents are altruistic because children have an incentive to act as altruistically toward each other as their parents want them to, even if children are really egotistical."

73. Bergstrom (1989).

ioral benchmark, it need not *necessarily* be true. Bergstrom shows that it is logically possible for a child—equipped, for example, with powerful lungs and first-strike capability against a parent with no means of precommitment—to grab more than he was supposed to get.[74] Bergstrom and Carl Bergstrom exploit this possibility to further explore the biological implications of Trivers's approach to parent-child conflict.[75]

Becker opens the door to the study of family conflict still further with his elegant model of "preference formation," or what could be termed "taking behavior."[76] A "taker" is someone too poor to provide compensation for doing his bidding, so he manipulates people instead. He does this with some ambivalence, since he is also altruistic toward his victims, but not enough to justify giving transfers because of his limited means. Instead, he "turns up the heat," with behavior that could be construed as threats, wheedling, or guilt-tripping, to get his way. Vijayendra Rao, in presenting his work with Frances Bloch, on domestic violence in India, recounts an interesting example.[77] A husband who could not afford a down payment for a motorcycle threatens his wife with violence in order to get her to ask her parents for the money. A

74. Imagine, for example, that a child away from home pleads for help with February's rent, insisting it's the last time he'll have to ask, and his parent relents, but issues a warning that it will really have to be the last time. But come March, the child asks for help again, and the parent, an altruist, weakens and relents once again. See also Bruce and Waldman (1990).

75. Bergstrom and Bergstrom. 1996. "Rotten Kids, Squawky Birds, and Natural Selection." Ann Arbor, Mich. Mimeo. Trivers' approach has received some rather intriguing support from recent, and widely cited, findings by evolutionary biologist David Haig (1993). In the first few days in which an embryo's cells begin to divide, it must accomplish several things to thwart imminent doom: send signals to shut down the menstruation process, establish a connection to the mother's blood supply, and duck attacks from the mother's immune system; Elison (2001). Thus begins the cat-and-mouse game that is pregnancy. For example, the placenta secretes a hormone that blocks the sugar-reducing effects of insulin. The mother's system can respond by upping insulin levels, which is why obstetricians sometimes observe pregnant women with sky-high insulin levels and normal blood sugar. Sometimes these effects do not cancel, and the mother contracts gestational diabetes—while her baby gets ever fatter. Haig's evidence reads like an *in utero* version of the grabby kid in the supermarket candy aisle.

76. Becker (1993).

77. Bloch and Vijayendra. 1997. "Terror as a Bargaining Instrument: A Case Study of Dowry Violence in Rural India." Williamstown, Mass.: Williams College. Mimeo.

necessary condition for this "taking behavior" to work, as Becker shows, is for the wife's marginal utility of capitulation to increase with her husband's threats.

It is puzzling that Becker's approach has not caught on among those who study family behavior. In stark contrast to the avalanche of applied research stimulated by models of altruism, only a trickle of applied work has emanated from models of conflict. Part of the problem might be an obvious question that Becker ignores: "Who in their right mind would tether themselves to some manipulative ogre?" One obvious answer is that financial or psychological burdens from breaking up create fixed costs that deter easy escape. It is possible to add these to the model, however, and doing so can add both realism and additional insight.[78]

Evidence about family conflict based on survey data is mostly limited to studies of domestic violence.[79] Household surveys provide little information concerning other forms of conflict. A new source of evidence, however, has become available from a special module of the 2000 wave of the HRS. This module asks a number of "point blank" questions, designed to probe for some of the more subtle motivations for intergenerational transfer behavior. The questions are directed to a subsample of survey respondents, and they include two related to family conflict. Respondents are asked if they agree, disagree, or are neutral about the following statements:

—"My immediate family sometimes pressures me to do more than I want to do for them."

—"I sometimes have to ask over and over again to get my immediate family to help me."

Call those who agree with the first statement "pressured," and those who agree with the second "pressurers." A summary of the responses is shown in figure 6-5.

Only a little over two-thirds of the respondents can be certified "pressure free," in the sense that they neither applied nor felt pressure; 9 percent of the respondents agree with the first statement, but disagree with the second, so

---

78. For example, as with most rural Indian wives, those in Bloch and Rao's data set lived far from their parents and faced virtually infinite fixed costs of terminating the relationship. The more money they had access to, the worse their situation could become, if, for example, parental riches presented a target of opportunity for bullying husbands. This is not necessarily so in the United States, for example, where having a well-paying job and a credible escape plan could help keep a potential bully in check.

79. See, for example, the informative papers by Tauchen, Witte, and Long (1991); and Farmer and Tiefenthaler (1996).

Figure 6-5. *Pressure in HRS Families*

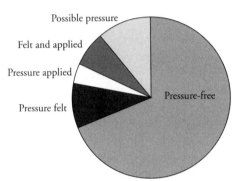

Source: Author's calculations using the Health and Retirement Study (HRS).

they feel pressure, but do not apply any pressure to others.[80] Of all the respondents, 4 percent disagree with the first statement but agree with the second; surprisingly, 7 percent agree with both statements, suggesting that pressure is not just a "one-way street." The rest of the sample, 11 percent, is in the "ambiguous" group; they give a "neutral" response to one or both of the statements.

These preliminary findings, along with the theoretical considerations discussed earlier, indicate that the door is open to further inquiry about family conflict. Further research in this area would be of potential policy and intellectual interest. The policy interest stems from the potential for crowding out. If for example, private income transfers are crowded out by public income transfer programs, does this mean that some familial strife would get crowded out too? Such possibilities could change the way we think about the relationship between private and public transfers.

Conclusion

The economic approach to intergenerational transfers often invokes the assumption that men and women have identical interests and capabilities in the reproductive realm. Often this assumption is harmless and convenient,

---

80. Note that the second question does not ask directly about applying pressure. Querying respondents about whether they asked repeatedly for help seemed a more diplomatic way to broach the issue, since it is unlikely that one would willingly describe oneself as a pest.

but it can sometimes stifle fruitful inquiry into family behavior. Relaxing it illuminates potentially valuable directions for research.

To see how existing work could be reinterpreted or built upon from considerations of reproductive biology, consider two examples referred to at the beginning, in the brief literature review: First is the evidence that putting more income into the hands of mothers increases spending on children. If this behavior is indeed driven, at least in part, by paternity uncertainty, then it should be weaker in cultures in which such uncertainty is low. It would be interesting, for example, to explore the relationship between the severity of regulations and norms about women's sexual behavior and the relative support of children coming from paternal versus maternal grandparents. Consideration of paternal uncertainty forges a link between these two disparate areas of family behavior.

Second is the existing evidence about favoritism of boys. Although little evidence for such bias exists in the United States, Trivers-Willard suggests that such bias can interact with relative socioeconomic status. It is conceivable that leaving out such interactions could obscure such favoritism.

Another standard economic perspective on the family is that it is a place of harmony and agreement, forged either by altruistic ties or the possibility of Pareto-improving trades.[81] But more recent theoretical work, and fragmentary evidence as well, indicates that conflict, and the "taking behavior" that goes along with it, might occupy a significant niche in the familial landscape.

Many of these ideas are amenable to testing with existing household survey microdata. New sources of such information on families are becoming available all the time. Theoretical breakthroughs and advances in data collection make this an especially exciting time for economists interested in family behavior. Further progress will require harnessing insights from biology, and using new ways of looking for evidence. There is much to be done.

COMMENT BY
Theodore Bergstrom

As we all know, economists' models of the family are typically inhabited by asexual Kewpie dolls, with names like A and B or 1 and 2. That is not good enough for Donald Cox. He wants to play with anatomically correct Kens and Barbies.

81. Becker (1974); for example, see also Cox (1987).

Cox argues that biological differences between the sexes are likely to result in predictable differences in the economic relations among family members. Cox looks for testable implications of his theoretical speculations, and has found some intriguing, if not entirely persuasive, results. This puts him well ahead of most economists who speculate about such matters.

Cox's first lesson in the asymmetry of birds-and-bees concerns cuckoldry. Simple biology ensures that women can be much more confident than men about which children are theirs and which are not. Cox finds that there do not seem to be reliable estimates of the percentage of children who are fathered by someone other than their putative father. What evidence there is comes from blood samples taken for other purposes than determining parenthood. Blood tests can be expected to catch a fraction of instances of mistaken paternity. One source is quoted as saying that "between 5 and 30 percent of American and British babies have been adulterously conceived," but Cox reports that even these loose figures are poorly documented. It would be nice to know more about what these numbers are and what they have been through long spells of human history. In the future, perhaps DNA testing will give us sharper results. For the time being, according to Cox, we will have to speculate about magnitudes and look for the qualitative implications of a significant rate of cuckoldry.

Grandma's Bias

Cuckoldry rates are going to have important economic implications if people are more likely to treat their biological children and grandchildren better than stepchildren. Cox proposes an interesting test of the propositions that people are significantly less confident about paternity than about maternity, and that people allocate time and money among their descendants in such a way as to maximize their total contribution to the gene pool. It turns out that Grandma has been discriminating among her grandkids. Grandma appears to care more about the children in her daughters' households than she does about the children in her sons' households. According to the National Survey of Families and Households, maternal grandmothers had 35 percent more sleepovers and 22 percent more visits and calls-plus-letters than paternal grandmothers. On average, they also reported themselves as feeling "extremely close" to their maternal grandkids somewhat more often. All but one of these differences were statistically significant at the 1 percent level.

Cox observes that these effects are consistent with the hypothesis that Grandma is more confident that her daughter's kids are really her descendants than she is about her son's kids. He also notes that other explanations are possible. For example, mothers take a bigger share of the responsibility for childrearing than do fathers. Mothers are emotionally closer to their mothers than to their mothers-in-law and are more likely to ask the former for help with child care.

What about money transfers? For the population on average, the Grandma story is reversed. Paternal grandparents tend to contribute more money than maternal grandparents. But for the least wealthy 10 percent of the population, maternal grandparents contribute more. Cox offers some anecdotes in support of the proposition that confidence in paternity is lower for poor people than for rich people. This would be consistent with the poor favoring their maternal grandkids, though it would not explain away the observation that the well-off favor their paternal grandkids. This argument would be more convincing if the evidence of differential paternity confidence by income were more convincing. While I do not know a lot about the sex lives of wealthy people, I have heard a lot of stories that suggest that hanky-panky is as likely to be a normal good as an inferior good.

Even if Grandma's bias turns out to be explained by the fact that she gets along better with her daughter than with her daughter-in-law and not by Grandma's suspicions about her daughter-in-law's sex life, her discriminatory practices are likely to interest those who study the economics of the family.

It would be useful to investigate whether some of Grandma's apparent bias toward the matriline is explained by other variables. Does the sample include households that have experienced a divorce and where some of the children are children from an earlier marriage? I can see some reason for Grandma to have more dealings with grandchildren who live with her own child than those who live with her child's former spouse. If mothers are more likely to gain custody than fathers, this would explain some bias toward one's maternal rather than paternal grandchildren.

Although it is likely to be a small effect, it may be worthwhile to consider Grandma's age. Husbands are on average older than wives, so paternal grandmothers will on average be older than maternal grandmothers. If older grandmothers are less attached to their grandchildren than younger ones, this effect would explain some of the apparent bias.

It would also be worthwhile to check the effect of distance between Grandma's home and the grandchild's home. My guess is that there is some tendency towards patrilocality, which would favor attachments with paternal grandchildren, but this is an empirical question that should be checked out.

While we are thinking about the effects of genetic linkage on Grandma's generosity to children, we should not forget about a large class of test cases, namely stepchildren and adopted children. In these cases we know that the genetic links are zero. It would be useful to compare Cox's measurements of grandmaternal connections for stepchildren and for adopted children with those for putative biological children of sons and daughters.

Sons and Daughters

The Trivers-Willard hypothesis goes something like this: In many species, only the healthiest and most successful males are able to reproduce, and these lucky few hit the reproductive jackpot. Females on the other hand, are biologically constrained from having huge numbers of children; an impoverished female is much more likely to have some children than an impoverished male. Therefore, according to the hypothesis, if mothers find themselves to be well-fed and healthy at the time of conception, they are more likely to have male than female offspring, and if they find themselves in poor condition, they are more likely to have female children. Moreover, the theory predicts that "wealthy" animals are likely to bias their parental investment toward their sons rather than their daughters, while "poor" animals are likely to do the reverse. Ecologists claim to have observed evidence of the Trivers-Willard effect in some species of mammals, such as bison, reindeer, gerbils, red deer, and macaques.[82]

Cox finds that poor people are more likely to educate their daughters than their sons, while rich people are more likely to educate their sons. He suggests that one interpretation of this result is operation of the Trivers-Willard effect. I am dubious about the Trivers-Willard explanation, but finding a better explanation for this phenomenon is an interesting challenge.

Conflict among Family Members

Biologists are well aware that the biological interests of family members do not coincide. A child has a stronger genetic interest in himself than in his sibling and thus disagrees with his mother about how she should allocate her time between him and his sibling. A person's own children are twice as closely related to him as his siblings' children. And so on. Robert Trivers presents a clear discussion of this issue, along with many good examples.[83]

Cox suggests that economists should pay more attention to interfamilial conflicts of interest and to "inefficiencies" that result from these conflicts. Economists are well aware of Gary Becker's "Rotten Kid Theorem" that suggests that under certain circumstances, even totally selfish children may be forced to act in the reproductive interests of their parents.[84] A few years ago,

82. Clutton-Brock (1991).
83. Trivers (1985).
84. Becker (1974).

I wrote a paper called "A Fresh Look at the Rotten Kid Theorem: and Other Household Mysteries," in which I argue that Becker's conclusion holds only in very special situations, and that a litter of selfish children would be unlikely to act in such a way as to maximize the parents' reproductive success.[85] An interesting parallel discussion exists in the literature of evolutionary biology, with some biologists, such as Richard Alexander, advocating the view that evolutionary forces cause mammalian offspring to act in such a way as to maximize their parents' net reproductive success, and others, such as Robert Trivers and Richard Dawkins, taking the contrary view.[86] A paper that my son, Carl, and I wrote, offers a genetically based model of the evolution of behavior in games that involve parent-offspring conflict.[87]

I want to conclude by adding one more plaything to Cox's dollhouse. This is a case where relatives' reproductive interests are nearly coincidental, but for which there are interesting divergences. I am thinking of a monogamous husband and wife, each of whom trusts the other's sexual fidelity. Each of these two people has the same genetic stake in each of their children, and neither of them has any other children to spend resources on. So we can expect a good deal of harmony of interest. But even here, theory predicts a source of discord—a discord that may even be familiar to some of you: in-laws. The prediction of Hamilton's kin selection theory is that a wife will value her sibling's children half as much as her own, while her husband has no genetic stake in these children. And conversely for the husband.

In historical societies, even where cuckoldry and divorce may have been rare, marriages were frequently interrupted by the early death of one spouse or the other. Suppose that a woman with some children is considering whether it is in her biological interest to have another child or to stop having children. If she becomes pregnant again, she may die in childbirth. In this case, her other children become orphans, and if her husband marries again, they become stepchildren, with lower survival rates and lower reproductive potential than they would have had if she had stopped having children before this birth. The reproductive loss to her husband is less severe. He has the possibility of remarrying, and producing more children by a new and quite possibly younger wife. Thus the wife's reproductive interests would be served by having fewer children than would be optimal for her husband to have.

85. Bergstrom (1989).
86. See Alexander (1974, 1979); Dawkins (1976); and Trivers (1974).
87. Bergstrom and Bergstrom (1998).

COMMENT BY
Kathleen McGarry

These certainly are provocative ideas and make for a very interesting paper. Yet, Donald Cox is careful to note that many alternative explanations are possible for the phenomena he describes and that he is simply raising issues that ought to be addressed in future work. The basic idea, that our desire to pass along our genes drives our investments in children, is quite plausible and has a long history in the biological sciences. The crucial question is whether this evolutionary motivation is large enough to affect behavior.

Is the drive toward certain behaviors induced by evolutionary desires strong enough to have an effect in the presence of a myriad of other incentives, obligations, and desires? Making a financial transfer, or providing time help, is a decision reached after some thought, and not a biologically triggered response. Even if parents were genetically predisposed to a certain behavior, it is difficult to imagine that it is carried out impetuously, rather than chosen in a utility maximizing framework where other models come into play. For instance, it is hard to imagine that parents are unconsciously giving greater cash transfers to one child over another. While I have my doubts about whether an evolutionary motive is operable, Cox has succeeded in getting us to think about these issues and perhaps is spurring others to test some of the hypotheses he offers, and on that score, is to be commended.

Consider the motivation for transfers to children. The biological explanation is that parents transfer resources to children to help them succeed so they have successful children of their own, and so on. Through this mechanism, parents enable their genetic line to continue. This theory is in contrast to an altruism model wherein parents transfer to their children because they care about the child's happiness, or an exchange model wherein parents care about their own happiness and the observed transfers are part of a reciprocal agreement, representing payment for services provided by the child.

An important part of developing the model is devising tests that differentiate it from other hypotheses existing in the literature. Fortunately, this novel idea appears to be testable in several ways:

One test that Cox employs is the difference in transfer propensities between mothers and fathers. Because mothers are more certain of the biological link to their child, they should be more likely to make transfers than are fathers. Cox highlights this difference by examining transfers from grandmothers to their grandchildren. Because maternal grandmothers are certain of a genetic link to the grandchild, they are more likely to make transfers than paternal grandmothers, who might harbor some doubt about whether their son is the child's father. The empirical evidence supports this prediction, but is also consistent with other models of transfer behavior. As Cox notes, if childcare is the responsibility of women, the wife in the couple with young children may turn to her own mother for assistance simply because she feels closer to her than to her mother-in-law. This assistance from the maternal grandmother could be given freely as part of an altruism model or "purchased" in an exchange regime. In an exchange model, the maternal grandmother would be preferred to the paternal grandmother if the wife's mother can provide care at a lower price. For example, the daughter and mother might share similar child-rearing beliefs, or alternatively, if child care is provided in exchange for future home health care, then the daughter may be more efficient in caring for her own mother because she knows the mother's likes and dislikes, her medical history, and so forth.

An extension of this prediction about maternal grandmothers is that the same pattern should be observed for grandfathers. While a maternal grandfather might not be certain that his wife's daughter is truly his, he does know that his daughter's child is hers and therefore, he has only one level of uncertainty (that is, if he is the girl's father, he is most definitely the grandfather). In contrast, a paternal grandfather faces uncertainty in both generations; he does not know for certain that his wife's son is his child, nor does he know whether the grandchild belongs to his son. With these two levels of uncertainty, he is less sure of a genetic relationship with the child than is the maternal grandfather. Following the pattern observed for grandmothers, the data should show greater transfers from maternal grandfathers than from paternal grandfathers. Taking the two relationships together provides a ranking of giving probabilities: maternal grandmother first, then either the maternal grandfather or paternal grandmother (each of whom faces uncertainty in one generation), and finally the paternal grandfather.

This hierarchy is testable and can potentially reveal interesting patterns. For example, part of the reason for grandmothers providing childcare is likely to be the tradition of women caring for children. One can compare the behavior of maternal grandfathers and paternal grandmothers—people who are in some sense "tied" in the probability of genetic attachments—to help sort out some of the difference in sex roles versus genetic uncertainty. My guess is that sex roles would dominate as an explanatory variable.

However, maternal grandfathers and paternal grandmothers might possibly differ in their belief that they have genetic ties to the child. One could expand the model to allow for the uncertainty of genetic links to differ by the age of the child in question. It may be that as the child ages, certain physical and personality traits lead the (potential) father to become more or less certain that the child is his. Thus despite the fact that they each have one generation of uncertainty, a maternal grandfather might be more (or less) certain of a genetic link than a paternal grandmother and transfers might vary accordingly.

In contrast to the transfer of time, financial transfers are more likely made by the grandparent couple and not by a particular grandparent. In the hierarchy of giving established by the genetic linkages, the maternal grandparents dominate the paternal for both grandmothers and grandfathers. Thus all else constant, the total transferred from the maternal side should unambiguously be greater than that from the paternal grandparents. This relationship, too, can be checked, and in fact, such a comparison is mentioned in the paper. However, in contrast to the predictions of the model, the data show that overall, paternal grandparents give more in cash transfers. This is a straightforward rejection of the model, but consistent with the alternative explanation that the wife is "in charge" of the children and transfers involving child care come from her parents, while the husband is "in charge" of the couple's financial needs and his parents help out there. Similar work by Robert Schoeni comparing cash transfers from each set of parents does find a slightly greater probability of giving by the wife's parents, but the difference is not statistically significant.[88]

Cox's results provide an interesting twist. Couples at the lower point of the income distribution receive more from the wife's parents, while those higher up in the distribution receive more from the husband's parents. This difference echoes the work in other disciplines on the Trivers-Willard hypothesis that finds that the wealthy favor sons while the less wealthy favor daughters in the hope that daughters can "marry up."[89] Cox suggests that the difference in relative giving by income could also reflect greater uncertainty about paternity among low-income fathers.

Again, a host of other explanations are possible. The difference may simply be capturing the ability of grandparents to make a transfer. Note first that the income used in this tabulation is the income of the recipient generation, not the donor generation. It is not unrealistic to assume that the income of the recipient couple is more highly correlated with the income of the husband's parents than that of his wife. This relationship would result if the couple's income is determined largely by the husband's income and if his income is more highly correlated with his own father's than with his father-in-law's.

88. Schoeni (2000).
89. See Cox (this volume) for a detailed discussion of the Trivers-Willard hypothesis.

Thus since high-income husbands likely have high-income parents who can afford to make generous transfers, while low-income husbands likely have low-income parents who do not make generous transfers, it is unsurprising that among those with low incomes, the wife's parents dominate the giving. This relationship, too, could be tested but the data requirements are extensive. To do a good job one would need information not just on transfers from each set of parents, but also income for each set of parents and for the recipient couple.

It would be interesting to see the statistics for the upper end of the distribution as well as the lower end. The paper shows that overall, paternal grandparents are more likely to make cash transfers, while in the lowest decile, maternal grandparents are more likely. Is the pattern reversed in the top decile? How do the amounts vary with the income decile? Is there a clean switch from the wife's parents to the husband's as income increases? Note also that if the income of the recipient couple is highly correlated with that of the donor, then the relationship between income and amount should be positive rather than the negative relationship usually reported when incomes of both the donor and the recipient can be controlled for.

In addition to the income of each generation, other variables need to be controlled for to make the comparisons more credible. Because the data do not indicate which child (or grandchild) is receiving the assistance with childcare, the only way to separate care given to help daughters from care given to help sons is to restrict the comparison to grandmothers with daughters only and grandmothers with sons only. As noted earlier, maternal grandmothers give significantly more care. One alternative explanation is that childcare is the responsibility of the mother, who turns to her own mother for help. However, there are some other possible differences. For example, do daughter-only and son-only parents differ in the number of children they have (and therefore in the total amount given), in the propensity for parents and children to live near each other, or in other factors that could be correlated with transfers?

While favoritism toward daughters can be justified by the certainty of genetic linkage, the Trivers-Willard model provides an explanation for the difference in favoritism across the income distribution. The model argues that parents "control" the sex of their offspring to take advantage of environmental circumstances that favor one sex over the other. Furthermore, poor conditions are predicted to favor girls while good conditions favor boys. Cox argues that investments in education are one (less extreme) variation on this. According to the evolutionary biology hypothesis, parents vary how much they invest in children of each sex based on how successful the child will be

Table 6-1. *Educational Attainment, by Race*
Percent

	1968–78		1979–89		1990–98	
Decile	Whites	Blacks	Whites	Blacks	Whites	Blacks
Bottom 20	0.38	0.48	0.37	0.44	0.48	0.44
Middle 60	0.61	0.57	0.63	0.61	0.75	0.68
Top 20	0.87	0.82	0.90	0.89	0.93	0.91

in "going forth and multiplying." As with the cash transfers, he finds evidence that girls are favored among low-income families; boys among high-income. This is explained by the idea that girls from low-income families have a better chance of "marrying up" than boys. This result could also be consistent with differences between males and females in the returns to schooling.

One result to note is that a similar pattern exists by race (see table 6-1). Blacks, like women, have higher educational attainment than whites at low socioeconomic status levels, while whites, like men, have more education at high socioeconomic status categories.[90] Interestingly, over time, this difference has gradually disappeared, suggesting that changes in the labor market may eventually bring about similar changes for the differences in investment between boys and girls.

Because schooling level likely reflects market opportunities as well as parental desires to assist a child, a more straightforward comparison might be to examine *inter-vivos* giving, controlling for schooling. However, while we would expect matriarchal preference to lead to more transfers to daughters, most studies do not find a difference in the probability or amount of transfers to sons and daughters.[91] Even the most recent work that can examine transfers within families fails to find a difference in recipiency by sex.[92]

Bequests also present a puzzle with respect to biologically based giving. In the evolutionary approach, transfers to children should be made while children are young enough that the assistance influences their fertility. However,

90. Sandra Black, Stephen Cameron, and Amir Sufi. 2001. "Why Some Do Better: Understanding Black-White Differences in College Enrollment." Federal Reserve Bank of New York. Mimeo.
91. Altonji, Hayashi, and Kotlikoff (1997); Cox and Jappelli (1990); Cox and Rank (1992).
92. McGarry and Schoeni (1995, 1997).

bequests typically come too late in life to do so, yet are still a large part of lifetime transfers. Furthermore, bequests are overwhelmingly divided equally across children, not favoring those with more offspring of their own, or a particular sex. Estimates of the probability of equal division range from 70 to 90 percent, numbers difficult to reconcile in an evolutionary context. If parents are consciously helping daughters more with care, they should also do so with cash transfers and bequests.

Not only might evolutionary-minded parents differentiate between sons and daughters; they might also want to give more to those children who can provide more grandchildren. Such an approach would predict that stepchildren or adopted children should not only receive fewer transfers than biological children, but should be unlikely to receive anything at all. I have not seen any evidence that this is true. Perhaps more important, the evolutionary model is not consistent with the adoption of children in the first place. If individuals cannot or do not have biological children of their own, rather than adopting, their energies should be invested in caring for or supporting the children of their siblings since these children carry some of their genes, while an adopted child will carry none. Thus the evolutionary biology model would predict that people with siblings who themselves have children would be less likely to adopt than only children, and that adopted children and stepchildren should be significantly less likely to receive transfers than biological children, all else constant.

I am not aware of anyone who has specifically examined *inter-vivos* transfers to step or adopted children, although data from the HRS would allow such a study. Some evidence on the division with respect to bequests does exist and suggests that adopted and natural children are treated equally.[93]

The allocation of bequests from the National Longitudinal Survey of Mature Women does address the issue of division of bequests with respect to stepchildren. The survey asks respondents whether their estate would be divided equally, and if not, why not. While this is anecdotal only, and certainly not a formal test of the model, it does provide probably the first glimpse at such data for a nationally representative sample. Out of all those who give explanations for not dividing their estate equally across children, some list reasons related to altruism: "X needs it more," and some related to exchange: "X helps me more." In only a very few cases does the explanation in any way mention whether the children are biological, step, or adopted. Here are the relevant responses:

—"It will be divided between *biological* children."

93. Judge and Hrdy (1992).

—"X only has one daughter. Not leaving to stepchildren."

These two explanations sound like stepchildren or adopted children are written out of the will. However, the intention might not be to treat these children unfairly. Other responses state that:

—"I figured that my stepdaughter can get it from her mother, but my adopted daughter will just have me to get it from."

—"Because once we are gone, they will disown adopted son, so we want to be sure adopted son will be provided for."

—"Because adopted son would squander money, so his portion is going to his children."

These indicate some preference for biological children over stepchildren but not necessarily because of genetics; more likely because the stepchildren have another parent from whom to get transfers and the donor is trying "to be fair." What is interesting is the only comments on adopted children seem to indicate that they will not be treated differently from biological children.

With respect to the issue of infidelity, Cox argues that women cheat on their mates so that more than one man thinks he could be the father, and will potentially contribute to the welfare of the child. Having two potential fathers can work in either of two ways: The mother can decide which man would provide greater support and rely on him exclusively, or the two potential fathers could both provide care, each at a lower level than they would were they certain the child was theirs. The question then to ask is under what conditions would the expected value of assistance from multiple potential fathers be greater than the amount from one who is (nearly) certain? This is similar to the provision of public goods examined in public finance. Cox acknowledges this "paternity uncertainty creates a public goods problem. . . . Such prospects create externalities that, at least in principle, further dilute incentives for male investment." As in the classic case, investment is too low in a public good. So a woman might expect that if she gives her mate reason to doubt he is the father, she will likely end up with less total support for the child.

It would be interesting to see a model in which the two sides interact, wherein both men and women are trying to attract mates. Women certainly have a biological reason to focus on the quality of children instead of quantity since their capacity to increase quantity is limited. They can improve the quality by increasing the contribution from the father. This in turn can be done by maximizing the probability that he believes he is indeed the father.

However, it is not just the woman who needs to be concerned about strategic behavior. Men need to attract mates and depending on the model, they may well prefer to attract high-quality mates. To do so, the male needs to convince a woman (who is selective because of the quality issue) that he would be a good father. Philandering men would not be good fathers from the mother's point of view: First, because by spending time pursuing the opportunity to father more children, they spend less time with any one child. Second, because with more children, each child gets less time and money. Thus evidence of philandering would a priori make a man a less desirable partner. Therefore, both sides want to signal that they are monogamous to get the best mate despite countervailing incentives to act otherwise. This strategic behavior could make for interesting modeling.

This paper raises a number of interesting thoughts, supplies us with numerous testable predictions, and perhaps more than anything, spurs us to think of behaviors consistent with or in conflict with the model. I hope Cox pursues some of the issues presented here, but at the very least he has already provided us with enormous intellectual stimulation.

PART 3

Taxes, Pension Benefits, and Wealth Transfers

7

Tax Consequences on Wealth Accumulation and Transfers of the Rich

WOJCIECH KOPCZUK AND JOEL SLEMROD

After many years off the political radar screen, the U.S. estate and gift tax system has recently received a lot of attention, culminating in the scheduled repeal of the tax in 2010 contained in the 2001 tax legislation. Opponents of this tax routinely deride it as unfair and point to its deleterious effects on wealth accumulation and its impetus to tax avoidance. Supporters tend to minimize these effects, but at the same time often emphasize its large effects on other aspects of behavior, in particular charitable giving. Thus the policy debates often make strange bedfellows with regard to behavioral responses, taking seriously some margins of response, but minimizing others. These positions are not necessarily inconsistent, as it is certainly logically possible that some margins are more responsive than others. However, it would be of interest to assess the behavioral responses on a consistent basis. After all, the place of an estate tax within the overall tax system does depend, *inter alia*, on how it affects behavior.

Unlike some other contexts, quantifying these behavioral responses is not simply a matter of estimating the relevant elasticities within a well-accepted model of choice under constraint. On the contrary, macroeconomists are engaged in an ongoing and fierce debate about the very motivation for

We are grateful to David Joulfaian, Ray Madoff, and James Poterba for insightful comments on the first draft of this paper, and to David Lenter and Sherry Li for research assistance.

bequests and the underlying model of behavior. Moreover, because estate planning usually occurs in the context of a family, and depends on the preferences of both spouses and their relationship, studying estate tax returns may shed some light on the appropriate model of family decisionmaking. We investigate spousal bequest decisions and use of a particular kind of trust, QTIPs, with this issue in mind. Finally, estate tax planning represents forward-looking behavior in its most extreme form, as it pertains to what will happen after an individual's death and requires contemplating one's own death. Analysis of estate arrangements and their responsiveness to changes in tax policy might provide new evidence about the importance of various behavioral considerations as opposed to the "rational" and dynamically consistent standard model of behavior.

In this paper, we review and extend what is known about the effect of estate taxes on wealth accumulation, the timing of intergenerational transfers, and the volume and timing of charitable giving. We examine the findings with respect not only to their implications for optimal tax policy, but also their implications for the key macroeconomic controversies about the nature of intergenerational links, and by further implication, fiscal policies. In the process, we highlight findings that may be inconsistent with a unitary model of the family or with forward-looking, dynamically consistent behavior.

The one important caveat to all that follows is that estate taxes—at least the federal variety—are, and have always been, only for the rich. Over its history, the U.S. estate tax has applied to at most the richest 6 percent of decedents, and in recent years has applied to a much lower percentage. This fact has two implications: First, generalizing any insights gleaned from the population subject to the estate tax to the whole population may be misleading. Second, because the tax applies only to the rich, it may have important implications for the distribution of wealth, income, and well-being; for example, what to some observers is evidence of an unfortunate negative impact on wealth accumulation may to others be seen as evidence of a successful redistribution of wealth. The paper begins with a brief discussion of the U.S. estate and gift tax law and the population it applies to, and then turns to a discussion of its effects.

An Overview of Transfer Taxes

This section summarizes current law, presents the key features of the 2001 tax legislation, and provides some characteristics about estate tax returns.[1]

---

1. For information on the history of the U.S. estate and gift taxes, see appendix. See Joint Committee on Taxation (1998) for a more detailed treatment of current law

Current Law

Federal law imposes an integrated set of taxes on estates, gifts, and genera-tion-skipping transfers.[2] By law, the executor of an estate must file a federal estate tax return within nine months of the death of a U.S. citizen or resident if the gross estate exceeds a threshold that in 2002 is $1,000,000. The gross estate includes all of the decedent's assets, his or her share of jointly owned assets, and life insurance proceeds from policies owned by the decedent. The gross estate also includes all gifts made by the decedent in excess of an annual exemption that in 2002 is $11,000 per recipient per year, and is indexed for inflation. The estate may also include other property over which the dece-dent had control, wealth transfers made during life that were either revocable or provided for less than full consideration, and qualified terminable interest property (QTIP).[3]

Typically, assets are valued at fair market value. However, closely held businesses are allowed to value real property assets, up to a maximum allowed value, at their "use value" rather than their highest alternative market-oriented value. In addition, it is often possible to discount asset value when such assets are not readily marketable or the taxpayer's ownership does not correlate with control.[4] The estate is usually valued as of the date of death, but alternatively may be valued six months after the death, if the value of the gross estate and the estate tax liability decline during this period.[5]

The estate tax provides unlimited deductions for transfers to a surviving spouse and contributions to charitable organizations. Deductions are also allowed for debts owed by the estate, funeral expenses, and administrative and legal fees associated with the estate. In addition, interests in certain qual-

---

and the legislative history of transfer taxes. Parts of this and the next section draw on Gale and Slemrod (2001).

2. States may also impose estate, inheritance, or gift taxes. The laws that govern how and to whom property may pass are the exclusive domain of the states. For example, many states provide a surviving spouse and minor children with some pro-tection against disinheritance. In cases of intestacy, state laws provide a structure to guide succession.

3. Qualified terminable interest property (QTIP) is created when the estate of the first spouse to die receives an estate tax deduction for a wealth transfer that provides the surviving spouse an income interest only, and provides the remainder interest to someone else. When the second spouse dies, the QTIP is included in his or her estate.

4. See Schmalbeck (2001).

5. If the six-month alternative valuation date is used, assets that were liquidated in the interim are valued at their sale price.

ified family businesses were allowed an extra deduction for the value of the business being transferred.

After determining the value of the net estate—gross estate less deductions—the statutory tax rate is applied. In 2002, the lowest rate that any taxable return faces is 41 percent. The tax rate rises in several stages to 50 percent on taxable transfers above $3 million. A credit is given for state inheritance and estate taxes, but not for state gift taxes.[6] The credit rate is based on the "adjusted taxable estate," which is the federal taxable estate less $60,000, and as of 2001, the allowable credit ranged from zero to 16 percent of the base; the 2001 tax law, however, phases out this credit until 2005, at which time state estate and inheritance taxes become deductible from federal taxable estates. Most states now levy so-called soak-up taxes that exactly mirror the credit limit, so that the state transfer taxes shift revenue from the federal to the state treasuries without adding to the total tax burden on the estate.

Tax payment is due within nine months of the decedent's death, although a six-month filing extension may be obtained. However, the actual timing of the tax payment can be flexible, as the law provides for *ex post* spreading out of tax payments over fourteen years for closely held family businesses.[7]

To reduce tax avoidance under the estate tax, the federal gift tax imposes burdens on transfers between living persons that exceed the annual gift exemption of $11,000. Although the estate and gift taxes are unified, the taxation of gifts and estates involves some important distinctions. Gifts are taxed on a tax-exclusive basis, while estates are taxed on a tax-inclusive basis. This provides a sizable tax advantage to giving gifts rather than bequests.[8] The tax-

---

6. Additional credits are also allowed for gift taxes previously paid, and for estate taxes that were previously paid on inherited wealth. The latter is phased out over ten years, in two-year intervals, from the date the wealth was inherited, and is intended to reduce the extent of (double) taxation of recently inherited wealth.

7. Moreover, in the presence of a well-functioning market for life insurance, a one-time estate tax liability at an uncertain future date can be transformed into a series of annual premium payments. In this context, it is interesting to note that the original estate tax law passed in 1916 contained a provision allowing for prepayment of estate tax liability with a 5 percent discount per year. This provision was eliminated by the Revenue Act of 1918.

8. Formally, if the marginal estate tax rate is e, the effective marginal gift tax is $e/(1 + e)$. For example, suppose the applicable estate tax rate is 50 percent and consider the implications of giving a gift or a bequest that costs the donor $15,000, including taxes. If the funds are given as an *inter-vivos* transfer, the recipient would receive $10,000, and the donor would pay gift tax of $5,000 (50 percent of $10,000). If the

ation of *inter-vivos* gifts also involves a disincentive to giving. When an appreciated asset is transferred as part of an estate, the asset's basis is "stepped up"; that is, made equal to the market value at the time of death, thus exempting from future income taxation the appreciation during the decedent's lifetime. In contrast, if the asset is given *inter vivos*, the donor's cost basis (often, but not always, the original purchase price) is "carried over" as the asset's basis. In this case, if the recipient sells the asset, capital gains that accrued before the gift was made would be taxed under the income tax.

Federal law also imposes a tax on generation-skipping transfers (GSTs). Under the estate and gift tax, a family that transferred resources over more than one generation at a time—for example, from grandparent to grand-child—could in principle reduce the number of times the wealth was subject to tax over a given period, and could greatly reduce its transfer tax liabilities. To close this avoidance mechanism, generation-skipping transfers in excess of $1 million per donor generate a separate tax, at rates up to 55 percent, beyond any applicable estate and gift tax. The GST tax raises virtually no gross revenue, but does appear to successfully close the loophole noted above.[9]

The 2001 Tax Bill

George W. Bush campaigned on a pledge to eliminate the federal estate and gift tax over a ten-year period. The bill eventually passed by Congress and signed by President Bush did eliminate it, but only during the year 2010. Between 2002 and 2009, it provides for gradual reductions in tax rates and increases in the effective exemption level.[10] For 2002, it repeals the 5 percent surtax designed to phase out the benefits of graduated rates for large estates, and increases the exemption amount to $1 million. Between 2002 and 2009, it gradually decreases the top rate to 45 percent, and increases the exemption level to $3.5 million. Finally, the credit for state estate and inheritance taxes is also phased out and replaced with a deduction for any state taxes paid.

---

funds are given as a bequest, the recipient would receive only $7,500, and the estate would owe $7,500 in taxes (50 percent of $15,000). Thus in this example, the estate tax is 50 percent of the gross-of-tax bequest; the gift tax is 50 percent of the net-of-tax gift, but only 33 percent of the gross-of-tax gift by the donor.

9. See Schmalbeck (2001). Writing from the practitioner's perspective, Sherman (1992) claims that some estate plans are designed to make use of the $1,000,000 tax exemption.

10. Under previous law the exemption level was already scheduled to gradually increase to $1 million by 2006.

The new tax law provides for the repeal of estate and generation-skipping taxes in 2010. Also in 2010, the top gift tax rate becomes the top individual income tax rate of that year; this was designed to eliminate income tax avoidance opportunities opened up by the repeal of the estate tax itself. Repeal in 2010 is followed by reinstatement in 2011. Thus if the law were to unfold as legislated, the estate tax would have a top rate of 45 percent in 2009, disappear in 2010, and return with a top rate of 55 percent in 2011 and after.

Characteristics of Estate Tax Returns

In addition to shedding light on fundamental behavior patterns of families, the estate tax also serves a more prosaic role: it generates much interesting data. However, most of the published data about estate tax returns do not distinguish between returns with a surviving spouse, and those without a surviving spouse. Moreover, in the literature, the term "bequests" usually refers to an intergenerational transfer, and only rarely is it noted that most often it is a married couple making decisions about estate planning.[11]

In 1998, roughly 98,000 estate tax returns were filed, amounting to 4.3 percent of adult (age twenty or higher) deaths in the United States in 1997.[12] Total gross estate among 1998 returns equals $173 billion, or less than 0.5 percent of privately held net worth.[13]

The size distribution of gross estates is highly skewed. The 89 percent of returns with gross estate below $2.5 million account for 53 percent of total gross estates. The 4.1 percent of estates valued in excess of $5 million account for 32 percent of gross estate value. Taxable returns, that is, returns that paid positive taxes, account for 49 percent of all returns and 59 percent of total gross estates.

Personal residence and other real estate accounts for about 19 percent of gross estates, stocks—other than closely held—bonds and cash account for 61 percent, and small businesses—closely held stock, limited partnerships, and other noncorporate business assets—account for 8 percent. Farm assets account for 0.5 percent of all gross assets in taxable estates.[14]

---

11. Michael Hurd (1994) is an exception.

12. Hoyert, Kochanek, and Murphy (1999).

13. Federal Reserve Board (2000).

14. This figure excludes farm real estate, which accounts for 2.6 percent of gross estates. The remaining amount of gross estates is in insurance, annuities, and other assets. We thank Barry Johnson for providing this information.

Deductions account for 41 percent of gross estate on average, but this ratio varies dramatically with estate size. For estates with gross assets below $1 million, deductions account for 25 percent of gross estate. For estates above $20 million, deductions are 56 percent of gross estate. The composition of deductions also changes with estate size. Bequests to surviving spouses account for between 60 and 75 percent of all deductions in each estate size category. In contrast, charitable contributions represent 11 percent of deductions for estates below $1 million, but rise to 27 percent of deductions for estates above $20 million.

Because differences in deductions relative to gross assets are the main reason why some estates are taxable and some are not, it is not surprising that deduction patterns vary by taxable status. Among taxable returns, overall deductions, spousal deductions, and charitable contributions all rise as a share of estate as estate size rises. For nontaxable returns, deductions are much higher as a proportion of estate size, and in particular, bequests to a surviving spouse are substantial. Martha Eller, Barry Johnson, and Jakob Mikow provide extensive additional data on features of decedents and asset and deduction patterns in estate tax returns.[15]

The Impact of the Estate Tax on Wealth Accumulation and Avoidance

The estate tax increases the price of bequests relative to lifetime consumption. In the simplest model, an individual decides how to allocate resources (we denote them by W) between consumption (C) and a bequest (B). Both of these choices yield utility, as represented by the utility function $u(C,B)$. The individual is subject to a budget constraint that can be expressed as $C + X = W$, where X is the total estate. The estate finances both a bequest and the estate tax $T(\cdot)$, so that it is equal to $X = B + T(X)$. This last identity defines the estate as a function of the bequest $X(B)$, and using the implicit value theorem yields $X'(B) = (1 - T')^{-1}$, that is, an increase of bequest by one dollar requires increasing the estate by $(1 - T')^{-1}$ dollars. Setting the price of consumption to be one, the relative price of bequests to consumption is therefore $(1 - T')^{-1}$, so that high marginal estate tax rates increase the relative price of bequests. This trade-off is intuitive and well understood, although it should be pointed out that due to the interaction of income and substitution effects, the theory cannot unambiguously predict whether an increase in estate tax rates would increase or decrease the size of the estate.[16]

An enormous body of work attempts to measure the impact of various aspects of the tax system on various aspects of behavior. Some of it is relevant to the question of how the estate tax affects behavior, even if the estate tax is not explicitly mentioned. For example, the literature on the effect of taxes on labor supply, which for the most part finds a fairly small aggregate labor supply elasticity with respect to the real after-tax wage, suggests that the estate tax is unlikely to have a large effect on that margin of behavior. The literature on how the income tax affects saving, which is largely inconclusive and riddled with econometric difficulties, suggests that demonstrating an impact of the estate tax on saving will be a daunting endeavor. A useful characterization of this vast literature, discussed at length in Joel Slemrod, and Alan Auerbach and Slemrod, is that behavioral response conforms to a hierarchy.[17] Short-run timing decisions are the most responsive, followed by renaming and accounting responses, while real responses, such as labor supply and saving, are the least responsive.

Although the evidence is not compelling that taxes in general significantly reduce saving, the strong presumption is that estate taxes may influence saving because the implied marginal tax rates on the return to saving from the estate and income tax can be very high. The implication is that the tax reduces significantly the after-tax return to saving done with the goal of providing an intergenerational transfer. The actual impact, though, depends on the response of both potential donors and potential inheritors to the lower after-tax return. What is known about this?

A few theoretical, or simulation, treatments address this issue. Laurence Kotlikoff and Lawrence Summers estimate that a one-dollar decline in gross transfers reduces the capital stock by about 70 cents, but they do not

---

16. Note also that the presence of various means of avoiding the estate tax does not affect this relative price. On the margin, any avoidance activity will be performed to the point where its benefit (saving on the estate tax) is equal to its cost (consisting of direct administrative and tax planning costs, possible loss of control over assets, and other distortions). Therefore, as long as the estate tax is paid, the marginal tax rate is the marginal price one should concentrate on, just as the marginal income tax rate is the focus of attention in the modern analysis of income tax distortions. See Feldstein (1999). Slemrod (2001) qualifies this statement. Applying his argument in this context, if marginal wealth accumulation reduces the marginal cost of a dollar of avoidance, the effective tax on wealth accumulation is less than the statutory rate.

17. Slemrod (1990); Auerbach and Slemrod (1997).

estimate how transfer taxes affect gross transfer levels.[18] Jordi Caballe develops an altruistic model with endogenous growth, human capital, and bequests and finds that estate taxes reduce the capital stock.[19] This model, however, focuses only on the special case where taxes on estates and on capital income have identical effects. John Laitner provides the most sophisticated model of estate taxes to date, embedding them in an overlapping generations simulation model with altruistic bequest motives.[20] He finds that removing estate taxes would have a small positive effect on the long-term ratio of capital to labor. In addition, the growth effects of removing the estate tax would not increase revenue enough to offset the revenue loss from abolishing the estate tax, so that other tax rates have to increase to maintain revenue neutrality.

William Gale and Maria Perozek argue that the impact of transfer taxes on saving depends critically on why people give transfers.[21] If bequests are unintentional, estate taxes will not affect saving by the donor, but they will reduce the net-of-tax inheritance received by the recipient and thereby raise the recipient's saving. If bequests are payment for services provided by children, the impact of taxes depends on the elasticity of parents' demand for services. If demand is inelastic, higher taxes will raise total parental expenditure on services, and thereby raise their saving. If bequests are motivated by altruism, the effects are ambiguous, but simulations suggest that the effect will be positive or zero under many circumstances.

Empirical investigation of the impact of estate taxes is sparse, and the results are not definitive. That the latter is true should not be too surprising, in light of the generally inconclusive empirical literature regarding the effect of taxes on saving in general.[22] Most relevant is Kopczuk and Slemrod, who use estate tax return data from 1916 to 1996 to explore links between changes in the estate tax rate structure and reported estates.[23] These links reflect the impact of the tax on both wealth accumulation and avoidance behavior.[24] Figure 7-1 presents a plot of the dependent variable (total

18. Kotlikoff and Summers (1981).

19. Caballe (1995).

20. Laitner (2001).

21. Gale and Perozek (2001).

22. See, for example, Bernheim (1999).

23. Kopczuk and Slemrod (2001).

24. Especially in the years before the unified estate and gift tax, avoidance may include *inter-vivos* gifts, offering another reason why changes in reported estates need not correspond to changes in intergenerational transfers.

Figure 7-1. *The Reported Estate-Wealth Ratio and Estate Tax Rates, 1917–98*

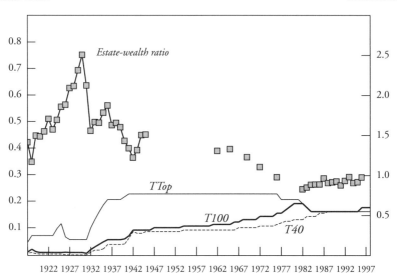

Source: Kopczuk and Slemrod (2001).

reported estates of the richest 0.5 percent of decedents, relative to aggregate wealth) and three measures of the tax rate: the top marginal tax rate (TTOP) and the tax rates evaluated at 40 and 100 times per-capita wealth in a given year (T40 and T100, respectively). This picture suggests a negative relationship between estates and the marginal tax rates. Regression analysis shows that this negative association remains, even holding constant other influences.

In pooled cross-sectional analyses that make use of individual decedent information, the relationship between the concurrent tax rate and the reported estate is fragile and sensitive to the set of variables used to capture exogenous tax rate variation. The negative effect of taxes does, however, appear to be stronger for those who die at a more advanced age and with a will, both of which are consistent with the theory of how estate taxes affect altruistic individuals. Strikingly, the tax rate that prevails at age forty-five, or ten years before death, is more clearly (negatively) associated with reported estates than the tax rate prevailing in the year of death. The estimated coefficient of the preferred specification implies that an estate tax rate of 50 percent reduces the reported estates of the richest half percent of the population by 10.5 percent when its effect is fully realized. The explanatory power of the tax rate at age forty-five suggests that future research should concentrate on developing appropriate lifetime measures of the effective tax rate.[25]

The Impact of the Estate Tax on Charitable Contributions

Because charitable bequests are deductible from the taxable estate, the estate tax lowers their price relative to a noncharitable bequest to $(1 - T')$. It also reduces the relative price of charitable donations made during life relative to a noncharitable bequest to $(1 - T')(1 - t)$, where t is the marginal income tax rate.[26] Since the total effect of the tax on charitable giving involves both income (negative) and substitution (positive) effects, determining whether the total effect is positive or negative is an empirical issue.

Econometric analysis of the impact of the estate tax on charitable bequests faces a difficult problem in distinguishing the impact of the marginal estate tax rate—which varies as a function of estate size—from the impact of variations in wealth. Charitable bequests as a fraction of the size of the gross estate increase with gross estate size. The key question is whether that empirical pattern is a result of a wealth elasticity greater than one, the result of a price elasticity, or some combination of the two. The problem is that the marginal estate tax rate is precisely, although nonlinearly, related to the taxable estate. If the taxable estate is used as the measure of wealth, the price and wealth effects can be identified only through assuming the functional form of the relationship that links these variables. Since this functional form is not known, this is an arbitrary identifying assumption.

Empirical work on charitable bequests has generally been based on a cross section of estate tax returns filed within a given year. Charitable bequests are specified simply as a function of estate size, the price of charitable bequests relative to other bequests, and other standard socioeconomic determinants of giving. Most studies calculate the marginal estate tax rate as a "first-dollar" rate, that is, the tax rate that would apply had the estate made no bequests to charity.[27]

25. Fiekowsky (1966); and Chapman, Hariharan, and Southwick (1996) also examine issues relating to the estate tax and saving.

26. These relative prices ignore the tax treatment of charitable gifts that include capital gains, and assume that the taxpayer is an itemizer for income tax purposes.

27. See Clotfelter (1985); McNees (1973); Boskin (1976); Joulfaian (1991); Auten and Joulfaian (1996); Joulfaian (2000b); and Joulfaian (2001). This "first-dollar" tax rate is sometimes used as an instrumental variable for the "last-dollar" tax rate that is presumed to determine the relative price of a charitable bequest relative to

Another important econometric issue is the treatment of spousal bequests, which are currently fully deductible in the calculation of the taxable estate. Almost all previous work calculates the marginal tax saving from a charitable bequest by assuming that spousal deductions are unchanged when charitable bequests increase: this means that nonspousal, noncharitable bequests are assumed to fall to offset the change. For a married decedent, the relative price of giving in terms of a nonspousal bequest is thus $(1 - T_1')$, where T_1' is the marginal tax rate that applies to that decedent's bequest. In terms of a spousal bequest, the relative price of a charitable bequest is exactly one, because both are deductible in calculating the taxable estate. In other words, increasing the amount of charitable bequests and exactly offsetting that with a decrease in the spousal bequest will have no effect on the estate tax liability of the first dying spouse. However, the reduced spousal bequest means that the second bequest will be lower as well—holding consumption constant—and ultimately the charitable bequest reduces the family's estate tax liability. In this case, the true relative price of a charitable bequest from the first estate would be less than one, and under a reasonable set of assumptions, the relative price becomes $(1 - T_2')$, where T_2' is the marginal estate tax rate of the surviving spouse.

Assuming that an increase in charitable bequests by a married decedent reduces the bequest to someone other than the spouse, so that its relative price is $(1 - T_1')$, helps resolve the problem of separately identifying the effects of price and wealth on giving. Because married decedents make substantial use of spousal bequests, the marginal tax (T_1') for married decedents is on average much lower for the same gross estate. This implies that if married decedents have on average lower charitable bequests relative to their gross estate (as they do), the regression analysis will tend to ascribe some of that to a price effect.

Of course, as David Joulfaian notes, being married may also affect the propensity to give in other ways besides lowering the apparent price of giving.[28] To deal with this, he separately controls for marital status in the regression analysis. The results of this exercise are revealing. Compared to married decedents, widowed decedents are estimated to have a gift-to-wealth ratio that is 11.1 percent higher, as seen in his table 6, column 1, controlling for the difference on price. The price of T_1' is estimated to have a significant independent effect on charitable bequests. When the sample is split between

---

a noncharitable wealth transfer. Note that this a separate issue from the identification problem addressed above.

28. Joulfaian (2000b).

married and unmarried decedents, the price term is not significantly different from zero for the unmarried, and the wealth term is not significantly different from zero for the married. This pattern of estimates strongly suggests that the assumption about the prevailing price is key to separately identifying the price and wealth effects.[29] It throws some doubt on the estimated price elasticity, because the effective marginal tax rate is clearer for the unmarried decedents.

The estate tax may well encourage giving during life as well. Indeed, this is precisely one of the avoidance techniques that Bernheim emphasizes could reduce both estate and income tax revenues.[30] Gerald Auten and David Joulfaian use a data set that matches the estate tax returns of 1982 decedents to both their 1981 federal income tax return and the 1981 income tax returns of their heirs.[31] They find that charitable bequests are sensitive to tax rates during life and at death. Joulfaian matches estate tax returns filed between 1996 and 1998 with the decedents' income tax returns for 1987 through 1996.[32] He notes that the relative composition of giving during life and at death changes markedly with wealth, with the extremely wealthy giving a much greater share of their contributions at death. His econometric analysis suggests that giving at death is sensitive to the marginal estate tax rate.

The difficulty of separating out price and wealth effects of the estate tax in a cross section suggests that much could be learned from examining the time-series evidence.[33] When the tax law changes, comparing data from both regimes means that families with the same wealth level faced a different set of relative prices. Their response to the different prices may help separate out the impact of the relative prices from the impact of the wealth level itself.

29. In a log-linear specification, the price elasticities remain significant when the sample is split between the married and unmarried decedents. Joulfaian (2000b) investigates two other procedures for calculating the effective tax price of charity. One calculates the marginal tax rate, setting the marital deduction to zero, with an allowance for an additional deduction of $600,000 at the spouse's death. This is justified as appropriate if the deceased retains full control over his or her estate and is certain that all spousal bequests will be transferred to the children by the surviving spouse. Finally, he calculates the tax price implied if all assets in a QTIP are planned to pass to heirs, and none are to be consumed by the spouse. To calculate this, he reduces the reported spousal bequests by the amount set aside in a QTIP and adjusts the marital deduction accordingly.

30. Bernheim (1987).

31. Auten and Joulfaian (1996).

32. Joulfaian (2001).

33. Alas, it is not likely panel data will be available in the foreseeable future.

Figure 7-2. *The Charity-Estate Ratio and Estate Tax Rates, 1916–98*

Charity-gross estate   Estate tax rate

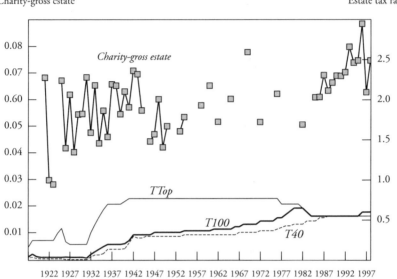

1922 1927 1932 1937 1942 1947 1952 1957 1962 1967 1972 1977 1982 1987 1992 1997

Source: Estate tax rates, Kopczuk and Slemrod (2001); other data, Internal Revenue Service, Statistics of Income Bulletins (1916–99), Washington, D.C.

Figure 7-2 shows charitable bequests as a fraction of total gross estates from the inception of the U.S. estate tax to now. The figure reveals year-to-year volatility in the ratio, as well as a noticeable upward trend over the entire period. Compare this pattern with the pattern of marginal estate tax rates, shown at the bottom of figure 7-2. The top estate tax rate has two major periods of change. The first is between 1931 and 1936, when the top rate increased from 20 percent to 70 percent. The second is from 1981 and 1984, when the top rate fell from 70 percent to 55 percent. Figure 7-2 does not reveal any clear response to either of these episodes. To be sure, inferring the relationship between taxes and reported estates is complicated, because factors other than the top estate tax rate also changed over this time. The real level of gross estate above which a return had to be filed changed, which means that the data of figure 7-2 refer to a different swath of the wealth population before and after the change. This is especially problematic because the biggest change in this threshold occurred between 1977 and 1987, when the filing threshold changed every year, increasing markedly from $120,000 to $600,000. Depending on the wealth elasticity and the price elasticity, this in itself could change the ratio of charitable bequests to total gross estates reported on estate tax returns.[34] During the same period, the top marginal estate tax rates fell from 77 percent to 55 percent. Thus it is difficult to separate out the impact of the filing threshold from the impact of the reduced marginal tax rate using only aggregate data. The analysis is further complicated because income tax rates varied markedly over this period, as well.

The following regression analysis attempts to control for some of the factors that could affect the ratio of charitable bequests to gross estates. The equations use as explanatory variables each of three measures of the marginal estate tax expressed as the logarithm of one minus the tax rate, the logarithm of one minus the top income tax rate lagged five years, the real level of total net-of-tax estates per estate tax return,[35] the ratio of estate tax returns filed to adult deaths as a measure of the effective filing threshold, and a measure of income inequality used in Kopczuk and Slemrod.[36]

The results of these ordinary-least-squares regressions are presented in table 7-1. Six separate regressions are shown, for three different measures of the estate tax rate, each with and without a linear time trend term. In the first panel of three regressions, those without a time trend, the results reveal a significant price effect. Based on the estimated coefficient using the TTOP price variable, a drop in the estate tax rate from 55 percent to 45 percent—the legislated decline between 2001 and 2010—is associated with a decline in the ratio of charitable bequests to gross estate of 0.004, or 5 percent of the 1996 value of 0.075. The regressions using the other two price variables produce similar price elasticities.

The coefficient on the log of real total net-of-tax estates per return reveals information about the wealth elasticity of charitable bequests. The first

34. Another factor is that, in part due to the changing rules regarding their tax treatment, the relative level of spousal bequests may have changed. With spousal bequests, the wealth of a family is in effect counted twice in these data. Because data on spousal bequests are not available over this entire period, this effect cannot be well controlled for.

35. In constructing this variable, we subtract from total gross estates the total amount of estate taxes before credits, on the ground that this best captures the reduction in disposable wealth due to state-levied estate and inheritance taxes. In order to remove a source of potential endogeneity, we also subtract the value of charitable bequests multiplied by the estate tax rate used in the appropriate regression; thus we are essentially disallowing the tax reductions that arise from the charitable bequests themselves. Because this variable controls for changes in purchasing power due to variations in tax rates, we can interpret the corresponding coefficient as the wealth (income) effect and the tax coefficient as the substitution effect.

36. Kopczuk and Slemrod (2001).

Table 7-1. Regressions of the Ratio of Total Charitable Bequests to Total Gross Estates Reported on Estate Tax Returns, for Three Measures of the Estate Tax: Selected Years, 1921–98[a]

	TTOP	T100	T40	TTOP	T100	T40
Log[(real value of net-of-tax estates – charity * tax rate) / returns]	0.026 (2.15)**	0.004 (0.42)	0.002 (0.18)	0.020 (1.67)	-0.006 (0.63)	0.002 (0.19)
Log(1 – TTOP)	-0.018 (2.48)**			-0.018 (2.65)**		
Log(1 – T100)		-0.017 (1.55)			0.032 (1.10)	
Log(1 – T40)			-0.022 (2.26)**			-0.025 (0.68)
Log(1 – top income tax) (5-year lag)	0.011 (3.82)***	0.005 (1.30)	0.004 (1.02)	0.005 (1.31)	0.004 (1.10)	0.004 (0.99)
Log(inequality)	-0.015 (0.99)	0.000 (0.00)	0.009 (0.43)	0.018 (0.90)	0.001 (0.03)	0.009 (0.42)
Time trend				0.000 (2.38)***	0.001 (1.82)*	0.000 (0.06)
Log(returns – deaths ratio)	0.015 (2.46)**	0.004 (0.67)	0.003 (0.65)	0.009 (1.37)	-0.003 (0.44)	0.004 (0.48)
Constant	-0.175 (1.22)	0.024 (0.23)	0.020 (0.21)	-0.235 (1.68)*	0.125 (1.08)	0.018 (0.18)
N	52	52	52	52	52	52
R^2	0.40	0.35	0.39	0.47	0.40	0.39

a. Absolute value of t statistics in parentheses. Inequality is defined as the share of income received by the top 5 percent of the income distribution, as calculated in Kopczuk and Slemrod (2001). The other variables are defined in the text.
***Significant at 1 percent.   **Significant at 5 percent.   *Significant at 10 percent.

regression, the one that uses TTOP as the measure of the estate tax, suggests that the wealth elasticity is significantly greater than one (because the ratio of charitable bequests to gross estates increases with an increase in wealth). The coefficient from the first column implies that a 10 percent increase in real after-tax wealth per return is associated with a 0.0026 increase in the charitable bequest ratio, a 3.4 percent increase over its 1996 value.[37] The magnitude of this coefficient suggests that, if the estate tax were a flat-rate tax (so that the after-tax estate was proportional to one minus the tax rate), the wealth effect would dominate the price effect; in this case, a tax decrease would increase charitable bequests, because the effect of higher disposable wealth would dominate the reduced incentive to donate disposable wealth. In reality, the estate tax is highly graduated, so for most tax reforms, the price variable will change proportionately more than the net-of-tax estate, implying that the price effect will dominate and a tax decrease would decrease charitable bequests. In any event, the second and third regressions feature a much lower estimated wealth elasticity, so that the overall predicted effect of a tax decrease in those cases is clearly to decrease charitable bequests.

The coefficient on the five-year-lagged top income tax rate is positive and significantly different from zero when the TTOP variable is used, and it is still positive although not significantly different from zero when either the T100 or T40 measure of relative price is used. The positive sign is consistent with the theory, as it implies that a higher income tax rate decreases charitable bequests by making charitable contributions during life relatively more attractive compared to charitable bequests.

The second group of three regressions highlights the importance of how one interprets the upward drift in the ratio of charitable bequests to total gross estates in figure 7-2. Recall that the critical issue is separating a price elasticity from a wealth elasticity. If the upward drift is ascribed to a wealth elasticity greater than one, then this can become part of a story that the charitable bequest to gross estate ratio was higher than otherwise when the tax rate rose beginning in 1931, and was lower than otherwise after 1981 through 1984 when the tax rate fell. Alternatively, if the upward drift in the ratio is attributed to a time trend unrelated to increasing wealth, these data shed less light. The regressions reveal that including a linear time trend as an explanatory variable eliminates the significant wealth effect when T100 and T40 are the price variables. Apparently T100 and T40 are too highly corre-

---

37. The 0.0026 is the estimated coefficient of 0.026 multiplied by a change in the logarithm of the independent variable of 0.1, corresponding to a 10 percent increase in the unlogged value.

lated with a linear time trend to confidently assert that the behavior of the charitable bequest ratio is not just an upward drift due to reasons that are not accounted for in the analysis.

Although these results are far from definitive, they offer some support for the view based on cross-section analysis that the estate tax induces more charitable bequests than would otherwise be made. The analysis surely does not account for many of the structural changes in the estate and gift tax over this period, suggesting a promising line of future research: to make use of the individual estate tax returns over time in a pooled cross-sectional analysis, while modeling the changing tax laws in more detail.

Bequests to Surviving Spouses Compared to Intergenerational Bequests

With just a few exceptions, both the theoretical and empirical investigations of how the estate and gift tax affects behavior have proceeded as if the potential bequeather is a single person who eventually dies, rather than addressing the pervasive reality of a married couple facing the eventual death of one and then, at an uncertain interval later, the other. This is in the tradition of modeling family behavior as if the spouses were a single agent maximizing a utility function that depends on their joint consumption, subject to a joint budget constraint, the so-called unitary model. But it goes beyond that, because it assumes that whatever preferences govern decisions while both spouses are alive, regardless of how these preferences are determined, are still applicable after the death of one of the spouses. It also ignores the changed situation that follows the first death, including lower consumption needs, altered preferences regarding consumption, and the acceleration of the time of expected death of the last-to-die spouse.

Unitary models are subject to increasing criticism on both theoretical and empirical grounds.[38] As Lundberg discusses, on the theoretical level, the unitary model is unable to analyze the actual or hypothetical formation and dissolution of marriages, nor can family decisions depend on conditions external to the marriage. Lundberg argues that this shortcoming is particularly important in analyzing retirement because long-term decisions must take into account the probability of widowhood. For example, since women typically live longer than men, women have more incentive than men to save for old age. On the empirical side, several recent studies have contradicted a central implication of unitary models—that the distribution of income among

38. Lundberg (1999).

family members does not affect family demands. For example, several studies have demonstrated that the larger the share of family income controlled by the mother, the greater the well-being of the children.[39]

Focusing on the disposition of the estate of the first-dying spouse is particularly intriguing for a number of reasons: From the perspective of the first-dying spouse, it is a disposal of that person's assets. However, from the perspective of the married couple, any bequests are *inter-vivos* transfers. It is also critical to understanding the effective tax margin on decisions made by both spouses of a married couple. Thus examining this issue can provide insights into the nature of lifetime and end-of-life decisions as well as into the effect of the estate tax on behavior. Additionally, marital bequest behavior may also provide insights into intra-family decisionmaking and preferences.

The Model

The simple model sketched above more accurately describes the decision of a widow or widower than that of a married individual, even though most households subject to the estate tax consist of married couples. How then should the estate of the first spouse to die be divided among a spousal bequest, a charitable bequest, and an ordinary bequest, perhaps to children? Two aspects of the tax system are relevant: First, since 1981, the estate tax has included an unlimited deduction for spousal bequests. Second, the graduated nature of the estate tax gives rise to an incentive to split the total nonspousal bequest between the two estates.

Let the value of giving be represented by the function $v(B_1, B_2)$, where B_i is the amount given by spouse i received by a child. We ignore gifts to charity for simplicity, and because they are nontaxable for both spouses their allocation among spouses has no direct estate tax consequences. A special case of this specification is $v(B_1 + B_2)$, which implies that gifts made by both spouses are perfect substitutes, so that it does not matter who leaves a bequest. Spouses, however, may have different tastes regarding transfers, in which case the gift made by a widow may be valued less by the husband. We do not take a stand on the appropriate form of the v function. One thing we explicitly allow for is that $v_1 > v_2$ *everywhere*, so that the husband prefers making a gift

---

39. Lundberg, Pollak, and Wales (1997) show that when a U.K. policy change effectively transfers ownership of the child allowance from fathers to mothers, without changing the size of the allowance, household spending on women's and children's clothing rises relative to spending on men's clothing. See also Thomas (1990, 1994).

himself rather than letting his wife do it.[40] Then the problem of the man facing the prospect of death may be expressed as

$$\max u(C_2) + v(B_1, B_2), \tag{1}$$

subject to

$$W_1 - D = B_1 + T(W_1 - D) \quad \text{and}$$
$$D + W_2 = C_2 + B_2 + T(D + W_2 - C_2), \tag{2}$$

where W_1 and W_2 are wealth controlled by the first and second spouse,
respectively, D is the bequest transferred to the second spouse, and C_2 is consumption of the widow after the husband's death.

Solving the constraints for B_1 and B_2, substituting in the objective function, and differentiating the resulting expression with respect to D yields the
first-order condition

$$-v_1(1 - T_1') + v_2(1 - T_2') + \left[u' - v_2(1 - T_2')\right]\frac{dC_2}{dD} = 0. \tag{3}$$

Here, T_1' denotes the marginal tax rate faced by the husband and T_2' by the
widow. The first two terms reflect the impact of the marital deduction on
bequests. A larger spousal bequest reduces the "regular" bequest and saves T_1'
in taxes on the margin. On the other hand, it increases the spousal bequest
and, holding C_2 constant, increases the widow's bequest at the marginal tax
cost of $(1 - T_2')$.

The third term is due to a possible difference in tastes regarding the choice
between consumption and bequests. If the widow's preferences regarding C_2
and B_2 coincide with the husband's preferences, then the last term disappears. Otherwise, the decision regarding the choice of the spousal bequest is
additionally affected by a misallocation (from the husband's point of view) of
the widow's resources.

Consistent Preferences

Consider first the case in which the spouses share the same preferences. In
this case, $u' = v_2(1 - T_2')$ and, if additionally the two types of gifts are perfect
substitutes, so that $v_1 = v_2$, the first-order condition yields

---

40. An example of such a utility function is $v(B_1 + sB_2)$, where $s < 1$. The following ignores interest rates and discounting, which could be easily added to the model
at the cost of additional notation.

$$1 - T_1' = 1 - T_2'. \tag{4}$$

The condition tells us that the two estates should be set so that the husband's marginal tax rate is equal to the wife's marginal tax rate. This plan, which is certainly not consistent with the man leaving all of his estate to the surviving wife, would fully take advantage of the opportunity of going through the graduated tax system twice.

Inconsistent Preferences

Husbands and wives may well not place the same values on bequests; the husband may trust his own judgment more than, or at least as much as, his spouse's (that is, $v_2 < v_1$). In that case, the husband would not leave as large a spousal deduction as otherwise since the condition becomes $1 - T_1' = (1 - T_2')(v_2/v_1)$. However, reasons exist to consider the opposite situation. Conditional on holding on to wealth until death, it is conceivable that not parting with resources during lifetime has an "option" value. This may be due to an uncertain lifetime of the surviving spouse and the need for financing future consumption, or it may be due to uncertainty about future healthcare and nursing costs. We will consider the implications of such types of uncertainty in what follows.

Overconsumption by the Spouse

If the widow does not trade off consumption and her own bequest exactly as her deceased husband would like her to, then the second term, $[u' - v_2(1 - T_2')]dC_2/dD$, becomes relevant.[41] If the husband believes his wife will overconsume, increasing the spousal bequest reduces utility. Thus the spousal bequest should be lower than otherwise.

Kinks in the Tax Function

We have proceeded thus far as if the tax function were differentiable. This is not the case in practice; in fact, the estate tax schedule is piecewise linear. One consequence of piecewise linearity is that husbands are likely to choose their marital deduction to be at the kinks of the tax function.[42] The most drastic jump in the marginal tax rate is at the point when the estate exceeds the exemption level and becomes subject to the tax, where the marginal tax

41. This term vanishes also when $dC_2/dD = 0$.

42. In the certainty case, kinks in the spouse's tax schedule should matter as well. In practice, however, due to the uncertainty of the time of death, this is only a theoretical curiosity.

rate schedule begins at 41 percent. The necessary condition for the marital
deduction to wipe out all of the husband's tax is

$$v_1\left(1-t^0\right) \leq v_2\left(1-T_2'\right) + \left[u' - v_2\left(1-T_2'\right)\right]\frac{dC_2}{dD},$$ (5)

where t^0 is the initial marginal tax. Limiting attention to the case without
overconsumption by the spouse (overconsumption additionally reduces the
incentive for using the spousal bequest deduction), this condition states that
$1 - t^0 \leq (1 - T_2')v_2/v_1$. Given that under the progressive tax schedule $t^0 \leq T_2'$,
it requires that $v_2/v_1 \geq 1$. In other words, for the husband to split a bequest
so as not to face any tax liability, what is required is a *preference* for postponing gifts until the wife's death.

Interaction with Other Taxes

One tax wrinkle ignored in the discussion above is that postponing estate
taxation by means of a spousal bequest allows for potentially tax-free accumulation of capital gains between the death of the husband and the death of
the widow. When an asset is transferred by the husband to a child, the child
assumes the asset's current value as the tax basis for measuring future capital
gains taxes. If instead the transfer is postponed until the death of the widow,
its then-current value will become the asset's basis, effectively allowing for the
accumulation of capital gains tax-free during the period between the spouses'
deaths. This strategy is valuable especially if the potential beneficiary does
not plan to sell the asset during this period.

   This may be a nontrivial benefit that can in some situations offset the
potential estate tax savings from estate splitting.[43] The precise value of it
depends on the number of factors, including expected future accumulation,
the expected frequency of reinvestment, the expected time between spouses'
deaths, and the capital gains tax rate. Denote the marginal cost of any additional capital gains tax if the asset is transferred to the child immediately by g,
and introduce it in the model as an additional cost of the husband's transfer,
so that

$$W_1 - D = B_1 + gB_1 + T(W_1 - D).$$ (6)

43. For example, the capital gains effect can dominate the estate splitting effect for
those very rich individuals who do not face significant progressivity, because the marginal tax rate for high estates is constant.

This decreases the net-of-tax rate to $(1 - T_1)/(1 + g)$ or, in other words, increases the cost of a transfer from T_1' to $(g + T_1')/(1 + g)$. It clearly reduces the benefit from transferring funds from the first-to-die spouse to the children, and therefore acts to increase the optimal spousal bequest. In particular, in the baseline case of no overconsumption, it yields

$$1 - T_1' = \left(1 - T_2'\right)\left(1 + g\right)\frac{v_2}{v_1} . \tag{7}$$

Even when the husband prefers making gifts himself, it can no longer be assumed that the marginal tax rate of the first spouse should exceed that of the second because the magnitude of g matters. The presence of this effect provides an incentive to increase the spousal bequest.[44] However, it does not imply transferring everything to the spouse, except for couples that are not much above the tax-paying threshold.[45]

Uncertainty

To address uncertainty, assume that the utility function is time-separable, and allow for uncertainty regarding future well-being, so that $v(B_1)$ + $E[m_i w(B_2)] + E[\Sigma d_i u(C_i)]$, where $E[\cdot]$ denotes the expectation operator, $w(\cdot)$ is the utility from bequests, and $d_i = 1$ (and $m_i = 1$) in the case of survival until (death in) period I and is equal to zero otherwise. The uncertainty considered here may pertain to the timing of death, as well as to various other

---

44. A qualification concerning the role of charitable bequests is in order. Charitable bequests are nontaxable and, because charities do not pay the capital gains tax, $g = 0$. The calculations sketched below apply to the level of wealth that is intended to be transferred to children or other taxable beneficiaries.

45. The upper limit for the value of g is the top (long-term) capital gains tax rate, which is now 20 percent. Abstract from the taste issue by assuming that $v_1 = v_2$. There is no benefit to estate splitting if $(1 - T_{min})/(1 + g) > (1 - T_{max})$, where T_{min} is the lowest marginal tax rate and T_{max} is the tax rate if all money over the exemption level is transferred to the spouse. In practice, until 2001 $T_{min} = .37$ and with $g = .2$ the left-hand side of this expression is .525. Therefore, the first spouse should pay no tax only if the transfer to the surviving spouse results in a tax rate below 47.5 percent. This is approximately the tax rate that applies to an estate of about $2 million. This limiting value applies only if the whole value of the asset consists of capital gains that had appreciated since the husband's death. Usually, g will be significantly below this top value.

events such as realizations of health care costs or financial variables.[46] C is a vector of future consumption. Expressed in this way, the solution to the spousal bequest problem is analogous to the one before:

$$-v'\frac{1-T_1'}{1+g} + E\left[w'\left(1-T_2'\right)\right] + E\left[\sum d_i\left(u_i' - m_i w'\left(1-T_2'\right)\right)\frac{dC_i}{dD}\right] = 0, \quad (8)$$

and the interpretation is similar to the certainty case. The last term is nonzero when the widow has different preferences on the consumption or bequest margin from the deceased husband. When their preferences are identical, the first-order condition becomes

$$1-T_1' = E\left[\left(1-T_2'\right)\frac{w'}{v'}\right], \quad (9)$$

which means that expected tax minimization applies except that future taxes are weighted by the marginal rate of substitution between the own and the spousal bequest. Introducing uncertainty may change the benefit to postponing giving, depending on the convexity-concavity of $(1 - T_2')w'$. In fact, with T_2', a step function that is neither convex nor concave, it is not clear whether the effect is positive or negative.

Availability of QTIP Trusts

At the same time as the unlimited marital deduction was introduced in 1981, Congress also introduced the QTIP exception to the rule that "terminable interest property" does not qualify for the deduction. Under a QTIP trust, the husband's estate is formally transferred to the widow. The widow must be given access to the earnings of the trust, but can be prevented from accessing the principal. The principal in the trust is transferred to ultimate beneficiar-

---

46. A separate consideration involves what is sometimes called the "peso" problem: the small probability of an event with a huge impact occurring, such that the effect on utility dominates the small probability. As an example, consider the possibility of a terminal illness that might be potentially cured if a sufficient amount of money is devoted to research. Such a possibility may not play any role in the plans of a typical individual, but may affect the decision of a rich, optimistic, and possibly eccentric person who would consider spending such an amount, as it creates a strong incentive not to part with wealth. Such events do not fit in the framework of our model, because they require that individuals be able to affect the chance of their death. They also require taking a stand about the form of utility from being alive.

ies at the death of the surviving spouse according to the will of the husband who originally elected to set up the trust. The tax consequences are exactly as with a regular spousal bequest: wealth put in the QTIP trust is taxed upon death of the widow. As pointed out by Johnson, Mikow, and Eller, and elaborated in the empirical section that follows, QTIP trusts are heavily used in practice.[47]

Why would a husband want to restrict the options of his wife in this way? One benefit of using the QTIP from the point of view of the husband is that he decides about the ultimate destination of the gift.[48] On the margin, this is valued as the difference between his value of giving and the value of his wife's giving, $v_1 - v_2$. Apart from that, the QTIP decreases the resources available to the spouse, which affects the magnitude of the overconsumption problem. There is, to be sure, the alternative of making a bequest to children, and transferring to the wife only what is truly intended to be transferred. In the context of our model, denoting the amount of money put in the QTIP trust by Q, the constraints of the individual optimization become

$$W_1 - D + Q = B_1 + T\left(W_1 - D\right),$$
$$D - Q + W_2 = C_2 + B_2 + T\left(D + W_2 - C_2\right),$$
$$D \geq Q \geq 0. \tag{10}$$

The first-order condition for the interior choice of Q is

$$v_1 - v_2 + \left[u' - v_2\left(1 - T_2'\right)\right]\frac{dC_2}{dQ} = 0. \tag{11}$$

When C_2 is a normal good and the widow is overconsuming, the last term in equation 11 is positive (because both factors are positive). If, as is likely, $v_1 - v_2 > 0$, the left-hand side of equation 11 is always positive and no interior solution exists: all of the spousal bequest should be in the form of a QTIP. In the baseline case of consistent tastes and no overconsumption, all of the terms in the above condition are zero and a QTIP accomplishes nothing and costs nothing.

---

47. Johnson, Mikow, and Eller (2001).

48. Of course, QTIPs could be used for other reasons. For example, they may be used to prevent a spouse who is financially inexperienced from making mistakes. See Sherman (1992) for a discussion of various circumstances that motivate the use of QTIPs. See also Madoff, Tenney, and Hall (2001, ch. 6) for the discussion of legal options in marital estate planning.

Without the availability of QTIPs, tax minimization is inextricably tied up with the decision about the transfer of resources to the spouse, and a trade-off between the two must be made. The QTIP option allows for separating these two decisions. Thus the spousal bequest can be selected so that taxes are minimized, and the QTIP implements the division of resources between bequests of both spouses. As a result, the estate tax does not affect the balance of power within the family.[49]

In sum, the graduated nature of the estate tax introduces an incentive to split the estate in order to go through the tax schedule twice. The incentive to do so would be weakened if the spousal bequest entailed losing control over who is going be the ultimate beneficiary. It is also weakened by the likelihood that the spouse will use intended intergenerational bequests for her own benefit. The effect of uncertainty is not clear. The availability of QTIPs resolves anxiety about the loss of control and overconsumption and restores tax minimization as the correct objective. An additional factor is the potential for avoiding capital gains taxes on the gains that accrue between the deaths of the two spouses. This effect increases the potential tax benefit to spousal bequests, but it is arguably not big enough to justify using the full marital deduction, with the exception of taxpayers who are only slightly above the filing threshold. Despite these offsetting considerations, tax minimization is a fairly robust prediction of the theory. We next confront these predictions with the data.

Basic Facts about the Estates of First-Dying and Surviving Spouses

Bernheim explores the sensitivity to estate tax provisions of the timing of transfers to one's ultimate heirs by comparing estate tax return data from 1977 and 1983.[50] Most of the former data are for estates treated under 1976 law, before the changes in the Tax Reform Act of 1976, and most of the latter data concern returns taxed under the Economic Recovery Tax Act of 1981, which removed the limitations on marital deductions. He finds that among estates with an approximately similar value, in 1977 married individuals left 48 cents out of every dollar to their spouses, but by 1983 this figure had

---

49. Similar reasoning applies when there is a corner solution for the marital deduction or for the QTIP. Interestingly, the QTIP not only implements the husband's objectives, but it also can reduce the welfare of the spouse. In our model, the QTIP simply increases spousal tax liability and, if it fully offsets the marital deduction, it does not bring any benefits to the spouse. In practice, the QTIP provides income to the spouse that, at least partially, compensates for the increase in tax liability.

50. Bernheim (1987).

increased to 59 cents. This change could be due to the introduction of the unlimited marital deduction. He also finds that the fraction of married individuals who claimed deductions for spousal bequests rose from 90 percent to 95 percent. This increase is not likely to be due to the increase in tax-free spousal bequests, but it is consistent with the lower estate tax rates in 1983 reducing the penalties associated with transferring wealth first to one's spouse, and then, upon the spouse's death, to one's children.

If the increased spousal bequests are not offset somehow, one would expect to see, over time, an increase in the share of decedents' wealth held by widowed decedents.[51] In 1983, married decedents accounted for 53.5 percent of estate tax returns and 56.7 percent of total estate value, while widowed decedents represented 36.1 percent and 33.0 percent of returns and estate value, respectively. By 1998, the proportions were dramatically different. Married decedents accounted for 43.9 percent of returns and 48.3 percent of total gross estate value, while widowed decedents accounted for 43.7 percent of returns and 40.9 percent of gross estate value. What we do not know, but would like to know, is whether this means that intergenerational transfers have been postponed.[52]

The second issue is whether the data are consistent with the tax-minimizing behavior our model predicts. We focus on the differences between the estate tax returns of the married and widowed decedents, shown in panel B and panel C of table 7-2. In 1998, these categories compose 43.9 percent and 43.7 percent of the total returns filed, respectively, and 48.3 percent and 40.9 percent of total gross estates, respectively. Notably, for the married decedents, spousal bequests are 58.8 percent of the total gross estate, and fully 86.5 percent (37,146 out of a total of 42,939) of the returns are nontaxable, predominantly because deductible spousal bequests push the taxable estate below the tax threshold. In fact, nontaxable returns constitute a significant share of all returns of married decedents even for the very rich, although their frequency falls with the size of gross estate. In particular, they are very

---

51. For example, by increased consumption by the spouse.

52. The Statistics of Income Division of the Internal Revenue Service publishes a voluminous amount of aggregated data from estate tax returns. However, in recent years none of these data differentiate the returns filed for married decedents from others. As table 7-2 shows, this differentiation reveals several interesting patterns. The top panel of table 7-2 aggregates all estate tax returns, while the next three panels disaggregate these data into categories depending on the marital status of the decedent: married, widowed, and single. We thank Barry Johnson of SOI for providing us with these data for 1998.

Table 7-2. Gross Estate, Spousal Bequests, Charitable Deductions, and Net Estate, by Marital Status of Decedents, 1998 [a]

	Gross estate, tax purposes		Bequests to surviving spouse			Charitable deductions			Net estate tax		
	Number	Amount (millions)	Number	Amount (millions)	Gross estate (percent)	Number	Amount (millions)	Gross estate (percent)	Number	Amount (millions)	Gross estate (percent)
Panel A. All decedents											
Total	97,868	173.8	41,463	49.4	28.4	16,983	10.9	6.3	47,483	20.3	11.7
Taxable	47,483	103.0	5,051	10.7	10.4	10,476	5.6	5.4	47,483	20.3	19.7
Nontaxable	50,385	70.8	36,412	38.7	54.7	6,507	5.3	7.5	0	0	0
Panel B. Married decedents only											
Total	42,939 (43.9)	84.0 (48.3)	41,463	49.4	58.8	2,506	1.5	1.8	5,793	3.7	4.4
Taxable	5,793	25.9	5,051	10.7	41.3	849	1.2	4.6	5,793	3.7	4.4
Nontaxable	37,146	58.1	36,412	38.7	66.6	1,658	0.3	0.5	0	0	0
Panel C. Widowed decedents only											
Total	42,722 (43.7)	71.1 (40.9)	0	0	0	10,590	6.9	9.7	32,938	13.8	19.4
Taxable	32,938	61.9	0	0	0	7,169	3.5	5.7	32,938	13.8	22.3
Nontaxable	9,384	9.2	0	0	0	3,421	3.4	37.0	0	0	0
Panel D. Single decedents only											
Total	12,156 (12.4)	18.7 (10.8)	0	0	0	3,887	2.5	13.4	8,751	2.9	15.5
Taxable	8,751	15.2	0	0	0	2,458	0.9	5.9	8,751	2.9	19.1
Nontaxable	3,405	3.5	0	0	0	1,428	0.3	8.6	0	0	0

a. Tabulations provided to authors by Barry Johnson of the IRS Statistics of Income Division. Numbers in parentheses are percentages for all decedents.

common in the $1 million to $10 million range, where estate splitting produces significant tax savings. Our model predicts such behavior only for couples that plan to leave only a small taxable bequest, and therefore the prediction of tax minimization does not appear to be supported by the data. Too little tax is paid by the first-dying spouse.

Spousal bequests also have implications for the proper calculation of the effective tax rate imposed on families' estates. According to table 7-2, the effective average tax rate is much lower for the married decedents: 4.4 percent for that group compared to 19.4 percent for the widowed decedents. An approximation of the average tax rate on families is obtained by calculating the ratio of the tax paid by both married and widowed taxpayers to the sum of the total gross estate of both groups net of spousal bequests. This procedure yields $17.5 billion ($3.7 + $13.8) divided by $105.7 billion ($84.0 billion + $71.1 billion − $49.4 billion), or 16.6 percent. This rate is significantly higher than the apparent overall average tax rate of 11.7 percent shown in panel A of table 7-2, and it is a more appropriate estimate of the overall average tax rate imposed on families' estates.

Table 7-3 presents the distribution of estate tax returns and gross estates by marital status and gender. In any given year, about the same number of men and women die, but as late as 1983, 61.3 percent (38,774 out of a total of 63,251) of estate tax returns were filed by men, representing 64.4 percent of total estate value. Because of the well-known longevity of women, it is perhaps less surprising to observe the relationship between gender and marital status at death. Within the population of estate tax filers, in 1983 only 18.7 percent (6,538 of 34,972) of ever-married males died as widowers, while 75.1 percent (16,284 of 21,685) of ever-married females died as widows. Note that this may simply reflect a bias in which spouse holds family wealth.

Table 7-3 documents that perhaps partly due to increased spousal bequests, the percentage of estates held by females has risen by more than one-fifth since the early 1980s. The share of gross estates held by females increased from 35.6 percent in 1983 to 42.9 percent in 1998. Most of this increase can be explained by the increase in the share of estates held by widowed individuals, who are predominantly female. Over this period, the composition of decedents' estates also shifted among married couples. Among married decedents, in 1983, 14.2 percent ($4.07 billion of $28.6 billion) of estates were held by females; by 1998, this had risen to 20.7 percent ($17.4 billion of $84.0 billion). This trend is consistent with the parallel trend of increasing female labor force participation and earnings, which would in itself probably increase the amount of wealth held by women.

Table 7-3. *Distribution of Estate Tax Returns and Gross Estate, By Marital Status, and Gender of the Decedent, 1983, 1989, and 1998*[a]

		All		Male		Female	
		Returns	*Gross estate (thousands)*	*Returns*	*Gross estate (thousands)*	*Returns*	*Gross estate (thousands)*
All	1983	63,251	50,390,376	38,774	32,429,386 (64.4)	24,478	17,960,990 (35.6)
	1989	50,376	87,171,506	28,031	52,273,459 (59.7)	22,345	34,898,047 (40.3)
	1998	97,868	173,817,315	52,015	99,332,317 (57.1)	45,854	74,484,818 (42.9)
Married	1983	33,835	28,552,205 (56.7)	28,434	24,484,130 (48.5)	5,401	4,068,075 (8.1)
	1989	23,897	44,748,218 (51.3)	18,554	36,172,087 (41.5)	5,343	8,576,131 (9.8)
	1998	42,939	83,987,450 (48.3)	32,253	66,579,251 (38.3)	10,687	17,408,199 (10.0)
Widowed	1983	22,822	16,643,974 (33.0)	6,538	4,792,632 (9.5)	16,284	11,851,342 (23.5)
	1989	20,342	32,128,779 (36.9)	6,075	9,799,980 (11.2)	14,267	22,328,799 (25.6)
	1998	42,772	71,092,804 (40.9)	13,509	22,361,078 (12.9)	29,264	48,731,725 (28.0)
Single	1983	4,171	3,164,920 (6.3)	n.a.	n.a.	n.a.	n.a.
	1989	3,952	6,116,650 (11.8)	2,153	3,782,278 (4.3)	1,799	2,334,374 (2.7)
	1998	12,150	18,736,881 (10.8)	6,253	10,391,987 (6.0)	5,903	8,344,894 (4.8)

Source: IRS Statistics of Income publications: 1983 and 1989. Barry Johnson of the SOI has provided 1998 data to the authors from tabulations.
a. Gross estate is measured in thousands of dollars. The term *n.a.* means that in that year the data were not classified into that category. Figures in parentheses are the gross estate in that category as a percentage of the gross estate in that year for all returns.

QTIPs

The fact that female decedents now account for a larger fraction of estates does not necessarily mean that they now exercise greater control over the disposition of wealth. As discussed earlier, for property to qualify as QTIP, the trust must provide a "qualifying income interest for life" to the surviving spouse, meaning that all trust income must be paid to the surviving spouse. Property qualifying as QTIP must be included in the value of the surviving spouse's estate.

As Johnson, Mikow, and Eller detail, QTIPs are now widely used.[53] For 1995 decedents, 27,066 married male decedents left bequests to surviving spouses, amounting to $33.5 billion. Of this total, 11,322 reported a QTIP trust, which totaled $16.4 billion. Among the decedents, 8,329 female married decedents left spousal bequests, totaling $7.4 billion. Of this total, 2,784 had QTIPs valued at $3.2 billion. Thus men were more likely to restrict the use of a spousal bequest through a QTIP: 41.8 percent of men used one, composing 49.0 percent of the value of their spousal bequests. Only 33.4 percent of women with a spousal bequest used one, covering 43.2 percent of the total spousal bequests.

Why are QTIP trusts so often used? As delineated in our model, one role they can play is restricting the spouse's control over assets. Whether this is an intended objective of the majority of QTIPs cannot be ascertained using our data, because QTIPs may (but do not have to) allow the surviving spouse to access more than the interest on principal. We expect that many QTIP trusts do in fact restrict decisions of the spouses. To the extent they do, this casts additional doubt on a unitary model of transfer behavior, but it is consistent with a number of alternative hypotheses, such as heterogeneous preferences regarding such issues as the most preferred charity; consumption versus bequests, and remarriage; or paternalistic preferences (the widow or widower may be perceived as being unable to handle financial matters).

As addressed in the discussion of our theoretical model, using QTIPs allows for greater flexibility in pursuing tax minimization strategies. Therefore, it is surprising to observe that although QTIPs are commonly used, the prediction of tax minimization does not seem to hold.[54]

53. Johnson, Mikow, and Eller (2001).

54. This conclusion is strengthened by the fact that nondeductible, that is, taxable, bequests of the first-dying spouse can be structured, using trust instruments, so that the surviving spouse can have limited access to the income and principal. As with the QTIP, this possibility weakens the connection between the tax minimization

Charitable Bequest Patterns by Marital Status and Gender

The patterns of charitable bequests vary markedly by marital status. The ratio of charity to gross estate is highest among the never-married taxpayers, at 13.4 percent, as seen in table 7-2. This is consistent with the hypothesis that noncharity heirs have a smaller pull on the resources of single, and presumably mostly childless, individuals. Among individuals married at one time, charitable bequests tend to be postponed until the second death. For married decedents, charitable bequests make up only 1.5 percent of gross estates, compared to 9.7 percent for widowed decedents. Even comparing charitable bequests to gross estate net of spousal bequests yields an average ratio of only 4.3 percent for married decedents. Note the striking contrast to the evidence from income tax returns that married individuals give more to charity than unmarried individuals, including in the year before the date of death.[55] Of course, the use of aggregate evidence to suggest that charitable behavior depends on marital status may be misleading if groups differ in other ways, such as the average level of wealth and the after-tax price of giving for a widowed decedent.

According to Eller, females are much more likely to have some charitable bequest, 23.4 percent compared to 13.7 percent for male 1992 decedents.[56] The recipient of charitable bequests also varies systematically by the gender of the donor. For male decedents, private foundations composed 37.6 percent of gifts, compared to only 18.7 percent for female decedents. Females gave much more to religious organizations: 14.3 percent versus 5.4 percent for men; and to educational, medical, and scientific organizations: women gave 34.5 percent versus 21.5 percent for men. The systematic gender differences in charitable giving patterns suggest that to the extent that the estate tax induces changes in the effective control over wealth, it will affect the volume and pattern of charitable giving.

Conclusion

The U.S. estate and gift tax significantly affects the relative reward of consumption, charitable giving, and bequests for those Americans prosperous

---

strategy and who may benefit from the bequest, and it makes the apparent failure of people to pursue tax minimization all the more puzzling. We are grateful to Ray Madoff for clarifying this issue for us.

55. See Randolph (1995) regarding giving during life; and Auten and Joulfaian (1996) on giving in the year before death.

56. Eller (1997).

5

WEALTH ACCUMULATION AND TRANSFERS OF THE RICH 245

enough to have wealth that exceeds the large exemption level. How it affects behavior depends on the motivation for bequests and charity, as well as how much people are willing to substitute among bequests, charity, and consumption when their relative prices change. Understanding the behavioral response is relevant to assessing the tax itself and possible reform, but also to shedding light on such critical economic issues as intergenerational altruism and rational behavior toward future, uncertain, and even existential events.

Sparked partly by the legislative attention to the estate tax, recently several studies have tried to assess the effect of the tax on wealth accumulation, *inter-vivos* giving, and charitable donations. Among the important tentative—and we emphasize tentative—conclusions are:

—The estate tax reduces the accumulation of estates—or at least the reporting of estates—by as much as 10.5 percent among the richest 0.5 percent of wealth owners.

—The estate tax increases charitable bequests by as much as 12 percent.

—In spite of substantial tax reasons to favor *inter-vivos* gifts over bequests, *inter-vivos* gifts, or at least those reported to the IRS, are small relative to bequests.[57]

This paper adds to the existing literature in two ways: First, it uses the time-series variation in tax rates to help separate out the price and wealth elasticities of charitable giving, providing corroborating evidence that the estate tax increases charitable bequests. Our preliminary results suggest that the effect could be larger than the 12 percent figure cited above. Second, it explores bequest decisions by married couples. The patterns of bequests among spouses suggest that the inter-spousal division of assets is responsive to tax considerations. However, nondeductible, that is, intergenerational, bequests of the first-dying spouse are much lower than a tax minimization strategy would dictate. This is so even though tax minimization appears to be a robust prediction of theory. Moreover, the evidence is inconsistent with a unitary model of behavior, in which the two spouses have identical tastes.

Taken together, these findings have implications for both estate tax policy and for more general economic controversies. Estate tax policy must confront the classic trade-off between equity and efficiency. Although the tax is by far the most progressive tax in the federal tax portfolio, it does have economic costs associated with reduced wealth accumulation, increased avoidance and evasion, or both. It probably also has the arguably socially beneficial impact of increasing charitable giving. To the extent that the tax reduces wealth

57. This finding, not discussed in this paper, is addressed in Poterba (2001) and elsewhere.

accumulation, it no doubt also reduces the concentration of wealth but in contrast to collecting tax from the most well-to-do without behavioral repercussion, it exacts some cost.

More generally, the results shed new light on the role of altruism, both intergenerational, interspousal, and with respect to charities. The responsiveness of estate planning to the price of intergenerational transfers is consistent with altruism—if bequests were accidental and unvalued, they would not be price-responsive.[58] However, some of the new evidence deepens the puzzle over why, if intergenerational transfers are motivated by altruism, they seem to be postponed to an extent that, for tax reasons, significantly reduces the eventual after-tax transfer. This phenomenon, which has previously been observed with respect to *inter-vivos* gifts, seems also to characterize the transfers made by married couples. Even more puzzling is that this strategy does not significantly benefit spouses because spousal bequests very often take the form of QTIP trusts that can be used to restrict the control of the spouse over their use. This suggests the need for future research that addresses intrafamily dynamics and the strategic interactions between spouses and children.

Appendix: Summary History of U.S. Estate and Gift Taxes

The modern estate tax began with the passage of the Revenue Act of 1916. That act imposed a tax on the estate of a decedent at rates ranging from 1 percent for net estates of up to $50,000 to 10 percent on net estates over $5 million. The law provided an exemption of $50,000 and permitted the value of the estate to be reduced by the amount of funeral and administration expenses, debts, losses, and claims against the estate. Under the 1916 law, the value of an estate for tax purposes equaled the fair market value of the decedent's property at death. The value of the estate was increased by certain lifetime transfers, including transfers made in contemplation of death.

Congress made numerous changes to the estate tax at various times from 1917 through 1926. The Revenue Act of 1917 increased rates by one-half, and later in 1917, Congress added two new rate brackets at the high end of the rate scale. At the end of 1917, estate tax rates ranged from 2 percent on net estates of less than $50,000 to 25 percent on net estates greater than $10 million. The Revenue Act of 1918 reduced the tax rates on estates of less than $1 million. The 1918 law also made charitable contributions deductible

---

58. It is conceivable that bequests are not valued but are price responsive, because they are useful as a strategic device to extract utility during life.

in computing the taxable estate, and broadened the tax base to include, among other items, the value of any property subject to a general power of appointment held by the decedent. In 1924 Congress increased the tax rates to a top rate of 40 percent on net estates of more than $10 million and instituted a gift tax—that is, a tax on gifts made during a person's lifetime. The new gift tax had the same rate schedule as the estate tax and permitted a lifetime exclusion of $50,000 in gifts and an annual exclusion of $500 in gifts per recipient. The 1924 changes also included certain adjustments to the estate tax base, and the granting of a credit against up to 25 percent of the federal estate tax liability for estate taxes imposed by states. In 1926, the gift tax was repealed. In that year, Congress also reduced estate tax rates, so that rates ranged from 1 percent on net estates under $50,000 to 20 percent on net estates of more than $10 million. It also increased the exemption from $50,000 to $100,000 and raised the maximum credit for state estate taxes from 25 percent to 80 percent of the federal estate tax liability.

The Revenue Act of 1932 increased estate tax rates at nearly all levels and added two new tax brackets for large estates. After the 1932 changes, rates ranged from 1 percent on net estates up to $100,000 to 45 percent on net estates of more than $10 million. The 1932 law also reduced the exemption to its 1924 level of $50,000, and reintroduced the gift tax and set rates at three-quarters of the estate tax rates. The new gift tax allowed a lifetime exclusion of $50,000 and an annual exclusion of $5,000 per recipient.

The Revenue Act of 1934 raised the maximum rate to 60 percent on net estates over $10 million, and the Revenue Act of 1935 further increased the highest rate to 70 percent on net estates of more than $50 million. The 1935 law reduced the estate tax exemption and the lifetime gift tax exemption to $40,000 each. The Revenue Act of 1940 imposed a 10 percent surtax on income, estate, and gift taxes. Another round of rate increases came in the Revenue Act of 1941: rates now ranged from 3 percent on net estates of $5,000 or less to 77 percent on net estates over $50 million. During this period, gift tax rates stayed at three-quarters of the estate tax rates.

Among other changes, the Revenue Act of 1942 increased the estate tax exemption to $60,000 and reduced the lifetime gift tax exclusion to $30,000 and the annual exclusion to $3,000 per recipient. The Revenue Act of 1948 introduced the estate and gift tax marital deductions. This change was intended to equalize the tax treatment of couples from non-community-property states with those from community-property states. The estate tax marital deduction permitted a decedent's estate to deduct the value of property passing to a surviving spouse. The deduction was, however, limited to one-half of the decedent's adjusted gross estate—that is, the gross estate less debts and administrative expenses—and community property was ineligible for the marital deduction. The gift tax marital deduction similarly allowed a donor spouse to deduct one-half of the amount of an interspousal gift, other than a gift of community property.

After 1948, few changes were made to the estate and gift tax laws until Congress passed the important Tax Reform Act of 1976. First, the 1976 act created a unified estate and gift tax framework: the law imposed a single graduated rate of tax on both lifetime gifts and testamentary dispositions. (Before the unified framework was established, gifts made during life were taxed at lower rates than gifts made at death.) Second, the 1976 act merged the estate tax exclusion and the lifetime gift tax exclusion into a single, unified estate and gift tax credit, which could be used to offset a donor's gift tax liability during his lifetime and, if not entirely used at death, could be used to offset the deceased donor's estate tax liability. The 1976 law retained the $3,000 annual, per recipient gift tax exclusion. The 1976 act also instituted a tax on generation-skipping transfers designed to ensure that transfers of wealth were taxed at each generation. It also increased the estate tax marital deduction available for certain taxpayers. The maximum deduction was increased to the greater of one-half of the adjusted gross estate or $250,000.

The Economic Recovery Tax Act (ERTA) of 1981 eliminated the quantitative limits on the amount of estate and gift tax deductions available for interspousal transfers, instead allowing unlimited tax-free interspousal transfers. ERTA also permitted a marital deduction for transfers of property in which the decedent's spouse had a life interest that was not terminable (property for which the spouse did not have the power to appoint beneficiaries at his death), so long as the property was "qualified terminable interest property"—that is, property in which the surviving spouse had the sole right to all income during life, but over which he had no power to transfer the property at death.

ERTA also raised the unified estate and gift tax credit from $47,000 to $192,800 over a six-year phase-in period. This increased credit effectively raised the tax exemption for estates and gifts from $175,000 to $600,000. ERTA also raised the annual gift tax exclusion to $10,000 per recipient and allowed an unlimited annual exclusion for payment of a recipient's tuition or medical expenses. And ERTA reduced the top tax rate on estates, gifts, and generation-skipping transfers from 70 to 50 percent for transfers of more than $2.5 million. The rate reduction was to be phased in over a four-year period, but legislation in 1984 and 1987 delayed the decrease in the top tax rate from 55 to 50 percent until after the end of 1992. The 1987 Act also introduced a phase-out of the initial exemption by imposing a higher 60 percent tax rate for taxable estates between $10 million and $21.4 million. In 1993, Congress decided not to decrease the top tax rates to 50 percent, retroactive to December 31, 1992.

COMMENT BY
Ray D. Madoff

Wojciech Kopczuk and Joel Slemrod, in their important and nuanced research, analyze estate tax returns to assess the effect of estate taxes on wealth accumulation, the timing of intergenerational transfers, and the volume and timing of charitable giving. While the questions they tackle are important, the answers are difficult to obtain because some of the data involving spousal and intergenerational transfers give the appearance of offering more information than they in fact do.

What We Can—and Can't—Learn from Analyzing Tax Returns

Estate tax returns provide an enormous amount of information about the amount and type of assets that people own at death and the timing of taxable transfers made during life. Moreover, since they are typically prepared after a careful review of all assets and signed under penalties of perjury, the information reported on returns is likely to be more reflective of truth than information obtained from people's memories.[59] Estate tax returns appear to provide significant information about people's dispositive plans in that estate tax returns include:

   —How much is included in a person's gross estate;
   —How much of a marital deduction has been claimed; and
   —How much of a charitable deduction has been claimed.

From this information, it is natural to draw the following conclusions:

   —The amount included in the decedent's gross estate reflects the value of all property owned or controlled by the taxpayer;

   —The amount claimed as a marital deduction reflects the amount transferred for the benefit of the decedent's spouse,

   —The amount claimed as a charitable deduction reflects the amount transferred for the benefit of charity; and

   —The amounts that are included in the gross estate that are not eligible for the charitable or marital deduction reflect transfers to other noncharitable beneficiaries (typically the decedent's children)

59. The executor of the decedent's estate is assigned the task of preparing the estate tax return in I.R.C. §6018.

As tempting and natural as these conclusions are—with the exception of the third assumption involving charitable transfers—they are not necessarily accurate.[60] The reason is that the governing statutory structure offers a tremendous amount of pliancy such that:

—A person can have a great deal of control and access to property, and that property will not necessarily be included in his gross estate for tax purposes;

—A transfer can qualify for the marital deduction, and the surviving spouse may have only limited access to the property; and,

—Even when a transfer is not eligible for the marital deduction, the surviving spouse may have significant access to the property.

Another Side of the Elephant . . .

Kopczuk and Slemrod start with the end product—the estate tax return— and find the following:

—Among married decedents, the vast majority, that is, 86.5 percent of returns, are nontaxable predominantly because spousal bequests push the taxable estate below the tax threshold (the unified credit exemption amount);

—QTIP trusts are extremely popular; and

—Married taxpayers are not equalizing their estates even though doing so could result in significant tax savings.

Kopczuk and Slemrod draw a number of conclusions based on their analysis of state tax returns. However, drawing definitive conclusions from these findings about the effect of estate taxes on people's dispositive plans is extremely difficult, given the inherent flexibility of the estate tax system. To appreciate this flexibility, it is helpful to understand the most common estate planning techniques.

ESTATE PLANNING 101. The most important estate and gift tax rules for estate planning are:

—The ability to make significant tax-free transfers by gift through the $10,000 annual exclusion;[61]

---

60. Before 1969, this same concern would have applied to charitable transfers as well. However, the Tax Reform Act of 1969 closed a number of loopholes with the goal of providing "a closer correlation between the charitable contributions deduction and the ultimate benefit to charity." Senate Finance Committee Report 91–552.

61. I.R.C. §2503(b). This amount is indexed for inflation, and as of January 1, 2002, was increased to $11,000.

—The large unified credit that provides a $675,000 threshold for the application of estate and gift taxes;[62]

—The ability to make unlimited tax-free transfers to spouses and charities;[63] and

—The ability to provide financial security to an individual while keeping assets out of her estate for tax purposes.[64]

In addition, two other tax-planning devices are very valuable from the point of view of saving overall taxes, but are much less commonly used by taxpayers. These are the ability to save significant taxes through making taxable gifts during life, and the ability to save significant taxes by paying some taxes upon the death of the first spouse (equalizing estates).[65]

PLANNING FOR MARRIED COUPLES. Estate planning for married couples primarily involves ensuring use of each spouse's unified credit exemption amount, and taking advantage of the marital deduction. Taken together, these techniques allow all taxes to be deferred until the death of the surviving spouse, while still reducing the couple's overall tax liability. This bifurcated technique can also be used for estate equalization by transferring more than the unified credit exemption amount to a "credit shelter trust." As such, this bifurcation of the decedent spouse's estate is the most common estate planning technique for married couples, regardless of their dispositive wishes.

Consider the case of a married couple where neither spouse has children from outside the marriage. It is common for couples in this situation to request an estate plan in which all assets pass to the surviving spouse upon the first spouse's death, and upon the death of the surviving spouse, the assets

62. In 2001, the unified credit exempted the first $675,000 from estate and gift taxes. In 2002, this amount increased to $1 million. I.R.C. §2010.

63. I.R.C. §§2056 and 2523; and I.R.C. §§2055 and 2522, respectively.

64. The exceptions found in I.R.C. §2041 provide the framework for many of these provisions.

65. One of the most significant differences between the estate tax and the gift tax is that the cash used to pay estate tax is itself subject to estate tax, whereas the cash used to pay gift tax is not subject to gift tax. In other words, the estate tax is tax inclusive, and the gift tax is exclusive. As a result, the gift tax rate is effectively lower than the estate tax rate, despite the fact that a single rate schedule applies for both taxes. In large estates, significant tax savings can by achieved by forgoing complete deferral of taxes in favor of equalizing the estates of the spouses. The reason for this is that estate tax rates are progressive. By paying taxes in the first spouse's estate, that estate takes advantage of the run up the tax brackets.

pass to the couple's children.[66] These so-called I love you wills have been found to be so reflective of people's wishes that the Uniform Probate Code changed its intestacy rules to provide for that disposition for people who die without wills.[67]

Although these are the wills many married people want, these are not the wills they will get from an experienced estate planner, because they fail to take advantage of the unified credit exemption amount of the first spouse to die, and therefore result in a significantly greater tax liability to the couple's children. If a married person transfers all of his property to his spouse in a manner that qualifies for the marital deduction, the tax benefit that he would otherwise obtain by using his unified credit is entirely lost.

> *Example*: H and W have simple wills that provide that upon death, all property goes to the spouse, if living, and if not, the property goes to H and W's children. H holds $1 million in assets and W holds $300,000.
>
> H dies in 2001 and W dies later in the same year. In 2001, the unified credit amount sheltered $675,000 in assets, and therefore could potentially shield up to $1,350,000 of a couple's assets. However, upon H's death, all of the property went to W, and due to the marital deduction, none of H's unified credit was used. When W died, she had $1.3 million in her estate: her original $300,000 plus the $1 million from her husband's estate. The unified credit only sheltered $675,000 from tax, resulting in a tax liability in W's estate of $249,250.

If a couple holds assets in excess of the unified credit exemption amount, significant tax savings can be achieved by limiting the marital deduction bequest to the amount in excess of the unified credit exemption amount. Giving the spouse only that portion, and transferring the unified credit exemption amount in a way that avoids taxation in the surviving spouse's estate, ensures that both spouses' unified credits are used.

> *Example*: H and W have an estate plan: It provides that the amount of the unified credit exemption will pass to a credit shelter trust—which was structured in such a way that it was funded with assets that were

66. Mary L. Fellows, Rita J. Simon, and William Rau, "Public Attitudes about Property Distribution at Death and Intestate Succession Laws in the United States," *Am. B. Found. Res. J.* 319, 351–54, 358–64, 366–68 (1978) found the majority favored granting the entire estate to the spouse regardless of the level of wealth involved.

67. Unif. Probate Code §2-102, 8 U.L.A. 274 (1998).

subject to tax in H's estate, but would not be subject to tax in W's estate—and that the remainder of the property will pass to the spouse.

H dies in 2001, and W dies later in the same year. Assuming H holds $1 million in assets and W holds $300,000, upon H's death, $675,000 would pass to the credit shelter trust, and the remaining $325,000 passes to W. Upon W's death, her gross estate would include her $300,000 plus the $325,000 transferred to her by H. This $625,000 could then be transferred free of tax to their children since it is less than the unified credit exemption amount for 2001.

This common estate planning technique of dividing the estate of the first spouse to die into a credit shelter share and a marital share does not by itself answer the question of the extent to which spousal bequests are affected by tax considerations. The reason is that tremendous flexibility is available within the constructs of a credit shelter share and a marital share such that the surviving spouse can be given a very small bequest or a very large bequest and both can be accomplished within this framework.

Range of Choices for Credit Shelter Trust

A credit shelter trust is a trust created for the purpose of using the decedent spouse's unified credit. In order for a credit shelter trust to accomplish its tax objective, it must apply to assets that are subject to tax in a decedent spouse's estate, and transfer them in such a way that they will not be subject to tax in the surviving spouse's estate upon her death. One way of doing this is to give the credit shelter portion of the bequest to someone other than the surviving spouse. For example, a bequest to the decedent spouse's children will use the unified credit of the decedent spouse and will avoid being taxed in the surviving spouse's estate. However, where this may be suitable for some people— particularly those with significant assets and adult children—many couples will not want to have to make the choice between saving taxes and providing sufficient support for the surviving spouse. Luckily for spouses, this choice need not be made since the credit shelter trust can be structured to provide the surviving spouse with access to the trust assets. The only limitation is that the surviving spouse cannot be given so much control that the assets will be subject to tax in her estate.

In general, the rules for credit shelter trusts provide a trade-off between control and withdrawal powers. That is, if the surviving spouse is the sole trustee of the trust, the trust property will be included in her estate unless her rights of withdrawal are limited. If, on the other hand, an independent trustee exercises discretion in distributions, the surviving spouse can be given unlimited benefits from the trust property. Maximum spousal control trusts and discretionary trusts are two common structures for the credit shelter trust.

MAXIMUM SPOUSAL CONTROL TRUSTS. Under a maximum spousal control trust, a surviving spouse can be made the trustee and given any or all of the following interests in the trust, and none of the trust property will be included in the surviving spouse's estate, except to the extent that it has been distributed to the surviving spouse:

—All income from the trust property for life, or in the case of real property or tangible personal property, the use of the property for her life;

—Power to invade principal subject to an ascertainable standard relating to her support, maintenance, health, or education.[68] An example of a qualifying standard would be the ability to invade principal to support her in her accustomed manner of living.[69] If the spouse is trustee, she can have power to distribute trust property to herself subject to this standard.

—Ability to invade up to the greater of $5,000, or 5 percent of the trust property each year for any purpose, without being limited to an ascertainable standard.[70] This power is sometimes referred to as a "five and five power." A five and five power can build flexibility into a plan by providing the option for the surviving spouse to get additional assets from the credit shelter trust without being limited by the ascertainable standard.[71]

—Power to appoint property to anyone other than herself, her estate, her creditors, or creditors of her estate.[72] This power can be exercisable either during life or at death or both. If the decedent spouse wants to maintain some control over the property, he can limit the power of appointment to being exercisable in favor of a specific group of people, such as their children.

DISCRETIONARY TRUSTS. The most flexible credit shelter trust is a discretionary trust giving the trustee complete discretion in making distributions.

68. I.R.C. §2041(b)(1)(A).
69. Treas. Reg. §20.2041-1(c)(2).
70. I.R.C. §2041(b)(2).
71. If the surviving spouse holds a five and five power, the trust property will not be subject to tax in her estate except to the extent of any unexercised power held at the time of her death. The estate tax exposure in this situation can be reduced by providing that the power can only be exercised during a limited period of time (for example, the last week in the calendar year.) In that way, none of the trust property will be included in the surviving spouse's estate for estate tax purposes unless she dies during the exercise period.
72. 2041(b) (1).

In order to prevent the trust from being included in her estate, the surviving spouse cannot be the sole trustee of this trust. However, one of her relatives or close friends can be trustee, and the surviving spouse can be the co-trustee for purposes of making investment decisions for the trust property. Under a discretionary trust, the independent trustee makes the decision as to how much, if any, should be distributed to the surviving spouse. Since the surviving spouse does not have the power to make discretionary distributions to herself, none of the trust principal is taxed in the surviving spouse's estate except to the extent that it has been distributed to the surviving spouse.

A discretionary trust can be established with a number of beneficiaries—discretionary trusts are commonly established for the benefit of the decedent's spouse and children—and can provide greater flexibility than the maximum benefit trust. For example, under a discretionary trust, the surviving spouse can be given distributions of principal that are not limited to the ascertainable standard or the five and five powers. The trust can instruct the trustee to give preference to the surviving spouse if that is the donor's wish. Alternatively, if the surviving spouse is financially secure, greater tax savings can be achieved by distributing trust assets to individuals other than the surviving spouse, thereby reducing the surviving spouse's taxable estate at the time of her death.

Range of Choices for Marital Trust

Just as a range of options is available for structuring the credit shelter trust, so too is a range of choices available for structuring the marital trust. For individuals interested in providing maximum benefit to their spouses, the marital portion can be structured as an outright bequest of property to their surviving spouse. For individuals who are concerned about their spouse's ability to manage property, they can transfer the interest in a trust and give the spouse the right to all of the income from the property and a power to appoint principal either during life or at death. Finally, if an individual is interested in providing only minimum access and control of the property to the surviving spouse, the marital portion can be structured as a QTIP trust, in which the surviving spouse is given only the income from the property for life. The transferring spouse can maintain complete control over who gets the property after the surviving spouse's death.

Kopczuk and Slemrod contend that the QTIP trust separates tax minimization from the decision about transfer of resources to the spouse, since it enables the transferrer to obtain the full marital deduction and retain control over the ultimate disposition of the property. While a QTIP can be used for this purpose, this is not its primary value from the estate planner's perspective, and use of a QTIP does not necessarily reflect a lack of control on the part of the surviving spouse.

The greatest value of the QTIP trust from an estate planner's perspective is its flexibility. Under the QTIP trust provision, a transfer to a surviving spouse will qualify for the marital deduction if the surviving spouse is given income interest in the property for life and the executor elects to treat the interest as a QTIP interest and claim the marital deduction. The decision as to whether to elect QTIP treatment need not be made until nine months after the decedent's death. This ability to defer the decision as to whether to pay taxes upon the death of the first or second spouse is the primary value of the QTIP from the estate planner's perspective.

Moreover, use of the QTIP trust imposes little restriction on the donor in terms of his dispositive wishes. As noted by Kopczuk and Slemrod, through the use of a QTIP trust, the donor spouse can give a very limited interest to the surviving spouse. However, what Kopczuk and Slemrod fail to point out is that QTIP provides flexibility in the other direction as well: If the donor wants to provide extensive access to the surviving spouse, the donor can give the surviving spouse all of the same interests in the QTIP trust that she could have in the credit shelter trust without compromising any flexibility in terms of the ability to opt out of QTIP treatment. In particular, in addition to the income interest for life mandated by the QTIP provision, the surviving spouse can also be given any or all of the following:

—Right to invade the principal of the QTIP trust for her health, education, maintenance, and support;

—Right to invade the greater of 5 percent of the trust principal or $5,000 from the QTIP trust each year;

—Right to receive discretionary payments from the QTIP trust, assuming there is an independent trustee; and

—Power to appoint principal of the QTIP trust during life or at death to anyone other than herself, her estate, her creditors, or creditors of her estate.

Summing Up

Kopczuk and Slemrod conclude that interspousal division of assets is responsive to tax considerations. Although they are correct that the technical division of assets is responsive to tax considerations, the technical division itself reveals little about the transfer of resources. A spouse interested in minimizing the interest given to the surviving spouse could limit her bequest to annual income from the marital portion, and provide her no interest in the credit shelter trust, whereas a spouse interested in maximizing the interest given to the surviving spouse could give her:

—Outright ownership of the marital portion;

—All income from the credit shelter trust;

—The right to invade principal of the credit shelter trust for her health, education, maintenance, and support;

—The right to invade the greater of 5 percent or $5,000 from the credit shelter trust each year;

—The right to receive discretionary payments from the credit shelter trust (assuming there is an independent trustee);

—The power to appoint principal of the credit shelter trust during life or at death to anyone other than herself, her estate, her creditors, or creditors of her estate.

Yet, these bequests would appear identical on the tax returns. Thus the question of the extent to which taxpayers respond to tax considerations in this area is perhaps a false question since it suggests a trade-off where none is required. That is, the husband can take full advantage of the unified credit and spousal deductions regardless of how much of his resources he wants to leave to his wife.

Understanding this lack of trade-off sheds light on the conundrum noted by the authors that "nondeductible bequests of the first spouse dying are much lower than a tax minimization strategy would dictate . . . even though tax minimization appears to be a robust prediction theory." Tax equalization, unlike allocations of interests between spousal and nonspousal transfers, imposes a real cost to the taxpayer. In order to garner the benefits of estate equalization, actual dollars need to be paid upon the death of the first spouse to die. This payment of taxes will reduce the total tax liability paid by the combined spouses, but the timing of the payment determines who bears the burden of the tax. If the tax is paid at the time of the first spouse's death, the surviving spouse's interest is truly diminished by the amount of the tax liability. If instead, the estate plan is an optimal marital deduction bequest in which only the unified credit of the decedent spouse is used, the combined tax liability may be greater, but the effect of the tax will not be felt by the surviving spouse; it will instead be borne by the couple's children. This reluctance to pay taxes at the death of the first spouse helps explain the popularity of the QTIP trust. The QTIP trust structure provides the flexibility to defer the decision about paying taxes in order to reduce the couple's overall tax liability until nine months after the death of the first spouse. At that time the surviving spouse may herself be in poor health, or may even have died, and the taxes can be paid with little emotional cost to the surviving spouse. Finally, this model resonates with the findings about people's reluctance to make taxable gifts even though the effective tax rate on gifts is significantly lower than the effective rates on transfers at death.

COMMENT BY
James Poterba

The emergence of estate tax reform as an active subject of tax policy debate in the late 1990s coincided with an outpouring of academic research on the economics of the estate tax. The theoretical research of past decades was supplemented with a host of empirical studies investigating how estate and gift taxation affects charitable giving, the choice between *inter-vivos* transfers and bequests, and the rate of saving and wealth accumulation. Empirical researchers had long dismissed the estate tax as very difficult if not impossible to study, because the tax affects only a small set of very high net worth households. In spite of this, recent investigators have found ways, either by working with confidential Statistics of Income data files compiled by the Internal Revenue Service, or by using household surveys that target the high net worth population, to provide insight on the economic effects of this tax.

Throughout the 1990s, the top marginal estate and gift tax rate was 60 percent—roughly double the top marginal income tax rate that was embodied in the Tax Reform Act of 1986, and one and one-half times the top marginal income tax rate of the late 1990s. As a result, the estate tax has attracted extraordinary attention from tax planners and the financial service professionals who assist high net worth households. The associated behavioral effects of the tax, and the distortions to economic decisions, may have consequently risen in the last two decades of the twentieth century.

Wojciech Kopczuk and Joel Slemrod offer three strands of empirical evidence on how the estate tax affects taxpayer behavior: The first concerns variation in the ratio of taxable estates to total wealth, which may depend on the marginal estate tax rate. The second focuses on the relationship between charitable bequests, total estate values, and the top marginal estate tax rate. The third, which represents a quite novel element of this research, explores the use of qualified terminable interest property (QTIP) trusts. Each strand of empirical research offers interesting new insights on the impact of the estate and gift tax system. My discussion comments on each line of research in turn.

The Effect on Wealth Accumulation

The first empirical issue the authors consider is the effect of the estate tax on wealth accumulation. As the authors note, this is a very difficult issue to address in a comprehensive fashion, since the estate tax could affect accumulation at all stages of the life cycle. No currently available data set offers researchers information on the estate tax expectations of currently young households. It is therefore not possible to relate their current wealth accumulation to a measure of the tax burden they expect to face if they accumulate substantial resources and ultimately face the estate tax. The empirical evidence presented in this paper is nevertheless suggestive. It shows that the total reported estates of the top one-half of one percent of decedents, as a share of total wealth in the economy, are negatively related to marginal tax rates on estates of various sizes.

Interpreting this finding in terms of an impact on capital accumulation is difficult because two distinct behavioral effects contribute to the reported estate value of high net worth households. The first is the level of lifetime saving done by these households, and the second is the level of estate tax avoidance. Finding that estates are smaller when the estate tax rate is greater is consistent with reduced saving when the estate tax rate is high. Such reduced saving could take many forms: potential estate tax payers might consume more while they are alive, or they might change their investment mix in a way that reduces the expected value of their bequest. However, a negative association between estate values and the level of estate tax rates could also be the result of greater estate tax avoidance when the estate tax rate is high.

High net worth households may use a variety of strategies to reduce their reported estates. They may involve the use of trusts, sophisticated insurance products, or programs of lifetime giving. Virtually all of these strategies involve relinquishing some degree of control over assets before death in order to remove the assets from the reported estate, and thereby reduce the estate tax bill. When the estate tax rate is higher, the optimal level of control to relinquish is presumably greater, and therefore the reported amount of estates will be smaller than during periods with lower estate tax rates.

A growing body of empirical research suggests that transfer behavior is particularly sensitive to the estate tax rate. Douglas B. Bernheim, Robert J. Lemke, and John Karl Scholz document a change in the likelihood of transfers between the early and late 1990s for the type of households that were affected by the estate tax changes of 1997.[73] In particular, households with net worth in the range that would have been taxable when the unified estate and gift tax credit was $600,000, but that might not be taxable when the credit was $1,000,000, reduced their *inter-vivos* giving between 1995 and 1998. This is consistent with an incentive effect of estate taxes on transfers. Several earlier studies by Kathleen McGarry and James Poterba also suggest that the level of transfers depends on the rate of tax at death.[74]

Estate planning strategies have the effect of reducing the size of the estate

73. Bernheim, Lemke, and Scholz (2001).
74. McGarry (2001); and Poterba (2001).

that is observed on the estate tax return, relative to the wealth that the decedent effectively controlled at some earlier date. An ideal research plan would track households beginning at an age when their behavior might not have been substantially distorted by the estate tax—maybe at forty or fifty—and follow their saving, transfers to charities, and *inter-vivos* transfers to individuals who might be potential bequest recipients. Needless to say, no data set provides all of the information needed to track these potential effects of the estate tax on household behavior!

One important unresolved issue is the cost of the economic distortions associated with estate tax avoidance. Standard models of tax avoidance, drawn largely from the literature on income taxes, suggest that households engage in avoidance or evasion activities until the point at which the marginal cost of avoiding another dollar of estate and gift taxes equals the marginal tax burden. The cost of avoidance includes the direct costs, such as the legal fees associated with creating new legal entities to hold assets that were previously part of the estate. It also includes the indirect cost in terms of potentially reduced returns on the assets in question and reduced control of assets by the potential decedent. The potential avoidance response underscores the difficulty of linking measured changes in the ratio of taxable estates to total net worth to a conclusion about the effect of the estate tax on capital accumulation.

The Effect on Charitable Giving

The second strand of empirical research in the paper focuses on charitable giving, and the sensitivity of such giving to the estate tax rate. The authors present valuable new evidence from time-series regressions showing that when the marginal estate tax rate is higher, the ratio of charitable bequests to the gross value of estates is higher. The authors acknowledge, however, that the empirical results are fragile, and that they are particularly sensitive to whether or not one controls for a possible secular trend in the fraction of estates going to charitable bequests. When one does introduce a time trend into the empirical model, the relationship between the estate tax rate and the charitable giving share disappears. Open issues about the data on charitable giving also exist, and the extent to which complicated gift arrangements before death, such as charitable remainder trusts, are captured on estate tax return filings or any other data sets that include information on lifetime gifts and charitable bequests is not clear.

Substantial evidence from income tax returns and from household surveys suggests that charitable giving before death is sensitive to marginal income tax rates. It consequently seems very likely that giving at death should also be sensitive to the relevant tax rates that apply to charitable bequests. Evidence from past income tax reforms is particularly suggestive of the importance of tax incentives for the high income, high net worth population. In the aftermath of the Tax Reform Act of 1986, for example, when the favorable tax rules on gifts of appreciated property were eliminated, charitable giving of appreciated property plunged. Well-to-do households with appreciated securities, or other items such as paintings, that can be donated, usually carry out this type of giving.

A number of difficult empirical problems arise in trying to measure the impact of estate tax rates on charitable giving. One of the most difficult is tracking the wealth available for donation on the part of high net worth households. The portfolio holdings of the highest net worth households are often quite different from the holdings of those lower in the wealth distribution. Their portfolios are more concentrated in corporate stock and in equity in privately held businesses, and they have lower holdings of fixed income instruments and residential real estate. A second empirical difficulty involves sorting through the effect of income taxes, as well as estate taxes, on the pattern of charitable giving. If income tax rates were high, while estate tax rates were low, one would expect taxpayers to emphasize charitable gifts during their lifetime, when the gifts generated income tax deductions, rather than gifts at the time of death. If households develop a lifetime giving plan, conditional on their lifetime resource endowment, then the entire pattern of marginal income tax rates over the course of the life cycle could affect the size of charitable bequests.

Controlling for the impact of past marginal income tax rates on current charitable giving is difficult. For example, just before the marginal income tax rate reductions in the Tax Reform Act of 1986 took effect, many high income and high net worth households made significant contributions to charitable foundations. The assets in these foundations have been used to fund charitable donations in subsequent years. In many cases, the strong growth in asset values in the years since 1986 may have left households with larger charitable foundations than they expected *ex ante*. Such "overfunded" foundations may provide households with a source of transfers at their time of death, thereby reducing the level of charitable bequests that one might otherwise have observed.

The most difficult question raised by the empirical findings on charitable bequests concerns the interpretation of the change in results when the time trend is included. The most prevalent view would probably hold that results without the time trend are impossible to interpret, since they might be driven by a spurious correlation between the marginal tax rate variable and slowly changing aspects of the economic system, such as the taste for charitable giving. This view raises difficulties for virtually any study of time series movements in tax rules and the associated effects on household behavior. Most tax rate measures show relatively little time variation, and removing trend variation can make it difficult to identify behavioral effects. It is unfortunate that careful study of behavior at the time of sharp changes in tax policy, such as the change between 1931 and 1936, does not offer clear evidence of the sensitivity of charitable giving to the marginal estate tax rate.

What conclusion should we draw from the empirical work on charitable bequests, both the work presented in this paper, and the work of others? Caution is clearly needed in drawing any strong inferences, but it seems that charitable giving is quite responsive to marginal tax rate changes. This is consistent with great concern on the part of universities, hospitals, museums, and other recipients of charitable bequests about the potential negative effect of estate tax elimination on the flow of charitable bequests. The open question is whether the price effects associated with changes in estate tax rates are larger than the wealth effects associated with changes in the net-of-tax size of estates.

The Effect on Bequests to Surviving Spouses

The last major issue the paper addresses concerns the role of bequests to surviving spouses, and the insights that such bequests provide about the effective operation of the estate tax. The authors draw attention to the important role of the treatment of surviving spouses. They emphasize that while many previous theoretical and empirical discussions of the U.S. estate and gift tax proceed as though all potential decedents were single persons, in fact, most estates are derived from assets accumulated by married couples. Married couples have several ways to structure their affairs before death, and to arrange for asset transfers at the death of the first- and the second-to-die spouse. These decisions have potentially important effects on estate tax burdens. Studying how households choose among these various options can potentially inform our understanding, not just of estate tax avoidance decisions, but more generally of economic decisions within married households.

The authors present a very careful analysis of the economic factors that may induce married couples to choose different levels of spousal bequests. These include potential differences between the spouses in their relative preferences for different bequest recipients, the option value of resource retention by the surviving spouse, and various tax considerations. They note that the optimal estate tax avoidance strategy is likely to differ across married couples, with factors such as the age disparity between members of the couple, and the relative importance of appreciated assets, for which the value of basis step-up at death is substantial, playing a key role.

The paper offers a particularly interesting discussion of QTIP trusts, which permit the first-to-die member of a married couple to direct the transfer of assets, but to have this transfer of assets take place at the death of the surviving spouse. The QTIP trust provides the survivor with access to the income from the trust assets, but the principal is transferred in accordance with the wishes of the first-to-die. The authors have broken important new ground by recognizing the role of QTIPs in the bequest-generation process, and they raise important questions about the factors that limit the use of these trusts.

Several factors warrant consideration. First, it is potentially critical to distinguish between married couples in which both partners have only been married once, and married couples in which at least one of the partners has been married before. In the latter case, the QTIP provides a very natural mechanism through which the first-to-die can provide a bequest to his or her natural children without concern that the surviving spouse may choose to reduce transfers to her or his stepchildren. Second, in some cases the QTIP may be motivated by factors that are unrelated to the estate tax, but rather involve the concerns about asset management. In some married couples, one spouse has substantial business and financial acumen, while the other has very little experience with such matters. This may provide a rationale for using a QTIP, since it provides the more financially savvy spouse with an opportunity to transfer asset management to experienced trustees, while at the same time providing resources for the surviving spouse.

Finally, an important issue that underlies the discussion of QTIPs concerns the extent to which surviving spouses would choose resource allocations different from those that are provided under the terms of the QTIP. This issue has two elements. One is the degree to which the restriction to income from the QTIP assets constrains the consumption of the surviving spouse below the level that the survivor would otherwise choose. The second is the extent to which the preferences of the surviving spouse regarding the allocation of the bequest would in fact differ from the allocation chosen by the first-to-die in creating the QTIP trust.

Conclusion

The authors provide a valuable guide to what we know about the economic effects of estate and gift taxation. Their description of existing empirical work also suggests the potential value of additional studies, not necessarily using tax return data. Such studies might address a number of unresolved issues:

the apparent failure of a substantial group of households to take advantage of opportunities to reduce their estate tax liability, and the interplay between lifetime gifts to both charity and relatives, and gifts at death, are two leading issues. Studies on these and other issues could improve our understanding of how households make decisions about how much of their wealth to bequeath, how to control the transfer at death, and whether to direct transfers to charities or to surviving individuals.

8

The Impact of Defined Contribution Plans on Bequests

ALICIA MUNNELL, ANNIKA SUNDÉN,
MAURICIO SOTO, AND CATHERINE TAYLOR

> That men labour and save chiefly for the sake of their families and not
> for themselves, is shown by the fact that they seldom spend, after they
> have retired from work, more than the income that comes in from
> their savings, preferring to leave their stored-up wealth intact for their
> families.
>
> Alfred Marshall, *Principles of Economics*, 1938

This paper explores the shift from defined benefit to defined contribution plans and considers how it might affect bequests and thereby consumption and saving. Our hypothesis is that both intended bequests and unintended bequests will increase as retirees receive more of their pension benefits as lump sums rather than as annuity payments. We also contend that

The authors would like to thank Sean Barrett, Elizabeth Lidstone, Mireille Samaan, and Long Tran for extraordinary research assistance; they were all full participants in the enterprise. Early work by Jeremy Zipple also contributed to this effort. Many people were very generous in providing data, expertise, and computer code during the preparation of this paper: Alan Gustman, Tom Steinmeier and Courtney Coile provided their computer programs for calculating pension wealth. The authors would also like to thank Bill Gale, Jonathan Gruber, Alan Gustman, James Poterba, and Tom Steinmeier for helpful comments on an earlier draft.

workers recognize they may not consume their lump-sum payments and react differently to accumulations in defined benefit and defined contribution plans during their lifetime.

We argue that unintended bequests will rise because people are reluctant to spend accumulated wealth. This reluctance is evident in the small size of the U.S. annuity market, the aversion of older homeowners to reverse annuity mortgages, the holdings of life insurance by retirees, and the limited dissaving in retirement. In the past, any reluctance to turn assets into income streams was mitigated by the fact that most retirement wealth—Social Security and private pensions—came in the form of annuity payments. Today, the story is different because more and more private sector pension plans provide lump-sum benefits. Privatization of Social Security would reinforce the private sector trend. Interestingly, proponents of privatization frequently cite the potential for leaving a bequest as a major advantage of individual accounts.

We also hypothesize that intended bequests will rise, because people's interest in bequests increases when they gain access to accumulated assets. Accumulating wealth out of current income to leave a bequest is too difficult, but if people receive a pile of wealth, leaving a bequest becomes a plausible option. Thus intended as well as unintended bequests are likely to increase.

The following sections of the paper spell out the various facets of the story about pensions and bequests and their implications for the welfare of older people. The first section describes the shift from annuities to lump-sum payments that corresponds to the shift from defined benefit to defined contribution plans and argues that people prefer lump sums to flows of income. The next section documents the extent to which retirees try to hold onto their assets, by reviewing the evidence on the reluctance of the elderly to take advantage of annuity and reverse mortgage opportunities, the limited dissaving among retirees, and their holdings of life insurance. Given people's general preference for piles of wealth rather than flows of income, the third section discusses how the shift to defined contribution plans might affect both intended and unintended bequests. Section four estimates the potential increase in the amount of wealth transferred from one generation to another through unintended bequests, using data from the Survey of Consumer Finances (SCF). Section five explores whether intended as well as unintended bequests might increase as people get a growing share of their pension wealth as lump sums, by testing whether the composition of pension wealth affects people's subjective probability of leaving a bequest. The last section investigates whether the increase in bequests will be financed by lower consumption in retirement or by greater saving during the work life. This requires estimating the effect of defined contribution plans on the saving and wealth accumulation of households, using data from the Health and Retirement Study (HRS).

We conclude that the effect of pensions on bequests is potentially large and significant. First, in 1998 bequeathable wealth in the hands of decedents was $15 billion higher (3.2 percent) as a result of the increase in defined contribution plans as a share of pension wealth between 1992 and 1998. Thus the shift in pension form has already significantly increased the potential for unintended bequests, and the transition to defined contribution plans was far from complete in 1998. Second, interest in leaving a bequest among respondents in both the SCF and HRS is positively related to the proportion of pension wealth received as lump sums rather than annuities. Thus it appears that lump-sum payments affect intended as well as unintended bequests. Third, workers react very differently to their defined contribution accumulations than they do to the present value of annuity pensions. They do not reduce their other saving in anticipation of payments from defined contribution plans as they do in response to promised Social Security and defined benefit pension payments. Finally, the most significant increase in lump-sum pension accumulations occurs in the middle and lower quintiles of the wealth distribution, so that the increase in bequests should help to reduce wealth inequality.

This summary may overstate the story, but our goal is to raise the possibility that a reluctance to spend lump sums may be a problem as serious as the conventional worry that recipients will spend their entire pension accumulation on a trip around the world. If people save more in anticipation of leaving their pension accumulations as bequests, they will have lower consumption during their working years. If they do not boost their saving, they will have lower consumption in retirement. In either case, a reluctance to spend accumulated pension wealth will reduce lifetime consumption.

Similarly, it may seem strange to worry simultaneously about people cashing out their defined contribution accumulations when they change jobs during their work lives, and to worry about people's reluctance to spend defined contribution accumulations in retirement. In fact, different worries may be appropriate for different types of people. Those who make it to retirement with large accumulations are likely to be the savers, while those with a propensity to cash out during their working years are likely to be the spenders. In any event, an increasing number of people will receive lump-sum payments from their pension plans, and this change has important implications for both this generation and the next.

It's Becoming a Lump-Sum World

The nature of pension coverage in the United States has changed sharply from defined benefit plans to defined contribution plans. Defined benefit plans generally provide retirement benefits based on a percentage of final salary for each year of service, and pay the benefits in the form of a lifetime annuity. For example, a worker with a final salary of $40,000 might receive 1.5 percent a year for thirty years of service, producing an annual pension of $18,000. The employer prefunds these benefits by making pretax contributions into a pension fund; employees typically do not contribute. The employer owns the assets, directs the investments, and bears the risk. Benefits are insured by the Pension Benefit Guaranty Corporation (PBGC).

In contrast to defined benefit plans, defined contribution plans are like savings accounts. The employer, and often the employee, contributes a specified dollar amount or percentage of earnings into the account. These contributions are usually invested, at the direction of the employee, in elections from a menu of mutual funds, stocks, and bonds. When the worker retires, the balance in the account determines the retirement benefit.

Within the defined contribution world, the fastest growing type of plan is the 401(k). These plans were authorized in 1978, but became popular only after the IRS proposed clarifying regulations in 1981. The defining characteristics of 401(k) plans are that participation in the plan is voluntary, and that the employee as well as the employer can make pretax contributions to the plan. These characteristics shift a substantial portion of the burden for providing for retirement to the employee; the employee decides whether or not to participate, how much to contribute, how to invest the assets, and how to withdraw the money at retirement. Despite the fact that 401(k) plans shift the risk to the employee, they are more appealing to a younger, more mobile work force. For these workers, greater portability clearly outweighs the predictability of benefits for the career employee under a defined benefit plan.

Given their popularity and growth, one would have thought the introduction of 401(k) plans should have boosted pension plan coverage in the United States. However, overall pension coverage has remained virtually unchanged. This means the enormous expansion of defined contribution plans has accompanied a sharp decline in the percent of the work force covered under traditional defined benefit plans.[1] The SCF shows that the pro-

1. Researchers attribute about half the decline in defined benefit coverage to shifts in employment from manufacturing to service industries, and half to employers substituting defined contribution for defined benefit plans. Ippolito and Thompson

Figure 8-1. *Percentage of Households Covered by a Pension, by Pension Type, SCF 1992, 1995, and 1998*

Percent

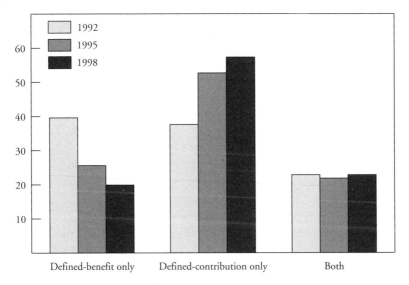

Source: VanDerhei and Copeland (2001).

portion of households with only a defined contribution plan increased during the 1990s from 37 percent to 57 percent of those households with coverage as shown in figure 8-1. Over the same period, the proportion with a defined benefit plan dropped from about 40 percent to 20 percent, while the proportion with dual coverage remained unchanged. Because defined contribution plans are becoming the only pension arrangement for more and more households, how beneficiaries receive their pension accumulations at retirement is becoming an increasingly important issue.

At retirement, defined contribution plans typically offer lump-sum payments, installment payments, or a life annuity, and generally allow the participant choice over the form of the distribution. According to the Employee Benefit Survey for Medium and Large Firms, in 1997 only 27 percent of 401(k) plan participants had an option to choose a life annuity as their method of distribution. The most common distribution option is

---

(2000); and Gustman and Steinmeier (1992). Poterba, Venti, and Wise (2001) show that defined contribution coverage has mainly replaced defined benefit coverage among younger cohorts of workers.

lump sum followed by some form of phased withdrawal. The pattern is similar for thrift and savings plans. In the future, the percent of plans offering only a lump-sum option is likely to increase sharply, because the Internal Revenue Service issued regulations in 2000 permitting sponsors of defined contribution plans to discontinue all options other than lump-sum payments.[2]

Lump-sum payments are also becoming more frequent options among defined benefit plans in large part due to the conversion of conventional defined benefit plans to so-called cash balance plans.[3] The most recent official statistics report that 6 percent of full-time employees at medium and large private establishments had a "cash account" benefit formula in 1997. But surveys suggest that significant conversion has occurred since then.[4] The key point is that cash balance plans—like defined contribution plans—provide lump-sum payments at separation. Assuming only modest growth in cash-balance plans, lump-sum pension benefits should exceed annuity payments from defined benefit plans for those retiring in 2010.[5]

Even though some defined contribution plans offer participants distribution in the form of an annuity, retirees frequently do not take advantage of the option.[6] This is not surprising; numerous examples from everyday life

2. U.S. Department of the Treasury, Internal Revenue Service. 2000. "Special Rules Regarding Optional Forms of Benefit under Qualified Retirement Plans," Treasury Decision 8900, Internal Revenue Service 26 CFR Part 1. (www.fedworld.gov/pub/irs-regs/td8900.pdf [August 2000]).

3. Legally, cash balance plans are defined benefit plans where employers prefund contributions, own the assets, select the investments, and bear the risk. And, like other defined benefit plans, the PBGC insures the benefits. To the employee, however, cash balance plans look very much like a defined contribution plan. Contributions made for the employees are recorded in an account. The employees receive regular statements showing the balance in their notional account, and the benefits tend to accrue as a constant percentage of compensation. The plans are attractive to employees, therefore, because they provide visible and portable benefits like a defined contribution plan, while securing accrual and government insurance like defined benefit plans.

4. By 2000, 16 percent of pension plans among the Fortune 100 were cash balance plans, and more generally, cash balance plans may have increased from 5 percent to 12 percent of all defined benefit plans between 1998 and 2000. Elliot and Moore (2000).

5. VanDerhei and Copeland (2001).

6. Analyzing a subsample of the Health and Retirement Study, Brown (2000) finds that less than half (48 percent) of households expect to annuitize even a portion

suggest that given the choice of either a lump sum or a stream of payments of equal value, people generally prefer the lump sum. Employers often exploit this preference by offering athletes and many professionals immediate signing bonuses, rather than streams of future payments, to induce them to accept positions. The great majority of taxpayers—75 percent—overpay their income taxes to ensure themselves a lump-sum refund, when they could easily adjust their withholding to avoid making an interest-free loan to the IRS.

In addition to anecdotal evidence, several empirical studies confirm that individuals have a marked preference for lump sums. In a survey conducted by David Fetherstonhaugh and Lee Ross, participants were offered either a pension that pays an annuity of $12,500 per year or one that offers $10,000 annually plus a lump-sum bonus of $25,000 disbursed immediately upon retirement.[7] Although the two plans are virtually equivalent at a real interest rate of 2.8 percent, more than 75 percent of the respondents to the survey preferred the one-time bonus to the increased annuity.[8]

The preference for lump-sum payments may reflect a higher discount rate than the one that pension plans use to compute present values, or it may reflect more complicated departures from the traditional neoclassical model. For example, Richard H. Thaler finds that the median respondent was willing to give up $3,000 immediately in exchange for a payment in ten years only if the delayed payment was at least $10,000, implying a discount rate (continuously compounded) of 12 percent.[9] He also finds that the survey evidence is inconsistent with standard theory; discount rates appear to vary depending on the size of the prize, how the proposition is phrased, and the time horizon. Such departures from standard discounting may explain the preference for lump sums. Higher discount rates can reflect the desire for

---

of their defined contribution accounts. Brown contends that the 1994 pension supplement to the Current Population Survey yields a comparable number.

7. Fetherstonhaugh and Ross (1999).

8. For the typical male born in 1960, the expected present value of the $2,500 additional annuity payment at a 3 percent discount rate is roughly $30,000, which is larger than the lump-sum payment. For the typical woman, the expected present value of the increased annuity is even larger, at roughly $35,000. The large majorities favoring the lump-sum payment are thus strong evidence that real discount rates are higher than 3 percent or that some other departure from the classical discounting model is present.

9. Thaler (1994).

immediate gratification at the expense of long-term well-being, or concerns about longevity expectations, or the belief that the utility of money will decline over time. An immediate lump sum also allows for big-ticket purchases, such as paying off a mortgage or taking a vacation, which are not possible with small annuity payments.

Not only will people generally take their defined contribution benefit in the form of a lump sum if offered, but they will also think differently about it than if they received a stream of payments. Specifically, the marginal propensity to consume from a lump sum is substantially lower than from a periodic annuity payment. This observation contradicts life-cycle theory, which operates on the assumption that money is fungible. Thaler, and Thaler and Hersh M. Shefrin, provides a plausible explanation for this deviation from standard theory in the notion of mental accounting.[10] In their model, households keep a series of mental accounts, partly in an effort to control their own behavior. A lump sum would raise consumption less than an annuity payment, because large gains relative to income are thought of as saving, and thus the recipient places the sums in the assets mental account. Annuity payments, which are smaller gains relative to income, are coded as current income, and available for spending.

In short, the psychological literature suggests that people want lump sums, and once they receive them, are reluctant to spend them. The following section looks at real-world opportunities for individuals to turn their lump sums into streams of income for consumption, and speculates about possible reasons for their reluctance to do so.

The Elderly Like to Keep Their Assets

In theory, the shift in how pension plans provide benefits need not have any implications for bequests. Individuals could always simply spend their assets or turn them into annuities. Our argument is that this is not going to happen. The failure of retirees to take advantage of annuity opportunities, their lack of enthusiasm for reverse mortgages, their minimal dissaving from bequeathable wealth, and their holdings of life insurance all suggest that the elderly hold on to their assets. We further contend that one of the important reasons they hold on to assets is to leave bequests.

---

10. Thaler (1985, 1990); Thaler and Shefrin (1981).

The Annuity Story

Annuities are contracts between insurance companies and individuals that protect individuals against the risk of outliving their savings. They provide a stream of monthly or annual payments in exchange for a one-time premium.[11] Economic theory would suggest that people should annuitize a lot of their wealth. Life-cycle consumers uncertain about how long they will live, with no bequest motives, and with access to an actuarially fair annuity market, should always chose to annuitize 100 percent of their wealth.[12] After all, consumers face a choice of a traditional market security with a return of *r*, or an annuity with a return of *r* plus a "mortality premium." This mortality premium arises because the assets from deceased annuitants are paid out to those who survive. The only cost to consumers is that the annuity payments stop at death, but if they place no value on wealth after death—that is, they have no bequest motive—the cost of the annuity is zero.

The gains from access to an actuarially-fair annuity market are substantial. Consider two identical sixty-five-year-old men with $100,000 of accumulated assets.[13] The first man purchases an actuarially fair annuity that, with a nominal interest rate of 7 percent, provides a monthly income of $927 for the rest of his life. The other man tries to duplicate the consumption of $927, investing the rest of his wealth at 7 percent. Unfortunately, the second man will run out of money after thirteen years and eight months, at which point he has a 60 percent chance of still being alive. Without annuitizing, the second man would have to cut consumption by one-third: from $927 to $624 in order to avoid running out of money before age 100.

Researchers have calculated that access to an actuarially fair annuity market is equal to roughly a 50-percent increase in unannuitized financial wealth

11. The following discussion focuses on the single premium immediate annuity (SPIA), since it is designed specifically to insure against longevity risk. Other types of annuities exist: For example, the rapid growth in variable annuities, sales of which increased from $5 billion in 1985 to $122 billion in 1999, has received considerable publicity. LIMRA (2000). But variable annuities, where payouts are linked to returns on stocks or other underlying assets, are more like mutual funds and generally purchased while people are working, as a form of tax-deferred investment. The payouts from these annuities are not required to be converted to a stream of payments, but rather can be taken as a lump sum and may ultimately not play an important role in protecting against the risk of outliving savings. Mitchell and others (1999). Hence the focus on SPIAs.

12. Yaari (1965).

13. Brown (2000).

for a sixty-five-year-old male with log utility and average mortality.[14] Despite the enormous potential gains from annuitization, the market for annuities in the United States is minuscule. In 2001, sales of so-called single-premium immediate annuities amounted to only $10.3 billion.[15] The question is why.

ADVERSE SELECTION AND ADMINISTRATIVE COSTS. If an insurance company imposes high enough load factors on annuities, these factors can off-set the benefits of annuitization. The load factors come from two sources. The first is the company's need to cover administrative costs and desire to earn a profit. The second is that those with longer life expectancies are more likely to buy the product. Olivia Mitchell and others found that the net present value of future annuity payments for a sixty-five-year-old male in 1995 was about 80 percent of the required premium, implying a load factor of 20 percent.[16] Using the difference between the mortality table for the whole population, and that used by insurance companies for the annuity group, the researchers concluded that of the 20 percent, approximately 10 percent was due to mortality differences, and 10 percent due to administrative costs. Although recent evidence suggests that load factors are declining, these costs are one reason why individuals might not buy annuities.[17]

ABILITY OF FAMILIES TO POOL RISK. If individuals can share mortality risk within their families, they will be less likely to buy an annuity.[18] In the case of marriage, husband and wife generally agree to pool their resources while both are alive, and to name each other as the major beneficiary in the

14. Brown (2000); Brown, Mitchell, and Poterba (2000b). Moreover, in a recent paper, Brown (2001) shows that when evaluating annuitization on a utility-adjusted basis, as opposed to a financial basis, complete annuitization is optimal even when annuities are not actuarially fair, so long as there are no administrative costs or bequest motives. That is, even with large financial transfers away from high-mortality groups, these groups gain in terms of utility from eliminating the risk that they might exhaust their assets should they live longer than expected.

15. LIMRA (2002).

16. Mitchell and others (1999).

17. Mitchell (2001) reports that in 1998 the net present value of annuity payments for a sixty-five-year-old male was 83.5 percent of the required premium; roughly 10 percentage points due to differential survival values between annuitants and the general population and 6.5 percentage points for marketing and administrative expenses.

18. Brown and Poterba (2000); Kotlikoff and Spivak (1981).

case of death. With this arrangement, the potential death of each spouse somewhat hedges the risk of the other spouse living too long and exhausting his or her resources. If one spouse lives to be very old, the probability is high that the other spouse has already died and left a bequest to help finance consumption. In addition to the exchange of wills, the two can increase their well-being by agreeing on a consumption path that takes account of the expected bequest. Simulations suggest that for a fifty-five-year-old individual, marriage provides 46 percent of the protection offered by a fair annuities market.[19] Similar types of risk sharing can occur between parents and children. Moreover, the comparisons are made in the context of a perfect annuity market. In an insurance market subject to adverse selection and significant administrative costs, it may be more efficient for the family to self-insure than to purchase annuities in the market.

PRECAUTIONARY SAVING. Individuals will be reluctant to annuitize if they want to keep a pile of financial wealth to cover uncertain future expenses. Full annuitization limits the amount that people can spend to their monthly benefits, and leaves them without a buffer to cover large unexpected expenditures. Thus retirees may want to retain at least some wealth to cover large bills, such as outlays for uninsured medical costs.

BEQUEST MOTIVE. A bequest motive is the most obvious reason that people might be reluctant to annuitize their wealth. Without a bequest motive, individuals get no utility from any wealth that they hold at death, so it would be irrational for them not to select the higher return on annuities that arises from the mortality premium. However, with a bequest motive, individuals do value the wealth left to their heirs, and therefore will not want to annuitize all their assets. Menahem Yaari makes this point in his original article.[20]

Benjamin Friedman and Mark Warshawsky attempt to sort out the importance of a bequest motive as opposed to the load factors in explaining why so few persons purchase annuities.[21] In the absence of a bequest motive, the decision to purchase an annuity would hinge simply on whether the

19. Kotlikoff and Spivak (1981).
20. Yaari (1964).
21. Friedman and Warshawsky (1990). In earlier research, the authors concluded that the interaction of the bequest motive, and annuity prices that were not actuarially fair, explain the reluctance of most individuals to buy annuities. Friedman and Warshawsky (1988).

return on a one-period annuity falls short of a market interest rate. On the other hand, a bequest motive is likely to eliminate the demand for annuities even when the return exceeds the market rate. The authors' simulations of an extended life-cycle model show that the yield differentials alone can explain the rarity of annuity purchases during the early retirement years. At older ages, however, it is necessary to add a strong bequest motive to the differentials to explain behavior.

The Reverse Mortgage Story

Housing equity is the most important asset for the vast majority of Americans; 14.5 million households age sixty-two and over own their home free and clear.[22] In principle, this asset might be used to support consumption in retirement. Reverse mortgages were envisioned as a mechanism that would allow older people to consume their housing equity without selling their homes. Yet this market is extremely small—less than one percent of qualified homeowners have a reverse mortgage.

The most important reverse mortgage currently on the market is the Home Equity Conversion Mortgage (HECM). The HECM program emerged from the National Housing Act of 1987 when Congress authorized the Department of Housing and Urban Development (HUD) to institute a pilot program and issue 2,500 reverse mortgages. From the outset, Fannie Mae agreed to purchase all HECM loans, and today is still the sole purchaser. Congress made the program permanent in 1998 and increased allowable outstanding loans to 150,000.[23] Nevertheless, through May 2001, the agency had issued only about 50,000 mortgages under the HECM program.[24]

In addition to the HECM, two private sector products are available. First, since 1995 Fannie Mae has offered its own reverse mortgage, the HomeKeeper. One advantage of the HomeKeeper is that the borrowing limit is

22. SCF (1998).

23. Abt Associates (2000).

24. Under the HECM program, homeowners receive payments secured by the equity of their home. The reverse mortgage becomes payable when the borrower sells the property, moves out, or dies. HECM loans are available to all homeowners age sixty-two and older who own their primary residence free and clear, or who can pay off their mortgage easily with the proceeds of the loan. The maximum amount of the loan depends on the lesser of appraised value of the home or the FHA insurance limit, the expected average mortgage rate, and the age of the borrower. Borrowers can take their money in regular payments for a fixed term, regular payments for as long as they stay in their house, a line of credit, or some combination of these choices.

higher—$275,000 in 2001—than the HECM's FHA loan limit, which currently ranges from $132,000 to $239,250, based on geographic area. On the other hand, the HomeKeeper does not offer the option of receiving payments for a specified term, and does not raise the loan limit on unused lines of credit.[25] On balance, borrowers eligible for both generally prefer the HECM to HomeKeeper loans. As a result, only 1,000 HomeKeeper loans were originated in 1999 compared to 8,000 HECMs. The second private sector reverse mortgage, which is provided by the Financial Freedom Senior Funding Corporation, is aimed at wealthier homeowners in that it offers a maximum loan amount of $700,000.[26] Adding private sector products to the 50,000 outstanding HECMs suggests that roughly 60,000 reverse mortgages exist in the United States compared to a potential market of 14.5 million households age sixty-two and over who own their home free and clear.[27]

The hypothesis of this study is that people want to retain ownership of their homes in order to leave them to their children. In fact, researchers find that the elderly tend to hold on to their homes, which is consistent with a desire to leave the homes as bequests.[28] Typically, the house will be the only significant asset in the bequest. Critics, however, look at these same facts and question whether housing bequests are intended. For example, they argue that it is highly unlikely that the value of a house, often unknowable in advance, would exactly equal the desired amount of a bequest in all cases.[29] Indeed, a host of other factors could also explain the small size of the reverse mortgage market.

HIGH UP-FRONT COSTS. For the median HECM borrower in 1999, the principal loan amount available ranged from $52,500 to $63,000, assuming

25. Under the HECM program, the unused balance of a line of credit grows over time at the same interest rate used for the loan. So borrowers selecting this option see an increase over time in the amount available to them.

26. Currently, Financial Freedom loans are available in only twelve states, although the company has announced its intentions to expand to thirty-five states. The product differs from the HECM and HomeKeeper in that borrowers receive a lump-sum payment at closing, which they can turn into an annuity whose payments can continue even after they sell their home.

27. SCF (1998).

28. Venti and Wise (2000). Even those who contest that most elderly hold on to their homes estimate that at least 42 percent of households will leave behind a house in their estate when the last member dies. Sheiner and Weil (1992).

29. Caplin (2000).

an interest rate range of 7 to 9 percent.[30] The typical costs for a loan of this amount include an origination fee of $1,800, closing costs of $1,500, and a mortgage insurance premium of $2,100. Unlike the case of forward mortgages, HUD does not offer a "no points, no fee" option, so these costs may look out of line to many potential borrowers. In addition, while servicing fees are paid over the life of the loan, the expected present value of these fees, which can range from $3,000 to $5,000, is subtracted from the amount borrowed. Thus closing costs may be perceived as even larger than they really are, especially when compared to the value of the loan.

CONCERN ABOUT FUTURE MEDICAL EXPENSES. Some have argued that retirees may be reluctant to take on reverse mortgages because they are worried about future medical expenses.[31] To the extent that they spend down housing equity early in retirement, they will have less available to cover a serious bout of illness. A period of sickness is also the time that an elderly person might reconsider the optimal living arrangement, and depleting equity early may make moving difficult.[32] On the other hand, most people with reverse mortgages opt for payment in the form of a line of credit, and it could be argued that this reserve offers the elderly precisely the safety cushion they need in case of illness.

FEAR OF DEBT. In addition to the specific arguments, elderly persons may fundamentally be unwilling to take on debt of any sort except in the case of dire emergencies. Many of those who own their homes outright have spent their entire adult lives paying off their initial mortgages. Aversion to debt may be particularly prevalent among the current generation of retirees who lived through the Great Depression and view debt as risky. Moreover, the counseling offered by HUD may itself discourage homeowners from taking on a reverse mortgage, since it emphasizes to potential borrowers that reverse mortgages involve complexities that may come back to haunt them.[33] In

---

30. Abt (2000).

31. Caplin (2000).

32. Feinstein (1996).

33. Moreover, according to several lenders, the media message about reverse mortgages tends to focus on the potential costs rather than the potential benefits. Abt (2000). A focus group of borrowers said that they feel reverse mortgages involve a stigma suggesting dire financial circumstances; for example, according to one participant, relatives viewed taking out a reverse mortgage as equivalent to losing a home.

short, retirees may simply prefer to live in a house they own outright and consume at a lower level than to have somewhat more consumption and the insecurity that comes from housing debt.

SUPPLY SIDE ISSUES. Despite substantial government subsidies and protections, many originators have been unable to generate sufficient volumes of these mortgages to justify maintaining a trained staff for this specialized product, and have exited the market. Low origination fees, the risk that elderly borrowers will not maintain their homes, and regulatory and legal uncertainties are all possible explanations, but many of these obstacles could be overcome if demand for reverse mortgages were strong. In the end, it may come down to a simple preference to hold onto to one's major possession and preserve a legacy for one's heirs.

The Savings Story

The life-cycle theory suggests that individuals accumulate resources during their working years that they will draw upon to support themselves in retirement. The accumulated resources consist of credits under Social Security, accrued benefits under employer-sponsored defined benefit plans, accumulations in defined contribution plans, housing wealth, and financial assets. Wealth in the form of Social Security and defined benefit plan accruals are automatically drawn down in retirement since they are paid out in the form of monthly benefits and generally consumed. Since for most of the population, pension promises constitute the bulk of total wealth at retirement, this drawing down of pension wealth means that savings behavior of most of the elderly more or less conforms with the life-cycle hypothesis.

The controversy about dissaving in retirement centers on the elderly's handling of their nonannuitized or bequeathable wealth. The tendency of the elderly to retain their home is discussed above in the context of reverse mortgages, and the evidence suggests that retirees are reluctant to draw down their financial assets as well. Part of the explanation is that individuals do not know when they are going to die, and therefore conserve their resources, or they are concerned about the possibility of a costly illness and hang onto assets for this reason. But the hypothesis of this paper is that the desire to leave a bequest is also an important factor.

A series of studies looking at panel data for the 1960s, 1970s, and early 1980s finds that the elderly draw down their nonannuitized financial assets at a relatively slow rate of between 1 and 5 percent per year.[34] Not surprisingly, households headed by a married person have a slower rate of decumulation than households headed by a single person, since the life expectancy of a married couple would normally be greater.

The results for the late 1980s and 1990s differ from the earlier studies in that they show either no change or increases in the assets of the elderly. For example, Erik Hurst, Ming Ching Louh, and Frank Stafford, using the Panel Study of Income Dynamics, find that individuals over sixty-five, during the period 1989 to 1994, actually increased the value of their bequeathable wealth.[35] Similar results emerge from a study by Steven Haider and others based on two data sets: the New Beneficiary Data System (NBDS), and Asset and Health Dynamics among the Oldest Old (AHEAD).[36] The NBDS contains interviews of new Social Security beneficiaries in 1982, when they were in their sixties, and again in 1991.[37] The results for the NBDS show changes in nonannuitized wealth to be fairly flat between 1982 and 1991, since mean wealth grew by less than 1 percent per year, and median wealth declined by a quarter of one percent per year. AHEAD contains information on households who were in their seventies in the first year of interviews in 1993. The AHEAD results show that most households experienced a significant increase in their nonhousing wealth between 1993 and 1995. This anomalous outcome may reflect the inability of older households to quickly adjust their spending plans in response to the rise in stock prices.

While rising stock prices may have dominated the most recent studies, the evidence taken as a whole clearly indicates that retirees are reluctant to draw down their accumulated saving. This reluctance may be due to fear of large medical expenses, to uncertainty about how long they will live, or to the

---

34. Mirer (1980); Diamond and Hausman (1984); Hurd (1987, 1991). Early work on dissaving uses cross-sectional as opposed to panel data because these were the only data available. Results from cross-sectional data can be misleading, however. First, younger cohorts are typically richer than older ones due to productivity growth. Second, the wealthy live longer than the poor. If rich and poor households had the same pattern of dissaving, this would not be a problem, but in fact, their patterns differ. Jianakoplos, Menchik, and Irvine (1989) create cross-sectional estimates from panel data, and demonstrate that it is not possible to correct cross-sectional data for these biases.

35. Hurst, Louh, and Stafford (1998).

36. Haider and others (2000).

37. The sample consists of newly retired workers, those claiming benefits as a wife or widow, new disability beneficiaries, and a Medicare-only sample; the authors limit the analysis to retired workers, wives, and widows born between 1914 and 1920.

desire to leave a bequest. In any event, the reluctance to draw down accumulated financial assets is fully consistent with older people's aversion to annuities and reverse mortgages.

The Life Insurance Story

Life insurance holdings by retirees shed some light on the strength of the
bequest motive, although the phenomenon is slightly different. We are interested in whether people hold on to their assets once they have them, while
the life insurance debate focuses on whether people attempt to turn annuitized income streams back into wealth by buying insurance. As Yaari shows,
purchasing life insurance is equivalent to selling off one's annuities.[38]

Life insurance is a useful instrument to protect working-age individuals
against the loss of earned income, but does not seem appropriate for retirees
who are living off accumulated wealth. They have no earned income to protect and should, if anything, be purchasing annuities in order to ensure that
they do not exhaust their resources before they die. If people are interested in
leaving bequests, they could simply not annuitize a portion of their wealth,
and invest it in stocks and bonds. Nevertheless, the majority of married couples in retirement own life insurance. Douglas B. Bernheim contends that
these elderly households hold life insurance to offset excessive annuitization
through Social Security, so that they will have assets to bequeath to their children or other beneficiaries.[39] People could feel they were overannuitized for
reasons that have little to do with bequests. For example, they could be concerned about unforeseen health expenditures. The response in this case, however, would not be to purchase life insurance, since its proceeds would not be
available to cover health care costs.[40]

---

38. Yaari (1965).

39. Bernheim (1991) tests his annuity-offset model using the 1975 Retirement
History Survey and finds support for two of three implications of his model: First, he
finds that higher Social Security benefits are correlated with higher probability of
owning life insurance and with higher amounts of coverage. Second, he finds weak
support that life insurance coverage is a decreasing function of lifetime resources, and
therefore an inferior good. He finds no support for the implication that people would
not simultaneously hold life insurance and annuities. Based on these results, Bernheim concludes that 25 percent of the elderly have too much of their wealth annuitized, and they are using term life insurance to sell these annuities in order to leave a
bequest. This would suggest a strong bequest motive, and a reluctance of people to
spend assets accumulated in a defined contribution plan.

40. In essence, Bernheim treats married couples as single agents who purchase life
insurance not to protect the surviving spouse, but solely as a means of providing

Jeffrey Brown reexamines the annuity-offset hypothesis using the first wave of the AHEAD survey, and finds no support for the theory.[41] AHEAD has advantages over Bernheim's Retirement History Survey because it includes only retirees and allows for the distinction between term life—pure insurance—and whole life—a combination of insurance and tax-deferred savings. AHEAD, like the Retirement History Survey, shows substantial ownership of life insurance among the elderly: 78 percent of couples own some form of life insurance, and 50 percent have term insurance. However, in the empirical analysis, Brown finds the positive correlation between Social Security benefits and life insurance disappears once life insurance is limited to term, and finds no support for any of the other implications of the annuity-offset model. Brown suggests several alternative hypotheses for the large fraction of elderly households that own life insurance. These include simple inertia in that many of the policies have been held for decades, an effort to prepay death expenses, a source of liquidity to pay estate taxes, or a way to ensure an adequate stream of consumption for spouses.[42]

While much of Brown's criticism has merit, the insurance holdings of older people are simply too large to dismiss. Table 8-1 shows the holdings by age of both term and whole life insurance as reported in the 1998 SCF. Although the mean value of term life insurance held by those sixty-five and older is much smaller than that held by younger age groups, it still averages $32,766. Moreover, it is unclear whether whole life holdings should be totally excluded from consideration, since whole life policies contain both an insurance and a tax-favored saving component. Since people have other tax-favored ways to save, such as variable annuities and IRAs, selecting whole life suggests that the insurance aspect has some value. In fact, households sixty-five and over are not only holding whole-life policies but actually buying them. In 1997, this group purchased 5 percent of the policies sold and received 25 percent of the premiums paid.[43]

---

bequests for children. Auerbach and Kotlikoff (1987) consider the demand for life insurance to protect the surviving spouse, and find no evidence that households use life insurance to offset government increases in annuitization. Specifically, they report that survivor insurance protection provided by Social Security does not lead to offsetting reductions in the purchase of private life insurance.

41. Brown (1999).

42. The majority of policies held by married individuals name their spouse rather than their children as beneficiaries.

43. LIMRA (1998).

Table 8-1. *Life Insurance Policies, by Age Groups, SCF 1998*

Age group	Term		Whole life		
	Percentage with	Mean value[a]	Percentage with	Mean cash value[a]	Mean face value
65 and older	41.2	$32,766	36.0	$22,435	$45,721
55–64	57.4	120,251	36.0	22,338	124,773
45–54	55.6	203,435	32.9	33,743	173,689
35–44	58.5	194,238	29.0	38,093	148,112
Younger than 35	50.4	167,475	18.1	25,015	122,670

Source: Authors' calculations using the SCF 1998.
a. Mean values are for households holding insurance.

How the Shift to Lump-Sum Payments Could Affect Bequests

Although researchers have offered a host of reasons for the reluctance of the elderly to purchase annuities and reverse mortgages, their limited dissaving, and their holdings of life insurance, the desire to leave a bequest is a common theme. Actually, people leave bequests for two reasons: a positive bequest motive described above, which produces intended bequests, and unintended bequests due to uncertain lifetimes. The shift to defined contribution plans could affect actual bequests through either mechanism.

With uncertain lifetimes and no access to life annuities, elderly individuals would conserve wealth to self-insure against the risk of outliving their resources or having to severely curtail consumption. Although a well-developed market for annuities exists in the United States, as we discussed earlier, most people do not buy them. Shunning annuities in a world of uncertain lifetimes creates precautionary saving, which produces significant unintended bequests. Simulation exercises suggest that the purchase of annuities could increase the consumption of the elderly by one-third.[44] In the context of this study, these results suggest that the movement away from annuitization in the private pension system could have a significant negative effect on consumption and a resulting positive impact on bequests.

A shift to defined contribution plans could also have an impact on intended bequests.[45] People may have an unsatisfied demand for leaving a

44. Kotlikoff and Spivak (1981); Davies (1981); Abel (1985).
45. Researchers have developed several theories about why decedents leave intended bequests. One defined by Barro (1974) and Becker (1974) is altruism. This means parents bequeath because they gain utility from the welfare of their children. The implication of altruistic behavior is that bequests will be compensatory. Parents

bequest, but find it too difficult to accumulate assets for that purpose. Given assets, however, their tendency is to preserve them and to increase the amount they intend to leave their children or other beneficiaries. One question is how prevalent is the desire to leave a bequest.

Two types of evidence shed some light on the importance of a bequest motive: The first is survey data.[46] Both the HRS and the SCF ask respondents virtually the same questions: "Do you (and your spouse) think it is important to leave an inheritance to surviving heirs?" and "Do you (and your spouse) expect to leave a sizable inheritance to your heirs?"[47] The responses show 67 to 78 percent of families think leaving an inheritance is very important, important, or somewhat important, and 42 to 50 percent responded either yes, probably, or possibly, to expectations about leaving a sizable inheritance.[48]

---

will leave greater amounts to children with low earnings, and bequests will compensate for intergenerational differences, with parents providing more to compensate for the lower average earnings of their children. A second motivation for bequests is strategic. Bernheim, Shleifer, and Summers (1985). Parents use the prospect of bequests to elicit more attention by threatening to disinherit any wayward child in favor of his or her siblings. A third motivation for bequests is the so-called joy of giving hypothesis, where decedents leave bequests solely because they receive utility from the size of the bequest. Yaari (1964). Of course, bequests are not the only way to transfer assets to one's children; *inter-vivos* giving is also important and could be as large as bequests. Cox (1987) finds that among those who make transfers, *inter-vivos* transfers increase as the income of the recipient increases. This is consistent with a theory of exchange between parent and child, but not with altruism.

46. Early surveys asked whether people were saving in order to leave a bequest. Only 4 percent of respondents to the 1962 Survey of Financial Characteristics cited "providing an estate" as a saving objective. Projector and Weiss (1966, table A30); Projector and Weiss (1966). Survey of Financial Characteristics of Consumers. Washington, D.C. Board of Governors, Federal Reserve Board. The Brookings Survey of Affluent Families ($10,000 and above in 1965, or $56,000 in 2001) found only 23 percent were saving to make a bequest. Barlow and others (1966).

47. Since the interviewer addresses the bequest questions to the respondent and spouse simultaneously, we assume that the couple in answering the questions is referring to bequests to children, or others outside of the household.

48. We have interpreted positive responses to these questions as an indication of a bequest motive. This seems reasonable because 80 percent of those who "expect" to leave a bequest view leaving a bequest as "important." Critics, nevertheless, suggest that positive responses to the questions simply reflect the recognition that any household with nonannuitized wealth will end up leaving a bequest, unless its members live for an exceedingly long time, or have large nonreimbursed medical expenses.

Not surprisingly, interest in bequests is greater among those with greater wealth.

The second method for determining the strength of a bequest motive is through empirical tests. John Laitner and F. Thomas Juster find significant interest in leaving estates in a sample of 1988 TIAA-CREF annuitants.[49] The households in this sample generally fall within the top 10 to 20 percent of the income distribution, but exclude the super-rich. The authors restrict their sample to male respondents, who compose 425 cases, and whose average age is seventy. About half of these individuals are interested in leaving an estate, and their net worth is several hundred thousand dollars higher than those with no interest in bequests.[50]

Many researchers argue that a strong bequest motive helps explain why the rate of dissaving among the elderly is so low.[51] The main critic of this position is Michael Hurd, who has examined dissaving among the elderly using a vast array of data sets.[52] Like other researchers, he finds a very small amount of dissaving among the elderly, and sometimes even a growth in wealth. In each study, Hurd tests whether this pattern can be attributed to a bequest motive by comparing the savings patterns of households with children to those without children. He finds no significant difference in the savings patterns between the two types of households and concludes that no evidence for a bequest motive exists.[53]

Brown also uses the presence of children to test whether a bequest motive has a significant effect on people's plans whether or not to annuitize proceeds

49. Laitner and Juster (1996).

50. Laitner and Juster (1996) are particularly interested in determining the extent to which intergenerational altruism explains saving for bequests. They find that among households for whom leaving a bequest is important, the projected bequest tends to be largest for those with the lowest assessment of their children's likely earnings, suggesting substantial intergenerational altruism. In the sample as a whole, however, altruism does not appear to be the major motive for saving.

51. See, for example, Juster and Laitner (1996); and Gale and Scholz (1994).

52. Hurd has analyzed the Longitudinal Retirement History Survey (1987, 1989, 1990, 1992); the Survey of Income and Program Participation (1991); the Health and Retirement Study (1999); the Asset and Health Dynamics among the Oldest Old (1999, 2000); the New Beneficiary Data System (2000). Hurd (1991). "The Income and Savings of the Elderly." Manuscript. Final report to AARP Andrus Foundation.

53. In collaborative work with Haider and others (2000), using AHEAD and NBDS, Hurd and his co-authors once again test whether parents dissave more slowly than nonparents. Again, they find no difference and conclude that a desire to leave a bequest is not the motive for the slow rate of dissaving.

Table 8-2. *Percent of Households Aged 51–61 with and without Children Interested in Leaving an Inheritance*[a]

	Respondents with children	Respondents without children
Panel A: Do you think it is important to leave an inheritance to surviving heirs?		
Very important or important	23	20
Somewhat important	48	36
Not important	28	40
Panel B: Do you expect to leave a sizable inheritance to your heirs?		
Yes or probably	28	25
Possibly	15	11
Probably not or no	55	59

Source: Authors' calculations using the Health and Retirement Study (HRS) (1992).

a. Totals may not equal 100 because a small number of respondents answered "don't know" or "not applicable" to these survey questions.

from their 401(k) plan.[54] Using the HRS, he constructs a subsample of about 900 people with defined contribution plans, and then estimates the probability of their annuitizing payouts based on "annuity equivalent wealth," mortality risk, risk aversion, fraction of wealth preannuitized, and marital status.[55] He finds that adding either the presence of children or the response indicating it is very important to leave an inheritance does not have a statistically significant effect on the probability of annuitizing.

The difficulty with these studies is that they implicitly assume that childless couples never leave intentional bequests. This assumption is not consistent with most survey data. Laitner and Juster's data on TIAA-CREF annuitants show a significant fraction of households without children believe leaving a bequest is either very or quite important.[56] Table 8-2 presents information from the HRS on attitudes about leaving inheritances for households with and without children. The differences between the two groups are small.

Moreover, in a recent paper, Hurd and James Smith test for the importance of children in another context and find that children have little explanatory power in the likelihood of leaving a bequest.[57] The data come

54. Brown (2000).

55. Annuity equivalent wealth measures the amount of additional wealth a household would require to follow its optimal path of consumption in the absence of annuitization.

56. Laitner and Juster (1996).

57. Hurd and Smith (1999).

from "exit" interviews with proxies, often relatives of the deceased, for 774 people in the AHEAD survey who died between the first and second wave. About 80 percent of these decedents left an estate of significant value.[58] Hurd and Smith attempt to explain the factors affecting the probability of leaving an estate and the magnitude of that estate. They find that the number of living children, grandchildren, or great-grandchildren has no statistically significant effect on either the probability of leaving a bequest or the amount. Hurd and Smith interpret this finding as supporting earlier evidence that a bequest motive is not important, because behavior does not differ between those with children and those without. We think this finding raises the question once again whether one should expect a systematic difference in behavior based on the presence or absence of children.

Another angle on the bequest issue is to estimate how much of the current stock of wealth is a result of bequests as opposed to life-cycle saving. Such an exercise, of course, cannot distinguish between bequests as a result of uncertain lifetimes and a bequest motive. Franco Modigliani and Richard Brumberg recognize the existence of bequests, and incorporate bequests into their model in the second of two papers laying out the life-cycle hypothesis.[59] Nevertheless, estimates by Kotlikoff and Summers, and by Kotlikoff, showing that inheritance and gifts account for 80 percent of total wealth generated considerable controversy.[60] Modigliani responded that inherited wealth accounts for no more than 20 percent of total wealth.[61] Much of the difference between the two estimates hinges on whether college tuition and other transfers to young adults should be included in the total, and whether the interest earned on inheritances should be included in the original transfer. Our preference is to exclude tuition, but include interest on the transferred wealth, which suggests that bequests account for 30 to 50 percent of total wealth.[62]

58. In total, the estates were worth $73 million, but interestingly, only one quarter of that value appears in estate tax files.
59. Modigliani and Brumberg (1980).
60. Kotlikoff and Summers (1981); Kotlikoff (1988).
61. Modigliani (1988). Laitner and Juster (1996) estimates for TIAA-CREF annuitants attribute about 20 percent of lifetime private net worth to intentional estate building. Their numbers, however, exclude unintentional bequests and *inter vivos* gifts. They also ignore the effect on overall wealth accumulation of the receipt of an inheritance.
62. Aaron and Munnell (1992). The inclusion of earnings on previous inheritances simply standardizes—in present value terms—inheritances received at various times in the past. The standard definition of life-cycle income is simply the present discounted value of earnings plus inheritances. The treatment of college tuition is

All the evidence taken together suggests that the desire to leave a bequest is widespread, and that the combination of intended and unintended bequests is large. This implies that a major increase in lump-sum payments from private pension plans could have an important impact on the total volume of bequests. The following three sections use data from the SCF and the HRS to explore the implications of the growth in defined contribution plans on various aspects of bequests.

The SCF is a triennial survey sponsored by the Federal Reserve Board in cooperation with Statistics of Income of the Department of the Treasury. The SCF collects detailed information on approximately 4,000 households' assets, liabilities, and demographic characteristics as well as on pension coverage, participation, and pension plan characteristics such as contribution levels. To provide reliable estimates of highly concentrated assets, the survey oversamples wealthy households. In the following analyses, we use data from the 1992 and 1998 surveys.

The HRS is a nationally representative sample of 7,607 families who had at least one member born between 1931 and 1941. Respondents were interviewed initially in 1992 when they were fifty-one through sixty-one years old, and have been interviewed every two years since; at this writing, five waves of the HRS are available. Because the HRS follows households over time, it is possible to calculate saving and then explore how saving responds to different types of pension coverage. The HRS also has the best pension data of any survey. In addition to self-reported data on pension benefits, it includes highly detailed employer-provided plan descriptions for pensions covering many workers in the sample, which allows more accurate estimation of pension values than is possible with only self-reported data. Social Security records are also available for 70 percent of the sample. HRS respondents also provide comprehensive information about assets other than pensions and Social Security. The survey deals with the typical high nonresponse rates when respondents are asked about the value of their stock holdings, IRA balances, or other narrow asset categories by following an open-ended question about value with a series of bracketed questions.[63]

---

more difficult. At some point, parental gifts to adult children should be treated as bequests. On the other hand, parental support of dependent children is usually viewed as consumption. A continuum exists between these extremes. If tuition has to be put in one category, however, our view is that it should be treated as an expenditure on dependent children.

63. The HRS changed the way in which it used the bracketed information to determine asset values between the 1992 through 1994 surveys and subsequent years.

The Potential Impact of the Shift to Defined Contribution Plans on Unintended Bequests

The argument that the extent to which retirement wealth comes as lump sums rather than flows will affect bequests is not new. In fact, Alan J. Auerbach, Kotlikoff, and David Weil make the same argument in reverse.[64] They contend that increasing annuitization of retirement wealth reduces bequests and lowers inequality. Their story is straightforward: Consider the case where individuals have no bequest motive at all, but leave accidental bequests because annuities are not available. Introducing annuities in this environment will allow retirees to increase their consumption and reduce their bequests. Without bequests, wealth holdings would look more like the distribution of human capital as reflected in wages, which is much more equally distributed than the current distribution.

The wealth of the elderly certainly did become increasingly annuitized as Social Security expanded and private pension coverage increased. Data from the Current Population Survey show that pension and Social Security income rose from 36 percent of the income of those sixty-five and over in 1958, to 57 percent in 1998.[65] To make a general argument about the overall level of annuitization would require careful consideration of Medicare.[66] Medicare represents a sizable health care annuity, where benefits have grown rapidly and are projected to continue to grow in the future. Including Medicare as part of annuities would probably show that the annuitized portion of total wealth would continue to grow despite the shift from defined benefit to defined contribution plans. But the focus here is not general patterns of annuitization, but rather the shift within the pension component from streams of payments to bequeathable assets.

The HRS is in the process of revising the 1992 and 1994 imputation procedures to make them consistent with subsequent surveys but at this writing has completed only 1994. The wealth data in this paper come from the 1992 and 1994 surveys, and since the 1992 imputation has not yet been modified, we have used the version of the 1994 data that contains the original imputations.

64. Auerbach, Kotlikoff, and Weil (1992).

65. Alicia H. Munnell and Annika Sundén (2001). "Private Pensions: Coverage and Benefit Trends." Paper prepared for "Conversation on Coverage," Conference of the American Institute of Architects, Washington, D.C., July 24–25, 2001.

66. Earnings also merit consideration in assessing the overall level of annuitized versus bequeathable wealth among the elderly. In part, the rise of pension annuities was accompanied by a decline in earnings, which are also a survival-contingent source of income.

To determine the potential impact on unintended bequests of the change in annuitization due to the growth of defined contribution plans, we estimate the annual flow of bequests using the 1998 SCF. To calculate wealth in the hands of decedents, we multiply respondents' nonannuitized assets by their age-sex-specific mortality probabilities. This exercise shows decedents holding $492 billion in 1998. Since we are interested in transfers outside of the couple, we eliminate bequests to spouses, bequests to charity, funeral expenses, and taxes, using data from 1998 federal estate tax returns, which indicate that about 48 percent of net worth is transferred across generations. Applying the 48 percent to wealth in the hands of decedents produces estimated bequests of $236 billion.[67]

To examine how the shift to defined contribution plans affects annual bequests, we reestimate bequests in 1998, replacing the 1998 ratio of defined contribution to total pension wealth with the 1992 ratio. The results are presented in table 8-3. This reduces wealth in the hands of decedents by $15 billion, and bequests across generations by $7 billion. In other words, the shift from defined benefit to defined contribution plans that occurred between 1992 and 1998 increased the wealth held by decedents in 1998 by $15 billion and transfers across generations by $7 billion. Of course, the shift to defined contribution plans had not run its course in 1998, at which point defined contribution assets accounted for only 53 percent of total pension wealth (compared to 36 percent in 1992). Assuming that defined contribution assets increase by another 17 percentage points to 70 percent of total pension wealth between 1998 and 2004, wealth held by decedents will be $13 billion higher each year and transfers to the next generation will increase by $6 billion by 2004.

67. The transfer rate was calculated by taking the total gross estate of all estate filers in 1998, and subtracting allowable deductions and tax liability. Johnson (1992) and Eller and Johnson (2000) also estimate a similar intergenerational percentage rate of 47 percent and 45 percent respectively. The intergenerational transfer rate for the whole population is probably higher than that for those who file federal estate tax returns. The estate tax returns undoubtedly overstate taxes paid by the whole population since only about 2 percent of decedents file estate returns. They also probably overstate deductions such as gifts to charity and expenses related to the funeral, as those with higher net worth tend to give more to charity and have more extravagant funeral expenses. However, the percentages generated by the federal estate tax returns appear to be the only estimates of wealth passed to the next generation. Eller and Johnson (2000). "Using a Sample of Federal Estate Tax Returns to Examine the Effects of Audit Revaluation on Pre-Audit Estimates." U.S. Department of the Treasury, Internal Revenue Service, Statistics of Income Division, Statistics of Income Research Paper.

Table 8-3. *Increase in Wealth in the Hands of Decedents due to Growth of Defined Contribution Plans between 1992 and 1998*[a]
Billions of dollars, unless otherwise noted

Quintiles of nonpension net worth	1998 increase of wealth in the hands of decedents	1998 wealth in the hands of decedents with 1992 pension ratios	Increase as a percent of 1998 wealth in the hands of decedents with 1992 pension ratios
Top	11.1	393.9	2.8
Second	2.0	60.9	3.3
Third	1.2	18.5	6.6
Fourth	0.4	3.4	10.9
Bottom	0.2	0.2	118.3
Total	14.9	476.8	3.2

Source: Authors' calculations using the SCF 1998.
a. Households are allocated among quintiles based on nonpension net worth with 1992 ratios.

This exercise also makes it possible to explore how the increase in bequests might affect the distribution of wealth. Table 8-3 shows the distribution across wealth quintiles of the $15 billion increase in the wealth in the hands of decedents due to the growth of defined contribution plans between 1992 and 1998. It also shows this increase as a percent of total net worth in the hands of decedents in 1998, assuming defined contribution plans had not grown. The percentages reveal that the increase in bequeathable wealth between 1992 and 1998 is far more important for lower quintiles than for the upper quintiles. This means the shift from defined benefit to defined contribution plans should help to reduce wealth inequality.

The Impact of the Shift to Defined Contribution Plans on Intended Bequests

The previous exercise demonstrates how unintended bequests could potentially increase as individuals receive more of their pension benefits as bequeathable wealth. We also hypothesize that intended bequests will rise, because people's interest in bequests changes when they gain access to a pile of assets. Accumulating wealth out of current income to leave a bequest is too difficult, but if people receive a pile of wealth, leaving a bequest becomes a plausible option.

It is possible to test this hypothesis using data from both the SCF and HRS, since both surveys collect information on households' expectations of leaving bequests. The SCF asks if the household expects to "leave a sizable estate to others." In addition to this simple yes-or-no question, the HRS asks households about their subjective probability of leaving a bequest of $10,000 or more. Households that expect to leave a bequest of $10,000 or more are then asked about their subjective probability of leaving a bequest of $100,000 or more.

Our hypothesis is that an increase in the share of pension wealth provided in the form of bequeathable assets will increase the probability of leaving a bequest. We test this hypothesis by estimating two sets of bequest equations, including the ratio of defined contribution and IRA wealth to total pension and Social Security wealth. The dependent variable in the first set is an indicator variable with a value of one if the household expects to leave a bequest, and zero if the household does not. The equations are estimated for the HRS and for a 1998 SCF sample of households with at least one member aged fifty-one to sixty-one. In addition to the share of pension wealth that is bequeathable, the explanatory variables include coverage under a defined benefit or defined contribution plan, income, total pension wealth, nonpension net worth, receipt of an inheritance, college degree, children, good health, race, and self-employment status. Total pension wealth, income, and net worth are entered as logs because changes of income and wealth at low levels would be expected to have a larger impact on bequest plans than at higher levels. The indicator variable for coverage under a defined benefit or defined contribution plan should not have a significant effect on the probability of leaving a bequest, since the hypothesis is that the share of nonannuitized pension wealth is the important factor, not pension coverage.

Since the same socioeconomic variables are used in all the following empirical work, it is useful to explain why each is included. We expect that the receipt of an inheritance will have a positive effect on the probability of leaving a bequest. The assumption is that families who benefit from earlier generations' generosity are more likely to help later generations. A college degree is expected to have a positive effect, since education may broaden one's time horizon. As we discussed earlier, the presence of children is unlikely to affect the probability of leaving a bequest, but we include it in the equation, because children are a test variable for a bequest motive in so much recent research.[68]

Good health could have a positive or negative effect. A person in good health may be less likely to deplete household assets to cover medical expenses,

68. Some reviewers suggest that the number of children would be more relevant than the presence of children. Using the number of children has virtually no impact on any of the results reported below.

Table 8-4. *Probit Regressions for Those Aged 51–61, HRS 1992 and SCF 1998*[a]

Variable	HRS 1992 Marginal effects	SCF 1998 Marginal effects
DC as a share of total SS	0.206	0.185
and pension wealth	(4.52)	(2.46)
DB or DC coverage	−0.030	−0.143
	(−1.37)	(−3.75)
Log income	0.016	0.054
	(2.07)	(3.41)
Log total SS and pension wealth	0.061	0.012
	(5.15)	(0.84)
Log nonpension net worth	0.040	0.047
	(10.86)	(5.48)
Received inheritance	0.100	0.123
	(4.80)	(3.29)
College education	0.008	0.052
	(0.42)	(1.37)
Have children	0.086	0.215
	(2.94)	(3.80)
Good health	0.056	0.072
	(2.64)	(1.57)
White	−0.200	−0.065
	(−9.69)	(−1.35)
Self-employed	0.074	0.073
	(3.12)	(1.86)
Pseudo R^2	0.09	0.28
N	4,794	1,008

Source: Authors' calculations of HRS (1992).

a. *t* statistics are in parentheses. See appendix table 8A-1 for variable definitions. The 1st tercile includes households with the lowest incomes. In the HRS, cohort 1 is for those born between 1935 and 1937, and cohort 2 is for those born between 1938 and 1941. In the SCF, cohort 1 is for those born between 1941 and 1943, and cohort 2 is for those born between 1944 and 1947.

and be more likely to leave a bequest. On the other hand, a person in good health may live longer, and therefore consume some of the assets available for bequests. We have also included a race variable. Our expectation is that the non-Hispanic white households (hereafter referred to simply as white) will be more likely to leave a bequest, since whites have a history of higher income and wealth, and therefore, more of a tradition of passing assets from one generation to the next. Finally, self-employed status should have a positive effect, since bequests are a way to continue the business across generations.

Table 8-4 presents the first set of equations. The values reported in the table are the change in the probability of leaving a bequest from a one-unit change in a continuous variable evaluated at the mean or the shift in a dichotomous variable from zero to one. For example, respondents who are in good health have a 5.6 percentage point higher probability of leaving a bequest than respondents in poor health.

As hypothesized, bequeathable pension wealth—defined contribution assets and IRAs—as a share of total pension wealth has a positive and large effect on the probability of leaving a bequest. If the defined contribution-IRA share of pension wealth increases by 10 percentage points, the respondent's subjective probability of leaving a bequest increases by 2.1 percentage points in the HRS and by 1.8 percentage points in the SCF.[69] This is not simply a "pension effect," since the equation contains a variable to control for coverage under a defined contribution or defined benefit plan.

In general, the results are consistent between the two surveys and with earlier studies.[70] As expected, an increase in income or wealth raises the probability of leaving a bequest in both the SCF and HRS. Having received a bequest in the past is positive and significant in both surveys. College education is not significant in either survey. Children and good health are positive and generally significant. Surprisingly, in both surveys, white households have a lower subjective probability of leaving a bequest. Self-employed households are more likely to plan on leaving a bequest.

The second set of equations employs the more specific bequest expectations included in the HRS. Asking families about the possibility that they will leave a bequest of certain amounts is likely to provide better information about bequest intentions and a better framework for testing the importance of the share variable. The equations are estimated for the probability of leaving a bequest of $10,000 or more, and the probability of leaving a bequest of $100,000 or more as shown in table 8-5.[71]

Again, the results indicate that the share of pension wealth that is in bequeathable form is a very important determinant of the probability of leaving a bequest of $10,000 and $100,000. The magnitude of the effect is somewhat higher than in the more general equations in table 8-4. For

---

69. The estimated coefficient is 0.206 in the HRS and 0.185 in the SCF. Because the share of defined contribution wealth in total pension and Social Security wealth is measured as a fraction between 0 and 1, the coefficient has to be divided by 100 to get the effect of a 1 percentage point change in the defined contribution or IRA share on the probability of leaving a bequest.

70. For example, see Smith (1999).

71. Since the probabilities range from zero to one, the equations are estimated using a Tobit regression.

Table 8-5. *Probability of Leaving a Bequest in the HRS; Tobit Estimates*[a]

Variable	Probability of leaving a bequest of $10,000 or more[b]	Probability of leaving a bequest of $100,000 or more
DC as a share of total SS	0.337	0.285
and pension wealth	(4.51)	(6.73)
DB or DC coverage	0.130	−0.008
	(3.39)	(−0.33)
Log income	0.081	0.544
	(6.16)	(6.09)
Log total SS and pension wealth	0.110	0.107
	(5.72)	(8.49)
Log nonpension net worth	0.083	0.065
	(15.70)	(15.90)
Received inheritance	0.072	0.058
	(2.05)	(2.85)
College education	0.169	0.205
	(5.08)	(10.62)
Have children	0.052	0.039
	(1.05)	(1.26)
Good health	0.169	0.163
	(4.55)	(6.47)
White	0.120	0.105
	(3.37)	(4.46)
Self-employed	0.265	0.135
	(5.68)	(5.07)
Constant	−2.591	−2.730
	(−11.32)	(−18.16)
Pseudo R^2	0.16	0.22
N	4,095	4,078

a. Authors' calculations of HRS (1992).

b. *t* statistics are in parentheses. See appendix table 8A-1 for variable definitions. The 1st tercile includes households with the lowest incomes. In the HRS, cohort 1 is for those born between 1935 and 1937, and cohort 2 is for those born between 1938 and 1941. In the SCF, cohort 1 is for those born between 1941 and 1943, and cohort 2 is for those born between 1944 and 1947.

bequests of $10,000 or more, a 10 percentage point increase in the share raises the probability by 3.4 percentage points; for $100,000 or more, a 10 percentage point increase in the share raises the probability by 2.8 percentage points. The higher impact for smaller bequests is consistent with the fact that pensions are a more important component of wealth for lower-wealth households. The coefficients on the other explanatory variables are generally consistent with the table 8-4 equations. One important exception is the race variable. In contrast to the previous equations, but consistent with James Smith, whites are more likely to leave bequests.[72] Another exception to the results in table 8-4 is that having children does not increase the probability of a bequest.

The conclusion from this exercise is that the form in which respondents receive their pension wealth affects their subjective probabilities of leaving bequests. The greater the share of pension benefits received as a lump sum, the greater the likelihood of a planned bequest.

The Impact of the Shift to Defined Contribution Plans on Saving and Wealth

If the elderly are not going to spend their lump-sum payments from defined contribution plans, the question arises as to whether they will reduce consumption in retirement, or save more during their working years. One way to answer this question is to explore whether people react differently to their defined contribution plan than to their defined benefit plan.

The starting point for this part of the analysis is a simple life-cycle model.[73] Households choose current and future consumption to maximize lifetime utility subject to lifetime resources:

$$\max \sum_{t=s}^{d} U(C_t)$$

$$s.t. \sum_{t=s}^{d} C_t = \sum_{t=s}^{r} (E_t + I_t) + \sum_{t=r}^{d} PEN_t - B_{d+1} , \tag{1}$$

where C is consumption, s is age at start of work life, d is age at death, r is age at retirement, E is earnings, I is inheritances received, PEN is pension and Social Security benefits, and B is intended bequests. In this simple model, utility is a concave function of only consumption, and lifetime consumption equals the sum of total earnings, inheritances, and pension benefits less intended bequests. This model serves as the basis for both the saving and

---

72. Smith (1999).

73. Although we have selected the life-cycle model of saving, other saving models exist. Two prominent examples are "consumption under uncertainty," in which savings arise from surprise changes in income (Hall, 1978), and the "buffer stock" model, which attributes a significant portion of saving to a precautionary motive. Carroll (1997).

wealth equations. In each set of equations, the focus is whether households react differently to pensions that will be received as lump sums as opposed to annuities.

The Impact of Pensions on Saving

Maximizing utility subject to the budget constraint yields annual consumption for the household at time t equal to a constant share of its lifetime resources:[74]

$$C_t = \frac{1}{LE}\left[E_t + \sum_{t=t+1}^{r} E_t + SSW + DBW + DCW + W_{t-1} - B_{d+1}\right], \quad (2)$$

where LE is remaining life expectancy and W_{t-1} is the sum of past saving. Savings in period t is income in period t less consumption in period t:

$$S_t = E_t - C_t. \quad (3)$$

Substituting (2) into (3) yields:

$$S_t = E_t - \frac{1}{LE}\left[E_t + \sum_{t=t+1}^{r} E_t + SSW + DBW + DCW + W_{t-1} - B_{d+1}\right], \quad (4)$$

$$S_t = E_t - \frac{1}{LE}\sum_{t=t}^{r} E_t - \frac{1}{LE}SSW - \frac{1}{LE}DBW - \frac{1}{LE}DCW$$
$$- \frac{1}{LE}W_{t-1} + \frac{1}{LE}B_{d+1}. \quad (5)$$

We estimate equation 5 for the HRS, where saving is the annual difference in net worth between the 1992 and 1994 surveys. The constructions of future earnings, Social Security wealth, defined benefit wealth, defined contribution wealth, nonpension net worth, and intended bequests are described in appendix table 8A-1. To test this model for household behavior, each household's future earnings, wealth, and expected bequests are entered into the equation divided by life expectancy of the highest earner in the household.[75] If households are perfect life-cycle savers, the coefficients of income and

74. This model is similarly presented in Munnell (1976).
75. For married households, we use the highest earner's life expectancy as a measure of the household's life expectancy. An alternative definition is to use the average life expectancy for the couple. The results using the two measures are similar.

assets divided by the life expectancy should be +1 and −1, respectively.[76] The equations also include the same socioeconomic variables used in the equations for the probability of leaving a bequest: college degree, children, good health, race, and self-employment status.[77]

The results reported in table 8-6 are remarkably consistent with the theory. The coefficient of current income is positive, albeit less than +1, while that on future earnings is negative and very close to −1. Nonpension net worth has a negative effect, while the amount expected to be left as a bequest has a positive effect, both as theory predicts although the coefficients are larger than the expected −1 and +1 shown in equation 5. In terms of the pension variables, the coefficient on defined benefit wealth is significant and close to −1, while that on Social Security wealth is not significantly different from zero.[78] In contrast, the coefficient on defined contribution wealth is positive and statistically significant. This suggests that households view their different forms of pension very differently in making their saving decisions.

Since the hypothesis is that pension wealth disbursed as a lump sum has a different effect from pensions paid as annuities, equation 2 combines defined benefit and Social Security wealth. The combined variable has a negative effect on net worth, although with a coefficient of less than 1. Defined contribution wealth continues to have a coefficient that is positive and significant. The results support the hypothesis that annuitized pension wealth has a different effect on savings than pension wealth paid as a lump sum.[79]

Since defined contribution plans are voluntary, and allow workers to decide how much to contribute, individuals with a taste for saving may be more likely to participate and contribute higher amounts to these plans. Sim-

---

76. An underlying assumption of the model is that households are in a steady state. This assumption may not hold because, as we have noted, defined contribution plans are relatively recent developments, and households may not yet have adjusted their consumption and savings plans fully. For a general example of analyzing general equilibrium effects, see Stiglitz (1978).

77. We also examine whether two-earner households behave differently from single-earner households, but an indicator variable for two earners had a statistically insignificant coefficient.

78. This is broadly consistent with Munnell (1976).

79. One reader suggests that households with both defined benefit and defined contribution plans might behave differently from those with only one type of plan. To test this hypothesis, we included an indicator variable for households with both types of plans and found that the savings behavior among these households does not differ from households with only one type of pension plan.

Table 8-6. *Regressions of Annual Savings between 1992 and 1994; HRS*[a]

Variable	Equation 1	Equation 2	Equation 3
Current earnings	0.301	0.393	0.394
	(1.60)	(2.21)	(2.21)
Future earnings	–0.813	–0.838	–0.839
	(–1.94)	(–2.00)	(–2.00)
Defined benefit wealth / LE	–0.906		
	(–2.16)		
Defined contribution wealth / LE	1.377	1.463	1.430
	(2.37)	(2.53)	(2.42)
Social Security wealth / LE	0.938		
	(0.87)		
(SSW + DB wealth) / LE		–0.619	–0.632
		(–1.65)	(–1.67)
Nonpension net worth / LE	–2.965	–2.947	–2.950
	(–14.77)	(–14.70)	(–14.69)
Expected bequest / LE	10.570	10.796	10.728
	(6.92)	(7.10)	(6.96)
Have IRA			2,180
			(0.28)
Expect to receive inheritance	11,519	11,853	11,798
	(1.67)	(1.72)	(1.71)
College	46,169	44,622	44,359
	(5.66)	(5.51)	(5.44)
Have children	–8,667	–6,170	–6,119
	(–0.72)	(–0.52)	(–0.51)
Good health	8,797	8,750	8,540
	(0.97)	(0.96)	(0.94)
White	13,368	14,373	13,953
	(1.54)	(1.66)	(1.59)
Self-employed	35,125	36,882	36,829
	(3.57)	(3.77)	(3.77)
Constant	–30,887	–29,696	–29,589
	(–2.04)	(–1.96)	(–1.95)
R^2	0.07	0.07	0.07
N	3,914	3,914	3,914

Source: Authors' calculations using the HRS (1992, 1994, and 1996).

a. t statistics are in parentheses. See appendix table 8A-1 for variable definitions.

ilarly, individuals with a taste for saving may be more likely to accumulate greater nonpension assets. Therefore, unless the equation controls adequately for a saving preference, the regression will show a positive relationship between defined contribution wealth and nonpension saving even if one does not determine the other. This is a difficult and to a large degree unresolved issue in the literature. Recent work by James Poterba, Steven Venti, and David Wise, and by Eric Engen and William Gale, has shown that 401(k) eligibility is exogenous with respect to taste for saving and can be used as an instrument for 401(k) accumulation.[80] Unfortunately, 401(k) eligibility is not available in the HRS. An alternative method of controlling for saving preference used by Gale is to include an indicator variable for having an IRA.[81] The results are presented in the last column of table 8-6. The combined variable for Social Security and defined benefit wealth continues to have a negative and significant effect on saving. A positive relation continues to exist between saving and defined contribution wealth, while the indicator variable for having an IRA is insignificant. The results support the earlier findings that defined benefit wealth has a negative effect on savings while accumulations in defined contribution plans do not reduce savings.[82]

The Impact of Pensions on Net Worth

The solution to the utility maximization described in equation 1 implies that people will smooth their consumption over their lifetime so that consumption in each period is a constant fraction of lifetime resources less planned bequests as shown in equation 2. Household consumption in period t can also be expressed as:[83]

$$C_0 = C_t = \frac{1}{LE}\left[\sum_{t=s}^{r}(E_t + I_t) + \sum_{t=r}^{d} PEN_t - B_{d+1}\right], \tag{6}$$

and after A periods consumption equals:

80. Poterba, Venti, and Wise (1995); Engen and Gale (2000).

81. Gale (1998).

82. To control for the fact that taste for saving may vary with earnings, Engen and Gale (2000) estimate the offset between 401(k) saving and other saving by earnings levels. They find that having a 401(k) plan has a positive effect on savings for individuals with low earnings while the offset is negative for higher earnings levels. We estimate equation 5 for different earnings levels, and the results are similar to Engen and Gale's.

83. The model for wealth accumulation follows Gale (1998).

$$\sum_{t=s}^{A} C_t = \frac{A}{LE_s} \left[\sum_{t=s}^{r}(E_t + I_t) + \sum_{t=r}^{d} PEN_t - B_{d+1} \right]. \tag{7}$$

This implies that nonpension wealth (W_A) at age A is equal to total earnings and inheritances accumulated to date less total consumption to date:

$$W_A = \sum_{t=s}^{A}(E_t + I_t) - \sum_{t=s}^{A} C_t. \tag{8}$$

Substituting equation 7 into equation 8 yields:

$$W_A = \sum_{t=s}^{A}(E_t + I_t) - \frac{A}{LE_s}\sum_{t=s}^{r}(E_t + I_t) - \frac{A}{LE_s}SSW - \frac{A}{LE_s}DBW$$
$$- \frac{A}{LE_s}DCW + \frac{A}{LE_s}B_{d+1}. \tag{9}$$

This model allows for an offset between pension wealth and nonpension wealth over the individual's lifetime, but at any moment in time, only a portion of that adjustment has occurred. For example, in the case of a dollar-for-dollar offset, a one-dollar increase in defined benefit pension wealth at time t will increase consumption in each period by $1/LE_s$. The increase in consumption is financed by a reduction in nonpension net worth of the same amount. After A periods, total consumption has increased and nonpension net worth has decreased by A/LE_s, which reflects where the household is in its life cycle. In estimating equation 9, therefore, we multiply the lifetime wealth variables for each household by the appropriate factor to reflect the adjustment process. The adjustment factor, A/LE_s, is calculated by dividing the number of years of labor force participation for the highest earner by the life expectancy at the start of the planning horizon.[84] In the case of a dollar-for-dollar offset, the coefficients of the modified wealth variables, as well as that on lifetime earnings, should be –1. The model allows, however, for the offset between pension wealth and nonpension wealth to be less than one for one.

84. For example, for a male who is currently fifty-five who started working at age twenty-five, and expects to live until age eighty-five, A is equal to 30 (55-25), and LE_s is equal to 60 (85–25).

We estimate the equation for net worth as specified in equation 9 for a sample of households from the HRS. The equations include the same socio-economic variables used in the earlier exercises: a college degree, children, good health, white, and self-employment status. As in the saving equation, our hypothesis is that defined benefit wealth and defined contribution wealth have different effects on wealth levels.

The results are presented in table 8-7. Generally, the variables enter with the proper signs, although the magnitudes often differ from the +1 on earnings to date and −1 on the adjusted lifetime resources that would be expected in the case of a dollar-for-dollar offset.[85] In terms of the pension variables, the estimated effect of defined benefit wealth is negative, and Social Security wealth enters with an insignificant coefficient. On the other hand, defined contribution wealth has a positive and significant effect on net worth. Since the hypothesis is that pension wealth disbursed as a lump sum has a different effect from pensions paid as annuities, we again combine defined benefit and Social Security wealth in a second regression, equation 2. The combined variable has a negative and marginally statistically significant effect on net worth, although the coefficient is less than 1.[86] We also attempt to control for a taste for saving, in the same manner as for the savings equation, by including an indicator variable for having an IRA, as in equation 3. The results are very similar to the earlier findings, and indicate that having a defined contribution plan has a positive effect on net worth, while defined benefit plans reduce nonpension net worth.

With regard to the other variables in the regression, the amount that the household plans to leave as a bequest has a positive effect on net worth, although larger than expected. The statistically insignificant coefficient for expecting to receive an inheritance indicates that households do not adjust

---

85. Earnings to date and lifetime earnings include inheritances received.

86. It is difficult to compare these results with those of earlier researchers, because either defined contribution plans were unimportant, or researchers did not look at the defined benefit and defined contribution plans separately. For example, Gale (1998) uses the 1983 SCF, where defined contribution plans are rare, and he finds no effect of combined pension and Social Security wealth on total wealth. This is roughly consistent with our finding for defined benefit and Social Security wealth. Gustman and Steinmeier (1998) use the 1992 HRS and find a positive and significant effect on net worth of combined defined benefit and defined contribution wealth. Combining the two types of plans, however, is fundamentally inconsistent with the thesis of this paper.

Table 8-7. *Net Worth Regressions; HRS 1992*[a]

Variable	Equation 1	Equation 2	Equation 3
Earnings to date	0.124	0.121	0.122
	(3.86)	(3.79)	(3.52)
Lifetime earnings * A/LE$_s$	−0.145	−0.130	−0.119
	(−3.47)	(−3.33)	(−3.05)
Defined benefit wealth * A/LE$_s$	−0.092		
	(−1.60)		
Defined contribution wealth * A/LE$_s$	0.310	0.312	0.251
	(3.91)	(3.94)	(3.11)
Social Security wealth * A/LE$_s$	0.145		
	(0.64)		
(SSW + DB wealth) * A/LE$_s$		−0.074	−0.096
		(−1.35)	(−1.75)
Expected bequest * A/LE$_s$	2.653	2.687	2.547
	(12.98)	(13.32)	(12.46)
Have IRA			57,952
			(3.94)
Expect to receive inheritance	−10,957	−10,758	−12,399
	(−0.84)	(−0.82)	(−0.95)
College	69,320	67,867	59,897
	(4.50)	(4.43)	(3.88)
Have children	−36,091	−32,822	−31,466
	(−1.58)	(−1.45)	(−1.39)
Good health	42,836	43,354	34,809
	(2.53)	(2.56)	(2.17)
White	48,628	49,953	38,639
	(3.01)	(3.10)	(2.37)
Self-employed	276,470	277,860	276,126
	(13.79)	(13.90)	(13.83)
Constant	−47,467	−44,909	−41,521
	(−1.67)	(−1.58)	(−1.47)
R^2	0.15	0.14	0.15
N	4,233	4,233	4,233

Source: Authors' calculations using the HRS (1992, 1994, and 1996).

a. *t* statistics are in parentheses. See appendix table 8A-1 for variable definitions.

their saving in anticipation of an inheritance.[87] The socioeconomic variables have the expected effects: college education, good health, white, and self-employed all have a large and significant positive effect on net worth.[88]

Although the wealth equations are not as consistent with theory as the saving equations, they support the contention that households react differently to the promise of lump sums as opposed to annuities in their saving and wealth accumulation decisions. Households appear to reduce their other saving in anticipation of an annuity, while they increase their saving and wealth when they anticipate a lump-sum payment.

Conclusion

This paper argues that once people get wealth, they are reluctant to give it up. This is evident in the reluctance to buy annuities, to take advantage of reverse mortgages, and to draw down financial assets in retirement. Life insurance holdings among the elderly may also reflect the desire to have bequeathable assets. The paper also argues that the desire to leave a bequest is an important motivation for acquiring and retaining financial resources and housing. Given these two factors, the shift from defined benefit to defined contribution plans should raise bequests to a significant degree. The estimates suggest that the increase in lump-sum payments over the period 1992 through 2004 will increase wealth in the hands of decedents by $28 billion *each year*.

In addition to the potential increase in unintended bequests, the growth in lump-sum payments also appears to raise the interest of households in leaving an intended bequest. Such a potentially large increase in bequests has important implications for the welfare of future retirees. The question is whether they reduce consumption during the working years or lower consumption in retirement. The results reported above suggest that households react very differently to their defined contribution accumulations than they do to the present value of annuity pensions. They do not reduce their other saving in anticipation of payments from defined contribution plans as they do in response to promised Social Security and defined benefit pension payments. Clearly, more work is needed to sort out these issues. Nevertheless, the evidence suggests that a reluctance to spend lump sums may be as likely as—if not more likely than—a tendency to squander accumulated pension resources.

87. This finding is consistent with preliminary research in Brown and Weisbenner (2002).

88. We also estimate the regressions separately for the self-employed and the non-self-employed. The results are consistent for the two groups.

Table 8A-1. *Variable Definitions; HRS*

Variable	Description	Mean
Nonpension net worth	Total assets minus total debts. Assets include checking, savings, and money market accounts, certificates of deposit, stocks, bonds, mutual funds, and other managed asset accounts, plus the value of all vehicles, property, and business assets. Total debt is defined as the sum of all mortgages, home equity loans, credit card debt, education loans, and installment loans.	$197,422
Savings 1992–94	Annual change in nonpension net worth between 1992 and 1994.	$18,382
Lifetime earnings	Sum of earnings to date and future earnings. Earnings are imputed for each year an individual has worked using an estimated wage equation from Gustman and Steinmeier (1998).	$1,426,630
Earnings to date	Sum of annual earnings from the start date to the current age.	$1,039,604
Future earnings	Sum of annual earnings for each future year until the self-reported retirement age.	$392,163
Inheritance received	Value of inheritances received. We assume a 5 percent return to calculate the present value.	$13,172
Defined benefit wealth	Present discounted value of defined benefit payments calculated using employer-reported information.	$130,794
Defined contribution wealth	Total value of all defined contribution plans and balances in IRAs.	$62,159
Social Security wealth	Present discounted value of Social Security benefits based on estimated lifetime earnings.	$150,978
Probability of leaving a bequest of $10,000 or more	Subjective probability of leaving a bequest of $10,000 or more.	0.728
Probability of leaving a bequest of $100,000 or more	Subjective probability of leaving a bequest of $100,000 or more.	0.390
DC as a share of total SS and pension wealth	Share of defined contribution and IRA wealth in total Social Security and pension wealth.	0.137
Expected bequest	An indicator variable that has the value of one if the respondent and his or her spouse expect to leave a sizable estate to others.	$86,445
Expected bequest amount	Based on a probability distribution from the subjective probabilities of leaving a bequest of $10,000 or more, and $100,000 or more. The probabilities are applied to the midpoints of the intervals (0–10,000), (10,000–100,000), and (100,000—mean bequeathable wealth above 100,000) to estimate the expected bequest amount.	$86,446

continued on next page

Table 8A-1. *Variable Definitions; HRS (continued)*

Variable	Description	Mean
Received an inheritance	Indicator variable with the value of one if the household has ever received an inheritance.	0.22
Expect to receive an inheritance	Indicator variable with the value of one if the household expects to receive an inheritance in the future.	0.38
College	Indicator variable with the value of one if the respondent received a college degree.	0.29
Have children	Indicator variable with the value of one if the household has at least one child.	0.91
Good health	Indicator variable with the value of one if the respondent indicates that his or her health is excellent, very good, or good.	0.81
White	Indicator variable with the value of one if the respondent reports being non-Hispanic white.	0.79
Self-employed	Indicator variable with the value of one if either the respondent or the spouse is self-employed.	0.12
Age	Age of the highest lifetime earner in the household at the time of the survey.	56.4
Start date	The year the highest lifetime earner in the household started working. The start date is defined as the age at which the highest earner started his or her first job. If the start date is missing, it is set to (years of education + 6).	23.1
Age at death	The expected age at death for the highest lifetime earner. Data on the expected age of death is collected from life tables.	81.5
Remaining life expectancy	The expected remaining number of years until death at the current age for the highest lifetime earner.	25.1
A/LE_s	Ratio that represents where the individual is in the life cycle. A is current age minus start date and LE_s is life expectancy at the start of the planning horizon, that is, age of death minus start date.	0.55

Source: *1992 Social Security Trustees' Report Intermediate Assumptions:* We used the assumptions from the 1992 Trustees' Report for consistency with Gustman and Steinmeier (1999) and the Pension Calculator.

a. Interest rate: 6.3 percent.
b. Wage growth: 5 percent.
c. Inflation rate: 4 percent.

COMMENT BY
Amy Finkelstein

The shift from defined benefit to defined contribution pension plans has been one of the most salient changes in nonwage compensation over the last twenty years. This shift has potentially important implications for a wide range of economic behavior, from labor force participation to capital accumulation. The authors have chosen to focus on the interesting issue of its effect on bequests and living standards in retirement, particularly by means of the decreased annuitization that accompanies the shift from defined benefit to defined contribution pension plans.

As the authors note, a common instinct in considering the implications of the change from defined benefit to defined contribution plans is concern that retirees may recklessly squander their lump sum in the first few years, and end up with drastically diminished consumption for the remainder of their lifespan. Instead, the authors point out a largely overlooked alternative hypothesis: namely, that the shift from defined benefit to defined contribution plans might result in an *increase* in bequests, both intended and unintended. This increase, they note, must be financed by some combination of decreased consumption in retirement and increased savings during working life. Their interpretation of their empirical work is a finding that the switch from defined benefit to defined contribution pension plans produces an increase in both unintended and intended bequests; they also find evidence that suggests that savings are reduced more in response to defined benefit pensions and promised Social Security payments than in response to defined contribution plans.

My comments address four main areas that I think deserve further consideration: The first concerns the different welfare and policy implications behind a potential rise in unintended bequests, and a potential rise in intended bequests associated with the shift to defined contribution pension plans. The second, relatedly, concerns whether or not these two types of bequests can be distinguished empirically. Third, some investigation of whether the relationships investigated in the data are likely to hold over time would be informative. The final area concerns the degree to which the share of pension wealth that is bequeathable reflects a general taste for saving, which makes it difficult to draw any causal inference about its impact on bequests and saving in the authors' regression analyses.

Unintended versus Intended Bequests: Welfare and Policy Implications

The paper would benefit from some attention to the important, and different, welfare implications of potential increases in unintended bequests, and potential increases in intended bequests that the authors note may result from the shift from defined benefit to defined contribution pension plans. Unintended bequests increase because the high loads in private annuity markets make it costly for individuals with defined contribution plans to replicate the annuitization provided through defined benefit plans. About half of these loads appear due to mortality differences between annuitants and the general population, and about half to administrative loads.[89] Because of these high loads, voluntary purchases of private annuities are quite minuscule.[90] It seems likely that many individuals who were previously annuitized through their defined benefit pension plan will not convert their defined contribution pension into an annuity. Faced with uncertainty about how long they will live, retirees will have to engage in precautionary savings to guard against the possibility of living a long time, and ending up impoverished in old age. Whatever is not consumed during their lifetime will be passed onto their heirs as an "unintended bequest." The increase in unintended bequests, stemming from the increased marginal cost of annuitization, therefore represents a welfare *loss*.

The increase in intended bequests, however, does not suggest a decrease in welfare. The authors suggest two possible mechanisms by which the decrease in annuitization associated with the switch to defined contribution pension plans would provide an increase in intended bequests. The first is that somehow the marginal utility of bequests increases with the share of assets that are bequeathable.[91] This is a novel hypothesis, and the model is not spelled out. However, it appears to be welfare neutral. Alternatively, however, the authors also suggest that intended bequests will rise because the decrease in "involuntary" annuitization with the shift away from defined benefit plans decreases the marginal cost of bequests.[92] The argument is based on the notion that individuals are overannuitized in defined benefit plans; to leave a bequest, they must therefore undo this overannuitization by purchasing life insurance. But life insurance is expensive—it has loads due to administrative costs and adverse selection as well—and thus undoing the annuitization provided by

89. Brown, Mitchell, and Poterba (2000a).

90. See, for example, Mitchell and others (1999); or Poterba and Warshawsky (2000).

91. The authors note, for example, that "people's interest in bequests increases when they gain access to accumulated assets."

92. Again, for example, the authors suggest that "accumulating wealth out of current income to leave a bequest is too difficult, but if people receive a pile of wealth leaving a bequest becomes a plausible option."

defined benefit plans is costly.[93] The shift to defined contribution plans therefore reverses this overannuitization, thus reducing the marginal cost of intended bequests, since individuals must no longer pay life insurance loads to leave bequests to their children. As a result, intended bequests should rise. The decreased marginal cost of bequests is welfare enhancing.

This distinction between the welfare loss implied by a rise in unintended bequests and the welfare neutrality or gain associated with a rise in intended bequests is important for the conclusions to be drawn from the authors' work. It influences whether the increased bequests are beneficial or problematic. It also has potentially interesting policy implications. If the rise in unintended bequests is large relative to the rise in intended bequests, policies that impose some mandatory annuitization requirements on the accruals from defined contribution pension plans could be welfare enhancing. The United Kingdom, for example, imposes annuitization requirements on most accruals from defined contribution pension plans; these appear to reduce the cost of adverse selection in the compulsory annuity market compared to the voluntary annuity market by half.[94] Similarly, a rise in unintended bequests associated with a move away from defined benefit private pension plans suggests that proposals to replace or supplement existing defined benefit Social Security programs with defined contribution systems might also want to consider a possible role for mandatory annuitization. On the other hand, if the shift from defined benefit to defined contribution plans produces a large rise in intended bequests relative to unintended bequests, this suggests that forced annuitization is welfare decreasing and should not be imposed on private or public defined contribution pension plans.

Unintended versus Intended Bequests: Empirical Distinctions

Because of the different implications of a rise in intended or unintended bequests in the authors' framework, it would be helpful to distinguish between changes in these two types of bequests in the empirical work. Unfortunately, the data do not permit this distinction. The first empirical analysis that the authors conduct is an illustrative calculation of the increase in bequests that would occur if bequeathable wealth estimated at 1998 levels, is reduced by replacing the 1998 ratio of defined contribution to total pension wealth with the 1992 ratio. The authors' interpretation that this represents

93. The argument is analogous to Bernheim's (1991), that the elderly hold life insurance to undo the forced annuitization of Social Security. Brown (1999) provides an empirical critique of this argument.

94. Finkelstein and Poterba (2002).

an increase in unintended bequests seems misplaced. The calculation, while an interesting attempt to examine how much bequests might rise, is incapable of distinguishing between unintended and intended bequests.

The second empirical analysis the authors undertake investigates the relationship between the household's expectations of leaving bequests, and the share of pension wealth provided in the form of bequeathable assets. The authors interpret answers to various questions in the SCF and HRS about the respondent's assessment of the likelihood of leaving a bequest (or a bequest of a certain size) as measures of intended bequests. I would again urge caution in the ability to distinguish in these data between intended and unintended bequests. The questions used do not directly measure intent but merely expectations. If individuals increase their precautionary savings in response to the decreased annuitization provided by the shift to defined contribution plans, they may realize that the probability of leaving an unintended bequest has risen. Therefore, while these data can potentially be used to shed light on the effect of bequeathable wealth on bequests, they cannot be interpreted—as the authors do—as evidence of an effect on *intended* bequests.

The Stability of Relationships over Time

Although the first two empirical exercises do not speak directly to differences in the effect of the shift to defined contribution plans on intended versus unintended bequests, they do potentially shed light on the relationship between the shift to defined contribution plans and bequests in general. It would be interesting for the authors to include some discussion of whether the relationships they estimate are likely to be stable over time. For example, in the first empirical calculation, the authors calculate that 48 percent of bequeathable wealth held by decedents in 1998 is transferred intergenerationally, rather than to other sources such as taxes or charities. When they calculate what the rising share of defined contribution pension plans between 1992 and 1998 is likely to have done to the size of intergenerational bequests, they assume the share of bequeathable wealth transferred intergenerationally is constant. In fact, it may vary as the share of pension wealth that is bequeathable increases. For example, as more of net worth is held in the form of assets that can be transferred at death, interest in charitable giving may also change. It seems difficult to estimate any such effects in the data, but some discussion of the possibility would be worthwhile.

Similarly, the effect of the shift to defined contribution plans on the intent to leave bequests may be a function of the financial experience of the respondents. While the authors focus on the decrease in annuitization that accompanies the shift to defined contribution plans, the shift to defined contribution plans also has other effects that may affect the desire to give bequests. For example, in defined contribution plans, unlike in defined benefit plans, the employee rather than the employer bears the performance risk of the pension fund. Individuals aged fifty-one to sixty-one, with defined contribution plans in the 1992 HRS and the 1998 SCF, have enjoyed an unprecedented run-up in stock market wealth. If individuals engage in explicit or implicit intergenerational risk sharing, these windfalls may increase the intention to leave bequests; the desire to leave a bequest may be lower if financial markets did not perform as well. Thus the relationship may not be stable over time. The available data do not permit direct examination of this issue, but some attention to the fact that the effect of the shift to defined contribution plans on intended bequests may vary with such things as the financial experience of the bequeathers would be helpful.

Endogeneity Concerns

Finally, a general empirical issue needs to be addressed in order to place any causal interpretation on the regression analyses. The authors examine, in a cross section, the relationship between the share of total pension wealth held in a bequeathable form and measures of intended bequests. A crucial issue with this analysis is the extent to which assets held in bequeathable form reflect a taste for savings. Therefore, these regressions cannot be interpreted as the effect of an exogenous change in the share of individuals' pension wealth held in bequeathable form.

As the authors themselves note, individuals can affect the amount of assets accumulated in bequeathable form in several ways, and these may very well be correlated with a taste for savings or the desire to accumulate bequeathable wealth. To begin with, individuals may select into firms that offer 401(k) plans because of a desire to save. In addition, participation in these plans is voluntary, and the amount that employees contribute to the plan is also at their discretion. As a result, how to identify the effects of defined contribution plans on savings and other outcomes is a difficult—and unresolved — issue in the literature.

Recent work has debated such issues as the validity of 401(k) eligibility as an instrument for 401(k) accumulation and how best to control for the relationship between income and taste for savings.[95] The authors have tried to address this issue, but the coefficients on pension wealth in defined contribution plans is probably biased upward in the regression analysis.

95. See Engen, Gale, and Scholz (1996) and Poterba, Venti, and Wise (1996) for an overview of some of the issues.

In sum, the paper raises the interesting hypothesis that the shift toward defined contribution plans may produce increases in both intended and unintended bequests. This hypothesis has implications for the national savings rate and the proportion of the capital stock that represents intergenerational transfers. I would urge the authors to pay greater attention in both the discussion of the theory and in the empirical evidence to the different welfare and policy implications of increases in intended and unintended bequests. The empirical analysis would also benefit from greater attention to the endogeneity of the key explanatory variable of interest.

COMMENT BY
Olivia S. Mitchell

In this provocative and interesting study, the authors seek to determine whether the national shift away from defined benefit toward defined contribution pensions might increase saving and wealth transferred by means of bequests. They analyze bequest intentions using two data sets on people in their fifties, namely the Health and Retirement Study (HRS) and the Survey of Consumer Finances (SCF). The paper argues that there is a positive relationship between the fraction of explicit retirement saving and older people's expressed intent to leave a bequest. Hence the work implies that the national movement toward defined contribution pensions could increase saving and bequests, assuming that expressed intentions to leave an inheritance actually translate into reality.

Understanding how bequests and saving are linked attracts social science attention for several reasons. One is that explaining old-age consumption patterns has become a popular industry in the economics profession over the last couple of decades, and many economists have tried to test the life-cycle theory using empirical data. Life-cycle theory predicts that old-age consumption can be smoothed by drawing down assets, perhaps with the aid of annuities to offset longevity risk. However, the small size of the private annuity market in the United States, and the apparent lack of asset drawdown, seems to imply that bequest motives may be important. That is, the desire to leave a bequest might lead some older people to set aside assets rather than consume them all. A second reason that bequest behavior interests social scientists is that wealth inequality may be to some degree explained by intergenerational transfers. Those focused on wealth distribution hence find the topic of substantial importance. A third reason bequests are of interest is that if national saving is deemed inadequate, then policies that boost bequests would be an instrument toward that end. Bequest policy is a focus in the Social Security reform debate, in part motivating President George W. Bush's effort to establish personal saving accounts as part of a restructured system. Recent U.S. estate tax changes also seek to make it easier for people to transfer wealth to others at death.

When evaluating determinants of bequest patterns, it is helpful to ask just how much wealth older people have, and what fraction of it might, in fact, be bequeathable. The HRS is an invaluable data set in this regard, since this nationally representative panel survey is matched with employer-provided pension records as well as Social Security earnings and benefits records, and also probes respondents with "unfolding" brackets in order to obtain better-quality data on wealth than ever before.

HRS evidence in table 8-8 shows that "full" retirement wealth for Americans on the verge of retirement is about $325,000 for the median household (in 1992 dollars). Two-fifths of this is the present value of Social Security benefits, an amount not legally bequeathable to heirs under current rules. Private-pension wealth constitutes another one-fifth of retirement wealth, most of which also cannot be bequeathed by this generation. As Munnell and others show, defined benefit plans are by far the dominant model for this cohort, with defined contribution wealth amounting to only about $10,000. This leaves only nonfinancial, nonpension wealth as potentially bequeathable, in a median amount of $60,000, plus another roughly equivalent amount in home equity. At this point, it might be asked whether there will be anything left over to bequeath when the HRS generation passes on. This is an issue since the HRS cohort was relatively young, around fifty-six years old, when surveyed at baseline. Wealth held by the cohort will therefore be used to sustain it for another fifteen to twenty (or more) years in the future. It is probable that little may actually be left over when the time comes to pass on.

This gloomy picture conflicts with tabulations of HRS respondents' views, where two-thirds of them say that leaving an inheritance is important, according to Munnell and co-authors. Additionally, some 78 percent of HRS respondents apparently expect to leave a bequest of at least $10,000; and 41 percent expect to leave a bequest of at least $100,000. My concern is that people's intentions are greatly at odds with what may be left by the time they die. In a related study, David Weir and Robert Willis determine that around 40 percent of low- and medium-wealth couples have insufficient assets to protect consumption if the HRS wives were to become widows, as shown in table 8-9.[96]

96. Weir and Willis (2000).

Table 8-8. *Mean Value and Composition of HRS Wealth, by Wealth Decile*

Wealth decile	Total wealth	Net housing wealth	Net financial wealth	Social Security wealth	Pension wealth
1	$39,470	$(5,719)	$1,520	$42,312	$1,356
		−14%	4%	107%	3%
2	97,452	$11,052	$10,579	$69,239	$6,583
		11%	11%	71%	7%
3	156,288	$24,951	$18,235	$93,920	$19,181
		16%	12%	60%	12%
4	219,797	$37,095	$32,632	$115,224	$34,845
		17%	15%	52%	16%
5	287,692	$53,787	$55,020	$128,377	$50,509
		19%	19%	45%	18%
6	364,802	68,637	$75,793	$136,116	$84,255
		19%	21%	37%	23%
7	459,858	$81,432	$109,811	142,981	125,635
		18%	24%	31%	27%
8	590,079	$95,414	$159,054	$149,310	$186,301
		16%	27%	25%	32%
9	804,934	$112,039	$265,967	$158,976	$267,953
		14%	33%	20%	33%
10	1,764,414	$180,894	$1,032,049	$161,605	$389,865
		10%	58%	9%	22%
Total					
Mean	478,313	$65,940	$175,974	$119,793	$116,606
		14%	37%	25%	24%
Median 10 %	325,157	$59,746	$66,530	$133,606	$65,275
		18%	20%	41%	20%

Source: Moore and Mitchell (2000).

Note: All values in 1992 dollars and calculated using HRS sampling weights for age-eligible households.

Since the descriptive analysis presented in the first half of the Munnell and others paper is well known, I turn next to the multivariate empirical analysis, which explores two sets of expectations questions: whether respondents expect to leave an inheritance, and whether the inheritance will be at least $10,000, or at least $100,000.[97] The authors regress these on a "defined con-

97. I do not go into the saving regressions in this paper since most HRS respondents are still working and are too young to draw inferences about retirement dissaving. In addition, inconsistent data imputes across waves imply that HRS public use data files should not be used to conduct saving regressions. More consistent impute

Table 8-9. *Percent of Wives Unable to Sustain Prewidowhood Consumption, by Couple Wealth*

Year	Low	Middle	High
1969	73	75	60
1992	55	39	20

Source: Weir and Willis (2000).

tribution share" variable, indicating how large defined contribution wealth is as a percent of Social Security and pension wealth, and a series of socioeconomic variables. The authors hypothesize that if defined contribution share has a positive and significant effect, then a continued national shift to defined contribution plans may boost bequests in the future—assuming intentions are carried out. The paper's empirical results indicate that, in most cases, the defined contribution share variable is positive and statistically significant.

A closer examination of the information on bequest expectations would be useful when interpreting results. One issue is whether respondents realized they were expected to exclude transfers to spouses, when estimating the chances of leaving an inheritance. No specific directions were given along these lines, so it might be useful to test whether differences in expected bequests vary for married and single persons. The authors could explore this issue by asking whether married couples are mutually consistent with regard to their bequest intentions. Previous research shows that men are more likely to report they intend to leave a bequest than women, which implies they must be including wealth for surviving spouses in their expectations.[98] Another issue is that respondents might not have consistently included housing equity when responding to the bequest question. It would therefore be useful to ask whether the results differ by home-ownership status, to see whether housing assets are in a different mental account than other wealth. A related question is how well respondents understand the expectations questions, since there is some dispute about whether they are telling the surveyor what they would "like to do" versus what they "expect to do." Previous research shows that responses to these questions also tend to pile up at several salient points including 0, 1, and one-half; whether one-half actually means fifty–fifty probability or "don't know" would warrant further exploration.

---

algorithms are being developed by RAND and promise to generate less error-ridden information on wealth changes between the waves.

98. Smith (1999).

Finally, four follow-up HRS waves are now available with several hundred decedents. It would be fruitful to compare people's expectations with the bequest realizations, before reaching policy conclusions.

Turning to the right-hand side variables in the multivariate analysis, here too there is room for more analysis. The labor economics literature has long argued that pension-covered workers tend to be more risk-averse, more productive, and have longer planning horizons than average. As a result, the defined contribution share variable may proxy for these, and other omitted worker and job characteristics correlate with having pension coverage. Fortunately, the HRS offers extensive measures that can readily be incorporated in the analysis. An even simpler test of the hypothesis would assess whether the same estimated effect holds for defined benefit wealth as a share of total wealth; if it does, it would undermine the notion that the degree of asset liquidity drives bequests. A related issue is that many pension-covered workers also have retiree health insurance; yet this variable is not included in the model. If the pension variable is correlated with omitted health insurance, this would bias the coefficient estimates. One other data concern is that spousal pension and other wealth should also be controlled in evaluating the probability of bequests, as long as housing and financial wealth are included.[99]

In sum, this is an ambitious effort to understand bequest intentions and link them to the national movement away from defined benefit toward defined contribution plans. Taken at face value, the results indicate that defined contribution wealth is more likely to be saved rather than spent, if expectations bear out. This is a provocative conclusion, and it stands in contrast to past studies showing that defined contribution participants take lump-sum cash-outs from their defined contribution plans and spend them. As employers move to automatic defined contribution plan enrollment, inertia may get them saving more during their working lives. What Munnell and others add is that retirees will continue to hold the funds in retirement as well. So the news may be good for individual accounts in Social Security, in that the results indicate that defined contribution plans help build wealth and can increase long-term saving.

---

99. All data tabulations and statistical results should also be weighted by sample weights and all HRS results should include only age-eligible respondents; the current version of the paper does not indicate whether this is done.

PART 4

Wealth Transfers and the Economy

9

The Impact of Gifts and Bequests on Aggregate Saving and Capital Accumulation

WILLIAM G. GALE AND SAMARA POTTER

The role of intergenerational transfers in aggregate wealth accumulation has received a substantial amount of attention and generated considerable controversy. The modern literature on this subject begins with the classic paper by Laurence Kotlikoff and Lawrence Summers.[1] In their own words, their paper has two goals: "The first is simply to answer an accounting question: namely can life-cycle savings alone account for the U.S. capital stock? The second goal is to answer an economic question: If, *ceteris paribus*, there were no intergenerational transfers, how large would the U.S. capital stock be? That is, if all such transfers were taxed in a confiscatory way, by how much would capital accumulation be reduced?"

Kotlikoff and Summers conclude that what they call "life-cycle saving" cannot account for more than 20 percent of U.S. capital formation, and intergenerational transfers therefore play a dominant role in wealth accumulation, accounting for 80 percent or more of observed wealth.[2] They also estimate that each dollar of reduced private intergenerational transfers due to tax policy reduces aggregate wealth in the steady state by 70 cents. Thus their

The authors thank Peter Diamond, Larry Kotlikoff, John Karl Scholz, Jonathan Skinner, and Joel Slemrod for helpful comments.

1. Kotlikoff and Summers (1981, p. 707).
2. Kotlikoff and Summers (1981).

estimates imply that if all transfers were abolished, aggregate wealth would fall by more than half.

Subsequent to Kotlikoff and Summers, a sizable literature has attempted to address various aspects of these issues. Franco Modigliani sharply criticizes the Kotlikoff and Summers methodology and conclusions.[3] Alan Blinder, Denis Kessler, and André Masson provide insightful critiques of the debate.[4] As discussed below, a variety of other researchers propose modifications and extensions of the findings.

At the most general level, this literature is aimed at two key questions: What motivates people to accumulate wealth and give transfers? What are the effects of government policies on wealth accumulation? Our conclusions regarding this literature are somewhat mixed: On the one hand, it is difficult to quarrel with Kotlikoff and Summers's conclusions that intergenerational transfers play an important role in wealth accumulation and need to be studied more carefully. It is also clear that the methodology and findings in Kotlikoff and Summers deserve credit for sparking interest in these broad and important issues and for spurring a research growth industry. Researchers have made significant progress in the past twenty years in understanding both the motivations for saving and the effects of public policies on wealth accumulation. Other papers in this volume attest to this finding.

But it is also the case that the methodology developed by Kotlikoff and Summers and their estimates, as well as the estimates in the subsequent literature on transfers and aggregate wealth accumulation, provide only limited guidance on the two key questions: First, estimates of the magnitude of "life-cycle wealth" or its counterpart, "transfer wealth," in overall wealth have proven difficult to pin down empirically. Second, even if transfer wealth and life-cycle wealth were known with precision, that information would not be sufficient to distinguish among the different motives for why people accumulate wealth. Third, the effects of government policies regarding wealth accumulation, for example estate tax policy, depend in large part on the *motives* for transfers on the margin.[5] Thus estimates of the size of aggregate transfer wealth and life-cycle wealth are useful in motivating and framing the relevant questions, but by themselves they do not provide sufficient information to address the motivations for wealth transfers or the effects of government policies on wealth accumulation.

The paper is organized as follows: In the first section, we review the original

3. Modigliani (1988a, 1988b).
4. Blinder (1988); Kessler and Masson (1989).
5. Kaplow (2001); Gale and Perozek (2001).

Kotlikoff and Summers paper. Next, we discuss empirical estimates of life-cycle wealth and transfer wealth. The third section discusses the extent to which those estimates help answer the two key questions regarding motivations for saving and the impacts of public policies, followed by a short conclusion.

Conceptual Framework

Kotlikoff and Summers provide a two-part theoretical framework for analyzing the importance of transfers for wealth accumulation.[6] The first part of the framework defines life-cycle wealth and transfer wealth. The second part estimates the impact of transfers on total wealth accumulation.

Definitions of Life-Cycle and Transfer Wealth

The level of net worth held by individuals in an economy at a point in time can be decomposed into the difference between sources of wealth (earnings and gifts received) and uses of wealth (consumption and gifts given). This accounting identity can be expressed as:

$$W_s = E_s + I_s - C_s - B_s, \tag{1}$$

where W_s = aggregate net worth at time s, E_s = the accumulated value of lifetime earnings by individuals alive at time s, I_s = the accumulated value of lifetime gifts and inheritances received by people alive at time s, C_s = the accumulated value of lifetime consumption by individuals alive at time s, and B_s = the accumulated value of gifts and lifetime bequests given by people alive at time s.[7]

By combining a particular source of wealth with a particular use of wealth, Kotlikoff and Summers define two variables: "aggregate life-cycle wealth" and "aggregate transfer wealth." Aggregate life-cycle wealth is the net accumulation of earnings in excess of consumption to date for all people alive at time s. Dropping the time subscript, life-cycle wealth can be expressed as:

$$L = E - C. \tag{2}$$

Aggregate transfer wealth is defined as the accumulated value of net transfers received by all people alive at time s:

6. Kotlikoff and Summers (1981).

7. Accumulation occurs at market rates of return. E, I, C, B, and the rate of accumulation should be considered in after-tax terms. Transfers from public agencies or private charities and donations to private charities could easily be added without changing the results. I and B differ only because of transfers in earlier periods between people who are alive at time s and people who are not alive at time s.

$$T = I - B. \tag{3}$$

Substituting the definitions in equation 2 and equation 3 into equation 1, aggregate net worth can be expressed as the sum of life-cycle wealth, L, and transfer wealth, T:

$$W = L + T. \tag{4}$$

Equation 4 shows that all wealth existing in an economy at a given point in time can, in an accounting sense, be described either as life-cycle wealth—an accumulated excess of wages over consumption—or transfer wealth, an accumulated excess of transfers received over transfers given among people who are currently alive. As discussed below, Kotlikoff and Summers estimate that life-cycle wealth is at most 20 percent of net worth.

Determining the Impact of Changes in Transfers on Wealth

To evaluate the economic impact of changes in transfers, Kotlikoff and Summers note that using equations 2 and 4, the expression for wealth can be rewritten as the sum of transfer wealth and lifetime earnings less consumption:

$$W = T + E - C. \tag{5}$$

Taking derivatives with respect to T indicates how total wealth will respond to changes in transfer wealth:

$$\frac{dW}{dT} = 1 + \frac{dE}{dT} - \frac{dC}{dT}. \tag{6}$$

Equation 6 says that a one-dollar reduction in transfer wealth affects net worth directly by means of the reduction in transfer wealth, and indirectly by means of the effect of lower transfer wealth on earnings and consumption.[8] Dividing each side of equation 6 by the share of transfer wealth in total wealth yields the elasticity of total wealth with respect to changes in transfer wealth:

$$\frac{T}{W}\frac{dW}{dT} = \left(1 + \frac{dE}{dT} - \frac{dC}{dT}\right)\frac{T}{W}. \tag{7}$$

8. Earnings are the product of wages times hours worked. Kotlikoff and Summers assume that wages are constant, and hence interpret dE/dT as the negative of the change in leisure induced by transfers.

The elasticity shows the percentage change in overall wealth from a given percentage change in transfer wealth. It is equal to the product of the effect of a one-dollar change in transfer wealth on net worth, as in equation 6, and the share of transfer wealth in overall wealth.

To calculate the elasticity requires estimates of T, W, dC/dT and dE/dT. Estimates of T and W are discussed in the next section. To derive estimates of the effect of transfer wealth on consumption (dC/dT) and on earnings (dE/dT), Kotlikoff and Summers assume that households' utility is separable between consumption and leisure on the one hand, and intergenerational transfers on the other. This means that changes in households' preferences or in taxes on transfers that change the level of transfer wealth, but do not affect the relative price of consumption and leisure, affect consumption and leisure only through income effects. In the model, the income effect depends on the difference between the interest rate and growth rate. If the interest rate and growth rate are equal, the income effect is zero. If the interest rate exceeds (falls short of) the growth rate, a reduction in transfer wealth reduces (raises) consumption.[9]

Using equation 6, the assumption that the interest rate is 1 percentage point higher than the growth rate, and a particular parameterization of a life-cycle model, Kotlikoff and Summers estimate that the change in wealth from a one-dollar change in transfer wealth (dW/dT) is about 70 cents. Combined with an estimate that the share of transfer wealth in overall wealth, T/W, is at least 0.8, their findings imply that abolishing all transfers by means of taxation would reduce aggregate wealth by at least 56 percent in the long run.[10]

Estimates of Life-Cycle Wealth and Transfer Wealth

If aggregate wealth is known, then an estimate of life-cycle wealth is sufficient to establish the size of transfer wealth and vice versa. However, because of data problems, estimates of both life-cycle wealth and transfer wealth separately can be informative.

9. In a steady state economy growing at rate g, a household that receives a dollar in transfers when young, must give $\$(1+g)^n$ in transfers n years later. If the interest rate exceeds the growth rate, the household can consume some of the investment income on the transfer it receives, and still have sufficient accumulated wealth to make the required transfer n years later. If the interest rate is less than the growth rate, the household must dip into its wage income to supplement the transfer it receives in order to make the required transfer n years later.

10. Kotlikoff and Summers (1981).

Estimates of Life-Cycle Wealth

Kotlikoff and Summers provide estimates of life-cycle wealth using data on average earnings and consumption by age across different birth cohorts in the United States.[11] They estimate that life-cycle wealth accounts for at most 20 percent and under some assumptions less than 0 percent of U.S. net worth.[12] Modigliani adjusts the Kotlikoff and Summers calculations for a number of factors, and calculates that 80 percent or more of net worth can be explained by life-cycle saving.[13] In particular, Modigliani argues that parents' payments for college should not be counted as part of transfer wealth, that interest accrued on previous transfers received should be attributed to life-cycle wealth, not transfer wealth, and that Kotlikoff and Summers did not adequately measure the consumption of durable goods. Betsy Buttrill White and Michael Darby reach conclusions similar to Kotlikoff and Summers, while Albert Ando and Arthur Kennickell estimate life-cycle wealth to be between 60 percent and 85 percent of net worth.[14]

All of these direct estimates of life-cycle wealth are sensitive to a variety of assumptions concerning the ages of retirement and death, the shape and stability over time of age-earnings and age-consumption profiles and relative wages, and the definition of durable goods as consumption or investment.[15] In principle, it would now be possible to obtain better estimates of life-cycle consumption and wages by cohort because of the increase in data availability over the last twenty years. However, estimating life-cycle wealth with improved data still requires judgments about whether parental payments for higher education are considered a transfer to an adult household and hence included in transfer wealth, or an expenditure on a dependent child, and excluded from transfer wealth, and on whether interest earned on transfers is considered part of life-cycle wealth or transfer wealth. But in the absence of a coherent economic interpretation of life-cycle wealth and transfer wealth, such a judgment is vacuous. As Blinder notes, arguing over accounting definitions is probably not productive.[16]

---

11. Kotlikoff and Summers (1981).

12. Life-cycle wealth accounts for less than zero percent of observed wealth when the accumulated consumption of cohorts currently alive exceeds the cumulative wages of cohorts currently alive.

13. Modigliani (1988a, 1988b).

14. White (1978); Darby (1979); Ando and Kennickell (1987).

15. Blinder (1988).

16. Blinder (1988).

Estimates of Transfers Received

A second approach taken in the literature has compared survey respondents' net worth (W) to the amount of transfers they have received to date (I) or has used survey respondents' reports on the share of their wealth that comes from transfers received. These studies do not estimate transfer wealth, which is given by transfers received less ($I - B$). These studies generally suggest that the cumulative gross value of transfers received compose less than 20 percent of wealth.[17] However, these estimates face several problems: First, they focus almost exclusively on wealth received through inheritances, and ignore *inter-vivos* transfers. Second, transfers received are notoriously underreported relative to transfers given.[18] Third, it is unclear how respondents define transfers, and whether they adjust the value of transfers received in earlier years to reflect the present value of these transfers.[19]

Estimates of Transfer Wealth

In their estimate of transfer wealth, Kotlikoff and Summers used admittedly limited data and a series of strong assumptions, and found the share of transfer wealth in total wealth was about 50 percent. This is lower than the share implied by their finding that life-cycle wealth is between 0 and 20 percent of total wealth. They note that the transfer data are poorly measured and are undoubtedly underreported, which indicates that the share of transfer wealth should be higher than 50 percent.

As Kessler and Masson note, and foreshadowing the discussion in the next section, some transfers are likely to be unintended and tend to obscure the findings of direct estimates of transfer wealth.[20] Treating bequests as departures from the life-cycle model would be appropriate if the bequest had been intended. However, bequests can be accidental rather than intended. In a world with uncertain lifespans and imperfect annuity markets, life-cycle savers—that is, those who intend to die with nothing in their pockets—will sometimes die earlier than expected, and end up leaving bequests.[21] Thus including the contribution of bequests to net worth is perfectly appropriate for measuring the proportion of wealth derived from transfers, but may *not* be appropriate for determining whether the life-cycle model adequately describes aggregate wealth accumulation.

17. Modigliani (1988b); Hurd and Mundaca (1989).
18. For a discussion, see Gale and Scholz (1994).
19. Kessler (1989).
20. Kessler and Masson (1989).
21. Davies (1981); Abel (1985); Hurd (1987).

William Gale and John Karl Scholz address this concern, and provide the first microeconomic estimates of aggregate transfer wealth, by distinguishing intended transfers—such as gifts from parents to adult children living in a separate household—from possibly unintended transfers.[22] Using the 1983 and 1986 Surveys of Consumer Finances, they find that intended *inter-vivos* transfers are the source of at least 20 percent of aggregate wealth, and that transfers are highly concentrated among wealthy families. Actual wealth due to all intended transfers is likely to be higher, since bequests accounted for about 30 percent of net worth in their estimates, and at least some bequests are likely to be intended.

Jeffrey Brown and Scott Weisbenner use data from the 1998 Survey of Consumer Finances and find that transfer wealth accounts for approximately one-fifth to one-quarter of aggregate wealth and is highly concentrated.[23] These estimates include both bequests and *inter-vivos* transfers. One reason these results differ from Gale and Scholz is the substantial increase in equity markets and overall net worth between 1986 and 1998.

Simulation Estimates of Life-Cycle Wealth and Transfer Wealth

Another strand of the literature is based on simulation models of the behavior of overlapping generations.[24] This approach is useful for showing, in a particular model, how the shares of life-cycle and transfer wealth in total wealth depend on assumptions concerning behavioral elasticities, credit market constraints, and other factors. However, these models have generated such a wide range of estimates that simulations have done little to reduce the range of plausible estimates.

Discussion

The previous section shows that estimates of life-cycle and transfer wealth vary widely. For the rest of the paper, however, we assume that aggregate values of life-cycle and transfer wealth are known with certainty. The analysis below asks how economists' understanding of the real world would be changed if the true values of life-cycle and transfer wealth were known, or if their true values changed. We focus on three aspects of this question: What is

22. Gale and Scholz (1994).
23. Brown and Weisbenner (2002).
24. Andre Masson (1986); John Laitner. 1990. "Random Earnings Differences, Lifetime Liquidity Constraints, and Altruistic Intergenerational Transfers." University of Michigan (October 12). Mimeo; Lord and Rangazas (1991).

the economic content of life-cycle and transfer wealth? What does knowledge of life-cycle and transfer wealth imply about motives for wealth accumulation and the giving of transfers? What does knowledge of life-cycle and transfer wealth imply about the effects of government policy?

The Economic Content of Life-Cycle Wealth and Transfer Wealth

Although the accounting definitions of life-cycle and transfer wealth may be clear, their economic content is not. The definitions of life-cycle wealth in equation 2 and transfer wealth in equation 3 require that all transfers received are either saved or paid out as transfers, but not consumed, and that all wages earned are either saved or used for consumption, but not devoted to transfers. That is, as constructed, the definitions rule out the possibility that wage income might be saved in order to provide transfers or that transfer income might be consumed by the recipient.

This is problematic on a theoretical level. Since wealth is fungible, the assignment of one particular source of wealth to one particular use of wealth requires some further justification. It is also problematic on an empirical level. Substantial empirical evidence indicates that households consume a portion of the transfers they receive by means of increased leisure and increased consumption.[25]

These facts confound interpretations of life-cycle wealth and transfer wealth in several ways: First, as defined by the Kotlikoff-Summers model, life-cycle wealth does not correspond in general to what the life-cycle model indicates wealth should be. As a result, comparing life-cycle wealth as defined by Kotlikoff and Summers to total wealth does not inform the question of whether the life-cycle model—even if it is augmented to allow for unintended bequests—adequately explains aggregate wealth accumulation. It is true that if transfers were equal to zero, the measure of life-cycle wealth would correspond to wealth accumulation in the life-cycle model. But once transfers are introduced, the life-cycle model indicates that some transfers received might be consumed or result in changes in labor supply, or that some wages might be used to give transfers. This implies that no correspondence necessarily exists between life-cycle wealth as defined by Kotlikoff and Summers, and what the life-cycle model would predict.

Second, differences in life-cycle wealth and transfer wealth across households or societies do not provide information about the relative strength of life-cycle versus other saving motives. As Alan Auerbach notes, suppose two

25. See, for example, Brown and Weisbenner (2002); Holtz-Eakin, Joulfaian, and Rosen (1993, 1994a, 1994b); Joulfaian and Wilhelm (1994); Weil (1994).

households have the same wages and have received the same transfers, but one has a higher propensity to consume out of inherited wealth. A natural conclusion would be that the household that consumes more of its transfer wealth has less net accumulated transfer wealth and hence by any plausible definition has less transfer wealth than the other.[26] Using the Kotlikoff-Summers methodology, however, all of the consumption out of inherited wealth would be subtracted from earnings to form life-cycle wealth. As a result, the Kotlikoff-Summers methodology would show a household with a higher propensity to consume out of inherited wealth to have less overall wealth, but a *higher* share of wealth from transfers compared to the other household.

Third, the accounting definition of transfer wealth does not allow for households to spend transfer wealth on their own, or anyone else's consumption. This definition thus requires that a household's transfer wealth either accrues interest, which raises aggregate transfer wealth over time, or is given to another household, and accrues interest there. Either way, using the accounting definition of transfer wealth, aggregate transfer wealth—the sum of transfer wealth over all households—must rise continually over time. This property stems solely from the accounting definition of transfer wealth, and it holds regardless of whether people consume or save the transfers they receive.

This property leads to the following *reductio ad absurdum*: Suppose that 1 cent (in 2001 dollars) was transferred in year zero and has earned 3 percent real interest per year since then. The transfer wealth from that penny would now total more than 10^{23}, numerous orders of magnitude larger than current world wealth. Thus if one takes the accounting definition of transfer wealth seriously, and goes back in time far enough, transfer wealth should be virtually infinite, since it accrues continuously over time. This example illustrates that, because people can in fact consume out of existing transfer wealth, applying compound interest to initial transfer values can create values that are difficult to interpret in a meaningful way.

This issue is related to the appropriate treatment of interest on previously received transfers. Modigliani argues that the interest earned on net transfers received should count as life-cycle wealth.[27] Kotlikoff and Summers, Blinder, Gale and Scholz, and Brown and Weisbenner attribute the interest received

<hr />

26. Alan J. Auerbach. 2001. "Comments on Jeffrey Brown and Scott Weisbenner, 'Is a Bird in Hand Worth More than a Bird in the Bush?'" University of California, Berkeley (July). Mimeo.

27. Modigliani (1988a, 1988b).

to transfer wealth.[28] The Modigliani view denies that a transfer received in the past is more valuable to the recipient than a transfer of equal real (inflation adjusted) value received today. The others' view leads to the *reductio ad absurdum* mentioned above. The fact that either treatment of interest leads to an economically absurd conclusion suggests that the underlying concept is not well specified.

Finally, it is not even possible to retreat to the view that life-cycle and transfer wealth decompose wealth into parts that are earned and parts that are gifts. A worker's earnings, for example, depend on cognitive ability (a genetic transfer), acquired education (possibly a transfer), work habits and effort (some part of which may be inherited) and other factors that might be considered transfers, such as social connections or jobs in the family business. Likewise, not all transfers are gifts. In the exchange models of Kotlikoff and Avia Spivak; Douglas Bernheim, Andrei Shleifer, and Lawrence Summers; and Donald Cox transfers represent payment for goods or services provided and hence are earned.[29]

In summary, then, it is difficult to assign any economic interpretation to life-cycle and transfer wealth as defined by the accounting identity, except the fact that life-cycle wealth would be an estimate of what the life-cycle model would predict if transfers were zero. Once it is acknowledged that transfers do exist, however, the definitions of life-cycle and transfer wealth have no meaningful economic analogue. As a result, the findings in the next two sections—that life-cycle wealth and transfer wealth provide no information about motives for saving or gifts or about the effects of government policies —should not come as a surprise.

Motivations for Wealth Accumulation and Transfers

Kotlikoff and Summers note the difference between accounting and economic definitions, but nevertheless assert that empirical estimates of life-cycle wealth and transfer wealth provided key information in distinguishing motives for saving.[30] They write that ". . . comparing total wealth with life-cycle wealth indicates whether the life-cycle model alone can explain aggregate U.S. capital formation." In a similar vein, they note that their "first goal is to establish the relative magnitudes of the two components T and L, and

28. Kotlikoff and Summers (1981, 1988); Blinder (1988); Gale and Scholz (1994); Brown and Weisbenner (2002).

29. Kotlikoff and Spivak (1981); Bernheim, Shleifer, and Summers (1985); Cox (1987).

30. Kotlikoff and Summers (1981).

thereby determine whether U.S. wealth holdings can be predominantly explained by life-cycle savings."[31]

In fact, because the definitions of life-cycle wealth and transfer wealth are devoid of economic content, estimates of life-cycle and transfer wealth do not help distinguish different motives for saving or for giving gifts. A low value of life-cycle wealth relative to total wealth does not constitute evidence against the dominance of life-cycle motives for saving, because the transfers may be "accidental." In the accidental bequest model, people face uncertain lifespans and accumulate assets to provide for retirement. They do not plan or desire to give bequests—that is, they save for their own future consumption. But because of imperfect or missing annuity markets, or because they are also saving for precautionary reasons against, say, uncertain future health expenses or uncertain lifespan, people do not annuitize their wealth, as would occur in a simple life-cycle model. Under these assumptions, people will generally have positive asset holdings when they die, even if they do not plan to give bequests. The key point is that accidental bequests can account for a large fraction of aggregate wealth.[32] Thus even if transfer wealth is large, the operative model may be a life-cycle framework with uncertain mortality and imperfect annuity markets.[33]

It is likewise tempting, but equally wrong, to conclude that low values of transfer wealth mean that intentional transfer motives are not an important motivation for saving. Transfer motives refer to *behavior at the margin*. An individual can have a bequest motive at the margin without leaving large bequests. For example, a household may very much like to leave a bequest but not be able to earn enough money to provide for its basic needs, and at the same time make a sizable bequest. Yet, on the margin, that household would have a strong bequest motive.

The difficulty of using aggregate measures of life-cycle wealth and total wealth to distinguish motives for saving and transfers is highlighted by the plethora of microeconomic studies that do examine these issues. Substantial evidence from patterns of *inter-vivos* giving, life insurance purchases, and annuity choices shows that a significant portion of transfers are intended.[34]

---

31. Kotlikoff and Summers (1981, p. 707–09).

32. Abel (1985).

33. See also Dynan, Skinner, and Zeldes (2000).

34. Bernheim (1991); Bernheim, Lemke, and Scholz (2001); Gale and Scholz (1994); Kotlikoff (1989); Laitner and Juster (1996); McGarry (1997); Benjamin R. Page. 1997. "Bequest Taxes, Inter-Vivos Gifts, and the Bequest Motive." Congressional Budget Office (September). Mimeo.

The existence of estate planning and tax avoidance techniques further suggests that not all bequests are accidental.

Another group of studies tries to distinguish among different types of intentional transfers and finds evidence to support particular motives for saving or transfers. In the pure altruism model, parents care about their own consumption and the utility of their children.[35] Parents make transfers and leave bequests until the marginal cost in terms of their own forgone consumption is equal to the marginal benefit to the parents of the increase in their children's consumption. In this model, the size of bequests differs across children to compensate for differences in their endowments or outcomes. Variations of altruism, with and without a mechanism that allows a parent to commit to a given transfer level, are examined in Neil Bruce and Michael Waldman; Assar Lindbeck and Jörgen Weibull; and Maria Perozek.[36]

Nigel Tomes, and Becker and Tomes, provide support for the altruistic model.[37] But other researchers have found no evidence for various empirical implications of altruism. First, Joseph Altonji, Fumio Hayashi, and Laurence Kotlikoff show that the division of consumption between parents and children is not independent of the division of income between parents and children, contrary to the predictions of an altruism model with operative transfers.[38] Second, several studies find that, among families where parents make transfers to children, a one-dollar increase in parents' resources coupled with a one-dollar reduction in children's resources does not raise transfers by a dollar, although it should under altruism.[39] Third, under altruism, siblings with lower incomes should receive larger inheritances than siblings with higher incomes, but typically they do not.[40] In fact, equal division of estates among children appears to be the norm. Bernheim and Sergei Severinov show that this norm can arise if parental altruism is combined with the assumptions that bequests are observable, that a child derives utility from her perception

35. Barro (1974); Becker (1974).

36. Bruce and Waldman (1990, 1991); Lindbeck and Weibull (1988); and Maria G. Perozek. 1996. "The Implications of a Dynamic Model of Altruistic Intergenerational Transfers." University of Wisconsin. Mimeo.

37. Tomes (1981, 1988); Becker and Tomes (1979, 1986).

38. Altonji, Hayashi, and Kotlikoff (1992).

39. Altonji, Hayashi, and Kotlikoff (1997); Cox (1987); and McGarry and Schoeni (1995). Although, see McGarry (2000b), who considers a model of altruism where parents and children interact for several time periods and concludes that this test is misspecified.

40. Paul Menchik (1980, 1988); and Wilhelm (1996).

of parental affection toward her relative to her siblings, and that bequests are viewed as signals of parental affection.[41]

A variety of "exchange" models posit that bequests or transfers are the payment for some good or service provided by children. In the strategic bequest model, parents care about their own consumption, their children's utility, and services obtained from children.[42] These services may represent standard market goods or services (lawn mowing, for example) or more personal goods, such as visits, attention, or children's choices regarding marriage, childbearing, education, career, and location of residence. In the exchange model, parents pay for services with bequests, rather than *inter-vivos* transfers. By delaying payment, parents can control a child's actions for a longer period, and extract the entire amount of services that the child is willing to provide for a given bequest amount. Cox presents a model in which parents buy services from their children by means of *inter-vivos* gifts, and the exchange may be mutually beneficial.[43] In Kotlikoff and Spivak, families act as annuity markets: children ensure a flow of resources to parents who are in danger of outliving their resources, and the parents pay for this service by making *inter-vivos* transfers and bequeathing any resources they have at the end of their lives.[44] Empirical tests of exchange models have generated mixed results.[45]

In a third model of motives for transfers, James Andreoni argues that people obtain utility from the act of giving itself.[46] Other specifications simply assume that households acquire utility directly from wealth or from the after-tax bequest they leave. This specification is sometimes offered as a structural model. Henry Aaron and Alicia Munnell; Gurdip Bakshi and Zhiwu Chen; and Christopher Carroll, for example, argue that pre-estate-tax wealth may enter the utility function as a separate argument, above and beyond the conventional consumption goods it can finance, because wealth may also provide social status, power, social connections, and so forth.[47] A related case occurs if households care directly about the size of the after-tax bequest they provide.[48] Alternatively, the specifications using pre- or post-tax wealth may be thought of as reduced form models consistent with different structural

41. Bernheim and Severinov (2000).
42. Bernheim, Shleifer, and Summers (1985).
43. Cox (1987).
44. Kotlikoff and Spivak (1981).
45. Bernheim, Shleifer, and Summers (1985); Cox (1987); and Perozek (1998).
46. Andreoni (1989).
47. Aaron and Munnell (1992); Bakshi and Chen (1996); Carroll (2000).
48. Blinder (1976); Carroll (2000).

motivations for transfers. Carroll presents casual evidence consistent with the utility-of-wealth model, but no formal tests of either model exist.[49]

For purposes of this paper, the noteworthy point is that because the economic content of life-cycle and transfer wealth is difficult to sort out, virtually all values of life-cycle wealth and transfer wealth are consistent with virtually all transfer motives discussed above.

Effects of Government Policies

The second key question that motivates the study of transfers is understanding how changes in transfers would affect overall wealth accumulation. One of the few issues on which Kotlikoff and Summers, and Modigliani, appear to agree is that it should be possible to evaluate the economic effects of transfers independent of whatever accounting norms or definitions are used. While their point is correct in principle, it does not ease the concerns noted above that life-cycle and transfer wealth lack economic content unless the two types of wealth are placed in the appropriate economic framework.

We make two main points regarding the Kotlikoff and Summers estimates of the economic effects of changes in transfers: First, the economic framework used by Kotlikoff and Summers described above to assess the impact of transfer wealth is problematic. Second, plausible variations and extensions in the *economic* framework are likely to produce huge variation in the estimates of the importance of transfers for wealth accumulation. As a result, we conclude that the findings in Kotlikoff and Summers are not helpful for determining the impact of changes in transfers on wealth accumulation.[50]

We have at least four concerns with the underlying economic framework that Kotlikoff and Summers use to assess the impact of transfers on wealth accumulation: The most important is that Kotlikoff and Summers never specify *how* changes in transfers come about. One can imagine many sources for changes in transfers. People could have an exogenous shift in preferences away from giving or receiving transfers. The government could require annuitization of all wealth. The government could tax transfers. Certainly, each of these policies would have a different effect on wealth accumulation.[51] Yet, the

49. Carroll (2000).

50. Kotlikoff and Summers (1981).

51. Nor is there any reason to believe that such interventions would necessarily be effective in eliminating all transfers. For example, even if the government forced annuitization of all wealth upon retirement, people could still make sizable transfers by using their annuity income to pay premiums for life insurance policies that listed children as the beneficiaries. Yaari (1965); and Bernheim (1991).

framework used by Kotlikoff and Summers does not distinguish the effects of these alternative policies.

The second problem is that to the extent that the analysis is intended to deal with changes in transfers due to taxes on transfers, it does not account for the revenues that are collected.[52] While it is useful and important in any analysis of tax incidence to keep track of the revenues, it is particularly important in this case.[53] Due to the assumptions about functional form—that is, a separable utility function—in the Kotlikoff and Summers model noted above, changes in transfer taxes only have income effects on consumption and leisure.[54] But the aggregate income effects of the tax change would be zero if the revenues were recycled into the model, and this could fundamentally change the results. For example, if the revenues from a transfer tax were recycled by giving each household a lump-sum equal to the transfer taxes it paid, the income effect would be zero for all households and hence no change in consumption, leisure or wealth, would take place regardless of the values of life-cycle and transfer wealth.

The third problem is that the framework used by Kotlikoff and Summers is based on a partial equilibrium model. In another work, Kotlikoff shows that the partial equilibrium results for capital intensity can substantially overstate analogous general equilibrium outcomes.[55]

The fourth problem is that the motive for transfers can also affect the impact of transfer taxes on wealth. Kotlikoff and Summers use a utility function in which consumption and leisure are collectively separable from transfers.[56] Transfers are specified to affect utility either through an additive term that measures the log of transfers or an additive term that measures the utility of the next generation. Thus Kotlikoff and Summers build in a utility-of-bequests motive or an altruistic model in order to develop their estimate. But, as noted above, the literature provides literally no evidence to support

52. We thank Peter Diamond for bringing the importance of this point to our attention.

53. Indeed, as Kotlikoff and Summers (1981)) note in footnote 9, the compensated rather than uncompensated changes are the appropriate way to measure the impact of tax changes. One might think that with a 100 percent tax on transfers, transfers and revenues would be zero. However, to the extent that bequests are accidental, as defined above, taxable transfers would be positive even with a 100 percent tax.

54. Kotlikoff and Summers (1981).

55. Kotlikoff (1979). In the case of private transfers, however, there may be reason to believe that the general equilibrium effects could amplify the partial equilibrium effects. We thank Laurence Kotlikoff for several discussions on this point.

56. Kotlikoff and Summers (1981).

the former specification and much evidence to oppose the latter. If bequests were motivated by exchange considerations, as in Bernheim, Shleifer, and Summers, a separate argument—the services provided by the child—would need to be included in the utility function.[57] Alternatively, if bequests were accidental, in the sense described above, or if households obtain utility from the holding of wealth, different utility functions would need to be specified. Thus the formulation of the utility function specified by Kotlikoff and Summers does not enable the model to adequately capture all transfer motives, nor does it imply that the results are independent of transfer motives.[58]

Different motives for transfers can imply radically different effects of transfer taxes or government policies on wealth accumulation. The implications of different transfer motives for public debt policies are well known.[59] Gale and Perozek show that different transfer motives translate into different impacts of the estate tax on wealth accumulation. For example, with accidental bequests, changes in estate tax rates have no effect on saving by potential transfer donors. If bequests are altruistic, estate taxes will typically reduce saving by potential transfer donors. In both cases—for the estate tax and for public debt—the effects can vary dramatically by transfer motive.[60]

Conclusion

Estimates of the relative magnitude of life-cycle wealth and transfer wealth have stimulated substantial new research on intergenerational transfers, aimed at understanding both the motives for household saving and transfers, and the impact of government policies on such behavior. The focus on intergenerational transfers has proven to be a fertile research ground. Yet, with twenty years of hindsight, it is fair to say that the methodology used to develop estimates of aggregate life-cycle and transfer wealth appears to be unlikely to resolve either of the two key issues that Kotlikoff and Summers pose at the beginning of their paper, namely the motivation for household saving and transfers, and the impact of government policies on wealth accumulation.[61] The testing of hypotheses about alternative motives for saving and transfers, and direct tests of the impact of policies on behavior seem to be more promising avenues for future research.

57. Bernheim, Shleifer, and Summers (1985).
58. Kotlikoff and Summers (1981).
59. See Barro (1989); and Bernheim (1989).
60. Gale and Perozek (2001).
61. Kotlikoff and Summers (1981).

COMMENT BY
Peter A. Diamond

I start with the same quote that William Gale and Samara Potter do. Laurence Kotlikoff and Lawrence Summers have two objectives: "The first is simply to answer an accounting question: namely, can life-cycle savings alone account for the U.S. capital stock? The second goal is to answer an economic question: If, *ceteris paribus*, there were no intergenerational transfers, how large would the U.S. capital stock be? That is, if all such transfers were taxed in a confiscatory way, by how much would capital accumulation be reduced?"[62]

Gale and Potter argue that the accounting question does not shed much light on the economic questions of interest. I agree. Nevertheless, the calculation has obviously been of considerable rhetorical success, and the article by Kotlikoff and Summers has attracted a great deal of further work.

Gale and Potter discuss some of the issues that make it difficult to distinguish between life-cycle wealth and transfer wealth in total wealth. For example, they mention how earnings can be increased by gifts, particularly to finance education. Let me add another example. How should the returns from investing transfers be divided between life-cycle wealth and transfer wealth? People experience different realized rates of return: they choose different points on the risk-return trade-off, some people just invest better than others, and some people use labor to find better rates of return for a given risk. In his adjustment of the Kotlikoff and Summers estimates, Modigliani attributed earnings on previous transfers to life-cycle wealth. We might interpret Modigliani as saying that anything above a zero rate of return (which should be nominal, not real) is due to labor, choosing an investment other than cash, and should therefore be attributed to life-cycle wealth. Another option is to attribute the excess over the lowest safe rate available in the market to life-cycle wealth. Like the other issues Gale and Potter identify, it is not obvious how these types of adjustments should be made. Nor does an adjustment make the accounting exercise more interesting.

One accounting exercise that might be interesting is to examine how important are the receipt of bequests and *inter-vivos* gifts for people at different places in the lifetime income distribution. Transfers received could be compared to wealth at the time of receipt and to the lifetime budget constraint net of transfers. Both calculations are interesting since the model of lifetime utility optimization subject to a lifetime budget constraint is ade-

62. Kotlikoff and Summers (1981).

quate for only some of the population. The exercise should clearly separate different aspects of gifts: education, early *inter-vivos* transfers, and bequests. The variation in the importance of transfer wealth within the population would be interesting—probably more so than some aggregate measure.

Let me turn now to the second objective of Kotlikoff and Summers. First, they confuse an odd, incompletely specified question—what if intergenerational transfers were zero, with a logically consistent one—what if all such transfers were taxed 100 percent? The former refers to endogenous variables, and because endogenous variables do not just change, it is hard to make sense of it; the latter refers to a change in policy. Instead, Kotlikoff and Summers might ask what would happen if preferences change so that people stop leaving bequests. However, such a change is associated only with an income effect on the level of earnings and consumption in their model, and this model strikes me as implausible for a typical consumer.

How would a policy that taxes transfers at 100 percent be defined, and how would it affect wealth accumulation? One way would be to take current law, remove the exempt amount on gifts, remove the tax credit on estates, and make the tax rates 100 percent. Presumably we would still allow transfers for spouses, education, and medical expenses. Maybe we would still allow deductions for charitable gifts and bequests. If so, we would need to recognize that charitable endowments are part of wealth accumulation and might be much larger if you could not give money to your children. Indeed, some charities probably spend money more slowly than individual beneficiaries, leading to more capital as a result of displaced transfers. Moreover, we need to compare rates of return earned by charities and individuals, since a higher rate of return may lead to more savings. In addition, we would expect some people to simply evade the tax and some to find loopholes in a 100 percent tax law. Even a 100 percent tax on transfers would generate revenue for the government, but presumably less than with a lower tax rate. So we need to also ask what happens to that change in revenue. If the tax revenue were saved, it would have a different implication for wealth accumulation than if it were spent on public consumption, although the latter might also have savings implications depending on how households respond to public consumption.

To consider the impact of such a tax law, we need a model of behavior, preferably one we believe. Kotlikoff and Summers consider two simple models, both of which I think are implausible as models of general behavior. Instead, to answer the question, we need to consider different motives for accumulation, as indicated by Gale and Potter.

The motive I consider of particular interest is that some people simply like to hold wealth (wealth in the utility function in the usual formulation, as in

Carroll).[63] If holding wealth means dying with it, such a model would not produce results like the Kotlikoff and Summers conclusion. Indeed, if everyone were like this and had no bequest motive, 100 percent taxation of bequests would have no effect on lifetime consumption of bequeathers, although it would still affect recipients. It is difficult to see why anyone would be interested in such an extreme policy question today, since it is not on the agenda; indeed, what we have seen is moving in the opposite direction.

I want to suggest that the distinction between intended and accidental bequests, used by Gale and Potter and others, is not the most helpful for examining this issue.[64] Instead, I prefer the vocabulary, also used by Gale and Potter, of "distinguishing motives." Assume an individual derives utility from consumption and bequests and does not annuitize any wealth. Then the size of bequests, in present discounted value terms, is probabilistic. To call the excess of actual bequests over some measure of intended bequests—for example, bequests at the maximal possible age at death—accidental does not seem helpful; it was stochastically intended. Similarly, someone who derives no utility from bequests and also does not annuitize has a stochastic distribution of bequests, although one that would include zero at the maximal possible survival age—an age almost no one would reach. The issue of motivation relates to how the distribution of possible bequests responds to changes in the economic environment. Hence the term "a bequest motive" does not distinguish between a variety of different formulations with different responses to changing economic variables.

This leads to the issue of the connection between annuitization and bequest motives. The issues of some annuitization and bequest motives seem quite separate. An individual can annuitize and still have some bequest motive. If an individual annuitizes planned consumption, the bequest would be known with certainty, apart from other risks and their associated precautionary savings. If not annuitizing any wealth is a sign of a bequest motive, as some argue, then that bequest motive would be peculiar. Not buying any annuities means the bequest is stochastic in present-discounted-value terms. Unless people are risk neutral in their utility from bequests, some annuitization would be expected unless annuities were very expensive. Hence lack of annuitization may be evidence of failure to understand insurance rather than evidence of an odd bequest motive.

63. Carroll (2000).

64. For example, "Treating bequests as departures from the life-cycle model would be appropriate if the bequest had been intended. However, bequests can be accidental rather than intended." Gale and Potter (this volume).

This argument is similar to the argument that the common form of annuities that has a years-certain guarantee does not make sense as a response to a conventional bequest motive. The annuity with the guarantee has a higher price than the same annuity without the guarantee. This means that by buying the annuity with the guarantee, an individual is converting a certain bequest, equal to the price difference between the annuities with and without a guarantee, to a probabilistic bequest depending on the length of life. This does not look like a maximizing strategy in a standard utility function including bequests, unless the pricing is very far from actuarially fair. Indeed, from the perspective of standard economic theory, what is striking is the absence of many more investment vehicles with payouts conditional on survival; for example, certificates of deposit with the accounts of the deceased distributed to the survivors, just as CREF annuities spread mortality risk among annuitants. I take this absence to be a sign of limited demand, which then influences the particular structure of annuity products that are offered.[65]

To repeat my basic message, in order to analyze the role of transfers in aggregate wealth accumulation, the focus should be on different ways of modeling consumption, savings, and bequest decisions. I believe that no single consistent maximization problem will make sense of the diverse pattern of savings and bequests. Instead I think we will need multiple models and some of them will be other than simple utility maximizations.

COMMENT BY
Laurence J. Kotlikoff

It is now twenty years since my paper with Larry Summers on the role of intergenerational transfers in aggregate wealth accumulation appeared in the *Journal of Political Economy*. Twenty years is a long time in this business, and I am delighted that the paper is still being read and debated. Twenty years is also long enough in the past that my current self feels free to take a look at the work of my former self with some degree of dispassion.

The paper by William Gale and Samara Potter affords this opportunity. Their main point is that studying the importance of intergenerational transfers for wealth accumulation does not tell us what is generating those trans-

65. See Davidoff, Brown, and Diamond for more on this Arrow-Debreu-like approach to the puzzle of limited annuitization. "Annuities and Individual Welfare." MIT. Unpublished.

fers, or how certain government policies would influence wealth accumulation. I certainly agree with this complaint, but in defense of my former self, answering those questions is not the paper's point. Its point is to figure out if the whole process of intergenerational transfers is important enough to merit detailed investigation. The paper argues strongly that it is and may have helped kick-start what turned out to be a great deal of important research on intergenerational transfers.

As Gale and Potter detail, the profession has made some real progress understanding the determinants of intergenerational transfers. Of course, on any particular issue, one can cite papers that reach opposite conclusions, but on a quality-adjusted basis, the research speaks pretty clearly. We know today that the Ricardo-Phelps-Barro model of intergenerational altruism has essentially no empirical purchase. If you take resources from the young, and give them to the old, they will spend them, and vice versa. This is true for transfers across cohorts, transfers among extended family members, and, indeed, transfers among extended family members who are actively engaged in making transfers among themselves. We also know that neither cohorts nor extended family members engage in much, if any, risk sharing, which is an automatic implication of intergenerational altruism. Moreover, we know that parents generally ignore what are often huge differences in the economic resources of their children, and leave them all exactly the same bequests.

This is not to deny that some form of altruism operates in extreme circumstances, when a parent or child runs into substantial and verifiable financial hardship, or when a parent has vastly more resources than a child. But in the main, today's retiree's bumper sticker rings true: "I'm Spending My Children's Inheritance."

We also know that the degree of annuitization of the elderly's resources has increased dramatically over time, through the expansion of Social Security, Medicare, and Medicaid, and that the elderly have responded, not by increasing their life insurance holdings, but by actually reducing them as a share of their resources, thereby reinforcing, rather than offsetting, the reduction in bequests. Taking the risk out of living too long has also led the elderly to increase their propensity to consume.

Indeed, if one wants to explain the postwar decline in U.S. saving, all one needs to do is look at the elderly. Their consumption has risen dramatically relative to that of the young because of the level of transfers they have received from and not returned to the young, and from the annuitized form in which these transfers have arrived.

Thus my current self feels he knows a lot more about the determinants of intergenerational transfers than my former self knew. He feels that intergenerational transfers are not, in the main, determined by Barro-type intergenerational altruism. He feels that *inter-vivos* transfers are made by middle-class parents primarily in the form of college support and by the super-rich in the form of explicit or implicit gifts. This may be altruism at work, but seems better explained by parents caring about the particular thing they are giving, namely the college education or the partnership in Dad's business.

My current self feels that bequests are driven, in large part, by imperfect annuitization, and that the more we annuitize the elderly, the less they will leave their heirs, and the smaller will be our nation's stock of capital. He also feels that the failure of the elderly to voluntarily annuitize their remaining nonannuitized assets reflects their quite sensible desire to hold fungible wealth as a security blanket, together with imperfections in the annuity market, the fact that annuities are not fungible, the fact that indexed annuities are not available, and the legitimate fear that the insurance carrier may die in advance of the annuitant.

In making such strong assertions about what we know and do not know, my current self is influenced by the practice of his departed friend Fisher Black, who realized that pulling punches was not necessarily advancing collective wisdom.

My paper with Summers pulls no punches either. It "rules out life-cycle hump saving as the major determinant of capital accumulation in the U.S. economy." To be clear, we did not set out with the goal of reaching this conclusion. Indeed, my prior view was that life-cycle saving would explain essentially all of private wealth holdings, and I would be able to correct my then colleague Michael Darby, who was suggesting otherwise, based on a stylized cross-section analysis. Our accounting framework for dividing wealth into life-cycle and transfer components seemed quite natural, and certainly was not chosen with the intent of producing a result, which, at first glance, would be inimical to the life-cycle model. The idea was simply that if transfers were really small, private wealth should correspond pretty closely to the sum, across cohorts, of their accumulated earnings (net of taxes, but gross of transfer payments) less their accumulated consumption. The reality was and is that longitudinal net earnings profiles and consumption profiles do not differ much previous to roughly age forty-five, leaving little scope for hump saving to generate lots of private wealth, as measured by our national accountants.

Gale and Potter seem to call this conclusion into question. They claim that all "direct estimates of life-cycle wealth are sensitive to a variety of assumptions concerning the ages of retirement and death; the shape and stability over time of age-earnings and age-consumption profiles and relative wages; and the definition of durable goods as consumption or investment." I do not agree. In principle, one can accumulate the net earnings and consumption (adjusted for the implicit rent on durable goods) of a cohort and compare it with its wealth holdings. In my analysis with Summers, retirement and death are nonissues, since we are aggregating over all cohort members. Also, if one is using cohort-specific historic data on levels of earnings and consumption, those profiles do not need to be stable or have the same shape through time.

It is true that when we did our study, cohort-specific data were hard to come by, necessitating lots of assumptions. But today, we have annual Current Population Surveys taken over thirty years, and annual Consumer Expenditure Surveys going back over twenty years. Thus anyone who wants to track a cohort's life-cycle saving and compare it with its current wealth holdings is in a much better position to do so.

However, in suggesting that further analysis along the lines of our study could be done, let me stress that accounting measures of life-cycle and transfer components are not, in themselves, indicative of anything. Instead, they are just raw data that need to be used in an economic analysis to gauge the importance of intergenerational transfers. My former self was overly seduced by the accounting results. He would have done better by showing in the article that the accounting could have been set up in different ways, but still have yielded the same answer to the economic question we posed: namely, how much wealth would be lost, in the aggregate and in the long run, if the government banned intergenerational transfers. He would also have done better by pointing out that not only is the division of private wealth into transfer and life-cycle components arbitrary and therefore intrinsically uninformative, but so is the measure of private wealth, which one is trying to decompose.

Stated differently, by choosing different, but equally plausible, labels for government receipts and payments, one can make the accounting measures of life-cycle and total household wealth used in our study both rise and fall by the same amount, where the amount can be any positive or negative number. Let me also hasten to stress that each nomenclature for government receipts and payments will alter the level and shape of net age-earnings profiles and therefore, the amount of perceived hump saving. That is why I was careful in my remarks above about those profiles to refer to household wealth as measured by our national income accounts that use a particular set of labels. Franco Modigliani's recent work in which he seeks to raise the share of life-cycle wealth in total private wealth by defining total private wealth to include claims on Social Security benefits is an illustration of this proposition.

The bottom line here is that we do not have, as my paper with Summers suggests, a well-defined accounting question to answer because each accounting framework will deliver a different answer to that question. However, each accounting framework will deliver the same answer to the economic question if the accounting data are carefully constructed and appropriately used. In my paper with Summers, appropriate use of our accounting data requires considering how our measure of life-cycle wealth would change if intergenerational transfers were fully banned by the government. Gale and Potter suggest in their paper that this economic adjustment factor to our measure of life-cycle wealth is based on a specific and peculiar specification of preferences. That is not the case, as we discuss in the text of the paper and in footnote ten.

The main thing this adjustment is getting at is the lifetime income effect on the consumption and leisure of future generations of showing up in a world in which they neither receive nor are allowed to make intergenerational transfers. Our adjustment factor is based on the assumption that preferences for consumption and leisure over the life cycle are homothetic and separable from preferences over the utility of the next generation or over the amount left to the next generation.

My current self would pick a different bone with my former self's adjustment factor. The factor we use assumed that only leisure and consumption would change if intergenerational transfers were banned. However, this assumes that average wage and capital income tax rates would remain fixed, which, working through the government's intertemporal budget constraint, means the government would have to experience a change in its purchases. Had we kept those purchases fixed in forming our adjustment factor, my sense is it could have been larger or smaller than the one we used, depending on the fiscal response.

Yesterday, I visited with Franco Modigliani, who regretted greatly not being able to join us at the conference. I asked him if he had any messages I should pass on to our gathering. He said he never claimed the life-cycle model ruled out a role for intergenerational transfers, but that the role is small—only 20 percent.

To conclude, I never viewed our study as ruling out selfish life-cycle preferences at the margin. Indeed, my subsequent work has reinforced my view that those preferences are operational for most households. The fact that intergenerational transfers used to and may still play a large role in aggregate capital formation is, in my view, reflective, in the main, of incomplete annuitization. In an elaborate simulation study I did with Jagadeesh Gokhale, James Sefton, and Martin Weale, published in the *Journal of Public Econom-*

WILLIAM GALE AND SAMARA POTTER

ics, all bequests are due to incomplete annuitization, and parents care not a fig about their kids, or what they leave their kids.[66] All bequests go to surviving spouses, and when the last spouse dies, are divided evenly among children. In this model, we were able to generate a realistic flow of bequests relative to GDP, reproduce the U.S. wealth Gini coefficient, and reproduce the share of total wealth held by the top tail of the U.S. wealth holders. I showed this paper to Franco, who was pleased to think that I was finally seeing the light.

66. Gokhale and others (2001).

10

The Impact of Gifts
and Bequests on the
Distribution of Wealth

EDWARD N. WOLFF

The paper explores three issues: First, how has the distribution of wealth changed over time in the United States? Second, how does the United States compare to other developed countries in terms of wealth inequality? Third, to what extent have bequests contributed to the growing inequality of wealth in the United States?

The data in this study come from the Survey of Consumer Finances (SCF). The advantage of the SCF is that it provides detailed information on households' assets and liabilities, as well as on inheritances and gifts they have received. Households are asked to record the amount of the transfer received and the year it was received. In addition, they are asked to indicate whether their real estate or business holdings stem from an inheritance or gift. This information makes it possible to estimate the share of current wealth holdings that comes from transfers. This in turn allows us to estimate the effect of transfers on the distribution of wealth.[1]

The chapter is organized as follows: The first section describes the data.

---

1. Unfortunately, it is not possible to simulate what the distribution of wealth would have been in the complete absence of gifts and inheritances. This simulation depends on the elasticity of substitution between transfers and active savings for different income, wealth, and demographic groups. The data available in the Survey of Consumer Finances are insufficient to allow such econometric estimation.

The next section presents recent trends in household wealth inequality in the United States, and the third section presents international comparisons of wealth inequality. The fourth section reviews the literature on the effects of bequests on wealth accumulation and wealth inequality. The following section delves into inheritance and gift patterns in the United States over the period between 1989 and 1998, and a final section concludes the paper.

Data Sources and Methods

The data in this study come from the 1983, 1989, 1992, 1995, and 1998 Survey of Consumer Finances, conducted by the Federal Reserve Board in cooperation with Statistics of Income at the Department of the Treasury. Each survey consists of two components: a core representative sample and a high-income supplement.[2] The advantage of the high-income supplement is that it includes a larger share of very wealthy families than would a random sample of the population. Since wealth is highly concentrated, the oversample of rich households provides for a more accurate estimate of total wealth.[3]

The SCF imputes information for all missing data in the survey. Despite this procedure, some discrepancies remain between the total balance sheet value computed from the survey and the "Board of Governors of the Federal Reserve System Flow of Funds Accounts of the United States" (a quarterly statistical release). To account for these discrepancies, the results presented in this paper are based on my adjustments to the original asset and liability values in the surveys. These adjustments are made by aligning asset and liability totals from the survey data to the corresponding national balance sheet totals. In most cases, this means a proportional adjustment of reported values of balance sheet items in the survey data (see box).[4] The alignment has very little effect on the measurement of wealth inequality measured by the Gini coefficient and the quantile shares. However, it is important to make these

2. The supplement sample is drawn from the Internal Revenue Service's Statistics of Income data file.

3. Because the survey includes an oversample of wealthy households, weights have to be used to calculate population totals. See Kennickell (1999, 2000) and Kennickell and Woodburn (1999) for an overview on the construction of weights in the SCF. For this paper the weights for 1992 have been modified to conform to the distribution of income as reported by Statistics of Income. See Wolff (1996a) for details on the adjustments.

4. See Wolff (1987a, 1994, 1996a, and 1998) for details. No adjustments were made to other asset and debt components or to the 1998 SCF.

Adjustment Factors, by Asset Type and Year				
Survey of Consumer Finances	1983	1989	1992	1995
Checking accounts	1.68	...	...	...
Savings and time deposits	1.50	...	...	...
All deposits	...	1.37	1.32	...
Financial securities	1.20	...	...	...
Stocks and mutual funds	1.06	...	...	...
Trusts	...	1.66	1.41	1.45
Stocks and bonds	...	...	...	1.23
Non-mortgage debt	1.16	...	...	...

adjustments when comparing changes in mean wealth overall and by asset type.[5]

The main wealth concept used in this study is marketable wealth or net worth, which is defined as the current value of all marketable or fungible assets less the current value of debts.[6] This definition measures wealth as a store of value and therefore a source of potential consumption. I believe this is the concept that best reflects the level of well-being associated with a family's wealth holdings, since only assets that can be readily converted to cash—that is, "fungible" ones—are included. As a result, consumer durables, such as automobiles, televisions, furniture, household appliances, and other durables, which are not easily marketed, or whose resale value typically far understates their consumption value, are excluded.

The other notable exclusion from net worth is the value of future Social Security benefits or Social Security wealth, and the value of benefits from

5. It should also be noted that I have revised my adjustments for the 1989 SCF data, so that the results reported here for 1989 differ somewhat from my earlier figures; see Wolff (1994, 1996a).

6. Total assets are defined as the sum of: the gross value of owner-occupied housing; other real estate owned by the household; cash and demand deposits; time and savings deposits, certificates of deposit, and money market accounts; government bonds, corporate bonds, foreign bonds, and other financial securities; the cash surrender value of life insurance plans; the cash surrender value of pension plans, including IRAs, Keogh, and 401(k) plans; corporate stock and mutual funds; net equity in unincorporated businesses; and equity in trust funds. Total liabilities are the sum of: mortgage debt, consumer debt, including auto loans, and other debt.

defined benefit plans, or pension wealth. Even though these funds are a source of future income for the household, they are not in their direct control and cannot be marketed. Therefore, in the definition of wealth used in this paper, they are not part of marketable wealth. However, Social Security and pension wealth do enter into the lifetime resources available to families, since they are an important source of income in retirement. The estimation of Social Security and pension wealth in the SCF is beyond the scope of this paper.[7]

The second wealth measure used is financial wealth. Financial wealth is a narrower definition of wealth and is defined as net worth minus net equity in owner-occupied housing. Financial wealth is a more "liquid" concept than marketable wealth, since a family's home is difficult to convert into cash in the short term. Financial wealth thus reflects the resources that may be immediately available for consumption.

Trends in Household Wealth in the United States, 1983–98

Table 10-1 presents trends in mean and median wealth for the United States between 1983 and 1998. Median net worth was only 4 percent higher in 1998 than in 1989. After rising between 1983 and 1989, median wealth dipped by 17 percent from 1989 to 1995, but then increased between 1995 and 1998. Median financial wealth was less than $17,800 in 1998, indicating that the typical American household had very little savings available for its immediate needs. Financial wealth increased sharply between 1989 and 1998, mainly reflecting raising stock market values.

Table 10-2 presents the distribution of wealth between 1989 and 1998. In 1998, the top 1 percent of families (ranked by net worth) owned 38 percent of total wealth, and the top 20 percent owned 83 percent of total wealth. Financial wealth is even more concentrated, with the richest 1 percent, as ranked by financial wealth, owning 47 percent of total financial wealth, and the top 20 percent owning 91 percent. Median household income, based on Current Population Survey (CPS) data, shows a similar time pattern to median wealth. After surging by 11 percent between 1983 and 1989, it increased by only 2 percent from 1989 to 1998. Table 10-2 also shows that wealth inequality, after rising steeply between 1983 and 1989, increased at a slower pace from 1989 to 1998. The share of net worth held by the top 1

7. The inclusion of both Social Security and pension wealth in the definition of household wealth would result in a considerably more equal distribution of augmented wealth. See, for example, Wolff (1987b).

Table 10-1. *Mean and Median Wealth, 1983–98*[a]

Thousands of 1998 dollars

	Year					Percent change		
	1983	1989	1992	1995	1998	1983–89	1989–98	1983–98
Net worth[b]								
Median	54.6	58.4	49.9	48.8	60.7	7.0	3.8	11.1
Mean	212.6	243.6	236.8	218.8	270.3	14.6	11.0	27.1
Financial net worth								
Median	11.8	13.9	11.7	10.6	17.8	18.0	28.0	27.1
Mean	154.3	181.8	180.5	167.9	212.3	17.8	16.8	27.1
Income								
Median	34.2	38.0	35.6	36.4	38.9	11.2	2.3	13.8
Mean	41.6	48.0	45.1	48.1	51.9	15.5	8.0	24.7

Sources: Author's calculations from the 1983, 1989, 1992, 1995 and 1998 Surveys of Consumer Finances using population weights. Household income data come from the U.S. Bureau of the Census, Current Population Survey.

a. The 1983, 1989, 1992, and 1995 asset and liability entries are aligned to national balance sheet totals (see footnote 4).

Table 10-2. *The Distribution of Wealth, 1983–98* [a]
Percent

Year	Percentage share of wealth or income held by									Gini coefficient
	Top 1.0	Next 4.0	Next 5.0	Next 10.0	Top 20.0	Next 20.0	3d 20.0	Bottom 40.0	All	
Net worth										
1983	33.8	22.3	12.1	13.1	81.3	12.6	5.2	0.9	100.0	0.799
1989	37.4	21.6	11.6	13.0	83.5	12.3	4.8	-0.7	100.0	0.832
1992	37.2	22.8	11.8	12.0	83.8	11.5	4.4	0.4	100.0	0.823
1995	38.5	21.8	11.5	12.1	83.9	11.4	4.5	0.2	100.0	0.828
1998	38.1	21.3	11.5	12.5	83.4	11.9	4.5	0.2	100.0	0.822
Financial wealth										
1983	42.9	25.1	12.3	11.0	91.3	7.9	1.7	-0.9	100.0	0.893
1989	46.9	23.9	11.6	11.0	93.4	7.4	1.7	-2.5	100.0	0.926
1992	45.6	25.0	11.5	10.2	92.3	7.3	1.5	-1.1	100.0	0.903
1995	47.2	24.6	11.2	10.1	93.0	6.9	1.4	-1.3	100.0	0.914
1998	47.3	21.0	11.4	11.2	90.9	8.3	1.9	-1.1	100.0	0.893
Income	Top 5 percent		Next 15 percent							
1983	16.4		28.3		44.7	24.7	16.5	14.1	100.0	0.414
1989	18.9		27.9		46.8	24.0	15.8	13.3	100.0	0.431
1992	18.6		28.3		46.9	24.2	15.8	13.2	100.0	0.434
1995	21.0		27.7		48.7	23.3	15.2	12.8	100.0	0.450
1998	21.7		27.5		49.2	23.2	15.0	12.5	100.0	0.456

Sources: Author's calculations from the 1983, 1989, 1992, 1995, and 1998 Surveys of Consumer Finances using population weights. Household income data come from the U.S. Bureau of the Census, Current Population Survey.

a. In thousands, 1998 dollars. The 1983, 1989, 1992, and 1995 asset and liability entries are aligned to national balance sheet totals as in note 4. For the calculation of percentile shares of net worth, households are ranked according to their net worth; for percentile shares of financial wealth, households are ranked according to their financial wealth; and for percentile shares of income, households are ranked according to their income.

percent rose by 3.6 percentage points from 1983 to 1989, and the Gini coefficient increased from 0.80 to 0.83. Between 1989 and 1998, the share of the top percentile grew by a more moderate 0.7 percentage points but the share of the next 9 percentiles fell by 0.4 percentage points and that of the bottom two quintiles grew by 0.9 percentage points, so that the Gini coefficient fell from 0.83 to 0.82.

The trend is similar for the inequality of financial wealth. Between 1983 and 1989, the share of the top one percent gained 4.0 percentage points, and the Gini coefficient increased from 0.89 to 0.93. In the ensuing nine years, the share of the richest one percent grew by another 0.4 percentage points, but the share of the next 19 percentiles declined, as did the share of the second quintile. At the same time, the share of the bottom two quintiles grew by 1.3 percentage points, so that overall financial wealth inequality declined, with the Gini coefficient falling from 0.93 to 0.89. Household income inequality, based on CPS data, increased between 1983 and 1989, with the share of the top five percent rising by 2.5 percentage points, while the share of the next fifteen percent and that of the bottom four quintiles all fell.[8] The Gini coefficient rose from 0.41 to 0.43 over this period. Between 1989 and 1998, the share of the top five percent rose by another 2.8 percentage points, while the next fifteen percent and the bottom four quintiles again lost ground. As a result, the Gini coefficient again increased, from 0.43 to 0.46. All told, according to the CPS figures, no abatement occurred in the growth of inequality between 1989 and 1998 compared to the period between 1983 and 1989.

Despite the seemingly modest increase in overall wealth inequality during the 1990s, the decade witnessed a near explosion in the number of very rich households. The number of millionaires climbed by 54 percent between 1989 and 1998, the number of "pentamillionaires" ($5,000,000 or more) more than tripled, and the number of "decamillionaires" ($10,000,000 or more) almost quadrupled. The conclusion that emerges from table 10-2 is that the top 1 percent has become wealthier compared to all other groups. In fact, 53 percent of the increase in wealth between 1983 and 1998 went to the top 1 percent. The share for the next 4 percent decreased slightly over the period.

In sum, the results point to stagnating living conditions for the average American household during the 1990s, with median net worth growing by only 4 percent. Another salient finding is the sharp dip in both household

8. The CPS tabulations published by the U.S. Bureau of the Census do not include the income shares of the top percentile (2000b).

wealth between 1989 and the mid-1990s. Indeed, it was not until the late
1990s that the level of wealth attained in 1989 was restored. These results
indicate rather dramatically that the growth in the U.S. economy during the
period from 1983 to 1998 was concentrated in a surprisingly small part of
the population.

Comparisons with Other Countries

To gain some perspective on the U.S. wealth distribution, this section presents a comparison with some other countries. International comparisons of
household wealth inequality must be made cautiously due to different data
sources, definitions of household wealth, and accounting conventions. Nevertheless, the evidence seems to suggest that in the early part of the twentieth
century—the 1920s are the earliest period for which data are available—
wealth inequality in the United States was much lower than in the United
Kingdom, and roughly comparable to Sweden. By the early 1990s, the situation appears to have completely reversed, with much higher concentration of
wealth in the United States than in Europe.

United Kingdom and Sweden

In addition to the United States, long-term time series are available on household wealth inequality for the United Kingdom and Sweden. The most comprehensive data exist for the United Kingdom. The data are based on estate
duty, that is, tax returns, and use mortality multipliers to estimate the wealth
of the living.[9] Figures are available on an almost continuous basis from 1923
to 1991.[10]

The Swedish data are available on a rather intermittent basis from 1920
through 1992. The data are based on actual wealth tax returns. The principal
problem with using wealth tax returns is underreporting owing to tax evasion
and legal tax exemptions. However, some assets, such as housing and stock
shares, are extremely well covered because of legal registration requirements
in Sweden. Also, the deductibility of interest payments from taxable income

9. The mortality multiplier technique uses the inverse of the mortality rate for a
particular group to weight the estate tax return in the total population. For example,
since young persons have lower mortality rates than older ones, an estate tax return
from a young decedent will have a higher weight in constructing the population estimates than an estate tax return from an older person.

10. The data are for individuals rather than households. For an overview of the
data and methodology, see Shorrocks (1987).

Figure 10-1. *Share of Marketable Net Worth Held by Top Percentile of Wealth Holders: Sweden, United Kingdom, United States, 1920–92*

Percent of net worth

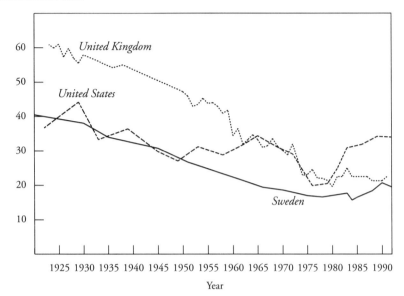

Year

makes it likely that the debt information is very reliable. On the other hand, bank accounts and bonds are not subject to similar tax controls, and it is likely that their amounts are underreported.

Figure 10-1 shows comparative trends in the holdings of marketable wealth for the top 1 percent for the United States, United Kingdom, and Sweden.[11] Wealth inequality declined dramatically in the United Kingdom from 1923 to 1974, but changed little thereafter. The top 1 percent share of net worth fell from 61 percent in 1923 to 23 percent in 1974.

Sweden also saw a dramatic reduction in wealth inequality between 1920

11. The U.S. series is based on household net worth excluding consumer durables (the "HWX" series). See notes to table A-1 in Wolff (2002) for sources and methods for the United States. Sources for the United Kingdom are: 1923–81: Anthony Atkinson, James Gordon, and Alan Harrison (1989), table 1; and 1982–91: Board of Inland Revenue (1993), series C, table 13.5. Results are based on marketable wealth for adult individuals. The 1982–91 Inland Revenue series is benchmarked to the 1923–81 data. Sources for Sweden are: 1920–75: Roland Spånt (1987), tables 3.7, 3.8, and 3.11; and 1975–92: Statistics Sweden (1994), table 42. The unit is the household, and wealth is valued at market prices. The 1920–75 data are benchmarked to the Statistics Sweden series.

and the mid-1970s. Over this period, the share of the top percentile declined from 40 percent to 17 percent of total household marketable wealth. Between 1975 and 1985, the concentration of wealth remained virtually unchanged. However, this was followed by a sharp increase in wealth inequality between 1985 and 1992, with the share of the top percentile increasing to 20 percent, a level similar to that of the mid 1960s.

Comparisons among the three countries are informative. The distribution of wealth became less concentrated in all three countries until the late 1970s, although the pattern was much more cyclical in the United States than in the other two countries. However, during the 1980s, both the United States and Sweden experienced a rather sharp increase in wealth inequality, whereas the trend was almost flat in the United Kingdom. The difference is surprising, since both the United States under Ronald Reagan, and the United Kingdom under Margaret Thatcher, pursued conservative economic policies, while the Social Democrats were in power in Sweden. Moreover, Sweden is the only country among the three with a direct tax on household wealth. This suggests that differences in public policy alone cannot account for trends in wealth distribution.

Other OECD Countries

Table 10-3 presents the distribution of wealth for six countries in the Organization for Economic Cooperation and Development (OECD) in the mid-1980s. The countries are grouped by the most comparable data sources. Panel A shows the distribution of household gross assets for France and the United States, based on a special study to create consistent databases between the two countries.[12] In France, the top 1 percent holds 26 percent of the total assets and the Gini coefficient is 0.71; while in the United States the top 1 percent holds 33 percent and the Gini coefficient is 0.77.

One reason that wealth is more concentrated in the United States than in France may be that French households keep a substantially higher proportion of their wealth in the form of owner-occupied housing, which is more equally distributed than most other assets, particularly bonds and corporate stock.

Panel B shows comparative statistics on net worth for Germany and the United States derived from two other consistent data sets. The results also show that net worth in the United States is more concentrated than in Germany.[13]

12. The French data come from the 1986 Enquete sur les Actifs Financiers, and the U.S. data from the 1983 SCF. See Kessler and Wolff (1991) for details on the survey.

13. The German data come from the Socioeconomic Panel, and the U.S. data from Panel Study of Income Dynamics Equivalent Data File for 1988. See Wolff (1996a) for details. See also Burkhauser, Frick, and Schwarze (1997).

Table 10-3. *The Inequality of Household Wealth in Selected Countries, Mid-1980s*

Source	Gini coefficient	Percent of total wealth held by	
		Top 1	Top 5
Panel A: Consistent data on gross assets			
France, Enquete sur les Actifs Financiers 1986	0.71	26	43
United States, Survey of Consumer Finances 1983	0.77	33	54
Panel B: Consistent data on net worth			
Germany, German Socioeconomic Panel 1988	0.69		
United States, Panel Study of Income Dynamics Equivalent Data File 1988	0.76	...	...
Panel C: Consistent household surveys on net worth			
United States, Survey of Consumer Finances 1983	0.79	35	56
Canada, Statistics Canada Survey of Consumer Finances 1984	0.69	17	38
Japan, Family Savings Survey 1981	0.58		
Japan, National Survey of Family Income and Expenditure 1984	0.52	25	...
Sweden, 1985–86	...	16	31

Source: Wolff (1996b). See the paper for details on sources and methods.

Panel C shows wealth statistics based on comparable household surveys from the United States, Canada, Japan, and Sweden.[14] Wealth inequality is greatest in the United States, with a share of the top percentile almost double that of Canada's. Estimates for Japan are shown for 1981 and 1984, and indicate that wealth concentration is lower in Japan than in the United States and Canada. Sweden has the lowest concentration of wealth among the four countries.

The conclusion is that wealth inequality in the United States is high by international standards. This result is perhaps not too surprising, since many

14. The U.S. data come from the 1983 Survey of Consumer Finances; the Canadian data from the 1984 Statistics Canada Survey of Consumer Finances; the Japanese data from the 1981 Family Saving Survey and the 1984 National Survey of Family Income and Expenditure; and the Swedish data from the 1985–86 Survey of Household Market and Nonmarket Activities. The source for the Canadian data is James Davies (1993, p. 162). The source for the Japanese data is Bauer and Mason (1992, pp. 416–17). The source for the Swedish data is Bager-Sjögren and Klevmarken (1993, pp. 208–10).

studies have shown that recent income inequality is greater in the United States than in most other industrialized economies.[15]

Literature Review on Bequests

Two approaches have been used to assess the contribution of bequests to household wealth. The first is based on household surveys, while the second relies on indirect inferences.

Survey evidence on the importance of bequests is fairly consistent, indicating that a fairly modest share of total wealth comes from bequests. Dorothy Projector and Gertrude Weiss, using the 1962 Survey of Financial Characteristics of Consumers, reported that 17 percent of families had received any bequest.[16] This compares with a figure of 18 percent reported by James Morgan, William David, J. Cohen, and Harvey Brazer.[17] The Projector and Weiss study also found that only 5 percent of households had received a "substantial" proportion of their wealth from bequests. However, among wealthier households, bequests were more important, with 34 percent of families with net worth exceeding half a million dollars indicating that they had received a substantial inheritance. Harvey Barlow, Brazer, and Morgan used the 1964 Brookings Survey on the Economic Behavior of the Affluent and found that only 7 percent of families with incomes of $10,000 or more mentioned gifts and inheritance as the source of most of their present assets.[18] They estimated that about one-seventh of the total wealth of this group came from bequests.

Paul Menchik and Martin David used probate records of men who died in Wisconsin between 1947 and 1978 and estimated that the mean bequest of all decedents was $20,000 in 1967 dollars.[19] This figure also includes interspousal and other transfers. David and Menchik (1982) estimated that the average interspousal transfer was $15,800, and about one half of all individuals died while still married.[20] Moreover, they calculated that about 60 percent of all non-interspousal bequests went to children. This means that the average intergenerational bequest was approximately $7,500 in 1967 dollars.

---

15. See, for example, Atkinson, Rainwater, and Smeeding (1995). Wolff (2000) shows that a strong positive correlation between the degree of wealth inequality in a country and its income inequality exists for the United States.

16. Projector and Weiss (1966).

17. Morgan and others (1962).

18. Barlow, Brazer, and Morgan (1966).

19. Menchik and David (1983).

20. David and Menchik (1982).

This is less than one fifth of average household wealth in 1967 and about 10 percent of the average household wealth of families 65 or over in age.

Michael Hurd and Gabriella Mundaca also analyzed data from the 1964 Survey on the Economic Behavior of the Affluent as well as data from the 1983 Survey of Consumer Finances on the importance of gifts and inheritances in individual wealth holdings.[21] Both surveys asked respondents about whether they had received gifts and inheritances, and how much these transfers were worth. In 1964, only 12 percent of the households in the top 10 percent of the income distribution reported that more than half their wealth came from gifts or inheritances. The corresponding figure from the 1983 data was 9 percent. Hurd and Mundaca concluded that intergenerational transfers were not an important source of wealth, even for rich families. However, William Gale and J. Karl Scholz, using the 1983 Survey of Consumer Finances, estimated that at least 51 percent of household wealth is accounted for by inheritances and other "intentional" wealth transfers.[22]

A similar type of analysis was conducted on French data by Denis Kessler and André Masson.[23] In a 1975 survey of 2,000 French families, respondents were asked whether the family had received any significant inheritance above $4,000, or gifts above $2,000. In the survey, 36 percent reported that they had already received some inheritance. Among all households, Kessler and Masson estimated that 35 percent of total wealth originated from inheritances or gifts. Most recently, Klevmarken computed that 34.4 percent of Swedish households reported receiving a gift or inheritance in the 1998 Swedish Household Market and Non-Market Activities Survey.[24] Using a three-percent capitalization of inheritances and gifts, as described in the next section of the paper, he calculated that 19.0 percent of the wealth of Swedish households in 1998 originated in wealth transfers.

Though direct survey evidence and econometric tests on household survey data or probate records failed to show a significant effect of bequests on household wealth accumulation, some indirect tests do find a substantial effect. Franco Modigliani and Richard Brumberg recognized the potential importance of inheritances in their original paper on the life-cycle model.[25]

---

21. Hurd and Mundaca (1989).

22. Gale and Scholz (1994).

23. Kessler and Masson (1979). See also Kessler and Masson (1989).

24. N. Anders Klevmarken. 2001. "On the Wealth Dynamics of Swedish Families 1984–98." Paper presented at the 21st Arne Ryde Symposium on Non-Human Wealth and Capital Accumulation. Lund University, Sweden. August 23–25.

25. Modigliani and Brumberg (1954).

Later, Modigliani estimated that only somewhere between one-tenth and one-fifth of all private wealth could be traced to inheritances.[26] This estimate has been challenged, by Betsy White, and by Laurence Kotlikoff and Lawrence Summers, among others.[27] Kotlikoff and Summers calculated that life-cycle savings accounted for only 19 percent of observed U.S. household wealth in 1974. The remaining 81 percent, by implication, was due to inheritance and intergenerational transfers.

Another model developed by James Davies augmented the standard life-cycle model with a bequest motive.[28] The starting point for the estimate was the actual distribution of wealth in Canada in 1970. Davies used data on the distribution of inheritances, mortality rates, and other factors to simulate the effects of inheritance on the distribution of wealth in Canada and concluded that inheritances were a major source of Canadian wealth inequality. In a follow-up paper, Davies and France St. Hilaire used the same model to estimate the proportion of total wealth accumulation in Canada that could be traced to inheritances.[29] Without cumulating interest on inheritances, they estimated that 35 percent of total household wealth was due to inheritances. With the interest on the inheritances added in, the proportion rose to 53 percent. John Laitner calibrated a model incorporating both life-cycle saving and bequests for the United States, and estimated the share of inherited wealth between 58 and 67 percent.[30]

In a simulation analysis, Daphne Greenwood and Wolff investigated the importance of four sources for household wealth accumulation: savings, capital appreciation on existing wealth holdings, bequests, and *inter-vivos* transfers—gifts from living parents to their children.[31] In the simulation, initial wealth holdings by age group, as reported in the 1962 Survey of Financial Characteristics of Consumers, were updated annually until 1983, based on savings rates computed from Consumer Expenditure Survey data, and capital gains by individual asset type. Based on mortality rates by age cohort, and age differences between generations, the study simulated the transfer of bequests between parents and children. Greenwood and Wolff estimated that 75 percent of the growth of overall household wealth between 1962 and 1983 arose from capital gains (appreciation) of existing wealth, and the

26. Modigliani (1975).
27. White (1978); and Kotlikoff and Summers (1981).
28. Davies (1982).
29. Davies and St. Hilaire (1987).
30. Laitner (1992).
31. Greenwood and Wolff (1992).

remaining 25 percent from savings (income less consumption expenditures). Bequests, including the capital appreciation on the assets in the bequest, accounted for a substantial portion of the wealth accumulation for households under the age of sixty-five in 1983. For ages forty to sixty-four as a whole, 34 percent of the wealth accumulated over this twenty-one-year period between 1962 and 1983 could be traced to bequests.[32] Even with bequests included in the model, the simulations systematically fell short of explaining the wealth of younger age groups and overstated that of older ones. The likely explanation appears to be that *inter-vivos* transfers are missing from the simulation. The wealth holdings of younger households in 1983 were much larger than could be explained by their savings, capital gains, and inheritances, while the wealth holdings of older households were much smaller than would have been the case if they kept all their wealth accumulation. The most reasonable explanation is that older parents have been transferring significant amounts of wealth to their adult children in the form of gifts. This means that inheritances and gifts together accounted for 40 percent of the wealth accumulation of age cohorts under the age of sixty-five, between 1962 and 1983. In a follow-up study, Wolff extended the period of analysis from 1962 through 1992.[33] He estimated that over the lifetime, bequests and *inter-vivos* gifts *each* contributed about one-third to the lifetime accumulation of wealth, while the remaining one-third was due to savings.

The question is what accounts for this sizable discrepancy in estimates between the direct survey evidence and regression analysis, and the simulation results. The direct survey evidence suggests that no more than about 20 percent of household wealth is due to intergenerational transfers. In contrast, the simulation models suggest that inheritances explain a large portion of total wealth accumulation. This subject was the source of a lively debate between Modigliani and Kotlikoff, and Kotlikoff and Summers, with commentary by Blinder, and Kessler and Masson.[34] The two approaches differ in three ways: First, direct survey evidence is hampered by recall bias and underreporting. It is hard for people to remember the amount of inheritances received five, ten, or, certainly, twenty years ago. As

---

32. Even this figure might be an understatement of the actual importance of inheritance, since no information was available on the sources of wealth before the calendar year 1962.

33. Wolff (1999).

34. Modigliani (1988a, 1988b); Kotlikoff (1988); Kotlikoff and Summers (1988); Blinder (1988); Kessler and Masson (1989).

a result, many respondents may understate the value of inheritances received, and this may bias the direct survey evidence on the importance of inheritances downward.

Second, the treatment of the appreciation of bequests is a crucial factor. Suppose a house was inherited ten years ago and its value doubles over the decade. Should its contribution to current wealth be valued at its original value or at its now appreciated value? Modigliani uses the former method, in which the appreciation of inherited assets is counted as savings, while Kotlikoff and Wolff include the appreciation on the inheritance as part of the contribution of inheritances to current wealth. This issue is definitional—it depends on the accounting framework one uses—but the difference in the assessment can be quite substantial.

Third, the role of *inter-vivos* transfers is often overlooked in direct tests of the bequest motive. In direct surveys, gifts, in particular, are subject to recall error since respondents typically do not have formal records of these transfers. Moreover, as the Greenwood and Wolff simulations suggest, *inter-vivos* transfers may be a particularly important source of wealth for young households. In a survey of the literature on the subject, Davies and Shorrocks surmise that between 35 and 45 percent of household net worth may be traceable to bequests.[35]

Trends in Inheritances, 1989–98

This section examines trends in inheritances using the 1989, 1992, 1995, and 1998 SCFs.[36] The data collection method in the SCF is based on recall. Respondents are asked to indicate whether they have received any inheritances, gifts, or other types of wealth transfers such as trust funds in the past, the value of the transfer, and the date at which it was received.

Questions on inheritances and gifts are asked in two different ways: First, the survey contains a section with questions on "general wealth transfers." These questions presumably refer to any type of gift or inheritance. Second, the survey includes specific questions on inheritances and gifts of real estate and businesses. These questions are asked in the sections of the questionnaire that deal specifically with the value of homes, other properties, and businesses. The questions on general wealth transfers are asked in a section on

35. Davies and Shorrocks (1999).

36. Data on inheritances are not available in comparable form from the 1983 Survey of Consumer Finances.

inheritances and incorporate the specific transfers indicated in the questions on real estate and businesses.[37]

The recall method is likely to have serious underreporting problems, as suggested in the previous section, and estimates of inheritances presented below are very likely to be biased downward. However, it is difficult to ascertain whether the underreporting is systematic by wealth class, by income class, or by demographic characteristics of the respondent.

Based on the reported value of wealth transfers and the date of the transfer, the present value of all inheritances received as of the survey year is computed by accumulating them at a real interest rate of 3.0 percent.[38] The value of inheritances is then converted to 1998 dollars. As indicated in the previous section, it is not clear whether interest or capital gains received on past inheritances should be counted as part of inheritances or as part of savings. My procedure is essentially a compromise. I assign a normal rate of return on assets received from wealth transfers, and count this part of the return in the inheritance portion of current wealth.[39] Returns on inherited assets above this normal rate are implicitly treated as part of savings.

Table 10-4 presents the share of households that had received transfers and the mean value of those transfers. In 1998, 20.3 percent of households indicated that they had received a general wealth transfer, a decline from 23.1 percent of households in 1989.[40] The data indicate that 3.1 percent of households had received their home in the form of a transfer. The mean present value of transfers was $220,200 in 1998 among households with transfers. The value of transfers declined over the period; in 1989 the mean value was $295,100.

37. Since the data are reported in two places in one survey, it is possible that respondents report an inheritance in one section, but then forget to report it in the second section as well. The SCF data are edited in order to correct for these inconsistencies. However, some inconsistencies do remain. To be on the conservative side, I have included the value of the specific wealth transfers in only two circumstances: first, if no general wealth transfer was reported; and second, if the value of the specific wealth transfer exceeds the value of the general wealth transfer (see below for details).

38. Technically, the date of receipt is rounded off to the nearest fifth year in the Public Use version of the SCF, so that some error is introduced into the calculations.

39. According to my calculations, the average real rate of return on the average household wealth portfolio between 1962 and 1998 was 3.07 percent. See Wolff (1999) for details on the computation.

40. Correcting the data for inconsistencies in reporting between the different sections on inheritances in the survey yields an estimate of 20.4 percent of households having received any inheritance.

Table 10-4. *Percent of Households Receiving Any Kind of Wealth Transfer and Mean Present Value of Transfer, 1989–98*

Recipients of	Households indicating a transfer of indicated type (percent)				Mean present value of wealth transfer by indicated type for recipients only[a] (thousands of 1998 dollars)			
	1989	1992	1995	1998	1989	1992	1995	1998
General wealth transfer questions	23.1	20.4	21.1	20.3	295.1	287.0	235.1	220.2
Owner-occupied housing[b]	2.8	2.2	3.6	3.1	141.7	162.5	155.7	189.5
Other real estate[c]	4.1	2.3	4.9	3.2	209.5	322.5	377.5	266.6
Business[d]	0.6	0.3	0.5	0.4	1,041.2	1,202.7	1,306.7	770.1
Real estate or business	7.6	5.0	8.6	6.6	247.5	303.8	412.4	262.0
Memo: General wealth transfer and/or real estate or business								
Low estimate: Include real estate or business only if no general wealth transfers; replace general wealth transfer by specific wealth transfer if the value of the specific wealth transfer is greater.					290.6	313.3	345.8	256.9
High estimate: Include real estate or business with all general wealth transfers					370.2	303.1	382.7	302.5

Source: Author's calculations from the 1989, 1992, 1995, and 1998 Survey of Consumer Finances.

a. The figures are based on the present value of all transfers as of the survey year that were received up to the time of the survey and accumulated at a real interest rate of 3.0 percent) for recipients only.

b. Includes mobile homes and sites as well as farm and ranch houses.

c. Includes vacation properties, time shares, and investment real estate.

d. Active businesses only. Transfer information is missing for passive businesses.

The general wealth transfer questions are likely to capture almost all of the specific wealth transfers, but to account for possible underreporting in the general wealth questions, I include two other estimates of total wealth transfers. The first, the "low estimate," adds the specific wealth transfers to the general wealth transfer in two cases: First, when no general wealth transfer was reported by the household, and second, when the sum of the specific transfers is greater than the sum of the general transfers. The second, the "high estimate," includes the value of the general wealth transfers plus the total value of the specific wealth transfers. The most sensible choice appears to be the low estimate, and I use these figures in the remainder of the paper.

Some general statistics on transfers are provided in the next two tables. Table 10-5 shows a breakdown of wealth transfers by type of transfers. Among households receiving a transfer in 1998, 80 percent of the value of these transfers came from bequests, 11 percent from gifts, and 9 percent from trusts. The importance of both bequests and gifts appears to have risen over time while that of trusts has declined.

In 1998, 66 percent of all wealth transfers came from parents, 21 percent from grandparents, 9 percent from other relatives, and 3 percent from friends and other sources, as shown in table 10-6. The share of total transfers coming from parents and grandparents rose during the 1990s, from 71 to 88 percent.

Table 10-7 presents the share of households receiving wealth transfers by income, total wealth, race, age, and education. As expected, the share of recipients rises very strongly with income and wealth level. In 1998, 39 percent of households in the highest income bracket, $250,000 or more, reported a wealth transfer, compared to only 14 percent in the lowest income bracket, less than $15,000; and 45 percent of households in the highest wealth bracket, $1,000,000 or more, received a transfer, compared to 10 percent in the lowest wealth bracket, less than $25,000.

The share of non-Hispanic white households reporting a wealth transfer in 1998 was more than twice as large as the share of non-Hispanic African Americans: 23.8 as compared to 10.8 percent. Only 4.2 percent of Hispanic households, and only 9.1 of Asian and other households, reported a wealth transfer.

As expected, the likelihood of receiving a wealth transfer also rises with age. In 1998, 12 percent of households whose head was under age thirty-five received a transfer while 34 percent of households whose head was between age sixty-five and seventy-four received a transfer. However, the fraction of recipients in age group seventy-five and over was only 28 percent. This pattern reflects both life-cycle and cohort effects. In the case of the former, the parents of older persons are more likely to have died than those of younger persons, so that older individuals are more likely to receive bequests than

Table 10-5. Distribution of Wealth Transfer Received, by Type of Transfer, 1989–98

Transfer type	Percent of wealth transfer recipients receiving indicated type of transfer[a]				Present value of transfer received as a percent of total wealth transfers[b]			
	1989	1992	1995	1998	1989	1992	1995	1998
Inheritances only	85.2	88.1	74.9	76.2	66.9	75.6	78.6	77.1
Gifts or transfers only	3.5	5.2	14.6	17.2	1.5	2.4	4.3	9.7
Trust funds or other only	7.7	3.3	6.2	3.0	10.6	8.6	5.7	6.0
Inheritances and gifts	0.6	1.7	2.5	2.2	0.6	1.1	1.6	1.6
Inheritances and trusts	2.9	1.4	1.7	1.3	20.4	4.9	4.0	5.2
Gifts and trusts	0.1	0.1	0.1	0.1	0.1	6.9	0.4	0.3
Inheritances, gifts, and trusts	0.0	0.3	0.0	0.0	0.0	0.5	5.4	0.0
All transfer recipients	100.0	100.0	100.0	100.0	100.0	100.0	100.0	100.0

Source: Author's calculations from the 1989, 1992, 1995, and 1998 Survey of Consumer Finances. Tabulations are only for general wealth transfer questions. See source to table 10-1 for technical details.

a. Inheritances include inherited trust funds.

b. The figures are based on the present value of all transfers as of the survey year that were received up to the time of the survey and accumulated at a real interest rate of 3.0 percent for inheritors only.

Table 10-6. *Distribution of Wealth Transfer Received, by Source of Transfer, 1989–98*

Transfer source	Percent of wealth transfer recipients by indicated source of transfer[a]				Present value of transfer received as a percent of total wealth transfers[b]			
	1989	1992	1995	1998	1989	1992	1995	1998
Parents only	49.2	48.0	60.1	61.0	35.9	36.7	49.7	50.7
Grandparents only	15.7	15.2	12.1	12.5	8.1	6.0	4.4	6.4
Other relatives only	13.8	17.7	14.0	11.2	4.5	9.3	19.3	6.3
Friends and others only	5.4	3.1	0.0	2.8	8.8	4.9	0.0	2.9
Two or more relatives	11.9	13.7	11.7	10.8	22.5	35.9	22.2	30.9
Relatives and friends or others	3.9	2.4	2.1	1.7	20.1	7.2	4.5	2.8
All transfer recipients	100.0	100.0	100.0	100.0	100.0	100.0	100.0	100.0

Source: Author's calculations from the 1989, 1992, 1995, and 1998 Survey of Consumer Finances. Tabulations are only for general wealth transfer questions. See source to table 10-1 for technical details.

a. Inheritances include inherited trust funds.

b. The figures are based on the present value of all transfers as of the survey year that were received up to the time of the survey and accumulated at a real interest rate of 3.0 percent, for recipients only.

Table 10-7. *Percent of Households Receiving Wealth Transfers, 1989–98*[a]

Category	1989	1992	1995	1998
All households	23.5	20.7	22.2	20.4
Income level				
Under $15,000	16.2	14.0	16.7	13.7
$15,000–24,999	21.0	17.9	23.3	21.9
25,000–49,999	22.4	21.8	19.5	19.9
50,000–74,999	28.1	24.6	22.6	21.5
75,000–99,999	30.3	24.3	31.5	20.5
100,000–249,999	32.1	31.1	41.0	32.2
250,000 or more	47.6	38.1	33.8	38.9
Wealth level				
Under $25,000	8.4	8.8	10.9	9.9
$25,000–49,999	24.9	20.4	18.7	20.0
50,000–99,999	26.3	22.5	21.4	19.6
100,000–249,999	33.1	25.3	29.3	26.0
250,000–499,999	37.6	37.7	41.4	31.7
500,000–999,999	46.2	44.5	53.2	35.5
1,000,000 or over	47.9	46.1	48.2	44.9
Race				
Non-Hispanic whites	27.6	24.2	25.2	23.8
Non-Hispanic African Americans	10.4	9.4	11.5	10.8
Hispanics[b]	5.8	6.7	9.3	4.2
Asian and other races	16.8	12.9	13.4	9.1
Age class[c]				
Under 35	15.4	12.8	13.3	11.8
35–44	18.7	15.7	19.1	15.5
45–54	24.4	21.0	23.9	19.4
55–64	26.4	30.5	26.7	27.7
65–74	34.9	26.8	32.0	34.5
75 and over	34.4	29.4	30.0	28.4
Education[d]				
Less than 12 years	17.7	14.4	14.4	13.5
12 years	19.8	19.3	18.7	17.8
13–15 years	22.2	19.4	21.5	20.9
16 years or more	34.4	27.0	32.4	27.3

Source: Author's calculations from the 1989, 1992, 1995, and 1998 Survey of Consumer Finances.

a. See source to table 10-1 for technical details. The figures record the share of households that indicate receiving a wealth transfer at any time before the time of the survey. The data are corrected for inconsistencies in reporting between the different sections on inheritances in the survey.

b. Hispanics can be of any race.

c. Households are classified according to the age of the head of household.

d. Households are classified according to the education of the head of household.

younger individuals. In the case of the latter, parents of those persons seventy-five and over in 1998 were more likely to be poorer than parents of younger people in 1998, so that the amount of the bequest is likely to be lower for older age groups. The likelihood of inheriting or receiving a gift also rises with education: from 13 percent for those with less than four years of high school to 27 percent for college graduates in 1998. This result is consistent with the patterns found by income and wealth class. Almost all income, wealth, and demographic groups saw a moderate decline in the share of transfer recipients between 1989 and 1998. However, there were some exceptions to this pattern. The highest income group experienced a precipitous drop in the share of recipients, from 48 to 39 percent. Even though the standard errors are large for this group, the change is statistically significant (see table 10A-1). The share of white households receiving a transfer declined by about four percentage points, whereas the share of African American households actually showed a slight increase. The change is statistically significant for whites, but not for black households. The results for black households may reflect the increasing economic resources of black families over the decade.

Table 10-8 shows the present value of wealth transfers received among recipients. In 1998, the mean present value of wealth transfers among recipients was $256,900, and the median was $54,500. The large difference in the mean and median value of transfers is of the same order of magnitude as that between mean and median household wealth, and indicates considerable skewness in the distribution of wealth transfers.

The patterns in the distribution of transfer wealth are similar to those in the previous table. Both the mean and median value of wealth transfers tends to rise with household income, with a big jump for the highest income class. In 1998, the mean present value of wealth transfers for the top income class, $250,000 or more, was almost 16 times as great as for the lowest, under $15,000, and the median transfer was seven times as large. Wealth transfers increase monotonically with wealth, with again a big jump for the top wealth class. The mean present value of wealth transfers for the highest wealth class, $1,000,000 or more, was more than twenty-five times as great as for the lowest, under $25,000, in 1998, and the median transfer was fifteen times as large.

Wealth transfers are also higher for non-Hispanic whites than for non-Hispanic African Americans. In 1998, the ratio of means between the two groups was 1.54 and the ratio of medians was 1.24. Both the mean and median value of wealth transfers tends to rise with age. The mean transfer for households age seventy-five and over was six times as great as that for the youngest age group, under thirty-five, while the median transfer was almost

Table 10-8. *Present Value of Wealth Transfers Received among Recipients, 1989–98*[a]

Category	Mean				Median			
	1989	1992	1995	1998	1989	1992	1995	1998
All households	312.2	313.3	345.8	256.9	51.8	50.0	51.9	54.5
Income level								
Under $15,000	95.9	155.9	165.3	155.4	32.3	31.0	0.0	33.9
$15,000–24,999	187.3	131.0	102.3	140.9	52.6	37.4	0.1	40.7
25,000–49,999	164.5	235.4	158.5	208.7	44.5	49.7	42.3	60.4
50,000–74,999	170.2	252.4	449.0	131.1	46.1	55.6	32.2	48.8
75,000–99,999	382.9	397.3	701.9	176.0	70.2	59.8	43.8	55.5
100,000–249,999	627.3	733.7	715.6	357.3	119.6	132.4	60.4	94.7
250,000 or more	3,180.7	2,490.9	3,065.1	2,416.8	363.1	168.2	76.4	237.8
Wealth level								
Under $25,000	65.7	35.5	30.1	52.7	14.5	12.2	80.5	19.0
$25,000–49,999	71.7	50.0	113.2	82.4	34.2	20.9	191.8	31.9
50,000–99,999	64.5	118.7	154.8	100.8	32.9	38.3	14.3	38.4
100,000–249,999	126.9	161.8	151.7	120.5	47.3	52.3	35.7	47.4
250,000–499,999	211.6	171.2	242.9	180.4	68.4	77.8	50.1	87.6
500,000–999,999	422.1	861.9	834.5	427.4	157.7	190.5	58.6	179.0
1,000,000 or over	1,720.0	2,049.8	2,137.3	1,325.9	328.6	290.4	110.0	277.4

Race								
Non-Hispanic whites	275.3	305.9	366.2	264.9	50.6	50.0	130.6	55.1
Non-Hispanic African Americans	122.2	72.9	178.3	171.6	39.6	30.6	271.4	44.4
Hispanics[b]	1,762.1	39.6	66.6	118.6	13.0	5.6	54.4	94.7
Asian and other races	243.5	327.9	333.7	272.6	51.8	42.2	35.0	76.1
Age class[c]								
Under 35	147.2	103.7	77.3	109.0	24.2	14.8	37.9	20.0
35–44	211.4	112.9	341.1	134.0	30.2	36.5	152.2	29.3
45–54	205.5	544.1	322.4	205.5	56.8	50.3	22.9	52.7
55–64	232.4	324.3	435.8	274.5	68.3	50.5	45.3	79.9
65–74	721.8	406.7	341.9	247.7	74.3	71.1	51.9	66.4
75 and over	309.3	405.8	588.6	609.1	79.1	89.1	54.4	73.0
Education[c]								
Less than 12 years	148.3	78.8	126.5	112.8	48.1	22.7	125.3	34.8
12 years	128.0	273.6	122.4	177.5	33.9	39.9	55.1	41.0
13–15 years	212.5	205.1	352.1	161.8	54.4	51.8	35.1	55.1
16 years or more	596.8	492.4	564.8	421.0	85.0	74.1	37.9	73.7

Source: Author's calculations from the 1989, 1992, 1995, and 1998 Survey of Consumer Finances.

a. Figures are in thousands, 1998 dollars. The figures show the present value of all transfers as of the survey year that were received up to the time of the survey and accumulated at a real interest rate of 3.0 percent for recipients only.

b. Hispanics can be of any race.

c. Households are classified according to the age and education of the head of household.

four times as great. The value of wealth transfers received also rises with the educational level of the households, and is particularly high for college graduates. In 1998, the mean transfer of the latter was almost four times as great as that for households with less than a high school education, and the median value more than twice as great.

The results of table 10-8 also indicate a sharp decline in the mean present value of wealth transfers between 1989 and 1998: almost 18 percent. The median value showed a moderate increase. The decline in the value of wealth transfers was especially marked among the upper two income classes and the top wealth class. Some of the lower income and wealth classes actually experienced a rise in the value of their wealth transfers.

Table 10-9 shows the present value of wealth transfers received as a percent of the current net worth of households. This figure is calculated by dividing the total transfers received by the group by the total wealth of the group. In 1998, transfers received as a share of net worth were 19.4 percent among all households. However, since net worth has risen during the 1990s in the United States, and the mean value of wealth transfers has fallen, this proportion has also fallen rather sharply over the decade. Indeed, the comparable figures were: 29.7 percent in 1989; 25.8 percent in 1992; and 35.5 percent in 1995.

Another surprising result is that, while both the percentage of households receiving a wealth transfer and the value of those transfers rise almost monotonically with income and wealth class, wealth transfers as a share of household net worth for a given group *decline* with both income and wealth. In 1998, the present value of wealth transfers amounted to 45 percent of total net worth of the lowest income class and only 18 percent for the highest income class. Likewise, the present value of these transfers accounted for 46 percent of total wealth of the second lowest wealth class: $25,000 to $49,999, compared to 17 percent for the top wealth class. The explanation for this result is that while the dollar value of wealth transfers is greater for wealthier groups, small gifts and bequests mean more to poorer families that receive them. Indeed, the inverse relation between wealth transfers as a share of a given group's current net worth and wealth level appears to have become more pronounced between 1989 and 1998.

Although the total value of wealth transfers tends to rise with the age of the household, wealth transfers as a share of current wealth tend to have a U-shaped relationship with age. The share is high for young households, because of their low savings, and for older households, because of the high absolute value of such transfers. It is low for middle-age households, because of their relatively small amount of inheritances and large level of savings.

Table 10-9. *Present Value of Wealth Transfers Received as a Share of Group's Net Worth, 1989–98*[a]

Category	1989	1992	1995	1998
All households	29.7	25.8	35.5	19.4
Income level				
Under $15,000	52.8	58.1	55.6	44.8
$15,000–24,999	35.1	27.6	30.7	35.2
25,000–49,999	26.7	39.6	27.8	33.8
50,000–74,999	23.1	32.4	49.1	12.6
75,000–99,999	27.0	25.2	65.0	11.0
100,000–249,999	25.7	26.6	34.6	13.0
250,000 or more	35.5	12.4	19.5	18.0
Wealth Level				
Under $25,000	−109.3	163.5	310.6	−9,896.9
25,000–49,999	48.1	27.3	58.5	45.5
50,000–99,999	23.5	36.7	45.9	27.1
100,000–249,999	26.2	25.2	28.0	19.6
250,000–499,999	23.0	18.7	28.8	16.5
500,000–999,999	29.0	53.5	65.5	22.6
1,000,000 or over	23.6	26.4	29.0	17.1
Race				
Non-Hispanic whites	25.7	24.7	36.2	19.7
Non-Hispanic African Americans	25.7	12.4	47.8	31.9
Hispanics[b]	217.4	4.0	11.5	6.3
Asian and other races	14.8	16.3	20.1	9.7
Age class[c]				
Under 35	34.6	26.9	30.6	21.8
35–44	20.3	10.0	46.5	11.4
45–54	14.5	32.3	25.7	11.6
55–64	15.8	21.8	29.9	14.7
65–74	65.4	27.5	29.7	18.8
75 and over	33.5	39.9	62.0	57.1
Education[c]				
Less than 12 years	13.7	14.4	23.4	20.8
12 years	21.1	38.8	17.6	20.8
13–15 years	25.5	19.3	41.9	16.2
16 years or more	40.2	25.4	40.7	19.9

Source: Author's calculations using the 1989, 1992, 1995, and 1998 Survey of Consumer Finances.

a. 1998 dollars. See source to table 10-1 for technical details. The figures show the present value of all wealth transfers as of the survey year that were received up to the time of the survey and accumulated at a real interest rate of 3.0 percent as a ratio to net worth.

b. Hispanics can be of any race.

c. Households are classified according to the age and education of the head of household.

   Instead of measuring wealth as current wealth holdings, wealth can be defined by lifetime resources, *LR*:

$$LR = LE + WT,$$

where *LE* is lifetime earnings, and *WT* is total wealth transfers. Lifetime resources consist of two components: lifetime labor earnings (*LE*), and total wealth transfers from other persons (*WT*).[41] This is a different measure from current wealth, which depends on lifetime resources, the household's savings rate, and the rate of return it receives on the assets it holds. Lifetime resources is thus a measure of the potential wealth available to a household, whereas current wealth holdings reflect the actualization of the resources at the disposal of the household.

   To calculate lifetime earnings, I estimate an earnings function by gender, race, and schooling level.[42] Future earnings are projected on the basis of the regression coefficients on age and age squared.[43] I also assume a 1.5 percent annual real wage growth in the future. This is the intermediate assumption made by the Social Security Administration in projecting future earnings in its annual Trustees' Report. A 3 percent real discount rate is used to calculate the present value. This means that future earnings will count less in the present value calculation than current or past earnings. Lifetime earnings are

---

   41. Technically speaking, gross Social Security and pension wealth should also be included in *LR*.

   42. To estimate the earnings function, the sample is divided into sixteen groups by the following characteristics: first, white and Asian as opposed to African American and Hispanic; second, male and female; and third, less than twelve years of schooling, twelve years of schooling, thirteen to fifteen years of schooling, and sixteen or more years. For each group, the following earnings equation is estimated:

$$\log(E_i) = b_0 + b_1\log(H_i) + b_2 X_i + b_3 X_i^2 + b_4 SE_i + \Sigma_j b_j OCCUP_{ij} + b_{10}MAR_i + b_{11}AS_I + \varepsilon_i,$$

where log is the natural logarithm; E_i is the current earnings of individual *I*; H_i is annual hours worked in the current year; X_i is years of experience at current age (estimated as age minus years of schooling minus 5); SE_i is an indicator variable indicating whether the person is self-employed or working for someone else, *OCCUP* is a set of five indicator variables indicating occupation of employment; *MAR* is an indicator variable indicating whether the person is married or not married; *AS* is an indicator variable indicating whether the person is Asian or not (used only for regressions on the first racial category); and ε is a stochastic error term.

   43. This implicitly assumes that deviations from the regression line in the current year are a result of a transitory component to current income only.

computed from the start of the person's work life to the person's last year, or expected last year, of work. Work history information is provided by respondents in the SCF. An adjustment is also made for part-time work.

Table 10-10 shows wealth transfers as a percent of lifetime earnings for 1998. The mean value of lifetime earnings is $665,000 in 1998, considerably higher than average marketable wealth of $270,000. Among all households in 1998, total wealth transfers as a percent of lifetime earnings amounted to only 8 percent. The ratio of transfers to lifetime earnings tends to have a U-shaped relationship with current income level. For the top income class, the ratio is almost 100 percent. On the other hand, the ratio of wealth transfers to lifetime earnings rises almost monotonically with wealth level, with a very sharp increase at the top wealth class, $1,000,000 or more. The ratio of transfers to lifetime earnings is highest for white households, followed by African Americans, Asian Americans, and lastly, Hispanics. Because lifetime earnings are inversely related to age and wealth transfers rise with age, the ratio between the two is increasing with age, with a big jump for the oldest age group.

The breakdown by lifetime earnings quantiles is illuminating. The ratio of wealth transfers to lifetime earnings declines monotonically as lifetime earnings increases, from a high of 51 percent for the lowest quintile to a low of 2 percent for the top 5 percent.

Conclusion

The most surprising finding of this study is that bequests and other wealth transfers make the wealth distribution more equal. Indeed, the addition of wealth transfers to other sources of household wealth has had a sizable effect on reducing the inequality of wealth. The results appear counterintuitive, because richer households do receive greater inheritances and other wealth transfers than poorer households. However, *as a proportion of their current wealth holdings,* wealth transfers are actually greater for poorer households than richer ones. That is to say, a small gift to the poor means more than a large gift to the rich.

Another surprising finding is that a higher fraction of the wealth of African American families comes from wealth transfers than that of whites and other races. Low-income households, and the young and old, also receive a higher share of their wealth from transfers relative to other groups.

While wealth transfers tend to equalize the distribution of household wealth, they are not equalizing with respect to lifetime resources. Indeed, the correlation between lifetime earnings and wealth transfers is virtually zero.

Table 10-10. *Present Value of Wealth Transfers as a Percent of Lifetime Earnings,*
1998[a]

Category	Mean wealth transfer for recipients	Mean lifetime earnings	Transfers as a percent of lifetime earnings
All households	256.9	665.1	7.9
Income level			
Under $15,000	155.4	275.9	7.7
$15,000–24,999	140.9	477.6	6.5
25,000–49,999	208.7	693.8	6.0
50,000–74,999	131.1	927.5	3.0
75,000–99,999	176.0	1,027.5	3.5
100,000–249,999	357.3	1,025.8	11.2
250,000 or more	2,416.8	949.7	99.1
Wealth level			
Under $25,000	52.7	547.9	1.0
$25,000–49,999	82.4	698.3	2.4
50,000–99,999	100.8	651.8	3.0
100-000–249,999	120.5	712.5	4.4
250,000–499,999	180.4	813.3	7.0
500,000–999,999	427.4	840.1	18.1
1,000,000 or over	1,325.9	854.1	69.8
Race			
Non-Hispanic whites	264.9	723.0	8.7
Non-Hispanic African Americans	171.6	404.9	4.6
Hispanics[b]	118.6	417.8	1.2
Asian and other races	272.6	780.2	3.2
Age class[c]			
Under 35	109.0	686.9	1.9
35–44	134.0	769.4	2.7
45–54	205.5	801.8	5.0
55–64	274.5	716.5	10.6
65–74	247.7	513.7	16.6
75 and over	609.1	223.8	77.4
Lifetime earnings			
Bottom quintile	191.0	60.8	51.4
2d quintile	466.1	284.9	31.7
3d quintile	237.7	589.9	9.4
4th quintile	189.5	913.5	5.0
Next 10 percent	175.5	1,242.0	3.5
Next 5 percent	241.2	1,486.3	2.9
Top 5 percent	190.4	1,917.8	1.6

Source: Author's calculations using the 1998 Survey of Consumer Finances.

a. See source to table 10-1 for technical details. The figures show the present value of all wealth transfers as of the survey year that were received up to 1998 and accumulated at a real interest rate of 3.0 percent as a ratio to the present value of lifetime earnings in 1998.

b. Hispanics can be of any race.

c. Households are classified according to the age of the head of household.

Thus wealth transfers widen the dispersion of resources available to different households.

Oddly enough, although wealth inequality has risen in the United States between 1983 and 1998, the increase may have been even greater were it not for the mitigating effects of bequests and gifts. Also, somewhat surprisingly, we might speculate that the lower wealth inequality found in European countries compared to the United States might be due to larger bequests, at least as indicated in the French and Swedish household surveys. Indeed, Pestieau reports in this volume that the share of bequests in total household wealth is higher in France and other European countries than in the United States.

The results also suggest that the current structure of the estate tax is quite good from the standpoint of equity. It exempts relatively small wealth transfers, including gifts, and taxes large ones. Small transfers are equalizing in terms of wealth, and should be maintained. Indeed, one might even speculate that an inheritance tax as found in many European countries, where individual inheritances are taxed rather than the full size of the estate, might be superior to an estate tax from the point of view of equity.

Two provisos for these results should be mentioned. First, we have assumed that the underreporting biases, which likely exist in the recall method, are not systematically correlated with the level of household wealth. If the underreporting bias is greater for richer households, then the equalizing effect of wealth transfers will be overstated. Second, we have used a three percent capitalization rule for all bequests and other wealth transfers. If we count the full capital gains received on wealth transfers, then this method might raise the value of wealth transfers of the rich relative to the poor.

Table 10A-1. *Number of Households Receiving Wealth Transfers: Sample Statistics*[a]

Category	Sample size				Standard error (percentage points)			
	1989	1992	1995	1998	1989	1992	1995	1998
All households inheriting	919	1,023	1,134	1,054	0.8	0.6	0.6	0.6
Income level								
Under $15,000	101	98	116	79	1.6	1.3	1.4	1.3
$15,000–24,999	91	80	120	104	2.1	1.8	1.8	1.8
25,000–49,999	180	197	220	194	1.5	1.4	1.2	1.3
50,000–74,999	129	133	136	134	2.2	1.9	1.7	1.7
75,000–99,999	87	82	94	76	3.0	2.7	2.7	2.3
100,000–249,999	140	183	207	186	2.5	2.1	2.1	2.0
250,000 or more	190	249	239	281	2.3	1.9	1.9	1.8
Wealth level								
Under $25,000	81	96	129	118	1.0	0.8	0.9	0.8
25,000–49,999	48	52	58	47	3.0	2.4	2.2	2.5
50,000–99,999	82	81	95	71	2.4	2.2	1.9	2.0
100–000–249,999	163	141	159	145	2.1	1.8	1.9	1.8
250,000–499,999	124	121	138	132	2.6	2.6	2.6	2.3
500,000–999,999	101	106	132	93	3.3	3.1	2.9	2.8
1,000,000 or over	320	426	423	448	1.8	1.6	1.6	1.5

Race								
Non-Hispanic whites	847	940	1,046	993	0.9	0.8	0.7	0.7
Non-Hispanic African-Americans	36	34	38	37	1.7	1.5	1.6	1.5
Hispanics[b]	13	15	17	12	1.8	1.7	2.1	1.3
Asian and other races	23	34	33	12	3.5	2.5	2.5	2.4
Age class[c]								
Under 35	95	116	119	99	1.6	1.2	1.1	1.1
35–44	154	165	201	165	1.5	1.3	1.3	1.2
45–54	185	205	256	232	1.7	1.5	1.4	1.3
55–64	198	211	213	241	1.8	1.9	1.7	1.7
65–74	179	208	216	200	2.2	1.9	2.0	2.1
75 and over	109	118	129	118	2.8	2.5	2.3	2.3
Education[c]								
Less than 12 years	125	90	81	74	1.5	1.4	1.4	1.4
12 years	177	179	211	186	1.4	1.3	1.2	1.2
13–15 years	156	177	217	207	1.8	1.5	1.3	1.3
16 years or more	461	577	626	588	1.4	1.1	1.1	1.1
Total sample size	3,143	3,906	4,299	4,305				

Source: Author's calculations using the 1989, 1992, 1995, and 1998 Survey of Consumer Finances.

a. The figures are based on households who indicate receiving a wealth transfer at any time.

b. Hispanics can be of any race.

c. Households are classified according to the age and education of the head of household.

COMMENT BY
John Laitner

Edward Wolff first characterizes the U.S. distribution of private net worth, from 1983 to the present, and changes in it, using data from the Survey of Consumer Finances. Next, he presents international comparisons. Then he presents information for the United States on inheritances received. Simulating the effect of eliminating the latter, he concludes that wealth equality might diminish. This paper is an informative addition to Wolff's distinguished list of publications studying various aspects of the distribution of wealth in the United States.

I limit my discussion to three topics: First, I examine the last result: that inheritances might play an equalizing role in the evolution of the distribution of wealth. Second and third, I comment on data quality issues.

Inheritances and Equality

The paper's most surprising finding is that inheritances and other wealth transfers tend to be equalizing in terms of the distribution of household wealth. Indeed, eliminating or reducing wealth transfers would have a sizable effect on raising the inequality of wealth. These results are counterintuitive. My comment first examines this result. I analyze Wolff's empirical finding on the basis of a theoretical model of household behavior from some of my own work and present a framework with four principal elements:[44] Each household has a finite life span and engages in life-cycle saving in youth and middle age, and life-cycle dissaving during retirement; the utility of each household depends on its own consumption and on the consumption of its descendants; a household's net worth must always be nonnegative, and the same is true for its transfers to its descendants (presumably, financial institutions and bankruptcy laws enforce this constraint); and each household is born with an earning ability, and such abilities vary across households.

In the theoretical model's equilibrium, parents with relatively high earning ability, or with large inheritances, accumulate wealth to build estates to share their good luck with their descendants through gifts and bequests. Parents with moderate or low earning ability, and little or no inheritance, on the other hand, move to a "corner solution" with no bequest, since they would ideally like to force their descendants to provide for them through a negative,

---

44. Laitner (1992); John Laitner. 2001. "Wealth Accumulation in the United States: Do Inheritances and Bequests Play a Significant Role?" University of Michigan. Mimeo.

or reverse, transfer. Indeed, in practice we would expect half or more of all households to leave no bequest at all.[45]

Laitner presents simulations of the long run, or steady-state equilibrium of such a model, calibrated to U.S. data.[46] The simulations imply that life-cycle saving explains most private wealth accumulation in the United States—perhaps two-thirds of the total. However, altruistic transfer behavior greatly increases the concentration of the steady-state distribution of wealth according to the simulations: life-cycle saving alone would leave the share of the top 1 percent of wealth holders at about 16 percent, whereas life-cycle saving combined with intergenerational transfer behavior raises the share of total wealth to 25 percent. The pure life-cycle outcome is consistent with earlier work, such as Huggett's; a 25 percent share for the richest 1 percent of households is generally consistent with U.S. data for 1995, provided the latter includes private pension wealth.[47]

Consider how intergenerational transfers work in the theoretical model: First, think about transfer donors. In a model without transfers, if household A has twice the earnings of household B, we might expect A's life-cycle net worth to be about twice as high at each age. In a model in which transfers are an option, however, household A is more likely to be well-off relative to its descendants. Hence A is likely to save for both life-cycle and estate building, whereas B may well only save for its own life-cycle needs. Thus in a model with transfers, household A is likely to accumulate more than twice as much net worth at each age as B. In other words, the behavior of potential donors will likely increase the inequality of the distribution of wealth.

Turn to recipients of transfers. As household A contemplates a bequest to its grown children, the lower the earning ability of the children, the larger the transfer will be. In other words, in an altruistic model, inheritances are "compensatory." It is true that positive intertemporal earning correlations within family lines will mean that at any given time, some lines will have consumption, saving, and transfer amounts which are large in absolute terms, while others will deal with small sums. Nevertheless, all else equal, lower earners will receive larger inheritances.

The theoretical model's finding—that bequest behavior increases long-run wealth inequality—encompasses the behavior of both donors and recipients of intertemporal transfers; in contrast, Wolff's paper only considers recipi-

45. For example, see Altonji, Hayashi, and Kotlikoff (1997); Laitner and Ohlsson (2001); and Wolff (table 10-10, this chapter).

46. Laitner (2001); see also Davies (1982).

47. Huggett (1996).

ents. The exclusive focus on recipients makes his finding that transfers augment equality much less surprising than it might first appear, since we have just seen that inheritances are compensatory for heirs in an altruistic theoretical framework. An interesting possibility is that this paper might yield valuable data for studying and testing one important aspect of integrated general equilibrium models of saving and transfer behavior.

Data Quality

The Survey of Consumer Finances is certainly one of the best, if not the best, data set for studying private intergenerational transfers and the U.S. distribution of wealth in general. The sample has two parts: One part is conventional, the so-called Census sample (about two-thirds of the total in 1995, for instance). The other part is what makes the survey especially useful: the IRS supplies a list of high-income tax filers, and the SCF draws its so-called list sample from these.

One would expect private transfer behavior to be most dramatic within the "list" sample. I have the following worry: Wealthy households are reluctant to participate in surveys; see, for instance, the comments made by Erik Hurst, Ming Ching Luoh, and Frank P. Stafford about the PSID's difficulties in this regard.[48] The SCF is not immune to these difficulties: in 1995, only 13 percent of families in the seventh, or highest, stratum of the "list" were eventually willing to participate in the SCF.[49] I worry that a person, rich from his own spectacular earning power, will more likely be proud enough of himself to want to participate in the Federal Reserve's wealth survey than a person rich because he has received a large inheritance.

The situation is not hopeless. The Statistics of Income provide information from the Federal estate tax about large estates. If one could correlate that information with the distribution of inheritances in the SCF, one's confidence in the latter might rise. The tax information can only provide a lower bound for aggregate private transfers, but it also can tell us how many transfers over, for example, $1 million, we expect to see in a given year. The question is: Are a credible number of large transfers reported in the SCF?

Aside from the issue of selection, I also worry about reporting error. Much earlier work with the Primary Care Physician Program (PCPP) survey sug-

48. Hurst, Luoh, and Stafford (1998).
49. See Arthur B. Kennickell. 1998. "Analysis of Nonresponse Effects in the 1995 Survey of Consumer Finances." Board of Governors of the Federal Reserve System. Mimeo.

gested that donors report larger aggregative transfers than recipients do.[50] Again, pride may play a role, though again IRS data conceivably could help to assuage worries.

International Comparisons

Wolff also presents international comparisons of the distribution of wealth. A general finding is that during the last several decades, the distribution is more unequal in the United States than in Europe, Canada, or Japan.

Again, I worry about data quality. The paper's footnotes imply that the Survey of Consumer Finances "list" sample is unique. If so, it is hard to see how much one can make, for instance, of foreign data on the wealth share of the top 1 or top 5 percent of households.

Wolff's previous work compares SCF aggregate net worth with the same variable from U.S. Flow of Funds tables.[51] It would be valuable to know if the international data sets have been subject to similar scrutiny and, if so, what the outcomes were. In the event of fairly large discrepancies, the ingenious imputation methods of Hurst and others might be useful; that is, if a survey's aggregative net worth total is, for example, 25 percent lower than the level from the corresponding flow of funds, one might want to allocate all of the difference to the top 1 percent of wealth holders, rather than simply making a proportional adjustment to the whole distribution.[52]

COMMENT BY
John Karl Scholz

This is a fun paper to read. It is packed with descriptive statistics on the distribution of wealth in the United States and other countries, and simple calculations about the effects of *inter-vivos* transfers and bequests on the distribution of wealth. Wolff has been an important contributor on this and related topics for a long time, and the paper reflects his deep knowledge. I organize my remarks into three parts: First, I briefly summarize central points of his paper. Then, as the discussant's job is to raise concerns, I do what is expected of me. Finally, I step back and raise some broader issues that are perhaps outside the scope of this paper, but fundamental to efforts to measure and interpret changes in the distribution of wealth.

50. For example, Cox (1987); and Kurz (1984).
51. Wolff (1987a).
52. Hurst, Luoh, and Stafford (1998).

Findings

Stock market performance in the 1990s was strikingly good. Between March 1, 1992, and March 1, 1998, the S&P500 increased nearly 200 percent.[53] The "wealth effect" associated with the stock market increase is frequently cited by Federal Reserve Board Chairman Alan Greenspan and others as fueling the longest economic expansion in U.S. history.[54] Consequently, the first result of the paper, that median net worth was only 4 percent higher in 1998 than in 1989 (table 10-1), at first seems surprising. This result is consistent with other evidence, however, (see, for example, Kennickell [2001]) and is explained by the fact that the typical (median) household does not own equity.[55] Only 27.2 percent of households in 1998 held equity in individual securities or in mutual funds, and the median holdings of these equity owners was only $22,000.[56] Clearly, strong stock market performance has little direct bearing on the net worth of the typical household in the economy.

However, some households did enjoy the benefits of the strong stock market performance. The mean equity holdings of households with stock held directly or in mutual funds was $153,192 in 1998. The difference in mean and median equity values, conditional on holding equity, is consistent with the well-known fact that the distribution of wealth is skewed toward wealthy households. With strong stock market performance, it is also not surprising that inequity in the distribution of wealth increased sharply over this period. Wolff offers several different ways to quantify these changes.

Readers familiar with the United States' "leading position" in income inequality across developed countries will not be surprised to learn that the United States also has a more unequal distribution of wealth than other countries. Again, Wolff offers an interesting perspective on the issue when he points out that wealth appeared to get more unequal in the United States during the 1980s, when Ronald Reagan was president, and that wealth appeared to get more unequal in Sweden during a time when the government

53. At the close of the first March trading day in 1992, March 2, the Vanguard Index 500 Fund (VFINX) was $33.0186. Six years later on March 2, the Vanguard index closed at $97.47, an increase of 195.2 percent. The percentage increases over the intervening two-year intervals were 17.6, 46.0 and 71.9.

54. See, for example, George Hager, "Greenspan's Caution about Stock Prices Again Puts Markets on Guard: Fed Likely to Keep Raising Rates to Curb Bull Market's 'Wealth Effect,'" *USA Today*, February 21, 2000, B6.

55. See Kennickell (2001).

56. This figure does not include equity held in 401(k)s. About half of Americans had equity either in specific securities, mutual funds, or through 401(k)s. The equity balance for the median household is nevertheless small.

was mainly controlled by Social Democrats. In contrast, wealth appeared to get less unequal in the United Kingdom when Margaret Thatcher was the leader. Wolff concludes that ". . . the differences in public policy alone cannot account for these trends in wealth distribution."

The paper then turns to the role of bequests and *inter-vivos* transfers in wealth. To motivate this topic, Wolff provides a brief survey of the literature, examining the degree to which intergenerational transfers affect wealth accumulation. He concludes that the direct survey evidence and regression analyses indicate a minor role for transfers in understanding wealth. However, he characterizes the simulation evidence as suggesting that transfers play a major role. He offers three reasons for the discrepancy: First, there may be pervasive, quantitatively significant underreporting in surveys. Second, different approaches for treating the appreciation of transferred assets can significantly affect conclusions. Third, some studies fail to account for *inter-vivos* transfers, which are an empirically significant component of aggregate transfers. These concerns, for the most part, add weight to the view that transfers are a significant component of wealth, which then motivates the last part of the paper, where Wolff examines trends in inheritances and the degree to which these transfers influence the distribution of wealth.

A thorny issue arises when trying to assess the current value of a transfer received in the past. Wolff assumes that transfers received previous to the date of the survey grew by an annual real interest rate of 3 percent. With this assumption, transfers accounted for only 16.5 percent of household net worth in 1998, down from 28.1 percent in 1989. This is presumably driven by a modest increase in the average net worth held by households, along with a decline in the fraction of households receiving a transfer and a reduction in the value of transfer conditional on receiving a gift.[57]

The final claim made in the paper is striking: That is, if intergenerational wealth transfers were eliminated, wealth inequality would *increase*. As I trust this brief summary makes clear, the paper includes a number of very interesting calculations and insights.

Concerns

I have four primary concerns with the paper: The first involves adjustments made to the core SCF data. Because of differences in aggregate asset and lia-

---

57. The paper notes there was a "precipitous drop in the share of recipients among the highest income group, over $250,000, from 48 to 39 percent." This is consistent with Bernheim, Lemke, and Scholz (2001), who argue that anticipated and actual estate tax changes significantly reduce *inter-vivos* giving.

bility totals in the Surveys of Consumer Finances and the Flow of Funds Accounts (FoF), Wolff proportionally adjusts SCF items to match Flow of Funds totals. In some cases, the adjustments are significant; for example, stocks and bonds are scaled by a factor of 1.23 in the 1995 SCF. As discussed in Rochelle Antoniewicz, these adjustments are tricky.[58] The household sector in the FoF is computed as a residual, so it does not provide an unassailable benchmark. Moreover, it is difficult to match asset and liability categories in the SCFs and FoFs. Last, the household sector in the FoFs includes nonprofit institutions, so the FoF benchmark needs to be adjusted to account for this discrepancy. The conclusion I draw from Antoniewicz is the SCFs and FoFs, once adjusted to account for differences in definitions and coverage, are strikingly close. Given this interpretation, Wolff's adjustments do not seem compelling.[59] Even if some change is needed, proportional adjustments implicitly assume there is uniform underreporting, in percentages, of the adjusted items. Nothing suggests that misreporting takes this particular pattern.

Along the same lines, the creators of the SCFs beginning in 1989 provide five separate imputed values for each missing variable. They also select 999 sample replicates from the final data in a way that allows users to capture important dimensions of sample variation. Accounting for these data features when calculating standard errors for parameter estimates is conceptually straightforward but involves a little programming. My experience is that accounting fully for imputation and sampling variation generally increases standard errors when working with wealth data.[60] Since Wolff does not mention using these features of the data (and incorporating them is not trivial), I suspect standard errors reported in the paper are inappropriately small. This is likely to be a particularly large concern at the extremes of the wealth distribution and for subpopulations, such as disaggregated statistics by race or ethnicity.

My second concern is prompted by one of the conclusions from the work on changes in the distribution of wealth. I quote: "In sum, the results point to stagnating living conditions for the average American household during the 1990s, with median net worth growing by only 4 percent. . . . These

58. Antoniewicz (1996).

59. In footnote 3, Wolff also mentions that he alters the SCF weights to better replicate the distribution of income found on tax returns. These adjustments also raise a number of difficult issues.

60. See, for example, Bernheim, Lemke, and Scholz (2001), which exploits these features of the SCF data.

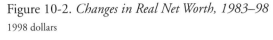

Figure 10-2. *Changes in Real Net Worth, 1983–98*
1998 dollars

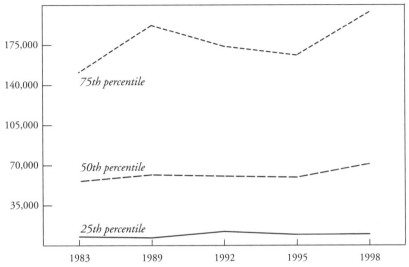

Source: Author's calculations from the 1983, 1989, 1992, 1995, and 1998 Surveys of Consumer Finances.

results indicate rather dramatically that the growth in the U.S. economy during the period from 1983 to 1998 was concentrated in a surprisingly small part of the population, the top 20 percent and particularly the top one or five percent."[61]

I think this is a misleading characterization of the economic changes over the past decade. Leave aside the fact that poverty rates fell during the decade, unemployment rates were at historical lows, and median money income increased. Let me focus on wealth changes:

Figure 10-2 shows the trend in real net worth for households at the 25th percentile, 50th percentile (median), and 75th percentile of the net worth distribution based on my own calculations for the SCF. The unadjusted, weighted measure of SCF net worth grew 15.3 percent between 1989 and 1998, and 26.9 percent between 1983 and 1998. Wolff's adjustments to net worth clearly affect the specific statistics on wealth changes, but the observed changes still only reflect a 1.6 percent annual growth rate—a slow rate. So while the specific numbers differ between my calculations and Wolff's, one would draw the same qualitative conclusion from this evidence.

61. Wolff (this chapter).

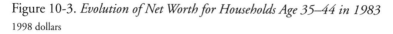

Figure 10-3. *Evolution of Net Worth for Households Age 35–44 in 1983*
1998 dollars

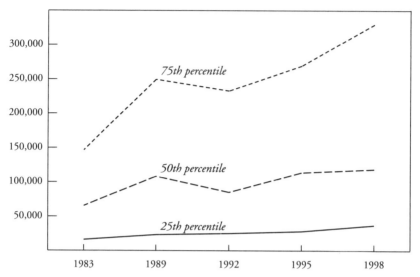

Source: Author's calculations from the 1983, 1989, 1992, 1995, and 1998 Surveys of Consumer Finances.

But this ignores that households move through the wealth and income distribution over their lifetime. As seen in figure 10-3, over the nine-year period from 1983 to 1992, real net worth grew at an annual rate of 3 percent per year for the median household age thirty-five to forty-four in 1983: from $65,449 to $85,049. Over the nine-year period from 1989 to 1998, real net worth grew at an annual rate of 3.3 percent per year for the median household age thirty-five to forty-four in 1989, from $72,850 to $97,520. Households are clearly accumulating wealth as they age, and the rates of accumulation seem to have increased slightly in the 1990s. Median wealth for thirty-five- to forty-four-year-olds in 1983 increased from $65,449 to $118,600 in 1998, when these households were fifty to fifty-nine. It seems clear that the typical household is accumulating wealth over this period. It also seems clear that their well-being, at least when measured by wealth, increased.

My third concern is prompted by Wolff's suggestion of significant disagreement between the empirical and simulation literatures on the importance of transfers. William Gale and John Karl Scholz accommodate all three concerns raised in the empirical literature on the importance of transfers: they account for *inter-vivos* transfers; they account for the underreporting problem by using data on transfers *given* (the dollar value of reported transfers given is much larger than the dollar value of reported transfers received, but we have no evidence that people underreport the transfers they give); and they do some sensitivity analysis on rates of return.[62] Gale and Scholz show that intended transfers can account for at least 20 percent of observed wealth, and if all bequests are intentional, transfers may account for at least 51 percent of observed wealth. The difference in the two figures (20 percent and 51 percent) raises a fundamental issue of whether bequests are intended or accidental.[63] Wolff's paper seems to interpret all bequests as part of a transfer motive. However, substantial bequests can arise purely because of uncertainty over life spans, as shown by James Davies among others.[64] Michael Hurd suggests most bequests arise from "accidental" reasons.[65] My idiosyncratic view is that we have a considerable amount of useful information about the empirical magnitudes on the importance of transfers and wealth accumulation and the issues over which disagreement exists are well understood.

My fourth concern has to do with the claim that transfers equalize the distribution of wealth. As with any calculation like this, the crucial issue is what the world would look like in the absence of the transfer. My understanding of Wolff's calculation is that a low-income household, who, for example, has $10,000 of net worth and a transfer received ten years ago, which in current dollars would be valued at $9,000, would be assumed to have $1,000 in the absence of the transfer. Similar numbers, with extra zeros, would apply for higher income households. But we have considerable evidence that the rich save more than others.[66] While transfers undoubtedly increase the economic well-being of low-income recipients, they almost surely have a modest effect on the observed wealth of low-income recipients because of their higher marginal propensity to consume.

In contrast, transfers presumably significantly increase the wealth of high-income recipients. If "eliminating transfers" means that the wealthy elderly

62. Gale and Scholz (1994).

63. The implications of some of the evidence presented in this paper will depend on the issue that motivates interest in the topic. If one's interest in this topic is driven by a concern with assessing the degree of altruism in the economy, perhaps motivated by an interest in which families might provide a safety net for those in need, then the issue of whether bequests are purposeful or simply a result of a failure in intertemporal optimization is central.

64. Davies (1981).

65. Hurd (1987, 1989).

66. See, for example, Dynan, Skinner, and Zeldes (2000).

would instead consume their wealth, or that the government would confiscate all transfers, or that all transfers would be donated to charity, the distribution of wealth would, in my view, result in a considerably more equal distribution. Affluent households would lose an important component of their observed wealth, while low-income, high-marginal-propensity-to-consume households (perhaps who are credit constrained) would have the same (or similar) wealth.

Other Issues

In closing, I want to mention two additional issues briefly: A limitation of the data used for the paper is that no data are provided on two significant sources of wealth: defined benefit pensions and Social Security. Data from the Health and Retirement Study indicate pensions are distributed far more equally than other sources of wealth, presumably because of the nondiscrimination rules imposed by pension plans. An important part of acquiring a comprehensive understanding of wealth inequality depends on learning more about the evolution of defined benefit pensions and the degree to which defined contribution pensions are displacing defined benefit plans. Second, Social Security equalizes the distribution of retirement resources. As labor force participation rates of poor, single-parent families have increased sharply over the past fifteen years, it seems likely that Social Security wealth has increased significantly at the bottom of the wealth and income distributions. It would also be interesting to see how these developments affect the evolution of wealth inequality.

Second, a large literature, to which Wolff has contributed, examines the determinants of white-black wealth differentials. The work is closely related to this paper and focuses on the factors that influence wealth accumulation and its evolution: income, demographic changes, changes in factors influencing consumption and saving, differences in rates of return, and intergenerational transfers.

My reading of the literature is that differences in intergenerational transfers can account for between 1 and 22 percent of the black-white wealth differential. If these estimates are true, it is likely that other factors play more important roles in understanding the distribution of wealth and changes in it. Learning more about these factors is an exciting topic for future research.

References

Aaron, Henry J., and Alicia H. Munnell. 1992. "Reassessing the Role for Wealth Transfer Taxes." *National Tax Journal* 45 (2): 119–43.

Abel, Andrew B. 1985. "Precautionary Saving and Accidental Bequests." *American Economic Review* 75 (4): 777–91.

———. 1987. "Operative Gift and Bequest Motives." *American Economic Review* 77 (5): 1037–47.

Abramovitz, Moses, and Paul David. 1973. "Reinterpreting Economic Growth: Parables and Realities." *American Economic Review* 63 (2): 428–39.

Abt Associates. 2000. "Evaluation Report of FHA's Home Equity Conversion Mortgage Insurance Demonstration." Final report prepared for Edward Szymanoski, U.S. Department of Housing and Urban Development.

Adams, James D. 1980. "Personal Wealth Transfers." *Quarterly Journal of Economics* 95 (August): 159–79.

Alesie, Robert, Annamaria Lusardi, and Arie Kapteyn. 1998. "Saving and Wealth Holdings of the Elderly." *Ricerche Economiche* 49: 293–315.

Alexander, Richard. 1974. "The Evolution of Social Behavior." *Annual Review of Ecology and Systemics* 5: 325–83.

———. 1979. *Darwinism and Human Affairs.* University of Washington Press.

Alston, Lee, and Morton Schapiro. 1984. "Inheritance Laws across Colonies: Causes and Consequences." *Journal of Economic History* 44 (2): 277–87.

Altonji, Joseph G., Fumio Hayashi, and Laurence J. Kotlikoff. 1992. "Is the Extended Family Altruistically Linked? Direct Tests Using Micro Data." *American Economic Review* 82 (5): 1177–98.

————. 1996. "The Effects of Income and Wealth on Time and Money Transfers between Parents and Children." Working Paper 5522. Cambridge, Mass.: National Bureau of Economic Research.

————. 1997. "Parental Altruism and Inter-Vivos Transfers: Theory and Evidence." *Journal of Political Economy* 105 (6): 1121–66.

American Association of Fundraising Council Trust for Philanthropy (AAFRC). 2001. *Giving USA 2001.* Indiana University, the Center on Philanthropy.

Anderson, Elijah. 1993. "Sex Codes and Family Life." In *The Ghetto Underclass,* edited by William Julius Wilson. Sage.

Ando, Albert, and Arthur B. Kennickell. 1987. "How Much (or Little) Life Cycle Is There in Micro Data? The Cases of the United States and Japan." In *Macroeconomics and Finance: Essays in Honor of Franco Modigliani,* edited by Rudiger Dornbusch, Stanley Fischer, and John Bossons. MIT Press.

Andreoni, James. 1989. "Giving with Impure Altruism: Applications to Charity and Ricardian Equivalence." *Journal of Political Economy* 97 (6): 1447–58.

————. 2001. "The Economics of Philanthropy." In *International Encyclopedia of the Social and Behavioral Sciences,* edited by Neil J. Smelser and Paul B. Baltes. Elsevier Science.

Antoniewicz, Rochelle. 1996. "A Comparison of the Household Sector from the Flow of Funds Accounts and the Survey of Consumer Finances." Finance and Economics Discussion Series 1996–26. Board of Governors of the Federal Reserve System.

Argys, Laura, and Elizabeth Peters. 2001. "Interactions between Unmarried Fathers and Their Children: The Role of Paternity Establishment and Child-Support Policies." *American Economic Review* 91 (2): 125–29.

Arrondel, Luc, and Anne Laferrère. 1992. "Les partages inégaux des successions entre frères et soeurs." *Economie et Statistique* 250: 29–42.

————. 1994. "La transmission des grandes fortunes." *Economie et Statistique* 273: 41–52.

Arrondel, Luc, and André Masson. 1991. "Que nous enseignent les enquêtes sur les transferts patrimoniaux en France?" *Economie et Prévision* 100–01: 93–128.

————. 2001. "Family Involving Three Generations." *Scandinavian Journal of Economics* 103: 415–43.

Arrondel, Luc, and Sergio Perelman. 1994. "Les opinions des Français sur l'héritage: sont–elles compatibles avec leurs comportements de transmission?" In *Héritage et Transferts entre Générations,* edited by Pierre Pestieau. De Boeck.

Arrondel, Luc, and François-Charles Wolff. 1998. "La nature des transferts *inter vivos* en France: Investissement Humain, Aide Financière et Transmission du Patrimoine." *Economie et Prévision* 135: 1–27.

Atkinson, Anthony B., James P. F. Gordon, and Alan Harrison. 1989. "Trends in the Shares of Top Wealth Holders in Britain, 1923–81." *Oxford Bulletin of Economics and Statistics* 51 (3): 315–32.

Atkinson, Anthony B., Lee Rainwater, and Timothy Smeeding. 1995. *Income Distribution in Advanced Economies: The Evidence from the Luxembourg Income Study (LIS).* OECD.

Auerbach, Alan J., and Laurence Kotlikoff. 1987. "Life Insurance of the Elderly: Adequacy and Determinants." In *Work, Health, and Income among the Elderly,* edited by Gary Burtless. Brookings.

Auerbach, Alan, and Joel Slemrod. 1997. "The Economic Effects of the Tax Reform Act of 1986." *Journal of Economic Literature* 35 (2): 589–632.

Auerbach, Alan J., Laurence Kotlikoff, and David Weil. 1992. "The Increasing Annuitization of the Elderly: Estimates and Implications for Intergenerational Transfers, Inequality, and National Saving." Working Paper 4182. Cambridge, Mass.: National Bureau of Economic Research.

Auten, Gerald, and David Joulfaian. 1996. "Charitable Contributions and Intergenerational Transfers." *Journal of Public Economics* 59 (1): 55–68.

Bager-Sjogren, Lars, and N. Anders Klevmarken. 1993. "The Distribution of Wealth in Sweden, 1984–86." *Research in Economic Inequality*, vol. 4. In *Studies in the Distribution of Household Wealth*, edited by Edward N. Wolff. JAI Press.

Baker, Robin R., and Bellis, Mark A. 1995. *Human Sperm Competition*. Chapman and Hall.

Bakshi, Gurdip S., and Zhiwu Chen. 1996. "The Spirit of Capitalism and Stock Market Prices." *American Economic Review* 86 (1): 133–57.

Bankers Trust Private Banking. 2000. *Wealth with Responsibility Study 2000*. Deutsche Bank.

Barlow, Robin, Harvey E. Brazer, and James Morgan. 1966. *Economic Behavior of the Affluent*. Brookings.

Barro, Robert J. 1974. "Are Government Bonds Net Wealth?" *Journal of Political Economy* 82 (6): 1095–1117.

———. 1989. "The Ricardian Approach to Budget Deficits." *Journal of Economic Perspectives* 3 (2): 37–54.

Barthold, Thomas A., and Takatoshi Ito. 1991. "Bequest Taxes and Accumulation of Household Wealth: U.S.-Japan Comparison." Working Paper 9692. Cambridge, Mass.: National Bureau of Economic Research.

Bauer, John, and Andrew Mason. 1992. "The Distribution of Income and Wealth in Japan." *Review of Income and Wealth* 38 (4): 403–28.

Becker, Gary S. 1974. "A Theory of Social Interactions." *Journal of Political Economy* 82 (6): 1063–93.

———. 1976. "Altruism, Egoism, and Genetic Fitness: Economics and Sociobiology." *Journal of Economic Literature* 14 (3): 817–26.

———. 1991. *A Treatise on the Family*. Harvard University Press.

———. 1993. "Nobel Lecture: The Economic Way of Looking at Behavior." *Journal of Political Economy* 101 (3): 385–409.

Becker, Gary S., and Nigel Tomes. 1979. "An Equilibrium Theory of the Distribution of Income and Intergenerational Mobility." *Journal of Political Economy* 87 (6): 1153–89.

———. 1986. "Human Capital and the Rise and Fall of Families." *Journal of Labor Economics* 4 (3): S1–39.

Behrman, Jere R. 1997. "Intrahousehold Distribution and the Family," In *Handbook of Population and Family Economics*, edited by Mark Rosenzweig and Oded Stark. Elsevier Science.

Behrman, Jere R., Robert A. Pollak, and Paul Taubman. 1986. "Do Parents Favor Boys?" *International Economic Review* 27 (1): 31–52.

———. 1995. "The Wealth Model: Efficiency in Education and Equity in the Family." In *From Parent to Child: Intrahousehold Allocations and Intergenerational Relations in the United States*, edited by Jere R. Behrman, Robert A. Pollak, and Paul Taubman. University of Chicago Press.

Ben-Porath, Yoram, and Welch, Finis. 1976. "Do Sex Preferences Really Matter?" *Quarterly Journal of Economics* 90 (2): 285–307.

Bergstrom, Theodore C. 1989. "A Fresh Look at the Rotten-Kid Theorem–and Other Household Mysteries." *Journal of Political Economy* 97 (5): 1138–59.

———. 1996. "Economics in a Family Way." *Journal of Economic Literature* 34 (4): 1903–34.

Bergstrom, Theodore C., and Carl Bergstrom. 1998. "Does Nature Punish Rotten Kids?" *Journal of Bioeconomics* 1 (1): 47–72.

Bernheim, B. Douglas. 1987. "Does the Estate Tax Raise Revenue?" *Tax Policy and the Economy* (1): 113–38.

———. 1989. "A Neoclassical Perspective on Budget Deficits." *Journal of Economic Perspectives* 3 (2): 55–72.

———. 1991. "How Strong Are Bequest Motives? Evidence Based on the Demand for Life Insurance and Annuities." *Journal of Political Economy* 99 (5): 899–927.

Bernheim, B. Douglas, and Sergei Severinov. 2000. "Bequests as Signals: An Explanation for the Equal Division Puzzle." Working Paper 7791. Cambridge, Mass.: National Bureau of Economic Research.

Bernheim, B. Douglas, Robert J. Lemke, and John Karl Scholz, 2001. "Do Estate and Gift Taxes Affect the Timing of Private Transfers?" Working Paper 8333. Cambridge, Mass.: National Bureau of Economic Research.

Bernheim, B. Douglas, Andrei Shleifer, and Lawrence H. Summers. 1985. "The Strategic Bequest Motive." *Journal of Political Economy* 93 (6): 1045–75.

Blattmachr, Jonathan G., and Mitchell M. Gans. 2001. "Wealth Transfer Tax Repeal: Some Thoughts on Policy and Planning." *Tax Notes* (January 15): 393–99.

Blinder, Alan S. 1976. "Intergenerational Transfers and Life-Cycle Consumption." *American Economic Review* 66 (2): 87–93.

———. 1988. "Comments on Chapter 1 and Chapter 2." In *Modeling the Accumulation and Distribution of Wealth*, edited by Denis Kessler and André Masson. Oxford: Clarendon Press.

Bloch, Francis, and Rao, Vijayendra. 2000. "Terror as a Bargaining Instrument: A Case Study of Dowry Violence in Rural India." Working Paper 2347. Washington: World Bank (May).

Blomquist, Sören. 1979. "The Inheritance Function." *Journal of Public Economics* 12: 41–60.

Board of Inland Revenue. 1993. *Inland Revenue Statistics, 1993*. Her Majesty's Statistical Office.

Bonfield, Lloyd. 1986. "Affective Families, Open Elites, and Strict Family Settlements in Early Modern England." *Economic History Review* 39 (3): 341–54.

Börsch-Supan, Axel. 1992. "Saving and Consumption Pattern of the Elderly: The German Case." *Journal of Population Economics* 5 (4): 289–303.

Boskin, Michael. 1976. "Estate Taxation and Charitable Bequests." *Journal of Public Economics* 5 (1–2): 27–56.

Boulding, Kenneth, E. 1962. "Notes on a Theory of Philanthropy." *Philanthropy and Public Policy:* 57–71.

Brenner, Gabrielle A. 1985. "Why Did Inheritance Laws Change?" *International Review of Law and Economics* 5: 91–96.

Brown, Jeffrey R. 1999. "Are the Elderly Really Over-Annuitized? New Evidence on Life Insurance and Bequests." Working Paper 7193. Cambridge, Mass.: National Bureau of Economic Research.

———. 2000. "Private Pensions, Mortality Risk, and the Decision to Annuitize." Working Paper 7191. Cambridge, Mass.: National Bureau of Economic Research.

———. 2001. "Redistribution and Insurance: Mandatory Annuitization with Mortality Heterogeneity." Working Paper 2001–02. Chestnut Hill, Mass.: Center for Retirement Research at Boston College.

Brown, Jeffrey R., and James M. Poterba. 2000. "Joint Life Annuities and Annuity Demand by Married Couples." *Journal of Risk and Insurance* 67 (4): 527–56.

Brown, Jeffrey R., and Scott Weisbenner. 2002. "Is a Bird in Hand Worth More than a Bird in the Bush? Intergenerational Transfers and Savings Behavior." Working Paper 8753. Cambridge, Mass.: National Bureau of Economic Research.

Brown, Jeffrey R., Olivia S. Mitchell, and James M. Poterba. 2000a. "Mortality Risk, Inflation Risk, and Annuity Products." Working Paper 7812. Cambridge, Mass.: National Bureau of Economic Research.

———. 2000b. "The Role of Real Annuities and Indexed Bonds in an Individual Accounts Retirement Program." In *Risk Aspects of Investment-Based Social Security Reform*, edited by John Y. Campbell and Martin S. Feldstein. University of Chicago Press.

Bruce, Neil, and Michael Waldman. 1990. "The Rotten-Kid Theorem Meets the Samaritan's Dilemma." *Quarterly Journal of Economics* 105 (1): 155–65.

———. 1991. "Transfers in Kind: Why They Can Be Efficient and Non-Paternalistic." *American Economic Review* 81 (5): 1345–51.

Buckley, John. 2001. "Transfer Tax Repeal Proposals: Implications for the Income Tax." *Tax Notes* (January 22): 539–41.

Burkhauser, Richard V., Joachim R. Frick, and Johannes Schwarze. 1997. "A Comparison of Alternative Measures of Economic Well-Being for Germany and the United States." *Review of Income and Wealth* 43 (2): 153–72.

Caballe, Jordi. 1995. "Endogenous Growth, Human Capital, and Bequests in a Life-Cycle Model." *Oxford Economic Papers* 47 (1): 156–81.

Cain, Mead. 1977. "The Economic Activities of Children in a Village in Bangladesh." *Population and Development Review* 13 (3): 201–27.

Caplin, Andrew. 2000. "Turning Assets into Cash: Problems and Prospects in the Reverse Mortgage Market." Working Paper Series 2000–13. Pension Research Council. University of Pennsylvania Press.

Carroll, Christopher D. 1997. "Buffer-Stock Saving and the Life Cycle/Permanent Income Hypothesis." *Quarterly Journal of Economics* 107 (1): 1–56.

———. 2000. "Why Do the Rich Save So Much?" In *Does Atlas Shrug? The Economic Consequences of Taxing the Rich*, edited by Joel B. Slemrod, 465–84. Harvard University Press.

Case, Anne, and Angus Deaton. 1998. "Large Transfers to the Elderly in South Africa." *Economic Journal* 108 (450): 1330–61.

Casner, A. James, and W. Barton Leach. 1969. *Cases and Text on Property,* 2d ed. Little, Brown.

Chapman, Kenneth, Govind Hariharan, and Lawrence Southwick Jr. 1996. "Estate Taxes and Asset Accumulation." *Family Business Review* 9 (3): 253–68.

Chu, C.Y. Cyrus. 1991. "Primogeniture." *Journal of Political Economy* 99 (1): 78–99.

Clay, Christopher. 1968. "Marriage, Inheritance, and the Rise of Large Estates in England, 1660–1815." *Economic History Review* 21 (3): 503–18.

Clotfelter, Charles T. 1985. *Federal Tax Policy and Charitable Giving.* University of Chicago Press.

———. 1997. "The Economics of Giving." In *Giving Better, Giving Smarter,* edited by John W. Barry and Bruno V. Manno. Washington: National Commission on Philanthropy and Civic Renewal.

Clutton-Brock, T. H.1991. *The Evolution of Parental Care.* Princeton University Press.

Cox, Donald. 1987. "Motives for Private Income Transfers." *Journal of Political Economy* 95 (3): 508–46.

———. 1990. "Intergenerational Transfers and Liquidity Constraints." *Quarterly Journal of Economics* 105 (1): 187–217.

Cox, Donald, and Tullio Japelli. 1990. "Credit Rationing and Private Transfers: Evidence from Survey Data." *Review of Economics and Statistics* 72 (3): 445–53.

Cox, Donald, and Frederik Raines. 1985. "Interfamily Transfers and Income Redistribution." In *Horizontal Equity, Uncertainty, and Measures of Well-Being,* edited by Martin David and Tim Smeeding. University of Chicago Press.

Cox, Donald, and Mark R. Rank. 1992. "Inter-Vivos Transfers and Intergenerational Exchange." *Review of Economics and Statistics* 74 (2): 305–14.

Cremer, Helmuth, and Pierre Pestieau. 1988. "A Case for Differential Inheritance Taxation." *Annales d'Economie et de Statistique* 9: 167–82.

———. 2001. "Non-Linear Taxation of Bequests, Equal Sharing Rules, and the Trade-off between *Intra-* and *Inter*-Family Inequalities." *Journal of Public Economics* 79 (1): 35–55.

Darby, Michael R. 1979. *The Effects of Social Security on Income and the Capital Stock.* American Enterprise Institute.

David, Martin, and Paul L. Menchik. 1982. "Distribution of Estates and Its Relationship to Intergenerational Transfers." *Statistics of Income and Related Administration Record Research.*

Davies, James B. 1981. "Uncertain Lifetime, Consumption, and Dissaving in Retirement." *Journal of Political Economy* 89 (3): 561–77.

———. 1982. "The Relative Impact of Inheritance and Other Factors on Economic Inequality." *Quarterly Journal of Economics* 97 (3): 471–98.

———. 1993. "The Distribution of Wealth in Canada." *Research in Economic Inequality*, vol. 4. In *Studies in the Distribution of Household Wealth*, edited by Edward N. Wolff. JAI Press.

Davies, James B., and Anthony F. Shorrocks. 1999. "The Distribution of Wealth." In *Handbook on Income Distribution*, vol. 1, edited by Anthony B. Atkinson and François Bourguignon. Elsevier Science.

———. 2000. "The Distribution of Wealth." In *Handbook on Redistribution*, edited by Anthony B. Atkinson and François Bourguigon. North Holland.

Davies, James B., and France St. Hilaire. 1987. *Reforming Capital Income Taxation in Canada. Efficiency and Distributional Effects of Alternative Options.* Economic Council of Canada, Ottawa.

Dawkins, Richard. 1976. *The Selfish Gene.* Oxford University Press.

Diamond, Jared. 1992. *The Third Chimpanzee.* Harper Collins.

Diamond, Peter A., and Jerry A. Hausman. 1984. "Individual Retirement and Savings Behavior." *Journal of Public Economics* 23 (1): 81–114.

Donahue, Charles, Thomas Kauper, and Peter Martin. 1993. *Property: An Introduction to the Concept and the Institution,* 3d ed. West Wadsworth.

Duflo, Esther. 2000. "Grandmothers and Granddaughters: Old Age Pension and Intra-Household Allocation in South Africa." Working Paper 8061. Cambridge, Mass.: National Bureau of Economic Research.

Dynan, Karen E., Jonathan Skinner, and Stephen P. Zeldes. 2000. "Do the Rich Save More?" Working Paper 7906. Cambridge, Mass.: National Bureau of Economic Research.

———. 2002. "The Importance of Bequest and Life-Cycle Saving in Capital Accumulation: A New Answer." *American Economic Review Papers and Proceedings* (forthcoming).

Edlund, Lena. 1999. "Son Preference, Sex Ratios, and Marriage Patterns." *Journal of Political Economy* 107 (6): 1275–1304.

Edlund, Lena, and Evelyn Korn. 2002. "A Theory of Prostitution." *Journal of Political Economy* 110: 181–214.

Elison, Peter T. 2001. *On Fertile Ground.* Harvard University Press.

Eller, Martha Britton. 1997. "Federal Taxation of Wealth Transfers, 1992–95." *Statistics of Income Bulletin* 16 (3): 8–63.

Eller, Martha Britton, and Barry W. Johnson. 2000. "Using a Sample of Federal Estate Tax Returns to Examine the Effects of Audit Revaluation on Pre-Audit Estimates." *Statistics of Income Research Paper.* U.S. Department of the Treasury, Internal Revenue Service, Statistics of Income Division.

Elliot, Kenneth R., and James H. Moore Jr. 2000. "Cash Balance Plans: The New Wave." *Compensation and Working Conditions* 5 (2): 3–11.

Engen, Eric M., and William G. Gale. 2000. "The Effects of 401(k) Plans on Household Wealth: Differences across Earnings Groups." Working Paper 8032. Cambridge, Mass.: National Bureau of Economic Research.

Engen, Eric M., William G. Gale, and John K. Scholz. 1996. "The Illusory Effects of Savings Incentives on Saving." *Journal of Economic Perspectives* 10 (4): 113–38.

Farmer, Amy, and Jill Tiefenthaler. 1996. "Domestic Violence: The Value of Services as Signals." *American Economic Review Papers and Proceedings* 86 (3): 274–79.

Feinstein, Jonathan. 1996. "Elderly Health, Housing, and Mobility." In *Advances in the Economics of Aging*, edited by David A. Wise. University of Chicago Press.

Feldstein, Martin. 1999. "Tax Avoidance and the Deadweight Loss of the Income Tax." *Review of Economics and Statistics* 81 (4): 674–80.

Fetherstonhaugh, David, and Lee Ross. 1999. "Framing Effects and Income Flow Preferences." In *Behavioral Dimensions of Retirement Economics*, edited by Henry J. Aaron. Brookings.

Fiekowsky, Seymour. 1966. "The Effect on Saving of the United States Estate and Gift Tax." In *Federal Estate and Gift Taxes*, edited by Carl Shoup. Brookings.

Finkelstein, Amy, and James M. Poterba. 2002. "Selection Effects in the United Kingdom Individual Annuities Market." *The Economic Journal* 112 (476): 28–50.

Fisher, Ronald A. 1958. *The Genetic Theory of Natural Selection*, 2d ed. Dover.

Fithian, Scott C. 2000. *Values-Based Estate Planning: A Step-by-Step Approach to Wealth Transfer for Professional Advisors*. Wiley.

Foner, Eric. 1985. *Free Soil, Free Labor, Free Men*. Oxford University Press.

Foundation Center. 2000a. *Foundation Growth and Giving Estimates: 2000 Preview*. New York.

———. 2000b. *Family Foundations: A Profile of Funders and Trends*. New York.

Friedman, Benjamin M., and Mark J. Warshawsky. 1988. "Annuity Prices and Saving in the United States." In *Pensions in the U.S. Economy*, edited by Zvi Bodie, John B. Shoven, and David A. Wise. University of Chicago Press.

———. 1990. "The Cost of Annuities: Implications for Savings Behavior and Bequests." *Quarterly Journal of Economics* 105 (1): 135–54.

Gale, William G. 1998. "The Effects of Pensions on Household Wealth: A Reevaluation of Theory and Evidence." *Journal of Political Economy* 106 (4): 706–23.

Gale, William G., and Maria G. Perozek. 2001. "Do Estate Taxes Reduce Saving?" In *Rethinking Estate and Gift Taxation*, edited by William G. Gale, James R. Hines Jr., and Joel Slemrod. Brookings.

Gale, William G., and John Karl Scholz. 1994. "Intergenerational Transfers and the Accumulation of Wealth." *Journal of Economic Perspectives* 8 (4): 145–60.

Gale, William G., and Joel Slemrod. 2001. "Rethinking the Estate and Gift Tax: Overview." Working Paper 8205. Cambridge, Mass.: National Bureau of Economic Research.

Gilleman, Gerard, S. J. 1959. *The Primacy of Charity in Moral Theology*. Westminster, Md.: Newman Press.

Gokhale, Jagadeesh, and others. 2001. "Simulating the Transmission of Wealth Inequality via Bequests." *Journal of Public Economics* 79: 93–128.

Greenwood, Daphne T., and Edward N. Wolff. 1992. "Changes in Wealth in the United States, 1962–1983: Savings, Capital Gains, Inheritance, and Lifetime Transfers." *Journal of Population Economics* 5 (4): 261–88.

Gustman, Alan L., and Thomas L. Steinmeier. 1992. "The Stampede toward Defined Contribution Pension Plans: Fact or Fiction?" *Industrial Relations* 31 (2): 361–69.

———. 1998. "Effects of Pensions on Savings: Analysis with Data from the Health and Retirement Study." Working Paper 6681. Cambridge, Mass.: National Bureau of Economic Research.

Haider, Steven, and others. 2000. "Patterns of Dissaving in Retirement." Prepared for the AARP Public Policy Institute.

Haig, David. 1993. "Genetic Conflicts in Human Pregnancy." *Quarterly Review of Biology* 68 (4): 495–532.

Hall, Robert E. 1978. "Stochastic Implications of the Life Cycle-Permanent Income Hypothesis: Theory and Evidence." *Journal of Political Economy* 86 (6): 971–87.

Hamilton, William D. 1964. "The Genetical Theory of Social Behavior." *Journal of Theoretical Biology* 7 (1): 1–32.

Hartog, Hendrik. 2000. *Man & Wife in America.* Harvard University Press.

Havens, John J., and Paul G. Schervish. 1997. "Our Daily Bread: Findings from the First Diary Study on Giving and Receiving Care Report." Working Paper. Chestnut Hill, Mass.: Social Welfare Research Institute at Boston College.

———. 1999. "Millionaires and the Millennium: New Estimates of the Forthcoming Wealth Transfer and the Prospects for a Golden Age of Philanthropy." Working Paper. Chestnut Hill, Mass.: Social Welfare Research Institute at Boston College.

Hirshleifer, Jack. 1977. "Economics from a Biological Viewpoint." *Journal of Law and Economics* 20 (1): 1–52.

Hochguertel, Steven, and Henry Ohlsson. 2000. "Compensatory *Inter-Vivos* Gifts." Working Paper 31. Göteborg, Sweden: Göteborg University, Department of Economics.

Holtz-Eakin, Douglas, David Joulfaian, and Harvey S. Rosen. 1993. "The Carnegie Conjecture: Some Empirical Evidence." *Quarterly Journal of Economics* 108 (2): 413–35.

———. 1994a. "Sticking It Out: Entrepreneurial Survival and Liquidity Constraints." *Journal of Political Economy* 102 (1): 53–75.

———. 1994b. "Entrepreneurial Decisions and Liquidity Constraints." *RAND Journal of Economics* 25 (2): 334–47.

Horioka, Charles Yuji. 2001. "Are The Japanese Selfish, Altruistic, or Dynastic?" Working Paper 8577. Cambridge, Mass.: National Bureau of Economic Research.

Hoyert, Donna L., Kenneth D. Kochanek, and Sherry L. Murphy. 1999. "Deaths: Final Data for 1997." *National Vital Statistics Report* 47 (19): 1–105.

Hrdy, Sarah Blaffer. 1981. *The Woman That Never Evolved.* Harvard University Press.

———. 1999. *Mother Nature.* Ballantine Books.

Huggett, Mark. 1996. "Wealth Distribution in Life-Cycle Economies." *Journal of Monetary Economics* 38 (3): 469–94.

Hurd, Michael D. 1987a. "Savings of the Elderly and Desired Bequests." *American Economic Review* 77 (3): 298–312.

———. 1987b. "Marginal Value of Social Security." Working Paper 2411. Cambridge, Mass.: National Bureau of Economic Research.

———. 1989. "Mortality Risk and Bequests." *Econometrica* 57 (4): 779–813.

———. 1990. "Research on the Elderly: Economic Status, Retirement, and Consumption and Saving." *Journal of Economic Literature* 28 (2): 565–637.

———. 1991. "The Income and Savings of the Elderly." Final Report to AARP Andrus Foundation.

———. 1992. "Wealth Depletion and Life-Cycle Consumption by the Elderly." In *Topics in the Economics of Aging*, edited by David A. Wise. University of Chicago Press.

———. 1993. "The Effect of Changes in Social Security on Bequests." *Journal of Economics*, Supplement 7: 157–76.

———. 1994. "Measuring the Bequest Motive: The Effect of Children on Saving by the Elderly in the United States." In *Savings and Bequests*, edited by Toshiaki Tachibanaki. University of Michigan Press.

———. 1995. "Mortality Risk and Consumption by Couples." Working Paper 7048. Cambridge, Mass.: National Bureau of Economic Research.

———. 1997. "The Economics of Individual Aging." In *The Handbook of Population and Family Economics,* edited by Mark R. Rosenzweig and Oded Stark. North Holland Press.

Hurd, Michael D., and B. Gabriela Mundaca. 1989. "The Importance of Gifts and Inheritances among the Affluent." In *The Measurement of Saving, Investment, and Wealth*, edited by Robert E. Lipsey and Helen Stone Tice, 737–63. University of Chicago Press.

Hurd, Michael D., and John B. Shoven. 1985. "Inflation Vulnerability, Income, and Wealth of the Elderly, 1969–79." In *Horizontal Equity, Uncertainty, and Economic Well-Being*, edited by Martin David and Timothy Smeeding. University of Chicago Press.

Hurd, Michael D., and James P. Smith. 1999. "Anticipated and Actual Bequests." Working Paper 7830. Cambridge, Mass.: National Bureau of Economic Research.

———. 2001. "Anticipated and Actual Bequests." In *Themes in the Economics of Aging*, edited by David A. Wise. University of Chicago Press.

Hurst, Erik, Ming Ching Luoh, and Frank P. Stafford. 1998. "The Wealth Dynamics of American Families, 1984–94." *Brookings Papers on Economic Activity* 1: 267–329.

Huston, James. 1993. "American Revolutionaries and the Political Economy of Aristocracy." *American Historical Review* 98 (4): 1079–1105.

Ippolito, Richard A., and John W. Thompson. 2000. "The Survival Rate of Defined-Benefit Plans, 1987–95." *Industrial Relations* 39 (2): 228–45.

Jianakoplos, Nancy A., Paul L. Menchik, and F. Owen Irvine. 1989. "Using Panel

Data to Assess the Bias in Cross-Sectional Inference of Life-Cycle Changes in the Level and Composition of Household Wealth." In *The Measurement of Saving, Investment, and Wealth*, edited by Robert E. Lipsey and Helen Stone Tice, 553–644. *National Bureau of Economic Research Studies in Income and Wealth*, vol. 52. University of Chicago Press.

Johnson, Barry W. 1990. "Estate Tax Returns, 1986–1988." *Statistics of Income Bulletin* 9 (4): 27–61.

Johnson, Barry W., and Martha Britton Eller. 1998. "Federal Taxation of Inheritance and Wealth Transfers." In *Inheritance and Wealth in America*, edited by Robert Miller and Stephen McNamee. Plenum Press.

———. 2001. "Federal Taxation of Inheritance and Wealth Transfers." *Statistics of Income Bulletin*. Internal Revenue Service.

Johnson, Barry W., and Jakob M. Mikow. 1999. "Federal Estate Tax Returns, 1995-1997." *Statistics of Income Bulletin*: 69–130. Internal Revenue Service.

Johnson, Barry W., Jakob M. Mikow, and Martha Britton Eller. 2001. "Elements of Federal Estate Taxation." In *Rethinking Estate and Gift Taxation*, edited by William J. Gale, James R. Hines Jr., and Joel Slemrod. Brookings.

Jones, Alice Hanson. 1980. *Wealth of a Nation to Be*. Columbia University Press.

Josephson, Matthew. 1934. *The Robber Barons*. Harper and Row.

Joulfaian, David. 1991. "Charitable Bequests and Estate Taxes." *National Tax Journal* 44 (2): 169–80.

———. 1994. "The Distribution and Division of Bequests: Evidence from the Collation Study." Working Paper 71. Office of Tax Analysis. Washington: U.S. Department of the Treasury.

———. 2000a. "Choosing between Gifts and Bequests: How Taxes Affect the Timing of Wealth Transfers." Working Paper 86. Office of Tax Analysis. Washington: U.S. Department of the Treasury (May).

———. 2000b. "Estate Taxes and Charitable Bequests by the Wealthy." Working Paper 7663. Cambridge, Mass.: National Bureau of Economic Research.

———. 2001. "Charitable Giving in Life and Death." In *Rethinking Estate and Gift Taxation*, edited by William G. Gale, James R. Hines Jr., and Joel Slemrod. Brookings.

Joulfaian, David, and Mark O. Wilhelm. 1994. "Inheritance and Labor Supply." *Journal of Human Resources* 29 (4): 1205–34.

Judge, Debra, and Sarah Blaffer Hrdy. 1992. "Allocation of Accumulated Resources among Close Kin: Inheritance in Sacramento, California, 1890–1984." *Ethology and Sociobiology* (13): 495–522.

Juster, F. Thomas, and John Laitner. 1996. "New Evidence on Altruism: A Study of TIAA-CREF Retirees." *American Economic Review* 86 (4): 893–908.

Kaplow, Louis. 2001. "A Framework for Assessing Estate and Gift Taxation." In *Rethinking Estate and Gift Taxation*, edited by William G. Gale, James R. Hines Jr., and Joel Slemrod. Brookings.

Kennan, John. 1986. "The Economics of Strikes," Chapter 19. In *Handbook of Labor Economics*, edited by O. Ashenfelter and R. Layard. Elsevier Science.

Kennickell, Arthur B. 1999. *Revisions to the SCF Weighting Methodology: Accounting for Race-Ethnicity and Homeownership.* Board of Governors of the Federal Reserve System.

———. 2000. "An Examination of Changes in the Distribution of Wealth from 1989 to 1998: Evidence from the Survey of Consumer Finances." Working Paper. Annandale–on–Hudson, N. Y.: Levy Economics Institute.

———. 2001. "An Examination of Changes in the Distribution of Wealth from 1989 to 1998: Evidence from the Surveys of Consumer Finances." Working Paper 2000–01. Washington: Federal Reserve Board, Survey of Consumer Finances.

Kennickell, Arthur B., and R. Louise Woodburn. 1999. "Consistent Weight Design for the 1989, 1992, and 1995 SCFs, and the Distribution of Wealth." *Review of Income and Wealth* 45 (2): 193–216.

Kessler, Denis. 1989. "Comment." In *The Measurement of Saving, Investment, and Wealth*, edited by Robert Lipsey and Helen Stone Tice, 141–52. University of Chicago Press.

Kessler, Denis, and André Masson. 1979. "Les transferts intergenerationales: L'aide, la donation, l'heritage." *C.N.R.S. Report.*

———. 1989. "Bequest and Wealth Accumulation: Are Some Pieces of the Puzzle Missing?" *Journal of Economic Perspectives* 3 (3): 141–52.

Kessler, Denis, and Pierre Pestieau. 1991. "The Taxation of Wealth in the EEC: Facts and Trends." *Canadian Public Policy* 17 (3): 309–21.

Kessler, Denis, and Edward N. Wolff. 1991. "A Comparative Analysis of Household Wealth Patterns in France and the United States." *Review of Income and Wealth* 37 (3): 249–66.

Kessler, Denis, André Masson, and Pierre Pestieau. 1991. "Trois vues sur l'héritage: la famille, la propriété, l'etat." *Economie et Prévision* 100–101: 93–128.

Keynes, John M. 1930. "Economic Possibilities for Our Grandchildren." In *Essays in Persuasion*, by John M. Keynes. Macmillan. Reprinted 1933.

Kohn, Meir. 2002. "The Origins of Western Economic Success: Commerce, Finance, and Government before the Industrial Revolution." Dartmouth University, Department of Economics.

Kopczuk, Wojciech, and Joel Slemrod. 2001. "The Impact of the Estate Tax on Wealth Accumulation and Avoidance Behavior of Donors." In *Rethinking Estate and Gift Taxation*, edited by William G. Gale, James R. Hines Jr., and Joel Slemrod. Brookings.

Kotlikoff, Laurence J. 1979. "Social Security and Equilibrium Capital Intensity." *Quarterly Journal of Economics* 93 (2): 233–53.

———. 1988. "Intergenerational Transfers and Saving." *Journal of Economic Perspectives* 2 (2): 41–58.

———. 1989. "Estimating the Wealth Elasticity of Bequests from a Sample of Potential Decedents." In *What Determines Savings?* edited by Laurence J. Kotlikoff. MIT Press.

Kotlikoff, Laurence J., and John N. Morris. 1989. "How Much Care Do the Aged Receive from Their Children?" In *The Economics of Aging*, edited by David A. Wise. University of Chicago Press.

Kotlikoff, Laurence J., and Avia Spivak. 1981. "The Family as an Incomplete Annuities Market." *Journal of Political Economy* 89 (2): 372–91.

Kotlikoff, Laurence J., and Lawrence H. Summers. 1981. "The Role of Intergenerational Transfers in Aggregate Capital Accumulation." *Journal of Political Economy* 89 (4): 706–32.

———. 1988. "The Contribution of Intergenerational Transfers to Total Wealth: A Reply." In *Modeling the Accumulation and Distribution of Wealth*, edited by Denis Kessler and André Masson. Oxford University Press.

Kurz, Mordecai. 1984. "Capital Accumulation and the Characteristics of Private Intergenerational Transfers." *Economica* 51 (201): 1–22.

Laferrère, Anne. 1991. "La taxation des héritages et donations: Eléments de comparaison internationale." *Economie et Prévision* 100–101: 177–88.

———. 1999. "Intergenerational Transmission Models: A Survey." *Geneva Papers on Risk and Insurance, Issues and Practice* 24: 2–26.

Laitner, John. 1992. "Random Earnings Differences, Lifetime Liquidity Constraints, and Altruistic Intergenerational Transfers." *Journal of Economic Theory* 58 (2): 135–70.

———. 2001. "Inequality and Wealth Accumulation: Eliminating the Federal Gift and Estate Tax." In *Rethinking Gift and Estate Taxation*, edited by William G. Gale, James Hines, and Joel Slemrod. Brookings.

Laitner, John, and F. Thomas Juster. 1996. "New Evidence on Altruism: A Study of TIAA–CREF Retirees." *American Economic Review* 86 (4): 893–908.

Laitner, John, and Henry Ohlsson. 1997. "Equality of Opportunity and Inheritance: A Comparison of Sweden and the United States." Paper prepared for conference "Wealth, Inheritance, and Intergenerational Transfers." 2001. England: University of Essex, June 22–23.

———. 2001. "Bequest Motives: A Comparison of Sweden and the United States." *Journal of Public Economics* 79 (2): 205–36.

Lav, Iris J., and Joel Friedman. 2001. "Estate Tax Repeal: A Costly Windfall for the Wealthiest Americans." Washington: Center on Budget and Policy Priorities (February 6).

LIMRA International. 1998. *The Buyer Study for the United States: A Market Study Of New Insureds and the Ordinary Life Insurance Purchased.*

———. 2002. The 2001 Individual Annuity Market: Sales and Assets.

Lindert, Peter. 1986. "Unequal English Wealth since 1670." *Journal of Political Economy* 94 (6): 1127–62.

Lindbeck, Assar, and Jorgen W. Weibull. 1988. "Altruism and Time Consistency: The Economics of Fait Accompli." *Journal of Political Economy* 96 (6): 1165–83.

Livi-Bacci, Massimo. 1992. *A Concise History of World Population.* Basil Blackwell.

Lord, William, and Peter Rangazas. 1991. "Savings and Wealth in Models with Altruistic Bequests." *American Economic Review* 81 (1): 289–96.

Lundberg, Shelly. 1999. "Family Bargaining and Retirement Behavior." In *Behavioral Dimensions of Retirement Economics*, edited by Henry J. Aaron. Brookings.

Lundberg, Shelly, and Robert Pollak. 1996. "Bargaining and Distribution in Marriage." *Journal of Economic Perspectives* 10 (4): 139–58.

Lundberg, Shelly, Robert Pollak, and Terrence Wales. 1997. "Do Husbands and Wives Pool Their Resources? Evidence from the United Kingdom Child Benefit." *Journal of Human Resources* 32 (3): 463–80.

Maddison, Angus. 2000. *The World Economy in Millennial Perspective*. OECD.

Madoff, Ray D., Cornelia R. Tenney, and Martin Hall. 2001. *Practical Guide to Estate Planning*. Panel Publishers.

Masson, André. 1986. "A Cohort Analysis of Wealth-Age Profiles Generated by a Simulation Model in France (1949–75)." *Economic Journal* 96 (381): 173–90.

Masson, André, and Pierre Pestieau. 1997. "Bequests Motives and Models of Inheritance: A Survey of the Literature." In *Is Inheritance Legitimate?* edited by Guido Erreygers and Tony Vandervelde, 54–88. Berlin: Springer-Verlag.

McElroy, Marjorie B., and Mary Jean Horney. 1981. "Nash-Bargained Household Decisions: Toward a Generalization of the Theory of Demand." *International Economic Review* 22 (2): 333–49.

McGarry, Kathleen. 1997. "*Inter-Vivos* Transfers and Intended Bequests." Working Paper 6345. Cambridge, Mass.: National Bureau of Economic Research.

———. 1999. "*Inter-Vivos* Transfers and Intended Bequests." *Journal of Public Economics* 73 (3): 321–51.

———. 2000a. "Inter-Vivos Transfers or Bequests? Estate Taxes and the Timing of Parental Giving." *Tax Policy and the Economy* 14 (1): 93–121.

———. 2000b. "Testing Parental Altruism: Implications of a Dynamic Model." Working Paper 7593. Cambridge, Mass.: National Bureau of Economic Research.

———. 2001. "The Cost of Inequality: Unequal Bequests and Tax Avoidance." *Journal of Public Economics* 79 (2): 179–204.

McGarry, Kathleen, and Robert F. Schoeni. 1995. "Transfers Behavior, Measurement and the Redistribution of Resources within the Family." *Journal of Human Resources* 30 (5): S184–226.

———. 1997. "Transfer Behavior within the Family: Results from the Asset and Health Dynamics Study." *Journal of Gerontology* 52B (2): 82–92.

McNees, Stephen. 1973. "Deductibility of Charitable Bequests." *National Tax Journal* 26 (1): 79–98.

Menchik, Paul L. 1980a. "Primogeniture, Equal Sharing, and the U.S. Distribution of Wealth." *Quarterly Journal of Economics* 94 (2): 299–316.

———. 1980b. "Effect of Material Inheritance on the Distribution of Wealth." In *Modeling the Distribution and Intergenerational Transmission of Wealth*, edited by James D. Smith. University of Chicago Press.

———. 1988. "Unequal Estate Division: Is It Altruism, Reverse Bequests, or Simply Noise?" In *Modeling the Accumulation and Distribution of Wealth*, edited by Denis Kessler and André Masson. Clarendon Press.

Menchik, Paul, and Martin David. 1983. "Income Distribution, Lifetime Saving, and Bequests." *American Economic Review* 73 (4): 672–90.

Menchik, Paul L., Frank O. Irvine, and Nancy A. Jianakoplos. 1986. "Determinants of Intended Bequests." Discussion Paper No. A–197. Michigan State University Press.

Mirer, Thad W. 1980. "The Dissaving Behavior of the Retired Aged." *Southern Economic Journal* 46 (4): 1197–1205.

Mitchell, Olivia S. 2001. "Developments in Decumulation: The Role of Annuity Products in Financing Retirement." Working Paper 8567. Cambridge, Mass.: National Bureau of Economic Research.

Mitchell, Olivia S., and others. 1999. "New Evidence on the Money's Worth of Individual Annuities." *American Economic Review* 89 (5): 1299–1318.

Modigliani, Franco. 1975. "The Life Cycle Hypothesis of Saving, Twenty Years Later." In *Contemporary Issues in Economics*, edited by M. Parkin. Manchester University Press.

———. 1988a. "Measuring the Contribution of Intergenerational Transfers to Total Wealth: Conceptual Issues and Empirical Findings." In *Modeling the Accumulation and Distribution of Wealth*, edited by Denis Kessler and André Masson. Clarendon Press.

———. 1988b. "The Role of Intergenerational Transfers and Life-Cycle Saving in the Accumulation of Wealth." *Journal of Economic Perspectives* 2 (2): 15–40.

Modigliani, Franco, and Richard Brumberg. 1954. "Utility Analysis and the Consumption Function: An Interpretation of Cross-Section Data." In *Post-Keynesian Economics*, edited by Kenneth Kurihara, 79–127. Rutgers University Press.

———. 1980. "Utility Analysis and Aggregate Consumption Functions: An Attempt at Integration." In *The Collected Papers of Franco Modigliani*, edited by Andrew Abel. MIT Press.

Moore, James, and Olivia S. Mitchell. 2000. "Projected Retirement Wealth and Saving Adequacy." In *Forecasting Retirement Needs and Retirement Wealth,* edited by Olivia S. Mitchell, Brett Hammond, and Anna Rappaport, 68–94. Pension Research Council. University of Pennsylvania Press.

Morgan, James N., and others. 1962. *Income and Welfare in the United States.* McGraw-Hill.

Mulligan, Casey. 1997. *Parental Priorities and Economic Inequality.* University of Chicago Press.

Munnell, Alicia H. 1976. "Private Pensions and Saving: New Evidence." *Journal of Political Economy* 84 (5): 1013–32.

Munnell, Alicia H., and Annika Sundén. 2001. "Private Pensions: Coverage and Benefit Trends." Prepared for "Conversation on Coverage," American Institute of Architects, July 24–25, 2001.

Murphy, Thomas B. 2001. "Financial and Psychological Determinants of Donor's Capacity to Give." *New Directions in Philanthropic Fundraising: Understanding the Needs of Donors: The Supply-Side of Charitable Giving* 28 (Fall): 33–49.

Murthi, Mamta, J. Michael Orszag, and Peter Orszag. 2001. "Administrative Costs under a Decentralized Approach to Individual Accounts: Lessons from the United

Kingdom." In *New Ideas about Old Age Security*, edited by Robert Holtzman and Joseph Stiglitz. World Bank.

National Opinion Research Center. 1998a. *Survey of Consumer Finances.*

———. 1998b. *General Social Survey.*

Nugent, Jeffrey. 1985. "The Old-Age Security Motive for Fertility." *Population and Development Review* 11 (1): 75–97.

Page, Benjamin R. 2002. "Bequest Taxes, Inter-Vivos Gifts, and the Bequest Motive." *Journal of Public Economy* (forthcoming).

Perelman, Sergio, and Pierre Pestieau. 1991. "Les Legs Volontaires en France." *Economie et Prévision* 100–101: 129–36.

Perozek, Maria G. 1998. "A Re–examination of the Strategic Bequest Motive." *Journal of Political Economy* 106 (2): 423–45.

Persson, Torsten, and Guido Tabellini. 2000. *Political Economics: Explaining Economic Policy.* MIT Press.

Piketty, Thomas. 2000. "Income Inequality in France 1901–98." CEPR Discussion Paper 2876. Paris: Centre d'Etudes Prospectives d'Economie Mathematique Appliquees (CEPREMAP).

Piketty, Thomas, and Emmanuel Saez. 2001. "Income Inequality in the United States, 1913–1998." Working Paper 8467. Cambridge, Mass.: National Bureau of Economic Research.

Pope, Stephen. 1991a. "Expressive Individualism and True Self-Love: A Thomistic Perspective." *Journal of Religion* 71 (2): 384–99.

———. 1991b. "The Order of Love and Recent Catholic Ethics: A Constructive Proposal." *Theological Studies* 52 (2): 255–88.

———. 1992. "Agape and Human Nature: Contributions from Neo-Darwinism." *Social Science Information* 31 (3): 509–29.

Poterba, James M. 2001. "Estate and Gift Taxes and Incentives for Inter-Vivos Giving in the United States." *Journal of Public Economics* 79 (1): 237–64.

Poterba, James M., and Mark Warshawsky. 2000. "The Costs of Annuitizing Retirement Payouts from Individual Accounts." In *Administrative Aspects of Social Security Reform*, edited by John B. Shoven. University of Chicago Press.

Poterba, James M., Steven F. Venti, and David A. Wise. 1995. "Do 401(k) Contributions Crowd Out Other Personal Saving?" *Journal of Public Economics* 58 (1): 1–32.

———. 1996. "How Retirement Saving Programs Increase Saving." *Journal of Economic Perspectives* 4 (10): 91–112.

———. 2001. "The Transition to Personal Accounts and Increasing Retirement Wealth: Macro and Micro Evidence." Working Paper 8610. Cambridge, Mass.: National Bureau of Economic Research.

Pritchett, Lant. 1997. "Divergence, Bigtime." *Journal of Economic Perspectives* 11 (3): 3–17.

Projector, Dorothy, and Gertrude Weiss. 1966. "Survey of Financial Characteristics of Consumers." Board of Governors. Federal Reserve Technical Papers.

Randolph, William C. 1995. "Dynamic Income, Progressive Taxes, and the Timing of Charitable Contributions." *Journal of Political Economy* 103 (4): 709–38.

Reil-Held, Anetta. 1999. "Bequests and Aggregate Wealth Accumulation in Germany." *Geneva Papers on Risk and Insurance, Issues and Practice* 24: 50–63.

Rosenthal, Paul A. 1991. "Pratiques successorales et fécondité." *Economie et Prévision* 100–01: 231–38.

Rosenzweig, Mark R., and Oded Stark. 1989. "Consumption Smoothing, Migration, and Marriage: Evidence from Rural India." *Journal of Political Economy* 97 (3): 905–26.

Saez, Emmanuel. "Income Inequality in the United States, 1913–98." Working Paper 8467. Cambridge, Mass.: National Bureau of Economic Research.

Schervish, Paul G. 2001. "The Spiritual Horizon of Philanthropy: New Directions for Money and Motives." *New Directions in Philanthropic Fundraising. Understanding the Needs of Donors: The Supply-Side of Charitable Giving* 28 (Fall): 17–31.

Schervish, Paul G., and John J. Havens. 1997. "Social Participation and Charitable Giving: A Multivariate Analysis." *Voluntas: International Journal of Voluntary and Nonprofit Organizations* 8 (3): 235–60.

———. 2001a. "The Methods and Metrics of the Boston Area Diary Study." *Nonprofit and Voluntary Sector Quarterly* 30 (3): 527–50.

———. 2001b. "The Mind of the Millionaire: Findings from a National Survey on Wealth with Responsibility." *New Directions in Philanthropic Fundraising, Understanding Donor Dynamics: The Organizational Side of Charitable Giving* 32 (Summer): 75–107.

———. 2002a. "The New Physics of Philanthropy: The Supply-Side Vectors of Charitable Giving. Part 2: The Spiritual Side of the Supply Side." *CASE International Journal of Educational Advancement* 2 (3): 221–41.

———. 2002b. "The Boston Area Diary Study and the Moral Citizenship of Care." *Voluntas: International Journal of Voluntary and Nonprofit Organizations* 13 (1): 47–71.

Schervish, Paul G., and Andrew Herman. 1988. *Empowerment and Beneficence: Strategies of Living and Giving among the Wealthy.* Chestnut Hill, Mass.: Social Welfare Research Institute at Boston College.

Schervish, Paul G., and Mary A. O'Herlihy. 2002. "The Spiritual Secret of Wealth: The Inner Dynamics by which Fortune Engenders Care." *New Directions for Philanthropic Fundraising* (forthcoming).

Schervish, Paul G., Platon E. Coutsoukis, and Ethan Lewis. 1994. *Gospels of Wealth: How the Rich Portray Their Lives.* Westport, Conn.: Praeger.

Schervish, Paul G., Mary A. O'Herlihy, and John J. Havens. 2001. "Agent-Animated Wealth and Philanthropy: The Dynamics of Accumulation and Allocation among High-Tech Donors." Chestnut Hill, Mass.: Social Welfare Research Institute at Boston College.

Schmalbeck, Richard. 2001. "Avoiding Federal Wealth Transfer Taxes." In *Rethinking Estate and Gift Taxation,* edited by William Gale, James R. Hines Jr., and Joel Slemrod. Brookings.

Schoeni, Robert F. 2000. "Support Networks within the Family as a Public Good Problem." Working Paper DRU–2294–NIA. Santa Monica, Calif.: RAND.

Sen, Amartya. 2001. "The Many Faces of Misogyny." *New Republic* 225 (33): 35–40.

Sheiner, Louise, and David Weil. 1992. "The Housing Wealth of the Aged." Working Paper 4115. Cambridge, Mass.: National Bureau of Economic Research.

Sherman, W. Richard. 1992. "A Half–Dozen Uses for a QTIP." *CPA Journal* 62 (3): 40–45.

Shorrocks, Anthony F. 1987. "U.K. Wealth Distribution: Current Evidence and Future Prospects." In *International Comparisons of the Distribution of Household Wealth*, edited by Edward N. Wolff, 29–50. Oxford University Press.

Sing, C. F., and others. 1971. "Studies on Genetic Selection in a Completely Ascertained Caucasian Population: Family Analyses of Eleven Blood Group Systems." *American Journal of Human Genetics* 23 (2): 164–98.

Siow, Aloysius. 1998. "Differential Fecundity, Markets, and Gender Roles." *Journal of Political Economy* 106 (2): 334–54.

Skinner, Jonathan. 2001. "Comment on Elderly Asset Management and Health." In *Rethinking Estate and Gift Taxation,* edited by William J. Gale, James R. Hines Jr., and Joel Slemrod. Brookings.

Slemrod, Joel. 1990. "The Economic Impact of Tax Reform." In *Do Taxes Matter? The Impact of the Tax Reform Act of 1986*, edited by Joel Slemrod. MIT Press.

———. 2001. "A General Model of the Behavioral Response to Taxation." *International Tax and Public Finance* 8 (2): 119–28.

Slemrod, Joel, and Wojciech Kopczuk. 2001. "Dying to Save Taxes: Evidence from Estate Tax Returns on the Death Elasticity." Working Paper 8158. Cambridge, Mass.: National Bureau of Economic Research.

Sloan, Frank A., Gabriel Picone, and Thomas J. Hoerger. 1997. "The Supply of Children's Time to Disabled Elderly Parents." *Economic Inquiry* 35 (2): 295–308.

Smith, James P. 1999. "Inheritance and Bequests." In *Wealth Work and Health: Innovations in Measurement in the Social Sciences*, edited by James P. Smith and Robert J. Willis. University of Michigan Press.

Smith, Roger S. 2001. *Personal Wealth Taxation and the European Union.* University of Alberta Press.

Social Welfare Research Institute. 1987. *Study on Wealth and Philanthropy.* Chestnut Hill, Mass.: Boston College.

Soldo, Beth, and Martha Hill. 1995. "Family Structure and Transfer Measures." *Journal of Human Resources* 30 (5): S108–37.

Soldo, Beth, and others. 1997. "Asset and Health Dynamics among the Oldest-Old: An Overview of the Survey," *Journal of Gerontology.* 52 (2):1–20.

Soltow, Lee. 1989. *The Distribution of Wealth and Income in the United States since 1798.* University of Wisconsin.

Spant, Roland. 1987. "Wealth Distribution in Sweden: 1920–1983." In *International Comparisons of the Distribution of Household Wealth*, edited by Edward Wolff. Oxford University Press.

Statistics Sweden. 1994. *Income Distribution Survey in 1992.* SCB Publishing Unit.

Stiglitz, Joseph E. 1978. "Notes on Estate Taxes, Redistribution, and the Concept of Balanced Growth Path Incidence." *Journal of Political Economy* 86 (2): 137–50.

Stoller, Eleanor P. 1983. "Parental Caregiving by Adult Children." *Journal of Marriage and the Family* 45 (11): 851–58.

Strauss, John, and Duncan Thomas. 1995. "Human Resources: Empirical Modeling of Household and Family Decisions." In *Handbook of Development Economics*, edited by Jere Behrman and T. R. Srinivasan. Elsevier Science.

Symons, Donald. 1979. *The Evolution of Human Sexuality.* Oxford University Press.

Tauchen, Helen V., Ann Dryden Witte, and Sharon K. Long. 1991. "Domestic Violence: A Nonrandom Affair." *International Economic Review* 32 (2): 491–511.

Tempel, Eugene R., and Patrick M. Rooney. 2000. "Repeal of the Estate Tax: Its Impact on Philanthropy." Indiana University: The Center on Philanthropy.

Thaler, Richard H. 1985. "Mental Accounting and Consumer Choice." *Marketing Science* 4 (3): 199–214.

———. 1990. "Anomalies: Saving, Fungibility, and Mental Accounts." *Journal of Economic Perspectives* 4 (1): 193–205.

———. 1994. "Some Empirical Evidence on Dynamic Inconsistency." Reprint. In *Quasi-Rational Economics*, edited by Richard H. Thaler. Russell Sage Foundation.

Thaler, Richard H., and Hersh M. Shefrin. 1981. "An Economic Theory of Self-Control." *Journal of Political Economy* 89 (2): 392–406.

Thomas, Duncan. 1990. "Intra-Household Resource Allocation: An Inferential Approach." *Journal of Human Resources* 25 (4): 635–64.

———. 1994. "Like Father, Like Son, Like Mother, Like Daughter: Parental Resources and Child Height." *Journal of Human Resources* 29 (4): 950–88.

Thompson, F. 1990. "Life after Death: How Successful Nineteenth-Century Businessmen Disposed of Their Fortunes." *Economic History Review* 43 (1): 40–61.

Tomes, Nigel. 1981. "The Family, Inheritance, and the Intergenerational Transmission of Inequality." *Journal of Political Economy* 89 (5): 928–58.

———. 1982. "On the Intergenerational Savings Function." *Oxford Economic Papers* 34: 108–34.

———. 1988. "Inheritance and Inequality within the Family: Equal Division among Unequals, or Do the Poor Get More?" In *Modeling the Accumulation and Distribution of Wealth*, edited by Denis Kessler and André Masson. Clarendon Press.

Toner, Jules. 1968. *The Experience of Love.* Corpus Books.

Trivers, Robert L. 1974. "Parent-Offspring Conflict." *American Zoologist* 14: 249–64.

———. 1985. *Social Evolution.* Menlo Park, Cal.: Benjamin-Cummins Publishing.

U.S. Department of the Treasury, Internal Revenue Service. 1999. *Instructions for Form 706 (Revised July 31 1999)* United States Estate (and Generation-Skipping Transfer) Tax Return.

———. 2000a. "Special Rules Regarding Optional Forms of Benefit under Qualified Retirement Plans." Treasury Decision 8900, Internal Revenue Service. 26 CFR Part 1 August 28.

———. 2000b. "Estate Tax Returns Filed in 1998: Gross Estate by Type of Property, Deductions, Taxable Estate, Estate Tax and Tax Credits, by Size of Gross Estate." *Statistics of Income Bulletin* (Winter 1999–2000).

———. 2000c. "Nonprofit Charitable Organizations, 1996." *Statistics of Income Bulletin* (Winter 1999–2000).

———. 2001. "Individual Income Tax Returns: Selected Income and Tax Items for Specified Tax Years, 1980–99." *Statistics of Income Bulletin.* (Summer 2001).

U.S. Trust. 1998. *U.S. Trust Survey of Affluent Americans:* XV (November).

VanDerhei, Jack, and Craig Copeland. 2001. "The Changing Face of Private Retirement Plans." *EBRI Issue Brief* 232 (April): Chart 2.

Venti, Steven F., and David A Wise. 1989. "Aging, Moving, and Housing Wealth." *The Economics of Aging,* edited by David A. Wise. University of Chicago Press.

———. 2000. "Aging and Housing Equity." Working Paper 7882. Cambridge, Mass.: National Bureau of Economic Research.

———. 2001. "Aging and Housing Equity: Another Look." Working Paper 8608. Cambridge, Mass.: National Bureau of Economic Research (November).

Weil, David N. 1994. "The Saving of the Elderly in Micro and Macro Data." *Quarterly Journal of Economics* 109 (1): 55–81.

Weir, David R., and Robert J. Willis. 2000. "Prospects for Widow Poverty." In *Forecasting Retirement Needs and Retirement Income,* edited by Olivia S. Mitchell, P. Brett Hammond, and Anna M. Rappaport. University of Pennsylvania Press.

White, Betsy Buttrill. 1978. "Empirical Tests of the Life Cycle Hypothesis." *American Economic Review* 68 (4): 547–60.

Wilhelm, Mark O. 1996. "Bequest Behavior and the Effect of Heirs' Earnings: Testing the Altruistic Model of Bequests." *American Economic Review* 86 (4): 874–92.

Willis, Robert. 1999. "A Theory of Out-of-Wedlock Childbearing." *Journal of Political Economy* 107 (4): 33–64.

Wilson, Margo, and Martin Daly. 1992. "The Man Who Mistook His Wife for a Chattel." In *The Adapted Mind,* edited by Jerome H. Barkow, Leda Cosmides, and John Tooby. Oxford University Press.

Wolff, Edward N. 1987a. "Estimates of Household Wealth Inequality in the United States, 1962–83." *Review of Income and Wealth* 33 (3): 231–56.

———. 1987b. "The Effects of Pensions and Social Security on the Distribution of Wealth in the United States." In *International Comparisons of Household Wealth Distribution,* edited by Edward Wolff. Oxford University Press.

———. 1992. "The Changing Inequality of Wealth." *American Economic Review* 82 (2): 552–80.

———. 1994. "Trends in Household Wealth in the United States, 1962–83 and 1983–89." *Review of Income and Wealth* 40 (2): 143–74.

———. 1998. "Recent Trends in the Size Distribution of Household Wealth." *Journal of Economic Perspectives* 12 (3): 131–50.

———. 1999. "Wealth Accumulation by Age Cohort in the U.S., 1962–92: The Role of Savings, Capital Gains, and Intergenerational Transfers." *Geneva Papers on Risk and Insurance, Issues and Practice* 24 (1): 27–49.

———. 2000. "Recent Trends in the Wealth Ownership, 1983–98." Working Paper 300. Annandale-on-Hudson, N. Y.: Levy Economics Institute.

Yaari, Menahem E. 1964. "On the Consumer's Lifetime Allocation Process." *International Economic Review* 5 (3): 304–17.

———. 1965. "Uncertain Lifetime, Life Insurance, and the Theory of the Consumer." *Review of Economic Studies* 32 (2): 137–50.

Contributors

Andrew B. Abel
University of Pennsylvania

James Andreoni
University of Wisconsin–Madison

Theodore Bergstrom
*University of California–Santa
    Barbara*

Charles Clotfelter
Duke University

Donald Cox
Boston College

J. Bradford DeLong
University of California–Berkeley

Peter A. Diamond
Massachusetts Institute of Technology

Amy Finkelstein
*National Bureau of Economic
    Research*

William G. Gale
Brookings Institution

Jonathan Gruber
Massachusetts Institute of Technology

John J. Havens
Boston College

Michael D. Hurd
RAND Center for Study of Aging

Wojciech Kopczuk
University of British Columbia

Laurence J. Kotlikoff
Boston University

John Laitner
University of Michigan

Ray D. Madoff
Boston College

Kathleen McGarry
University of California–Los Angeles

411

Olivia S. Mitchell
University of Pennsylvania

Alicia H. Munnell
Boston College

Peter R. Orszag
Brookings Institution

Pierre Pestieau
University of Liège

James Poterba
Massachusetts Institute of Technology

Samara Potter
University of Michigan

Paul G. Schervish
Boston College

John Karl Scholz
University of Wisconsin–Madison

Jonathan Skinner
Dartmouth College

Joel Slemrod
University of Michigan

Mauricio Soto
Boston College

Annika Sundén
Boston College

Catherine Taylor
Charles River Associates

Edward N. Wolff
New York University

Index

Aaron, Henry, 332
Abel, Andrew, 9–10
ACCF. *See* American Council for Capital Formation
Accounting: in capital/wealth accumulation, 62–63, 72, 321, 324–26, 342–43; definition of transfer wealth, 328–29; methods, 24, 72, 336–39, 341, 342–43
Age. *See* Demographic factors
Agricultural issues: acquired wealth and, 35; in France, 69; growth in productivity, 59; importance of land, 4, 5, 54–55, 57, 59; in Japan, 59–60; primogeniture and, 45–46, 57, 69
AHEAD. *See* Study of the Asset and Health Dynamics among the Oldest Old
Alessie, Robert, 77
Alexander, Richard, 201
Alston, Lee, 45
Altonji, Joseph, G., 75, 331
American Council for Capital Formation (ACCF), 86

Anderson, Elijah, 185
Ando, Albert, 324
Andreoni, James, 11–12, 13, 332
Annuities and annuitization: 401(k) plans, 285–86; bequests and, 25–26, 98, 124–26, 275–76, 338–39, 341, 343–44; compulsory and voluntary, 309; costs of, 273; defined contribution pension plans, 269, 289, 307; definition of, 273; as dominated assets, 123–24; economic factors, 273–74; load factors, 274, 275–76, 308; mortality premium, 273; payments of, 272, 273, precautionary saving and, 88, 275; pricing of, 106, 122–24, 339; purchases of, 9, 20, 29, 106, 107, 120–26, 266, 274–75, 283, 308, 330, 341; single premium immediate annuity (SPIA), 273; TIAA-CREF, 10, 124–25, 285, 286, 339. *See also* Medicare/Medicaid; Social Security
Antoniewicz, Rochelle, 384
Argys, Laura, 176